The Tourist's Guide to
Lost Yiddish New York City

The Tourist's Guide to Lost Yiddish New York City

HENRY H. SAPOZNIK

excelsior editions
State University of New York Press
Albany, New York

Cover credit: Kishke King, Brownsville, Brooklyn, © 1953 by N. Jay Jaffee. All rights reserved. Used by permission of the N. Jay Jaffee Trust at www.njayjaffee.com
Cover design: Henry H. Sapoznik

Published by State University of New York Press, Albany

© 2025 State University of New York

All rights reserved

Printed in the United States of America

No part of this book may be used or reproduced in any manner whatsoever without written permission. No part of this book may be stored in a retrieval system or transmitted in any form or by any means including electronic, electrostatic, magnetic tape, mechanical, photocopying, recording, or otherwise without the prior permission in writing of the publisher.

Links to third-party websites are provided as a convenience and for informational purposes only. They do not constitute an endorsement or an approval of any of the products, services, or opinions of the organization, companies, or individuals. SUNY Press bears no responsibility for the accuracy, legality, or content of a URL, the external website, or for that of subsequent websites.

EU GPSR Authorised Representative:
Logos Europe, 9 rue Nicolas Poussin, 17000, La Rochelle, France
contact@logoseurope.eu

Excelsior Editions is an imprint of State University of New York Press

For information, contact State University of New York Press, Albany, NY
www.sunypress.edu

Library of Congress Cataloging-in-Publication Data

Name: Sapoznik, Henry, author.
Title: The tourist's guide to lost Yiddish New York City / Henry H. Sapoznik.
Description: Albany : State University of New York Press, [2025] | Series: Excelsior editions | Includes bibliographical references and index.
Identifiers: LCCN 2024039356 | ISBN 9798855801736 (pbk. : alk. paper) | ISBN 9798855801743 (ebook)
Subjects: LCSH: Jews, East European—New York (State)—New York—Social life and customs. | Jews in popular culture—New York (State)—New York. | Jews—Music—History and criticism. | Theater, Yiddish—New York (State)—New York—History. | Yiddish language—New York (State)—New York. | New York (N.Y.)—Description and travel.
Classification: LCC F128.9.J5 S26 2025 | DDC 305.892/40747109—dc23/eng/20250225
LC record available at https://lccn.loc.gov/2024039356

The book is dedicated to the memory of
Peter Sokolow (1940–2023) ע"ה
"The Mayor of Yiddish New York City"

Contents

Acknowledgments ix

Introduction 1

Part 1. Essen! Eating!

1. *Kashrus*: The Quest for Kosher 7

2. Trotzky's Kosher Restaurant 13

3. The Jewish Delicatessen: "The Stronghold of Pungent Meat" 17

4. Of Knishes and Kishkes 35

5. Joseph Moskowitz and Romanian Restaurants 49

6. Yiddish Champagne: Seltzer and Dr. Brown's Celery Tonic 69

7. From Adjective to Noun: The Appetizing Store 77

8. Eat in Good Health!: Dairy and Vegetarian Restaurants 85

9. Fast, Crowded, and Cheap: The Cafeteria 99

10. Raisins and Almonds: Chunky Milk Chocolate 109

Part 2. Architecture

11. The Rise and Fall of the House of Jarmulowsky — 115
12. The *Forverts* Building: From Socialist to Socialite — 125
13. Harrison G. Wiseman: Builder of New York Yiddish Theaters — 129
14. Hotel Herzl: Max Bernstein and the Libby's Hotel and Baths — 139

Part 3. Music

15. "To Hear . . .": The First Yiddish Records — 159
16. The First Yiddish Recording Artists — 179
17. Jews and Jazz: From Before the Beginning — 193
18. Sam Ash and Shimele Blank: Two Music Stores — 207
19. *Khazntes*: Women Cantors of the Stage — 215
20. Thomas LaRue Jones, Gladys Mae Sellers, and the Lost World of Black Cantors — 231

Part 4. Theater

21. Yente Telebende: The Woman with the Wallop — 259
22. Uncle Thomashefsky's Cabin: The 1900s Yiddish Uncle Tom Shows — 273
23. Before Jolson: *The Jazz Singer*, Jessel, and the Jews — 279

Notes — 309

Bibliography — 345

Index — 349

About the Author — 369

Acknowledgments

Thanks to Richard Carlin and to those who generously helped, including, but not limited to, Zachary Baker (Yiddish); Shulamith Berger (Libby's Hotel); Sabina Brukner (Yiddish); Michele Clark (Schmulka Bernstein); Ken Cobb, assistant commissioner, NYC Department of Records and Information Services (NYC 1940 tax photos); Chip Deffaa (*The Jazz Singer*); Jeff Feinberg (Black cantors/kosher); Bob Foley (Fillmore East); Rochelle Friedlich, Rabbi Capers Funnye (Black cantors); Joe Fishstein Collection of Yiddish Poetry, Rare Books, and Special Collections; McGill University (Rolland Theater architects drawing); Aliza Gans (Russ & Daughters); Joel Grey (Mickey Katz); Walter Grutchfield (H. W. Perlman wall sign photograph); Michael Hilf (Frank Seiden), Barbara Kirshenblatt-Gimblett; Vince Giordano (*The Jazz Singer*, jazz); Eric Goldman (Yiddish films); Bernice Zuckerberg Gordon (khazntes); J. Hoberman (Yiddish film); Annice Jacoby (William Gropper cartoon of Abe Cahan/Yiddish Book Center); Cyrisse Jaffee (Kishke King photograph); Andy Lanset; Jeremiah Lockwood (khazntes); David Lynch (cover design consult); David Mazower (Yiddish theater); Charley Mays (Dr. Brown's Cel-Ray); Dr. Jesse McCarroll (z"l), Shahanna McKinney-Baldon (Goldye); Brian Merlis (Brooklyn); Ted Merwin (delicatessens); Robert F. Moss (Katz's delicatessen), Chaim Motzen (Black cantors); Jeremiah Moss (Jeremiah's Vanishing New York); Dan Morgenstern (z"l, Willie "The Lion" Smith); Keith Mueller ("Reconstructing the Fillmore East"); National Library of Israel (Yiddish and Anglo-Jewish newspapers); Chana Pollock (*Forverts* building); David Prager (Malavsky family); David Reinhold (cantorial); Rich Remsberg (maps and image research); Sharon Rivo/National Center for Jewish Film (Frank Seiden image); Ron Robboy (Yiddish theater/music); Joel E. Rubin (klezmer music); Cookie Segelstein (Macintosh troubleshooter); Dennis

Smith (Dr. Brown's Cel-Ray); Dick Spottswood (discography, jazz); Michael Sternberg (Oysher family); John Kuo Wei Tchen (research access); Harvey Varga (Yiddish); David Weider (headstone photos); Dave Willens (Chunky chocolate/Phil Silvershein); Sam Wieder (Black cantors); Cantor Josée Wolff (khazntes) Shoshke-Rayzl Yuni (Yiddish *komputeray*); Jai Zion (Libby's Hotel).

Introduction

In 1958, as part of its already extensive *Say It* traveler's phrase book series, Dover Publications issued *Say It in Yiddish*. Edited by Uriel Weinreich (later compiler of *The Modern Yiddish-English Dictionary*) and his wife Beatrice, the book follows the proscribed structure of every other tourist phrase book with expressions useful in a variety of situations: travel, shopping, assistance, and so on.

On its surface, publishing a Yiddish phrase book for travelers a little more than a decade after 85 percent of its speakers were murdered was mildly surreal. Questions in Yiddish aimed at railway conductors, police, ship captains, and government officials—things impossible to imagine even when Yiddish was in full flower—heightened that surreality.

And yet, while it appears to be a guide for phantom speakers, the book's bevy of quotidian phrases (best in any situation away or at home) and its careful attention to proper pronunciation, speaks to a living language. In its own modest way, it was an effort, despite the devastating blow of the Holocaust and subsequent Soviet repression, to maintain the place of Yiddish alongside other great world languages, even if just in a modest paperback.

So, in the spirit of the brave little Yiddish phrase book for a recently devastated people, I offer a tourist's guidebook for a lost Yiddish New York City, though not in any way a "traditional" guidebook given New York's voracious appetite for consuming itself. The task of identifying a physical Yiddish New York City requires the deft melding of past and present. Most of the physical evidence (buildings, blocks, neighborhoods) is long gone, although some original buildings survive in modified/altered use (Village East by Angelika, the Holy House of Prayer for All People, Nine Orchard, etc.). The rarest are those (like Katz's delicatessen, the Tenth Street Russian Baths, Russ & Daughters, B&H dairy, and Yonah Schimmel, etc.) that are where they've always been, doing what they've always been doing. Yet the Jewish food survivors have amazingly avoided becoming "forkloric" (a living history/reenactment) food offerings, as they do a living menu despite being from a phantom community, less Colonial Williamsburg than Williamsburg Bridge.

This "tourist's guide" also demands the deeper dive into the multitude of scattered jigsaw puzzle pieces of New York's golden age of Yiddish: tens of thousands of commercial 78s, photographs, films, posters, books, and newspapers, the essential materials of New York's Yiddish culture, made available through the accessible stewardship of, among others the YIVO Institute for Jewish Research, Yiddish Book Center, the National Center for Jewish Film, and the National Library of Israel newspaper collection. (This last was the source of over 2,500 period Yiddish advertisements, articles, and graphics downloaded in research for this book.)

And, while also illuminating the above objects, this has also been an opportunity to celebrate the now largely forgotten men and women who helped make Yiddish New York City: poet and singer Solomon Smulewitz, banker S. Jarmulowsky, vegetarian pioneer Sadie Schildkraut, architect Harrison G. Wiseman, black cantors Thomas LaRue Jones and Goldye Mae Sellers, and visionary hotelier Max Bernstein, among many others.

This book allows me to revisit subjects about which I have written much (Yiddish culture and klezmer music), a return I welcome given what has been discovered in the intervening years since my 2000 book *Klezmer! Jewish Music from Old World to Our World*. Conversely, I am equally excited to explore subjects about which I have long been passionate (food, architecture, film, crime, etc.) but have never written about. One was my wholly unanticipated immersion into the forgotten phenomenon of Black cantors (the so-called *shvartze khazonim*) thanks to the recent discovery of a long-sought period recording. My research during the Covid-19 lockdown in July and August of 2020 to uncover this lost history was documented in the blog of my newly launched website, whose six postings garnered over one hundred thousand hits, international news coverage, and a BBC documentary.

As a native Yiddish speaker, I also here indulge my interest in the linguistic intersection of Yiddish and English. In my translations, I have attempted to transmit some of the very approximate transcription attempts of English loan words by "re-romanizing" them as if they were Yiddish and placing them in italics as opposed to the translated Yiddish, in terms like "moving picture" / *muving piksher* / מווינג פיקשער or "up to date" / *ap-to-deyt* / אפ־טו־דעיט. I point them out because of what they reveal about the critical contact points between the two cultures.

And finally, while Weinreich's little phrase book was written in the aftermath of the Holocaust, I found myself writing in the aftermath of the October 7 Hamas pogrom, the dramatic rise worldwide of anti-Semitism, and a seeming end of the golden age of American Jewry. On the one hand, while as a historian and a child of Holocaust survivors, I cannot help but wonder if I have written a book about one lost Jewish world on the eve of another. Writing this book has been a much-needed refuge to temporarily deflect the current unfolding tragic events. I hope that reading it will do the same.

Henry H. Sapoznik
Olive Bridge, NY / Madison, WI

Part 1
Essen! Eating!

1
Kashrus
The Quest for Kosher

Defining Kosher Restaurants

The grand old man of New York kosher dining was Felix Marx (1825–1903). Born in Alsace-Lorraine, he came to New York in 1858.[1] While both census reports and city directories in the 1870s list Marx as running a "saloon," ads in the Anglo-Jewish press proudly describe it as "an old established and popular kosher resort," which, except for a few years, he ran until his death.[2] Marx's successor, David Wasser at 108 Bowery, is reported to have learned his cooking by way of a stint in the Austrian army and later in Berlin restaurants. A September 4, 1903, newspaper announcement notes that his Passover food will be "*yomtovdik* (holiday) cooking in its perfection."[3]

Another early eatery was Victor Steiner's kosher restaurant at 105 Delancey Street whose ads featured the handlebar-mustachioed Steiner and a bit of his poetry:

> Victor Steiner's restaurant
> Iz fir yorn arbayter bakant
> Als geshmak'haft un elegant
> Getrank un shpayzn
> Fimesige prayzn
> Lever's Union Beer
> Immer tsu bakumen bay mir

> Victor Steiner's restaurant
> The workingman's familiar haunt
> It's all tasty and elegant
> Food and drink and what's nice is
> The restaurant's prices
> Lever's Union beer
> Can't wait to see you here.[4]

Others like Simonoff's restaurant featured the motto "*strikli* kosher as by a rabbi / tasty as by your mother's table."[5] What that "mother's table" might have had can be gleaned from the 1871 *Jewish Cookery Book* by Mrs. Esther Levy, the first American kosher cookbook. Its pages display a continuity of imported German Jewish dishes (Frimsel, Sauer Krout, Ein Gefullter Magen, Matzo Coogle) but also point the way to acculturated cuisine, with recipes for mock turtle soup, mulligatawny soup, and toad in the hole.[6] For that matter, what was deemed "kosher" was anybody's guess. Boarding houses advertising "kosher" were less about "treyf" and more about "safe," that is, places where Jews felt comfortable to stop and where, if someone said they had a kosher home, then it was assumed to be, as in the Yiddish axiom: "Az zayn numen iz Mendel, meg men esn fin zayn fendl" (If Mendel's his name, you can both eat the same).

The outdatedness of kashrus was a hot topic in American Reform Jewish publications but surprisingly also in general readership publications like *The Galaxy: A Magazine of Entertaining Reading* from November 1874. While meticulously laying out the history of stringent kashrus practices, the writer W. M. Rosenblatt points to the inevitability of discarding kosher, stating that the circumstances "which created those adherences has passed," and that only among the declining number of those whom he calls "the sternly Orthodox" was there any further interest in it. Rosenblatt, like many reformers and progressives, felt that even those "sternly Orthodox" would decline with "sustained exposure to a Democratic and American way life."

For evidence, Rosenblatt talks about a recent national gathering of the B'nai B'rith in Chicago, ending in a banquet whose "cooking was done by Gentiles under Gentile supervision, and it was beneath a Gentile roof that the table was decked, although there were numerous Jewish inns and restaurants in the city." The meal included meat, shellfish, and milk. "It was," Rosenblatt noted "only necessary to set a juicy, roasted suckling pig upon the table, to complete this insurrection against the dietary authorities of Israel."[7]

This feast was only an opening course for the later infamous treyf banquet on July 11, 1883, of newly ordained rabbis at the Reform Hebrew Union College in Cincinnati. It was a multicourse banquet that eliminated pork but unabashedly included shrimp, oysters, and shellfish. Again, this was hardly an anomaly: in an editorial on April 4, 1895, in *The Jewish Voice*, Rabbi Isaac A. Wise, leader of the Jewish Reform movement, penned a paean (and a possibly purposely provocative one) to one of his favorite foods: oysters. In his rabbinic interpretation, Wise argued that oysters were permissible, as the shell was, in essence, a fish scale, making it kosher.[8]

Dr. Wise's adamant bivalve advocacy was not met everywhere with approval or good humor. In a *responsa* editorial in *The Jewish Voice*, a B. Younker noted that while he did not begrudge "any member of the clergy the full enjoyment of the oyster on the half shell or any preparation thereof, any more than we do any other of the multifarious forbidden luxuries enjoyed by them," he did however "protest emphatically against declaring the same permissible under and by Jewish law, when as a matter of fact, it is not."[9]

While Wise's fierce shellfish support may have been an attempt to update Judaism's ancient laws of kosher, it may also have been merely a feint aimed at his most vocal "kosher" opponent: Orthodoxy's Rabbi Jacob Joseph (1840–1906), the first (and last) Chief Rabbi of New York.

Sorting Out the Kosher Chaos: Rabbi Jacob Joseph

The Vilna-born Rabbi Joseph was brought to New York in 1888 in a misbegotten effort to bring Orthodox order to the religious inconsistencies and kosher chaos of a city with the country's largest growing Jewish population.[1] However, the bookish and insular Rabbi Joseph was ill-equipped to handle the rough-and-tumble New York fighting style, as he tried to attach Talmudic law and order to the wild west (and east) side of New York. Although installed at the most prestigious synagogue on the Lower East Side (Beys Ha'Medresh Ha' Godol), pretty much from the beginning Rabbi Jacob Joseph was in serious trouble.[2]

---

1. "Rabbi Wise and 'Rabbi' Dana," *Chattanooga Daily Times*, June 2, 1895, 12.
2. Abraham J. Karp, "New York Chooses a Chief Rabbi," Waltham, MA, Publications of the American Jewish Historical Society, Sept. 1, 1954, 129.

The organization that brought Rabbi Joseph (the Association of American Orthodox Hebrew Congregations) represented a mere dozen synagogues, so the vast number of Orthodox communities did not recognize his authority. For that matter, the organization did not even really represent kosher butchers. When butchers learned that Rabbi Joseph's salary and expenses were to be paid by a kosher tax increase, it triggered a bitter memory of an earlier "kosher tax" imposed on Jews by the Russian czar and so smacked of the very kind of abuse and corruption Rabbi Jacob was brought in to stop.[3] While Rabbi Joseph succeeded in advancing and standardizing religious Jewish education, the kosher meat experiment unraveled by the mid-1890s when he succumbed to the stress of his difficult work and, after two years in bed, died in 1902.[4]

Rabbi Joseph's funeral cortege of sixty thousand, wending its way through the Lower East Side, was set upon by anti-Semitic factory workers who, from the high loft building floors above, "rained missiles down upon the Hebrews" of chunks of iron, wood, and chamber pots. When the police finally intervened, it was the Jews they set upon.[5]

---

3. "Mosaic Meat," *Salt Lake Herald*, Jan. 12, 1890, 1. Over a century after the 1898 establishment of the first successful kosher certification agency, the Orthodox Union, the pendulum has now swung to the other extreme. As of 2019, there were 180 competing kashrus-granting agencies in the New York City area. Of those, 142—perhaps not surprisingly—are in Brooklyn.
4. "Death of Chief Rabbi Jacob Joseph," *New York Times*, July 29, 1902, 9.
5. "Riot at Funeral of Rabbi Joseph," *Brooklyn Times Union*, July 30, 1902, 1.

The Meat Riots

1902, in an odd nod to the recently deceased Rabbi Joseph, saw another Jewish riot on the Lower East Side, also over kosher. An agreement made in 1895 with the "big western meat packers"—the consortium who provisioned Eastern retail butchers—was abruptly changed in May of 1902, raising costs exponentially overnight.[10] At first, the six hundred or so New York City kosher butchers made a half-hearted attempt to protest the radical 50 percent increase in the cost of kosher meat. Failing that, they foolishly attempted to pass the entire increase directly onto their customers.

Figure 1.1. Kosher meat riots broke out over several years in the early 1900s. *Source:* National Library of Israel, Historical Jewish Press website (www.jpress.org.il), founded by the National Library and Tel Aviv University. Used with permission.

FIERCE MEAT RIOT ON LOWER EAST SIDE

Demonstration Caused by Rise in Kosher Beef Prices.

500 POLICE CALLED OUT.

Officers Attacked by Immense Mob Around Hall Where Women Were Holding Indignation Meeting.

Starting on May 15, in a spontaneous set of street actions, over twenty thousand Jews, mostly women, battled more than five hundred police officers and conducted actions against restaurants and butcher shops over the course of several weeks.[11] One result was the formation of ad hoc independent meat markets, many run exclusively by women. An article on June 13, 1902, in *The Hebrew Standard* mentions "the East Side Ladies Anti-Trust Association of the Sixteenth Assembly District's 'Anti-Trust Women's Suffrage Meat Market.'"[12]

The inevitable success of the meat boycott caused the beef trust to roll back its price increase. However, in 1904, it made another attempt, through a strike that cut off the supply of New York's kosher meat, which produced an even worse reaction. The multiday uprising (which broke for Shabbos) consisted of picket lines. Women who crossed it were called "scabs" and had their meat purchases snatched and doused with kerosene or carbolic acid.[13] It's no stretch to imagine that the 1906 Pure Food Law was helped along by these events, along with Upton Sinclair's tremendously popular 1905 meat industry exposé *The Jungle*, which was subsequently published in Yiddish.[14]

This meat moment was evoked in the May 4, 1946, issue of the *Forverts* in feature columnist Chaim Ehrenreich's "Vos yidn in Amerika hobn gegesn mit 50 yor tzurik, un vos zey esn haynt" (What Jews in America Ate 50 Years Ago and What They Eat Today): "The Jewish diet of that era did not merely include meat, was not merely dominated by meat, but consisted solely and wholly of meat. Lunch, for sure, was meat and 'sopper' (which the American Jews enthusiastically called the evening meal) is yet again, meat. Meat, meat, meat. Meat."[15]

2

Trotzky's Kosher Restaurant

Figure 2.1. Business card for Trotzky's Kosher Restaurant (here spelled "Trotsky") (ca. 1915). *Source:* Dovi Safir. Used with permission.

The Famous Restaurateur Hyman Trotsky
Who has been proprietor of the well-known strictly Kosher restaurant for so many years located at
NO. 235 MERCER STREET
is now located at the well-known
Broadway Central Hotel
663-673 Broadway, Bet. Bleecker & 3d Sts.
(On the Second Floor, One Flight Up)
conducting
THE LARGEST AND FINEST STRICTLY כשר RESTAURANT IN THE UNITED STATES
Out-of-town buyers and visitors to the city will thus be enabled to stop at a well-known hotel and at the same time be assured of Kosher meals.
Any question as to the reputation of Mr. Trotsky can be settled by referring to prominent Orthodox Rabbis of New York city.

On May 25, 1919, the *New York Tribune* ran "None Genuine Without This Sign," a full-page illustrated story about Trotzky's restaurant advertised as "the largest kosher dining room in America." Right off the bat, its owner was asked about any relation to another Trotsky:

Bah! That fellow, his name isn't even Trotzky. His name is Bronstein. When he lived in New York in 1917, he used to come here to eat. He liked my kosher dishes. He came often. He found that I was honest and respected. . . . This Bronstein knows he is not trusted and wants to be respected so he borrows my name. Bronstein calls himself Trotzky. What shall I do? Change my name every time someone takes mine? Bolshevik? Bah! How can an Orthodox Jew be a Bolshevik?[1]

But did they meet?

Thanks to the relentless folk process, the Trotzky/Trotsky myth continued to mutate: Trotsky taking rooms at the demimonde Broadway Central in order to eat at Trotzky's; Trotsky working as Trotzky's dishwasher; Trotsky being given the Trotsky moniker by New York comrades tired of his complaining about all other restaurants but Trotzky's kosher eatery.[2] Trotsky and Trotzky were both living in the Bronx while Trotsky's work at the Russian magazine *Novy Mir*, on St. Marks Place, put him just a few footfalls from Trotzky's restaurant in the Broadway Central. On the one hand, Trotzky's served meat, and some biographies cite Trotsky as a vigilant vegetarian, even identifying The Triangle, a kosher dairy restaurant on the Bronx's Intervale Avenue, as his regular haunt (to the chagrin of its proletariat staff thanks to his rigid refusal to tip).[3] While a number of articles claim that Trotsky took his name from the restaurant, in his memoirs he talks about taking his nom de guerre from that of a Russian jailer involved in his 1902 prison break. And the name Leon Trotsky appears on the 1916 passenger manifest of the SS *Monserrat* when he and his family first came to New York.

Despite being Orthodox and a passionate Zionist, Hyman Trotzky could not avoid being conflated with his sound-alike name-mate. A 1922 incident involved Hyman Trotzky and his wife on a European vacation being stopped at the border of a middle European country, an impasse that was not resolved until the American Embassy obtained a "personal letter" from US Secretary of State Charles Evans Hughes, "which settled all cases of mistaken identity."

Hyman Trotzky (1864–1930) was born north of Bialystok, Poland, and emigrated to the US in 1899, living in New Bedford, Massachusetts, and working as a peddler. In 1912, he and his family moved to New York, and in two years Trotzky went from owning a small café on Mercer Street to establishing a history-making strictly kosher restaurant at the once storied Broadway Central Hotel at 673 Broadway, off West Third Street.[4]

Built in 1870, the Broadway Central was at the time the world's largest and most lavish hostelry; building it cost $1.6 million (or $30 million today). A playpen for the rich and famous, the meeting place of the hoity-toity social "400," it saw celebrities like Lillian Russell, Mark Twain, and Diamond Jim Brady (who was famously shot making his way down the hotel's wide sweeping stairway). It was also the site of an occasional murder or suicide, and in 1876, thanks to a gathering of professional baseballers, it was the birthplace of the National League.[5]

It was only with the migration of the "400" uptown, and with it the decline of the hotel's sheen, that Hyman Trotzky even had a prayer in 1914 to inhabit the hotel's massive showcase second-floor dining space, where, with its seating capacity of six hundred, it was the first kosher restaurant in a world-class hotel. Trotzky's restaurant was *the* place for New York's Orthodox/kosher community, including celebrities like Cantor Yossele Rosenblatt and Rabbi Meyer "Max" Manischewitz of eponymous food fame.[6] So in August 1923, when Manischewitz acquired the Broadway Central, it at first appeared to be a validation of Trotzky's long years as the hotel's—and the city's—pioneering deluxe kosher outpost. Instead, the takeover showed that the restaurateur had more in common than he thought with his Bolshevik bête-noir, when, just as Stalin exiled Leon Trotsky upon Stalin's ascension to power, so Manischewitz did with his Trotzky.[7] Manischewitz turned out Trotzky, and with a vast makeover, turned the Broadway Central into New York City's largest kosher hotel. Its lavish interior was described in the October 6, 1934, *New Yorker* Talk of the Town column: "A $12,000 marble floor inlaid with a big six-pointed star in the lobby and decorating with special grandeur seven sets of period rooms for wedding purposes. . . . One of the bride's rooms where the Orthodox bride sits with her maid of honor before the ceremony is silver modern, and another, whose walls and ceilings are lined with pastel silks, has a special gold-brocade bridal throne."[8]

After leaving the Broadway Central, Trotzky moved uptown to the Garment District into the still extant Arsenal Building at 153 West Thirty-Fifth Street. After Hyman Trotzky died in 1930, his sons also opened a catering business at the Bronx's Concourse Plaza Hotel at 161st Street.[9] Trotzky's final location on West Forty-Sixth Street got a mention on October 13, 1938, in the *Daily News*, thanks to a sign in the restaurant's window: "No relation to Leon." The quip made it into syndicated gossip columns, so the Trotzky/Trotsky story was, yet again, carried nationwide.[10]

Amazingly, the Trotzky/Trotsky story surfaced in reportage of the August 3, 1973, collapse of the sorely neglected Broadway Central, long a welfare hotel. Not a few press reports noted the once historic hotel and its "Communist" connection.[11]

Trotzky and Trotsky would only ever meet in print.

3

The Jewish Delicatessen

"The Stronghold of Pungent Meat"

Figure 3.1. By 1873, Isaac Gellis had become the first dominant manufacturer, distributor, and retail outlet of kosher smoked and processed meats. *Source:* 1940 Tax Photograph Collection, NYC Municipal Archives. Used with permission.

The delicatessen—not "deli," its postwar weak-kneed, neutered diminution—is at the center of the concentric circle of historic Yiddish American dining. No Jewish-associated restaurant has a more gloried and storied history than do delicatessens. The popularity of kosher sausages and smoked meats can already be seen in an 1875 article in *The American Israelite*, crowing that demand has increased so much that kosher manufacturer Lowenstein Brothers had abandoned handmade sausages and "were obliged to put in a steam apparatus and now make the best quality sausages with a steam engine."[1]

Not long before the Lowenstein Brothers got its steam contraption, Isaac Gellis (1849–1906), the man who would put delicatessen on the New York Yiddish map and by extension onto tables around the country, first arrived. Claims have been made that Gellis supplied meat to Union troops during the Civil War, an oft repeated but unsubstantiated assertion. First, Gellis, who did not arrive in America until years after the war, received no mentions of this very patriotic act in any of his contemporary press or in any of his many obituaries. Also, it's unlikely the US government would approach a European exporter of exponentially more expensive kosher meat to feed its mostly Gentile troops, just as it was extremely unlikely that the Orthodox Gellis would jeopardize his flourishing wurst business—and his kosher certification—to fill orders for treyf meat.

By 1873, Gellis had become the first dominant manufacturer, distributor, and retail outlet of kosher smoked and processed meats. His first brush with national fame came wholly by accident. On January 22, 1895, newspapers across the country picked up the curious New York story of Temperance activist Rebecca Fream, who organized a campaign against Lower East Side stores desecrating the city's Sunday blue laws. Among the miscreant defilers hauled before magistrate's court (including a man selling pins and another hawking hot sweet potatoes) was forty-year-old butcher Isaac Gellis.[2]

Gellis expanded his business base from retail consumer in-store sales and wholesale orders in 1897 when his sons Henry and Samuel, in what is listed in the city directories as an "eating house," opened what was quite possibly the first modern Jewish delicatessen.[3]

Gellis was able to accomplish substantial growth amidst the chaos of the uncertainty of kosher food, because like his colleague and fellow self-made Lower East Side entrepreneur Sender Jarmulowsky, Gellis was widely regarded for his scrupulous Orthodoxy and active omnipresence in charitable projects. He and Jarmulowsky were founders of, and leaders in, the Eldridge Street Synagogue and trustees and founders of Lebanon, Mount Sinai, and Beth Israel hospitals. With Gellis's death in 1906 (his obituary was found above-the-fold in all New York Yiddish and English broadsheet newspapers), his wife Sarah and his sons assumed the business.[4]

Without question, the most famous ex–Isaac Gillis employee was Eddie Cantor, who as a child made deliveries for the shop, and who, despite being offered money for his services, only wanted to be paid in salami. "Salami," he said, "I was all salami. When I walked down the street, I was a sausage with eyes."[5] Cantor's affection for Isaac Gillis (mentioned in both of his autobiographies) led his longtime writer Matt Brooks to list Isaac Gellis Delicatessen in the professional trade journals as his faux Hollywood business address.[6]

Ads in the mid-1930s Yiddish press in honor of Isaac Gellis's sixtieth anniversary pointed out:

> Three Generations of Gellis
>
> Three Generations of Kosher
>
> Three Generations of Quality
>
> Older than the oldest Yiddish newspaper
>
> Older than all Orthodox synagogues in New York
>
> Older than all Jewish institutions
>
> And a decade older than the mass emigration from Russia and Poland.[7]

In the postwar years, Isaac Gellis increased its appeal to emerging American Jewish tastes. In 1950, the company began selling "beef fry," its bid in the ongoing chimera to create a market for kosher "bacon," and by the late 1950s, Gellis jumped on the frozen food bandwagon with pastrami.[8] But its glory days—and market share—were long behind it, with most of that market share gobbled up by a wurst company founded the year before Isaac Gillis's death.

Hebrew National

In what must be one of the most prescient bits of reportage, an article headlined "A Genuine Hebrew Wedding Feast Took Place in the Flushing Hotel

Yesterday Evening," while ostensibly about the 1896 Rabenowitz-Krainin wedding, was also the first press that would associate groom Theodore Krainin (and future founder of Hebrew National) with festive Jewish dining.[9]

Tanchum "Theodore" Krainin (1870–1946) came to the US in 1891 already a trained wurst maker and who, by 1900, owned his own sausage-making business. The following year Krainin founded Co-Operative Sausage Co. at 158 Monroe Street at a cost of $50,000 (approximately $1.5 million today). Soon, Krainin and partners opened new smokehouses at 47-49 Pike Street and changed the company name to Hebrew National Kosher Sausage. Over what appears to have been several tumultuous years, Krainin announced in a Yiddish display ad on February 26, 1909, "I hereby make it known to all in the city, the country and yes, even the entire nation, that the famous Hebrew National company in now under my full and complete control and I am the only boss at the kosher factory with not one partner."[10]

With that control, Krainin followed Gellis in both assuring stringent Orthodox kosher oversight and also instituting government inspections as per the 1906 Pure Food Act. Also like Gellis, Krainin's acts of charity on behalf of the community were plentiful. He was also a founder and president of the Eldridge Street Synagogue, several hospitals, and a number of religious organizations (including something called the Jewish Sabbath Alliance of America).[11] Indicative of Krainin's core kosher market outreach, the majority of Hebrew National display ads (plus announcements that feature the endorsement of noted rabbis) appeared in the religious *Morgn Zhurnal*, rather than the socialist *Forverts* or the more independent *Tog*.

Krainin modernized the Pike Street smokehouse (with canny, regular public tours to help reassure customers of its cleanliness) and—other than Saturdays—opened its adjacent retail outlet eighteen hours a day. With that, demand increased so that in 1911, the company moved to larger facilities at 155 East Broadway and opened yet another smokehouse factory/store in Harlem.[12]

In 1912, Hebrew National introduced Krainin's Kosher Canned Meats (roast squab, goulash, oxtail soup, and *tzimmes*). Announcing the new product by addressing some concerns about the kashrus of canned foods, the company stated, "To those who question the possibility of Kosher Food inside cans, we say this: The Jews of Palestine who, in the past, would not eat Canned Food of any kind, are now ready buyers of our meats. This because our name and brand are recognized there as everywhere not only as marks of purity but also as representing 100 per cent 'Kasheroth.' "[13]

Figure 3.2. Hebrew National kosher canned franks and beans were the first canned franks and beans to reach the market in 1915. *Source:* National Library of Israel, Historical Jewish Press website (www.jpress.org.il), founded by the National Library and Tel Aviv University. Used with permission.

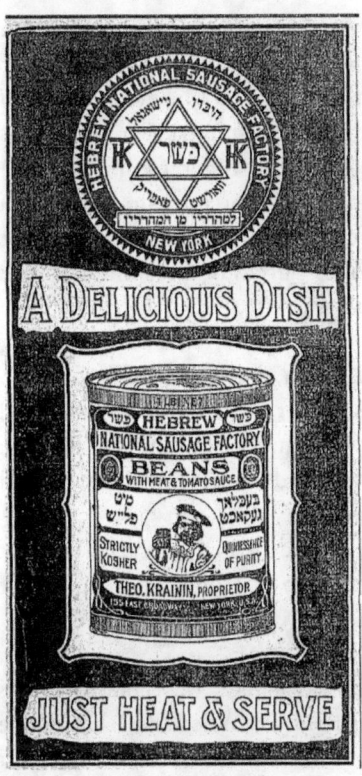

Krainin's entry into canned meats allowed him to counter the ubiquitous pork and beans marketed by rival Van Camp's. In 1915, Krainin produced the first canned franks and beans, more than thirty years before Van Camp's itself brought out their own franks and beans (Beenie Weenie) in the 1940s.[14] Krainin, in fact, was so bully on the canning end of Hebrew National that on his 1920 federal census he listed his profession as "manufacturer of canned goods."

In what appears to be the first example of product placement in Yiddish popular culture, Hebrew National (and a knish maker named Yonah) got unprecedented endorsements from the dean of Yiddish authors, Sholem "Sholem Aleichem" Rabinowitz. In 1916, the author was living out his final years in New York, where he began the second (and unfinished) half of his story "Motl peysye dem khazn's" (Motl Peysye, The Cantor's Son), which like its creator had now come to America:

> Have you ever heard of the "Hebrew National Wurst Company?" There's where they sell kosher Jewish meats: stuffed kishke, roast tongue, and smoked meats. On every corner of the city, they have *stores* where you can buy kosher sausages. If you're hungry and have time, you can order fresh, hot little kishkes which you eat with horseradish or mustard, just as you please. If you aren't short of money, you can order another portion. I, and my friend Mendl, once put away three orders and felt we could eat another two had we not run out of cash.[15]

On July 15, 1919, Krainin, following Isaac Gellis, opened a *brentsh stor*, Hebrew National Restaurant and Lunch Rooms, which soon grew to a half dozen locations in Manhattan—the one on Broadway off Waverly Place could seat 250 diners—and several in Coney Island, becoming the first kosher food sold there.[16]

English-language food writer Samuel Tenenbaum wrote about the rather recent transformation of Coney Island into a Jewish preserve thanks to delicatessen:

> Coney Island of olden days was famous for its clams and its chowder. It wasn't any wonder that the Jews made it a practice to load up with eatables, for if even they cared to pay the exorbitant prices asked they would have had to starve, that is. If they insisted on kosher food.
>
> All this has changed. Delicatessen as never before is Coney's popular food, and it is kosher, too. You can buy knishes and Hebrew National delicatessen next booth to the frozen custard on the Boardwalk.[17]

Hebrew National's growth in the aftermath of World War I was such that in 1922 Krainin started manufacturing sacramental wine at 125 First Street (across from where Katz's delicatessen is today), a curious choice given the at-best difficult time Jewish wine producers were having with the three-year-old Prohibition Act. The product line, however, would run for years.[18]

By 1925—the company's twentieth anniversary—the Krainin children had fully entered the Hebrew National workforce as head of sales, cashier, and export director. The company had built a new plant, one of the largest of its kind in the city, at a cost $150,000 (more than $1 million today) and was generating about $65,000 annually (approximately $1 million today).[19] However, within a few years, Krainin declared bankruptcy, selling his vast accrued resources for a mere $7,500, and disappeared from food business history.[20] In a lengthy display ad in the Yiddish papers, new owner Alter M. Brody claimed Krainin as the sole inventor of the modern kosher delicatessen and the creator of the brand's good name but also that the newly lightly renamed "'Hebrew National Food Products Corporation Company' has no connection, affiliation to the original company."[21]

By the middle of 1930, Brody flipped Hebrew National to Chicago's Sinai Kosher Wurst Company, bringing in local New York butcher Isidore Pinckowitz (1884–1936) as the face and president of the company.[22] In the 1910 census, the twenty-six-year-old Pinckowitz—who first came to the US in 1906, the year after Krainin founded Hebrew National—originally owned a necktie stand before opening a butcher shop at 407 Cherry Street. Pinckowitz's subsequent show of neighborhood civic generosity made him a member of the Locality Mayors of New York, a vestigial part of old local Tammany ward politics where well-to-do community members aided in neighborhood philanthropic acts. After Tammany, the "mayors" were described as "a group of cordial men who set themselves up as the benevolent despots in those districts where they live."[23] During the Depression, Pinckowitz ran a free soup kitchen on East Broadway out of a local Talmud Torah, and in 1931 he took over running an annual free seder for the Lower East Side's poor.[24]

Pinckowitz's presidency kept Hebrew National's kosher bona fides in place while expanding its outreach. In 1931, Hebrew National sponsored a Yiddish radio show on Brooklyn station WGBS featuring the Boibriker Kapelle, the noted klezmer orchestra led by fiddler Hirsh Gross.[25]

With Pinckowitz's death in 1936, his son Leonard (who Americanized the name to Pines) became president and continued to do outreach into the Jewish world (in the 1950s Hebrew National would be one of the rotating sponsors on WMGM's series *American Jewish Caravan of Stars*).

But, in 1953, Pines began the aggressive mainstreaming of Hebrew National, and succeeded in gaining more non-Jewish crossover than he was losing with the steadily declining number of delicatessens, by sponsoring radio coverage of the New York City mayoral results and "nonsectarian" programs for general audiences. Pines also did outreach into the African American community through Black newspapers and radio shows selling wine (by 1954, Hebrew National put over 90 percent of its wine advertising budget on the radio).[26]

Hebrew National (which *The New York Times* called "long a stronghold in pungent meats"[27]) spent annually as much as Dole Pineapple: $29,000 (a quarter million dollars today) on TV ads,[28] including commercials for a 1957 "Win Your Weight in Wieners" contest (a city-wide treasure hunt for "rubber franks hidden within 40 feet of delicatessens selling Hebrew National products").

In 1968, Pines sold 51 percent of Hebrew National to Riviana Foods[29] (makers of Carolina Rice) for $6.7 million dollars ($93 million today), which itself was soon consumed by Colgate Palmolive.[30] In 1977, Colgate Palmolive made advertising history when it hired ad agency Scali, McCabe, and Sloves (who had previously made a star of chicken magnate Frank Purdue with its "it takes a tough man to make a tender chicken" campaign) to spruce up the product's profile. The resulting ad featured Uncle Sam ("i.e., American food regulations") holding a frank and being told in a stentorian voice-over that although certain impurities were allowed by the US government, Hebrew National "answers to a higher authority." While it didn't catch on at first (*The New York Times* called it "obnoxious," with most complaints to the FCC coming from Jews), the ad (which is now considered a classic) later became so tied to the company's identity that Leonard Pines had it inscribed on his and his wife's headstone.[31]

In 1980 Colgate Palmolive put the company back on the market, where it was snatched up by Isidore "Skip" Pines, Leonard's son.[32] Skip's most fateful decision came in 1986 when, after a bitter strike at its Maspeth Long Island factory, he abruptly moved its operations, quite ironically, to a onetime ham processing plant in Indianapolis; an intrepid *Daily News* reporter journeyed to Indiana that August to ask local delicatessens if they carried pastrami, few of which did, with one explaining, "We're not Italian."[33]

In 1993, the company was acquired by culinary industrial complex giant ConAgra for $100 million during a market period when flagging mainstream sales made acquiring specialty niche food producers especially enticing.[34] ConAgra eventually acquired surviving kosher meat rivals like Isaac Gellis and putting them under the National Foods brand and quietly discontinued them, leaving Hebrew National the last of the old-time "pungent meat" brands. One of those acquired rivals was Zion National.

Zion National

Leopold Tarlow (1891–1953) came to the US around 1905, and by 1912 he opened a factory at 486 Austin Place in the Bronx, listing his occupation as "wholesale provisions." In the footsteps of Krainin and Gellis, Tarlow early on sought the approval of rabbinic authorities and underscored that connection by using כשר in his trademark registration.[35]

Around 1912, Zion National innovatively reinforced its identity among observant Jews by purchasing display space in Passover *haggadas*.[36] In 1915, Tarlow expanded his market by opening an exact duplicate "kosher style" factory right next door at 482 Austin Place with partner Max W. Anderson; Anderson and Tarlow and Zion Kosher Meats would run side by side for decades. By 1940, Tarlow's sons William and Jerome were both working for the firm in sales and as a shipping clerk.

As was common with food companies, Zion National sponsored a number of radio shows, including in 1936, a fifteen-minute program on WMCA dedicated to great singers of the stage and synagogue.[37] Zion was best known for its long-running soap opera *Uptown, Downtown* on WMCA and the *Zion Variety Hour*, an unusual combination of a choir, reenacted news of the day and a talent segment produced by Yiddish theater composer Abe Ellstein and choir leader Oscar Julius.[38]

Ironically, it was Zion's strict adherence to kosher that successfully enabled it to build large markets outside the Jewish world in both Islamic and African American communities. In 1940, on the heels of a meeting of Muslim religious leaders in Morocco that ruled that kosher was halal, Zion inked a deal to provide ten million frankfurters a month for Muslim troops serving in Allied armies in France and the Near East.[39] During the war, Zion underscored its connection to African Americans by funding a massive war bonds billboard looming over Times Square featuring a Black Uncle Sam.[40]

With the death of Leo Tarlow in 1953, his sons took over and Zion continued the connection to Muslim and African American communities thanks to the 1960s publication of the two-volume *How to Eat to Live* by the Nation of Islam leader Elijah Muhammed. As the Nation of Islam's nascent food industry geared up, Muhammed advised his followers to eat kosher food: "The Holy Quran teaches us that we can eat their food and they can eat our food."[41] Zion was able to sell directly to Nation of Islam temples and in bulk to their Shabazz stores until it built its own food infrastructure.

In 1972, Zion National was purchased by Mogen David Kosher products, which itself was purchased by ConAgra in 1995, and the brand name soon discontinued.[42]

Crime and Unions in the Kosher Food Industry

The cash-only nature of the prepared food industry made it a natural target for crime, and delicatessens rated more than their unfair share. In addition to facing periodic armed holdups, delicatessens were identified as one of the main locations for the work of white slavers, resulting in articles that warned "Dance academies and delicatessens are traps for young girls."[1]

In 1928, a group calling itself the Mogen Dovid Delicatessen Corporation (not the Mogen David company noted above), operating out of lower Second Avenue's Central Plaza, ran Yiddish newspaper ads calling for a mass meeting of all delicatessen owners in New York at the nearby luxe Libby's Hotel.[2] Prior to this, Mogen Dovid had been sending "salesmen" to Jewish delicatessens around the city, offering "membership" (i.e., "protection") in exchange for exclusively carrying Mogen Dovid's authorized Qualitessen brand "liverwurst, salami, pickles, pumpernickel, pretzels and a lot of other things that don't come in tin cans."[3] While Mogen Dovid managed to entrap 235 delicatessens (of the estimated three thousand throughout the city), it also managed to get the attention of a New York State grand jury inquiry, in which numerous witnesses told stories similar to that of Solomon Pomerance, who "when he tried to open a delicatessen store at 1492 Pitkin Avenue . . . was approached by a man named Drucker and ordered to pay $1,200 for the privilege of opening without interference."[4] The case would wither away, but so would the Mogen Dovid Delicatessen Corporation.

As Rabbi Jacob Joseph attempted to issue certification to restaurants that adhered to kosher practices, the rise of labor unions issued certification to restaurants that adhered proper labor practices. Soon, union certification rivaled kosher certification designating a place safe to eat

---

1. "Tantz-shuln un delicatessen *stors* als pastkes far yinge meydlekh," *Forverts*, Nov. 22, 1931, 5.
2. "Delikatesn *stor kippers*," *Morgn Zhurnal*, Aug. 16, 1928, 10.
3. "Turn Out the Guard! A Monopoly in Liverwurst Has Been Found," *St. Louis Star*, Mar. 3, 1928, 1.
4. "Says He Had to Pay $1,200 to Open Delicatessen Store," *Brooklyn Daily Eagle*, Mar. 1, 1928, 18.

for Jews. As a wurst maker's union struggled into existence, one of the first calls for a delicatessen worker's union came in a 1906 letter to the editor signed by "a delikatesn *kloyrk*," who threw down the gauntlet for the creation of a union:

> Comrades!
> How long will you remain slaves?
> How long will you continue to work 18-hour days with no time for a meeting, a lecture, in short, time for things for our uplift. . . .
> At the time that *veyters* and the *riteyl kloyrks* have all organized, why not us?[5]

The task would not be taken up until 1911, when a nascent grocery and delicatessen worker's union in Harlem spread to the rest of the city. The union would score its first major victory in 1913 when it overturned the same blue law, prohibiting stores to sell goods on Sundays, that brought Isaac Gellis his first blush of publicity eighteen years before.[6] By 1917 the New York Delicatessen Clerks Union counted over six thousand members, which, thanks to its first city-wide strike, in 1926 became the Delicatessen Counterman Union Local 302 of the American Federation of Labor.[7] From its peak when the 1927 city directory listed over sixty delicatessens on the Lower East Side alone, the union would disappear before most of the delicatessens.

---

5. "Fun folk tsum folk tsu ale delikatesn *kloyrks*," *Forverts*, Mar. 23, 1906, 5.

6. "Delikatesn *stors* muzn zayn ofn zuntog," *Forverts*, Apr. 24, 1913, 10.

7. "Di delikatesn *kloyrks yunyan* vert instolirt als *lokal* fun dem *amalgemeyted mit koters yunyan* fin America," *Forverts*, Aug. 5, 1925, 6.

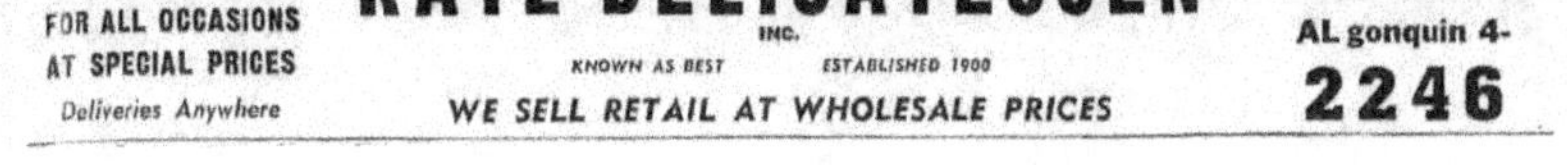

Figure 3.3. A 1943 phone book display ad for Katz's delicatessen with 1900 as the founding date. *Source:* New York Public Library Digital Collections. Public domain.

Katz's

Katz's enjoys bragging rights as the oldest Jewish delicatessen in New York (ergo, the world). Its founding goes back to brothers Herman/Hyman (1882–1955) and Morris (ca. 1886–1964) Iceland. Federal and state census records from 1905 and 1910 of the Icelands (alternately spelled "Island" and "Eisland") show they arrived in the United States ca. 1900, with the 1905 census showing both brothers working at delicatessens. By 1910, William Katz (b. Zev Wolf Katz, 1889–1943), who first arrived in the US in 1905, was Hyman Iceland's boarder and delicatessen employee. The 1915 New York City directory listing at 207 East Houston Street of "Eisland and Katz" showed Katz was no longer an employee but a partner.[43] After Katz took over in 1917, and enshrined his name on the business, the Iceland brothers left the restaurant business: Hyman would go into real estate and Morris moved to Saratoga Springs in 1920 and ran a series of kosher hotels.[44]

"Send a Salami"

Katz's had a lot of slogans. Some, like "Known As Best," were no better than those the delicatessen inherited from defunct eateries. ("From a sandwich to an institution" was from Arnold Reuben—he of decidedly unkosher eponymous sandwich fame—and Katz's "That's all" was from either pop song "At the Ball (That's All)" or Yiddish comedian Menashe Skulnik's famous exit quip "and det's all!")

But "Send a salami to your boy in the Army" more than made up for those.

Absenting its beloved forced rhyme of "army" with "salami," which can only be accomplished when using the all-but-defunct Bowery/Brooklyn accent, the slogan, like "Loose lips sink ships" and "We can do it," is inexorably tied to American World War II gung-ho. However, though it is ubiquitously reported as created as a wartime slogan—even on Katz's own website—the syndicated gossip column *Tales of Hoffman* on May 19, 1941, notes a "poem is displayed in the window of Katz's Delicatessen store, Ludlow and Houston streets: 'Send a salami to your boy in the Army'" more than half a year before Pearl Harbor, at a time when very few Americans had a boy in the Army.¹ This was still a time when American involvement against the Axis was no sure thing as antiwar isolationism (on both the left and the right) still held sway, thus marginalizing Jews, and so making the sign's pugnacious and prescient admonition to take up arms (and salamis) against the Nazis even more powerful and singularly amazing.

---

1. James Hoffman, "Tales of Hoffman," *Hollywood Reporter*, May 19, 1941, 3.

Katz's appeared never to have been kosher, unlike its better, down the street competitor Henry's delicatessen, but while Katz's may never have been kosher, it was, at one time, a union shop. A July 1918 notice in the *Forverts* announced that William Katz had complied with all union demands and Katz's would now sport a union placard in its window.⁴⁵ Katz would retain his union affiliations into the 1920s as a founding charter member of the Delicatessen Counterman's Union Local 302. But like the kosher designation, Katz's would do without the union too.

Katz's claims its founding year as 1888. As noted, the Iceland brothers, the acknowledged founders, only arrived in America around 1900, about a decade after the delicatessen's supposed 1888 opening. The 1903 Sanborn Fire Map (the bible of insurance company maps) identifies the business where Katz's should have been, not as a delicatessen but as a Chinese laundry.⁴⁶ None of Katz's interwar-years newspaper ads give an opening date, and a 1940 New York City tax photo of Katz's exterior back wall (taken from an empty lot on Orchard Street) shows extensive hand-painted advertising but no founding date.⁴⁷ The first documented "since" date is in Katz's 1943 Manhattan phone directory display ad, where it is given as 1900.

Sometime in the 1950s, the founding date was changed again when brown and tan baked enamel signs were installed on the delicatessen's Ludlow Street side, with the vertical panel reading "since 1898," at some point clumsily rendered into 1888.

The earliest print appearance of 1888 as the founding date occurs in an enthusiastic Craig Claiborne review from April 25, 1961.⁴⁸ Katz's enshrined the incorrect date into its publicity making it the lead line in its many subsequent reviews. (Internet searches for "Katz's delicatessen/1888" and "Katz's deli/1888" net nearly fifty thousand hits.)

But as "Send a salami to your boy in the Army" was a memorable slogan from Katz's wartime generation, it was joined by another memorable phrase in 1989: "I'll have what she's having," as Katz's (in a very strong supporting role) was the setting for that line in the wildly successful 1989 Rob Reiner rom-com *When Harry Met Sally*.[49] The movie assured not only the delicatessen's film immortality but likely its business immortality: in 2015 Katz's sold the air rights above its low-slung restaurant for $17 million, thus ensuring Katz's location on its own terms in perpetuity,[50] no matter what year it was founded.

Schmulka Bernstein/Bernstein-On-Essex Street

Another pioneering "pungent meat" purveyor in the early twentieth century was Schmulka Bernstein (1886–1968).

Born Shmuel Dmocher in the Polish town of Andrezejewo, he apprenticed to a butcher in Bialystok, where he met and married his wife, a cook for a rich family.[51] Dmocher, with $10 in his pockets, came to America in 1910, joined two years later by his wife and two children, taking up residence in a new land and with a new name: Bernstein.

The diminutive Schmulka Bernstein sported green tinted spectacles to aid with glaucoma, and was a pious man who adorned the walls of his store with a biblical mural and was known for openhanded philanthropy to religious institutions and people.

By 1930, Bernstein opened a butcher shop at 110-111 Rivington Street, adjacent to his smokehouse where all three sons worked as butchers.

Schmulka Bernstein's, known for all variety of delicatessen meats, also specialized in sugar-cured hickory smoked turkeys, geese, duck, and capons. In the late 1940s, Bernstein's produced kosher "bacon" (called "fry beef"), fashioned from textured strips of smoked steer belly. The audacious idea came via Bernstein's youngest American born son Murray (Morris), who was attuned to modern eating trends, unlike his traditional father. To heighten interest, they placed the fry beef's automatic slicing machine in their front window: "It is months now that a crowd, several rows deep, has been gathering . . . to watch 'Jewish Bacon' come off the slicing machine. . . . The crowd stands at the window oblivious to the burdens of parcels, of errands . . . no comments are made, they stand in silence, not to interfere with one another's contemplation, as they follow the course of the slices from the blade to the box."[52]

By the late 1950s, Schmulka stepped down, leaving his three younger sons the store and smokehouse, which they ran until 1966. In May 1945, oldest son Sol (1908–1992) opened Bernstein's Kosher Catering around the corner at 135 Essex Street, when in 1957 he dropped the catering to become the semi-schmancy Bernstein-On-Essex Street. For its first few years, it served solely standard delicatessen, but in 1960 made the unusual jump to augment the menu with kosher Chinese cuisine.[53]

Just as the Old World Schmulka heeded the advice of his American-born son to launch an idea attuned to modern tastes, so too did the European-born Sol heed the idea for kosher Chinese from his American-born store manager David Garfein (1907–1984).

Garfein was the son of kosher restaurateur Oscar Garfein, who came to America around 1902 and worked as a waiter. By 1914, he owned two restaurants: Garfein's Dairy Restaurant and the meat eatery Garfein's Jewish Family Restaurant on Avenue A. Following his father's death in 1930, David Garfein took over the Avenue A location, which he ran as a restaurant and catering hall until going to Bernstein's in the late 1950s.

The observant Garfein was a passionate advocate for the fusion cuisine idea:

"Young people from orthodox Jewish families have no opportunity to sample the food from New York's foreign restaurants. 'They get tired,' he explained, 'eating pastrami and corned beef sandwiches.'"[54]

Downtown Jews of an earlier decade were no strangers to Chinese food. From 1922 to 1926 *Forverts* readers would see a regular display ad for the Port Arthur Chinese restaurant on Mott street, touted as having a "brodveyer *dzhez bend*" (Broadway jazz band). "It is no rare occurrence," the *Forverts* later noted in 1928, "to go into a Chinese restaurant and see a *Yiddishe Momme* with a half dozen children having chow mein for lunch. . . . Chinese food has even invaded the home and many Jewish families are having Oriental fare instead of *kreplach* for dinner."[55]

The realization of kosher Chinese food was actually relatively easy given its near total absence of dairy (the Chinese, like Ashkenazi Jews, are widely lactose intolerant, thus avoiding the meat and milk conflict), while pork could be agilely bypassed with beef, chicken, and veal. For his kitchen,

Bernstein recruited Chinese cooks from Borscht Belt hotels already familiar with both kinds of cooking.⁵⁶

The menu recreated conventional Chinese American restaurant fare (Egg Foo Yung, BBQ spare ribs, Moo Goo Gai Pan) while creating fusions like Lo Mein Bernstein (David Garfein's concoction of fresh chicken livers, chicken breast, and sliced beef with Chinese vegetables).⁵⁷

Its swift growth can be seen in the Chinese menu going from only on Saturday nights to soon also Wednesday and, within a few months, nightly.

Bernstein's core clientele is identified in an early review:

> Last Saturday night eight Orthodox Jews came in wearing their traditional yamulkas, and not only ordered the Chinese specialties but also called for chopsticks, which they used with practiced ease. The manager asked them where they learned.
>
> "We were all born in Shanghai," answered one old gentleman. "I'm glad to see you have a Shanghai cook instead of Cantonese." Various other customers have identified themselves as having fled Germany and settled in China before and during the war.⁵⁸

The restaurant's male Chinese waiters were described by Schmulke Bernstein's granddaughter Michele Clark as "wearing black skullcaps with gold tassels that made them look simultaneously like observant Jews, and outtakes from the Mikado."⁵⁹ The Chinese waitstaff even became the source of a popular Borscht Belt gag: Two Bernstein customers, amazed at how well the waiters speak Yiddish, call over the manager to ask how he found them. "Shhhh," he shushed, "we told them we were teaching them English."

Bernstein-On-Essex Street (which, curiously, is widely misidentified as Schmulka Bernstein's) closed around 1992 but had already set a trend of kosher Chinese restaurants with the 1970s-era Moishe Peking (Manhattan) and Brooklyn's Shang Chai, both now closed.⁶⁰ There are currently some twenty kosher Chinese restaurants in New York City, with more than half in Brooklyn alone.⁶¹

Second Avenue Delicatessen: Abe Lebewohl (1931–1996)

Abe Lebewohl was a romantic. How else to explain someone who, after working for other delicatessens, decided to convert a bedraggled, generic corner luncheonette on the now equally bedraggled Lower East Side into a delicatessen—a kind of restaurant whose numbers were swiftly dwindling, and not only that but a kosher delicatessen, whose numbers were not particularly good to begin with. As noted, Abe Lebewohl was a romantic.

Born in the Ukraine, where his father Ephraim had been exiled to Siberia in 1940 for being a capitalist and exploiting the workers at his wool-dyeing plant in Lviv, Abe Lebewohl came to New York in 1950. After gaining experience, opened the Second Avenue Delicatessen in 1954 (the year before getting his US citizenship).[62] Although the neighborhood was in decline, Lebewohl benefited from nearby Manhattan Plaza being used for filming television shows, and his delicatessen was soon hosting numerous stars, many of whom would become regulars. In the mid-1960s, Robert Sylvester, who penned the syndicated *Daily News* column Dream Street, was mad for Lebewohl (whom he called "the Escoffier of Second Avenue") and would always find a way to slip in quips about the delicatessen in his column.[63] For example, in 1979, during the gas shortage, Sylvester reported that Lebewohl took to making local deliveries in a horse and wagon, and when New York City was on the cusp of bankruptcy, he advertised that proceeds for his salami sales would go to the municipal coffers.[64] Lebewohl was also a throwback to the old locality mayors, fiercely proud of his neighborhood and of the people in it, and with an outsized sense of responsibility for its collective well-being.

Indigent locals could sometimes outnumber paying customers. For years, for a few hours every day, Lebewohl would offer meals to those sixty-five or older at half price. He also hosted an annual Purim party for the blind, with Braille menus, MC'ed by comedian Sam Levenson.[65] He would also offer discounts to all. For one day in 1974 on his twentieth anniversary, Lebewohl lowered his prices to what they were when he first opened ("For every dollar coming in, a dollar twenty goes out," he joked).[66]

Lebewohl was also a romantic in his love for the Yiddish theater, which once thrived in his adopted neighborhood but fell long before he came to America. In 1980, in the delicatessen's cozy back, Lebewohl opened the Molly Picon Dining Room, its walls festooned with photos, sheet music, and posters of the grand dame of the Yiddish stage, who, living only a few blocks away, walked over for its opening.[67] In June 1985, in a nod to the Jewish Sid Grauman's Chinese Theater, Lebewohl unveiled his Yiddish theater walk of fame, a series of thirty-two plaques, each dedicated to two stars, embedded in the concrete sidewalk outside his restaurant. A live radio broadcast on WEVD marked the installation occasion, and although the event elicited a large turnout, not everyone knew what it was for. "One neighbor," Lebewohl noted afterward, "thought they were employees that died."[68] Given the Lebewohl family history of his father being punished by the Communists (Abe Lebewohl puckishly designed his family crest as a crossed hammer and pickle), his most quixotic idea was to open a kosher delicatessen in Moscow. Lebewohl made nearly a dozen trips there starting in 1968, but the plan was, ironically, scuttled by the fall of the Soviet Union.[69]

Lebewohl's tragic end was foretold in a series of signs that the insouciantly optimistic delicatessen owner repeatedly pooh-poohed. In an article on March 6, 1988, about a recent local murder, neighborhood booster Lebewohl waved off the danger: "I tell you it's very safe. My wife, she's an actress and she walks home alone late at night."[70] The next year, in the wake of a series of mob rubouts that proved to be a PR boon for the restaurants in front of which they occurred, reporters, who knew that John Gotti was a fan of the Second Avenue Delicatessen, approached Lebewohl for his opinion. "I only wish," he quipped, "that if they had to shoot my customer, they would have done it in front of my place."[71] And again, a few years later, a razor-wielding thief accosted and robbed Lebewohl, who, after handing over the money, calmly returned to work.

In 1996, Lebewohl, while depositing the weekend's $10,000 receipts, was held up. After he handed over the money, Lebewohl was shot twice at point blank range with a .38.[72] For nearly a decade after his death, the family continued to run the delicatessen, issued a cookbook in his memory, and had the vest-pocket park across the street named for him. But in 2006, the delicatessen was driven out by a steep rent spike (the space has since been replaced by one of a half dozen twenty-four-hour ATMs in the neighborhood).[73] Since the departure, Lebewohl's beloved Yiddish theater walk of fame is rapidly deteriorating. The plaques, shoddily constructed to begin with, required regular maintenance that stopped when the restaurant closed, and they have degraded to such a degree that many are no longer even legible.[74]

The Second Avenue Delicatessen reopened in 2007 off Third Avenue at Thirty-Third Street, with another location at First Avenue and East Seventy-Fifth. Despite a longstanding $150,000 reward, Abe Lebewohl's killer has never been found.[75]

4

Of Knishes and Kishkes

Knish-Story

Behold the humble knish, whose resilience lay in its Zelig-like adaptability to reappear in the same pastry shell but in different inner guises headed by potato, with kasha a very close second and other vegetable/fruit/cheese fillings bringing up the rear. And while knishes are generally vegetarian, liver was a significant exception: a knish recipe in the *Forverts* (April 8, 1950) includes liver, calves lungs and hearts, and *gribenes* (crispy minced chicken skins).[1]

A January 27, 1916, article under the headline "Rivington Street Sees War" was very likely the first time in the history of the *New York Times* that the word "knish" appeared. The "war" a was kind of Shmetfield-and-McOys feud, but instead of rifles and revolvers the antagonists used increasingly cheaper and cheaper knishes (or, as the reporter for the *Times* offered, "knishes—or knishi, or whatever the plural is"). The rivals were Max Green (with his United Knish Factory at 150 Rivington Street and reputedly the "inventor" of the knish) and a man with the same name as the Lower East Side's beloved Socialist congressman, Meyer London, across the street at No. 155.[2]

Over the course of weeks, the competitors enticed customers, first by steadily lowering the price of their five-cent knishes and then by escalating to more and more bombastic signage, and eventually augmenting selling knishes with live music: Max Green hosted a Jewish band, and Meyer London retaliated with jazz musicians, whose simultaneous playing resulted in what the *Literary Digest* said "suggests a performance of Schöenberg's 'Kammmersymphonie.'"[3] At one point, Green offered coupons that could be redeemed for prizes, resulting in one overeager eater (in a quick quest for a pocket knife) consuming twenty knishes in a sitting and having to be carried off.[4]

"Knish is one more esoteric word," the *Literary Digest* further informed its readers, "to add to the culinary vocabulary along with chop-suey, goulash and zabaglione."⁵

Curiously, and perhaps due to the snickering and condescending tone in the mainstream press, it appears that no New York Yiddish paper (*Forverts, Tog, Morgn Zhurnal*) covered the otherwise famous "knish war" going on in its own backyard.

The knish was, though, a dependable cultural Yiddish touchstone, like comic Aaron Lebedeff's hit 1926 Vocalion recording of Gilrod and Sandler's novelty song "Hot Dogs Un Knishes," whose chorus (replete with barking dog) advised:

> Hot dogs un knishes (Woof! Woof!)
> Hot dogs un knishes (Woof! Woof!)
> Es kost aykh bilig un s'iz git
> Un s'makht'n apetit
> Hot dogs un knishes (Woof! Woof!)
> Hot dogs un knishes (Woof! Woof!)
> V'et batrogn, yeder mogn
> Hot dogs un knishes!
> Hot dogs and knishes, Hot dogs and knishes
> It's cheap, it's good and made just right
> It's perfect for your appetite
> Hot dogs and knishes, Hot dogs and knishes
> There's no question about digestion
> Hot dogs and knishes!⁶

The knish, not surprisingly, crossed over into Jewish American popular culture not only as "Love and Knishes"—Mickey Katz's longtime signature valediction—but also in Lenny Bruce's arch 1960 takeoff routine on the Sidney Poitier and Tony Curtis film *The Defiant Ones*, where he riffs on the film's uplifting biracial message with the phrase "Yet. Knish."⁷ And equally ubiquitous to the knish is its dependable mispronunciation in the popular press, rendering it a polysyllable ("kah-NISH"), when it is קניש, not קאָניש or even a silent "k."

Yonah Schimmel

Yonah Schimmel, whose name has been prominently emblazoned on a large Lower East Side store sign since before Teddy Roosevelt was president, is a mystery hiding in plain sight. Disagreements abound: it is reported that he was a rabbi, a sofer (scribe), and/or a melamed (a children's teacher). Other accounts differ on where he was born, ranging from Romania to Bulgaria to Russia.[8] There is even uncertainty about the spelling of his name, with numerous variations such as on his 1901 naturalization papers ("Schimel") and on his headstone ("Shimel"). Between them, even the longtime store signs cannot seem to agree: the vertical yellow sign above the entrance reads "Shimmel," while the ones in the front window read "Schimmel."

What *is* known is that Schimmel (no matter how you spell it) was born in 1866 and came to the US in 1896. On his 1901 naturalization papers, Schimmel listed his occupation as "peddler" and his birthplace as Austria (i.e., Austro-Hungarian Empire/Poland). This corresponds with an article in the *Forverts* on June 21, 1920, about the postwar economic development in Lemberg (today's Lviv), which noted that one of its native business leaders, Marcus Shimel, "was the brother of the famous New York restaurateur, Yonah Shimel."[9]

By 1916, Yonah Schimmel had three bakeries on the Lower East Side, one just down the block from its current location on East Houston Street.[10] A measure of his success comes in the form of a 1913 *Forverts* comic strip featuring a trio of Getzl Tararam, Motl Bok, and the plump and portly "Yonah Knish."[11] Schimmel ceded ownership to his cousin/son-in-law Joseph Berger, who married Schimmel's younger daughter Rose in 1903; the couple worked as the knishery's bakers. Joseph Berger's son, Arthur Morris Berger, was brought in circa 1924, and upon Yonah Schimmel's death in 1931, Morris's wife Lillian joined.[12]

In the 1930s, the store was updated with the installation of a flashing sign whose two-story vertical "knishes" could be seen up and down East Houston Street. By 1950, branded with the rapper-like Snack Master Schimmel, the bakery successfully tuned in to the bite-sized zeitgeist and pioneered "cocktail knishes," which, with the other trade, were popular enough to enable the bakery to open a branch at 140 Delancey and (for a time) buy regular display ads in the *New York Times*.[13] After Arthur's death in 1974, Lillian Berger ran the business until 1985 when she sold to Ellen Anistratov and Ellen's father Alex Volfman, a Ukrainian immigrant who started working at Yonah Schimmel's as a busboy in 1979 and whose aunt was Yonah's granddaughter.[14]

The mixed-use building (residential and commercial) at 137 East Houston Street was only a decade old when Yonah Schimmel started renting there in 1910. The devastating collapse in 2000, during a restoration of its Siamese twin neighbor, resulted in a bland replacement, which, together with a new sleek glass-and-steel behemoth on its other side, makes the frowzy centenarian survivor look every nanosecond its age.[15]

In the long absence of visible capital improvements, the slow-motion decay of the building made it expeditious to exploit its shabby chicness. The interior—with the original shoulder-width bathroom, tin ceilings, and dumbwaiter system to the oven in the cellar—is frozen in time like a prehistoric insect trapped in amber. On the walls, displaying a tribute to long-forgotten Yiddish cultural neighbors, is a gallery of faded photographs and brittle clippings whose warm sepia tones evoke nothing more than the golden hue of a Yonah Schimmel knish itself. And while some bemoan the decay as a Yonah Schimmel 2.0 fan art version of its original, others see the knishery's resolute in situ resilience as an incredible—and edible—triumph.

SCHWARTZ'S FAMOUS POTATOPIE

Despite other Manhattan makers (and Queens' legendary Knish Nosh), the diverse and contentious story of the knish is a Brooklyn story.

In the book of Exodus, the Jews are led through the desert sands by Moses and sustained on manna. In America, the sand was at Coney Island, the manna was potato, and the "Moses" was Morris Schwartz, the forgotten father of the "Potatola," the original Coney Island knish.

Born in Russia, Morris Schwartz (1902–19??) set up his locavore Potatola Company in May 1925, selling Schwartz's Famous Potatopie from his home at 2807 Surf Avenue. Potatopies never sold outside of Coney Island, to honor the company's "one-hour factory-to-consumer" policy, which the Potatola Star of David coat of arms underscored with a solemn credo:

> Mir erloybn nit unzere *kustomers* tsu farkoyfn
> A knish vus iz nit itst gebakn un frish fun oyvn
> We promise our customers, this all above in
> That we'll never sell a knish not fresh from the oven.[16]

Schwartz took his outreach seriously (ads appeared only in the Yiddish press) and took his kosher ranking just as seriously, as he got the two major kosher delicatessen companies (Isaac Gellis and Hebrew National), who were then operating their own restaurants, to carry his knishes exclusively in Coney Island. Suddenly, you could not go anywhere on Surf Avenue, on the Boardwalk, or on the Bowery without seeing Schwartz's Famous Potatopie at twenty locations "in every good restaurant and stand."[17]

Figure 4.1 Coney Island's first knish, Morris Schwartz's Potatola (1925). *Source:* National Library of Israel, Historical Jewish Press website (www.jpress.org.il), founded by the National Library and Tel Aviv University. Used with permission.

Yet just as quickly, on February 9, 1926, Morris Schwartz stopped. Though his partners planned to revive the Potatola business, they never did.[18] By 1940, Schwartz was a syrup manufacturer, with his Potatola a brief, bright knish comet streaking across the Yiddish New York City skies.

GABILA

How much more fitting could it be for someone wholly identified with the knish as Elia Gabay (1889–1971) to be born in a town called Niš (pronounced "Nish") in today's Yugoslavia.[19] Yet how ironic that the person most identified with this iconic Ashkenazic food was himself not Ashkenazic, but Sephardic.

It's unclear the trajectory that took Elia Gabay from being trained as a high-end cobbler to coming to America around 1919 to become involved with food. And for a company known for knishes, Gabay's first "Gabila" branded product was not a knish but a "non-alcoholic maltless beverage" soft drink, as announced in the trade magazine *The Soda Fountain*.[20] Gabay produced the soft drink Gabila until 1926, when, after an attempt at a restaurant (in which wife Bella did all the cooking and baking), with a cash influx of $100,000 ($1.5 million today) he bought a three-story brick factory in downtown Brooklyn and switched to baking.[21] Gabay's business card around this time showed him astride a charging steed over the legend "The King of Potatopie," crowning himself with the same product name Brooklynite Morris Schwartz had just recently abandoned.

During the 1928 New York attorney general "Qualitessen" hearings, one of the state's witnesses was Gabay. In underscoring his testimony about being bodily threatened not to sell knishes to nonpaying "members," Gabay offered everyone in court from "a pan of thirty hot knishes," which the writer for the *New York Times* gamely described as "a kind of stuffed dumpling."[22]

The Ladino Gabay (he listed Spanish as his principal language in the 1925 census) was a devoted supporter of Sephardic charities. The pencil-thin mustachioed Gabay was also a dapper dresser who usually sported a derby and spats, and who once stopped a cattle stampede on the Williamsburg Bridge with his cane. And, in a footnote—as it were—to his former career as a high-end cobbler, Gabay and his wife Bella were fierce competition ballroom dancers who netted a showcase full of silver loving cups for their terpsichorean efforts.[23]

What Manischewitz did for matzo—industrializing what had been until then an entirely bespoke food while maximizing its portability, storability, and shelf life, thereby stabilizing profits—by altering its traditional shape from round to square, is what Gabay did for knishes. But Gabay went one step further and altered not only the traditional shape but also the traditional preparation from baking to deep frying.

It was perhaps thanks to the same hand skills, which made him a custom cobbler, that Gabay was also a tinkerer and inventor (e.g., he got his car horn to go "a-oo-GA" instead of the normal "a-OO-ga"). By 1932, Gabay switched from handmade knishes to knishes made on machines he himself designed with internals so proprietary, they were never patented for fear of revealing their workings. Gabila would soon produce a million knishes daily.[24] It was further fortuitous that Gabay's knish process also made them perfectly suited to the postwar American boom in frozen food, and his sales numbers again jumped exponentially. Despite some setbacks, including a 1996 fire at the plant that caused an acute knish crisis and a 1998 recall involving a quarter million pounds of knishes,[25] Gabila, in its fourth generation and with sales that would exceed twenty million knishes a year, left Brooklyn in 2006 for the south shore of Long Island.[26]

Gabila's knishes had a—literally—hidden part in the 1984 Sergio Leone Jewish gangster film *Once Upon a Time in America*. Principal shooting for the movie's important opening panoramic exteriors was done during some unexpectedly frigid spring days, only steps from Gabila's Williamsburg location. The factory's ventilation system bathed the 1910s-era movie set in a steady stream of warm, baked smells, as if someone nearby had set out a truck-sized pie to cool on a window sill. During a break—and looking everything like a pilgrimage to a holy site—hundreds of shivering "Hasidic" extras made their way to the factory to buy knishes because the pockets of the thin kapote (jacket) that were issued (myself and a friend included) neatly and unobtrusively fit the fresh, hot squares that now served as very much appreciated hand warmers.

Shatzkin's Famous

Gabila's was not, however, the only fried knishes. A variant was the lightly fried knish of Shatzkin's Famous.

Sam Shatzkin was born in 1902, two years after his family came from Lithuania, where his father Yosl "Alex" had been a tinsmith, becoming a plumber in America. The family recipe for fried knishes is credited to Alex's wife, who would sell them, as rhapsodized decades later by author Joseph Heller (*Catch-22*) who grew up in Coney Island and feasted on them: "Mrs. Shatzkin used to make these fabulous knishes with onions and peppers in her apartment and bring them down and sell them from a basket on Surf Avenue when she was about 70."[27]

However, the family business really took off when Sam Shatzkin (who trained and worked as a master electrician) changed careers after World War II. The 1950 census lists him as a "salesman" at a "frankfurter concession."[28] The concession was in an old building at Fifteenth Street and Surf Avenue, "which once saw a striptease bathed in sherry light," across the street from Nathan's, for whom Shatzkin supplied knishes.[29] Store number one would be joined by a second location at Twenty-First and the Boardwalk run by Sam Shatzkin's brother, who trained as a chemical engineer but could find no work in that field because he was Jewish.[30]

One time, in an attempt to break up a fight in his knishery, the five-foot-six, 190-pound Sam Shatzkin was "beaten about the head and body and struck on the back with a chair," resulting in "two black eyes, a fractured nose, a sore shoulder." In sentencing the assailants, who were also longtime customers, the trial judge ventured, "I guess there were too many vitamins in those knishes which gave you strength." "It wasn't the knishes," noted one of the assailants. "It might have been the few drinks we had before."[31]

Despite the success of its cooked knishes (lightly fried and round, as opposed to Gabila's deep fried and square), Shatzkin's felt the pull of baked knishes in the 1950s and started carrying Schimmel-style potato cocktail knishes, with cherry cheese and blueberry cheese but also more offbeat fillings like huckleberry cheese and pineapple cheese. However, as no one in the Shatzkin family knew how to bake knishes, they had to be made by a traditional knish baker.[32] Not everyone was a fan. In 1970, *Newsday* food writer Arthur Schwartz called Shatzkin's fruit and cheese knishes "something between a cheese strudel and a sugared doorstop."[33] However, two years later, travel writer Eric Newby's Time Off column in the *London Observer* (May 28, 1972) rhapsodized over Shatzkin's: "A delectable pastry filled with various fruits, cheese or potato and prepared before your very eyes."[34] Newby's column was picked up in a number of newspapers and generated a surge in traffic. By this time, Shatzkin's could no longer find experienced knish makers, so, like Gabila, it began mechanizing, and by the end of the decade was producing 100,000 knishes a week.[35]

In 1975, Shatzkin's pulled up stakes from Coney Island and moved to Mill Basin's new Kings Plaza shopping mall and soon "diversified into a wild orgy of 27 varieties," including a "chow mein knish, a pizza knish, and a 'Super Big Boodum' (a knish split open and filled with corned beef and pastrami)."[36] It is unclear when Shatzkin's closed.

Mrs. Stahl's: Fannie Stahl (1887–1961)

While Yonah Schimel wins for longest running, Gabila's for sheer multitudinous numbers, and Morris Schwartz for being the first Brooklyn manufacturer, no knish comes close to inspiring the kind of rhapsodic recall, the kind of eternal, ethereal devotional fidelity at the powerful crossroads of ambrosia and nostalgia, like Mrs. Stahl's knishes.

Fannie Stahl was born in Poland and married Hebrew teacher Samuel Stahl, twenty-two years her senior, around 1905. They arrived in the US between 1914 and 1920 and their census tell the whole story: the 1925–1930 reports show the Stahls as a typical Jewish immigrant family living in Ramapo, New York, with Sam teaching Hebrew, Fannie as a housewife, and two daughters Rae and Bela working as operators and finishers in the dress business. The 1930 census shows that the family moved to the Midwood section of Brooklyn, with Fannie's husband still teaching Hebrew. Sometime after that, he died.

The 1940 census picks up the story: Fannie is now head of the family with the daughters no longer operators and finishers in the needle trades but as a "counter girl" and a cashier in their mother's new restaurant. After her husband's death and with only a fourth-grade education, Fannie raised herself up Mildred Pierce–fashion, from selling homemade knishes out of a shopping bag to owning a store on Brighton Beach and Coney Island Avenues, the Brooklyn Jewish seashore's Saint-Tropez. Under the sharp curve of the BMT's overhead El where the steel wheels of the Manhattan-bound subway first begin their shrill metallic keening, Fannie Stahl's knishes—kasha, potato, potato mushroom, sweet potato, cabbage, cherry cheese, blueberry cheese, mushroom, potato-spinach, and more—were baked into the culinary consciousness of generations.

While businesses like Stahl's benefited from commercial industrial refrigeration, Mrs. Stahl's would be undone by the postwar residential offshoot of refrigeration: air conditioning. Gone were the days of vast beach crowds. This critical downturn in summer tourism, which had historically bolstered its bottom line through the slack winter months, was exacerbated by a steady erosion of its customer base for whom this was a year-round comfort food. While the influx of a new Russian Jewish population slowed Stahl's decline, evidence of the neighborhood's changing eating habits could be seen in the shrinking counter space for knishes, space gobbled up by other foodstuffs. The knishes were no longer sold at the high-volume/high-visibility streetside window but pushed into the back of the store, where the knish ovens had also been displaced by the pizza ovens up front. Even the store sign reflected the deleterious effects of that change: What at one time had been a ten-foot-tall sign with the proud, sweeping Spencerian signature "Mrs. Stahl's knishes" was now a tiny "Mrs. Stahl's" in the upper left, with "knishes" in an intermarriage with "pizza."

With Fannie's death, her capital stock and knish recipe were acquired by Morris and Sam Weingast, who continued to honor the Stahl legacy.[37] They made a few attempts to branch out, including opening an outpost on West Seventy-Second in 1988; in 1991, a pair of Brooklyn expats opened a store featuring the lowly knish on the otherwise tony and fashionable Wilshire Blvd in Beverly Hills. Both ventures only lasted a couple of years. Mrs. Stahl's closed in 2005.[38]

A middle-period Mrs. Stahl's store sign was its Gadsden flag, but instead of "Don't tread on me," it defiantly proclaimed "Baked, not fried," the battle cry in an increasingly futile rear-guard action against Gabila's sheer numbers. After decades of Gabila's palaver of being the "original" Coney Island knish, it was finally the only knish, because if a knish could be found in what was once the domain of Schwartz's Famous Potatopie, Shatzkin's Famous, and Mrs. Stahl's, it would be Gabila's.

The Kishke King

Kishke, the name of the intestine casing in which flour, schmaltz, onions, garlic, and spices are baked, did not get the same kind of love as knishes. A beloved Sabbath and holiday side dish, kishke was never quite ready for its delicatessen close-up.

Kishke had a kind of comic allure: the expression "a kishke un a dno" ("a casing without a closure") is about something that goes on forever. Borscht Belt comics dubbed the Catskills hotel circuit the "Derma Road" and the hotel's dining room side dish as "Hebrew haggis," while wedding musicians would call old-time klezmer repertoire "kishke music." And, of course, "kishke" was the favorite punch location offered by ringside boxing kibitzers.[39] It was a punchline even when not intending to be:

> A large restaurant on Second Avenue. Noontime. The tables were packed with men and women; fork and knife and plate and glasses clinked and hummed.
>
> Waiters fly back and forth, were they just silent; they yell, they holler, they bellow orders: "A half spring chicken! Boiled beef! Kreplakh! Hamburger steak! Chopped liver!"
>
> Suddenly, a pale young man with blue circles under his eyes stands up and begins to harangue the diners because they are eating meat and fish. Figs and raisins they should be eating!

And before he could get another word out, he is hit in the head with a piece of kishke.

Now the vegetarian becomes angry and starts yelling:

"Such people! You want to throw something at me? Alright, throw! I was expecting this. But please, people: you know I'm a vegetarian; throw me a baked potato, a tomato, an onion, a radish, a head of lettuce, some figs, a watermelon, a sour pickle, but no kishke!"

Which, of course, resulted, in a salvo from all directions of kishke.[40]

One of the early commercial kishke purveyors was "Papa" Joseph Burger, whose Avenue C restaurant, "Café Burger," hosted a 1911 Purim feast featuring the corpulent US president William Howard Taft upon his return from Panama. "Kishkes did that noble man eat," Burger boasted, while Papa's trained South American poll parrot Pokol chortled "Sholom Aleichum, Mr. President."[41]

Kishke found its modern champion in Jacob Sohn (1905–1969) the beloved self-proclaimed "Kishke King." Sohn's father Eleazar "Louis" trained as a wurst maker in the Kamanetz region of Ukraine, while the US census lists his occupation as "butcher" from 1905 to 1915. Then, at 1711 Pitkin Avenue ("the Broadway of Brownsville") he opened a wurst and kishke factory, which by 1930 employed six of the eight Sohn children including Jacob, and by 1940 the factory was Kishke King. Jacob Sohn, "a tall, heavy-set man with dreamy eyes,"[42] loved kishke and was its passionate partisan and poet laureate: " 'Ah,' he sighs, 'the kishke is to be eaten slowly, not gulped. The true lover of kishke never goes at it like he's running to a fire. He eats it delicately, like a true lover.' "[43]

Sohn made kishke a more common commercial finger food by 1949, when he reported selling four hundred kishkes (a.k.a. four thousand pounds) weekly in forty-cent increments: "On Saturdays and Sundays, the busiest days, the kishke sells in huge quantities. The 14 employees of the 'Kishke King' work like beavers as the cry 'Kishke!' is sung in Pitkin Ave., and Jacob himself stands behind the open counter, handing out kishke with pride."[44]

Yet as Sohn loved kishke, he loved Brooklyn—and Brownsville—just as much. Jacob Sohn could always be counted on to provide refreshments for any community event from a Salute to Israel parade to a March of Dimes fundraiser to a pre-Christmas celebration for orphans and even served as the grand marshal of the annual Brownsville Thanksgiving Day parade. In an acknowledgment of his evergreen civic pride, on October 19, 1949, Sohn was named "the mayor of Brownsville," the sixtieth New York City locality mayor. To honor this occasion, Sohn hosted a twenty-four-course banquet "with each course embellished with some form of kishke," while "the bill of fare itself was printed on kishke skins."[45] Sohn was as popular in the Jewish community as he was among African Americans (the *Amsterdam News* called him "one of Brownsville's most popular businessmen").[46]

The nineteenth-century three-story wooden building at the corner of Pitkin and Thatford Avenues had only recently ended some twenty-five years as Toback's Hall, when it was acquired by the Sohns for their wurst operation. It's likely that the first thing the Sohns did once they made the transition to being a restaurant was the installation of an industrial-strength horizontal neon כשר "delicatessen" sign over the Pitkin Avenue main entrance. But that was their last quotidian signage.

The building's focus shifted from the intended Pitkin Avenue side onto Thatford Avenue when the Sohns broke through the wall, not only creating some fifteen yards of outdoor counter space but also revealing the building's west facade as a tabula rasa in desperate need of filling. The Sohns soon capped the building with a two-story billboard visible from a half mile away on Eastern Parkway: a giant sign for a "Giant hamburger—enough food for a family of four." Other west wall signs included "A frank built for two / 12c 10 inches long 14 bites" accompanied by a thirty-foot-high portrait of a young couple caught in mid-bite who bear more than a slight resemblance to the grinning gap-toothed mascot of Coney Island's Steeplechase Park.

The cutouts were perhaps the most eye-catching of the building's commercial folk art: a massive כשר cow and a nearby trio of men: two muscular and beefy, atop the other's shoulders, one with an "Eat Franks," T-shirt and the other "Eat Hamburgers," and, standing off to the side, a smaller emaciated, drooping figure whose shirt reads: "I Didn't Eat at Kishke King." "The Most blatant establishment on Pitkin Avenue," was how *Brooklyn Daily Eagle* columnist Margaret Mara described the Kishke King facade in a column describing her recent slumming expedition to Brownville. She sniffed at the "delicatessen with this 30 foot sign across the entire face of the building."[47]

For everyone else, however, the bright, playful, and colorful Pitkin Avenue destination was a beloved local landmark and to no one more so than to the homegrown photographer who documented it for all time: N. Jay Jaffee. Born in Brooklyn, Jaffee was a trade school graduate and union

Figure 4.2. The dynamic façade of Kishke King captured the year the author was born around the corner. *Source:* Kishke King, Brownsville, Brooklyn, © 1953 by N. Jay Jaffee. All rights reserved. Used by permission of the N. Jay Jaffee Trust (www.njayjaffee.com).

typesetter before World War II, during which he experienced fierce fighting in the European theater.[48] As part of his subsequent recovery, Jaffee turned to photography, which soon became his career as a focused and attentive observer of New York street nuances. As the *New York Times* noted decades later: "His work is like a number of photographers who were very involved with trying to integrate art into a whole social scheme. . . . But his images are somewhat more lyrical and based on a kind of poetry of the street, it's more about memory than the present tense."[49] Jaffee's 1953 photo documents not only the iconic local landmark, but its deep biculturality: all the customers at the store's streetside window are Black. The picture was taken the same year I was born, around the corner on Chester Street, with that very Kishke King sight a powerful memory of my toddler years.

And as much as Sohn loved kishke, Brooklyn, and Brownsville, he also loved the Brooklyn Dodgers. One of the popular folk tales about Sohn was that as a diehard Dodgers fan he had long promised that if his beloved Bums ever won the World Series, he would treat everyone in Brownsville to one of his famous foot-long franks. In 1955, the Dodgers won the World Series. The story survives only anecdotally, with no news coverage to explain how the sheer physical impossibility to hand-produce the thousands of franks required was actually accomplished. After the Dodgers left Brooklyn in 1957, Sohn seemingly lost his inner light, and as his core clientele moved away, he disappeared from public view. Kishke King lasted for another few years after Sohn's death in 1969.

5

Joseph Moskowitz and Romanian Restaurants

The landscape of Jewish dining had clear demarcations of light and shadow: Kosher, the long-established standard of "pure food" was now joined in the light by the new breed of dairy/vegetarian restaurants equating the nourishing, humanist, and health-giving elements of their food with the clean, white, bright settings in which they were served. And underscoring their light, airy open spaces were their daylight and early evening hours. There were also Jewish restaurants in the shadows, open only at night, which, instead of large and airy, offered smoky and dark, and instead of the healthy and nourishing dairy/vegetarian (or the promise of כשר) would cap their bad-boy dining status as the only public display—such as it was—of Jewish drinking.

If dairy/vegetarian and kosher cuisine were the synagogues of Jewish restaurants, then Romanian restaurants were the Yiddish theater, offering the most lavishly sensory experience in the Jewish restaurant universe. On the one hand, the food sensory was fueled by karnatzlakh (Romanian broilings), coal-fired grilled meats, and the more modest Romanian steak (a skirt steak), joined by their omnipresent sidekicks: kishke, varenikes/kreplekh (dumplings), kashe varnishkes (groats and bow tie pasta) with shmaltz, and the binding mortar of Romanian gastronomic architecture, mamaliga (corn meal pudding). And wine: lots of wine.

And cheek by jowl with the culinary stimulation was the equally stimulating music. Not music in a passive digestif wallpaper sense or as a melodic metronome for rote dance, but music both plaintive and toe-tapping, rousing and reminiscent; music so brilliantly visceral, so essential in its connectivity that not infrequently it outweighed the food in importance.

That was due to the patron saint of New York Jewish Romanian restaurants/ cymbalom virtuoso, Joseph "Yossele" Moskowitz (1879–1954).

Joseph Moskowitz: Moskowitz & Lupowitz, Part I

Born in Galatz, Romania, Joseph Moskowitz (1879–1954) was a child prodigy musician and his family's early breadwinner. The twenty-eight-year-old Moskowitz was invited for a concert tour in the US in 1907 and then, joined by his wife only a few months later, never left.[1] From first setting foot on American soil, Moskowitz proved irresistible for a succession of English-language feature writers. An anonymous *New York Times* scribe (April 26, 1908) rhapsodized about Moskowitz's arrival in New York, while slightly mischaracterizing the restaurant's cuisine: "The café where he plays is several blocks east of 'Little Hungary' which is about all of East Houston Street that the uptown New Yorker knows. In this little eating room, from 7:00 p.m. to 2:00 a.m., Joseph Moskowitz discourses music by dexterous use of two little sticks for those who come partake of the raw meat and nudel soup served there."[2]

Moskowitz's success hinged not only on his virtuosic musical brilliance but on his timing: Romanian music was becoming a force majeure on Yiddish popular and dance music. Like rhythm and blues would be to rock and roll in the 1950s, Romanian music would influence how klezmer and Yiddish theater music would be played for decades. An excellent barometer of the renewable resource of Romanian music and food is Aaron Lebedeff's classic "Roumania, Roumania," whose paean to Romanian eats ("mamaligele, karnatzale, pastramale") in the energy-building doina-hora-bulgar structure was so popular that Lebedeff recorded it four times between 1919 and 1953 and it remains in standard Yiddish song repertoire.

In 1915, on the heels of opening his first restaurant at 113 Forsythe Street, Joseph Moskowitz (who listed "musician" on that year's New York census) recorded a jewel box collection of some twenty 78s of Yiddish, Romanian, Hungarian, Turkish, and even some very peppy rags for the Victor company. The records, the first cymbalom recordings ever made in the US, were so popular that they stayed in Victor's catalog for over a decade, until the new electrical microphone recording process made them obsolete.[3]

In 1916, Moskowitz joined forces with fellow Romanian Samuel Lupowitz (1882–1954), and opened Moskowitz & Lupowitz at 158 East Houston Street, soon a destination as noted in the syndicated column New

York Day By Day: "Over on the East Houston street there is a Roumanian restaurant where the music is provided by the proprietor who plays on the cymbaleme [sic]. The entertainment is extempore and ancient and modern songs are rendered by the patrons. An old man with a raisin wrinkled face may sing some weird chant to be followed by a rouged, henna-haired girl who sings 'The Vamp.'"[4]

On her 1920 census, spouse Rebecca Moskowitz demurely listed "housekeeper" as her occupation, yet more accurately on her passport application the same year she listed "restaurant keeper," as she was the baking and cooking backbone of the restaurant. Rebecca was also part owner: the previous year, she took out a ten-year lease at 90 Rivington Street for what was characterized by Joseph Moskowitz on that same 1920 census as a "wine cellar."[5] This was no doubt the same Rivington Street wine cellar thrillingly described in eyewitness detail in the 1930 roman à clef *Jews Without Money* by Michael Gold:

> There were dozens of Russian and Rumanian wine cellars on the East Side. They were crowded with family parties after the day's work. People talked, laughed, drank wine, listened to music. That was all, no one smashed chairs about in the Christian manner, or cursed or fought or slobbered.
>
> Moskowitz runs a famous restaurant now on Second Avenue. In those years he kept a wine cellar on Rivington Street. It was popular among Rumanian immigrants, including my father and his friends. Moskowitz was, and is a remarkable performer on the Rumanian gypsy cymbalom.
>
> I remember his place. It was a long narrow basement lit by gas-lamps hanging like white balloons. Between the lamps grew clusters of artificial grapes and autumn leaves. There were many mirrors and on them, a forgotten hand had painted scenes from Rumanian life—shepherds and sheep, a peasant, a horse fair, peasants shocking wheat, a wedding.
>
> At one end of the room, under a big American flag, hung a chromo showing Roosevelt charging up San Juan Hill. At the other end hung a Jewish Zionist flag—blue and white bars and star of David. It draped a crayon portrait of Dr. Theodore Herzl, the Zionist leader, with his pale proud face, black beard and burning eyes. To one side was an open charcoal fire, where lamb scallops and steaks grilled on the spit. Near this, on a small

platform, Moskowitz sat with his cymbalom. Strings of red peppers dried in festoons on the wall behind him. A jug of wine stood at his elbow and after every song he poured himself a drink.

As Moskowitz played, his head moved lower and lower over the cymbalom. At the crescendo one could not see his face, only his bald head gleaming like a hand mirror. Then, with a sudden upward flourish of his arms, the music ended. One saw his shy, lean face again, with its gray mustache. Everyone cheered, applauded and whistled. Moskowitz drank off his wine and smiling shyly, played an encore. (Moskowitz is a real artist, after twenty years he still makes restaurant music with his heart and has never saved any money.)

A hundred Jews in a basement blue as sea fog with tobacco smoke. The men wore their derby hats. Some were bearded, some loud sporty and young, some brown as nuts. The women were fat and sweated happily and smacked their children. Moskowitz played. The waiters buzzed like crazy bees. A jug of good red Rumanian wine decorated the oilcloth on every table. The cash register rang; Mrs. Moskowitz was making change. The artificial grapes swung from the ceiling. Teddy Roosevelt, with bared teeth, frightened the Spaniards. Moskowitz played a sad and beautiful peasant ballad. A little blubber-faced man with a red beard beat his glass on the table, wept and sang. Others joined him. The whole room sang.[6]

As brilliant as was Moskowitz's timing for introducing Romanian music, it was not as good for opening a Romanian "wine cellar" given the passage of the Volstead Act six months after opening, resulting in places like his soon being shuttered.

In 1926, Joseph Moskowitz left Moskowitz & Lupowitz to open Moskowitz's Little Roumanian Rendezvous at 76 Second Avenue.[7] Run as a cozy and easygoing extension of his own home ("Drop in any time between 11:00 a.m. and 3:00 a.m."),[8] Moskowitz did so well that he opened a larger restaurant in 1928 at 100 Second Avenue, and the following year, an even larger one ("You can dance as much as you want. We have plenty room!") at 219 Second Avenue, under the name the Original Moskowitz.[9] His third-person Yiddish and English newspaper ads all came with a similar disclaimer: "Disregard all other places on the Avenue, which wrongfully commercialize the name of Moskowitz in order to mislead the public. Moskowitz has no connection with any such places."[10]

Figure 5.1. "If you want delicious food and beautiful music come hear the world renowned tsimbler, Little Joe Moskowitz" (1926). *Source:* National Library of Israel, Historical Jewish Press website (www.jpress.org.il), founded by the National Library and Tel Aviv University. Used with permission.

Moskowitz leaving the restaurant as ". . . & Lupowitz" was news. *New York Evening Journal* columnist Louis Sobol reminded readers "to be sure [to] keep the 'Original' in caps for it appears there are other Moskowitz restaurants which are not original."[11] Perhaps the most unusual response to the new Original Moskowitz was a full-page Yiddish ad for Old Gold cigarettes. Beneath photos of the restaurant's exterior and of the maestro at his instrument was Moskowitz's signed statement soberly attesting to the official results of a "best American cigarette blind taste test held at the Original Moskowitz's restaurant." (PS, Old Gold won.) Sadly, in the Yiddish ad, Old Gold's famously nimble slogan ("Not a cough in a carload") was rendered: "In a gantsn vagon kent ir kayn hust oyf a refue nit krign / In an entire wagon you will never find a cough.[12]

Moskowitz's concert career continued: "Talent exists in all sorts of places and occupations. The proprietor of a Roumanian restaurant in the lower east side has been entertaining his patrons for many months by playing on a cymbalom. Uptowners who don't go in for what they call 'slumming' smiled when their more adventuring friends told them of their discovery of real music in the little eating place. Now that restaurant proprietor is to give a recital at our Town Hall later this month."[13]

Restaurants like Moskowitz's *were* magnets for slummers: the after-theater, top-hatted uptowners with their begowned arm candy who taxied down to the East Side to see how the other half lives in the half-light:

"Gotham's high society, always seeking for something novel as a relief from ennui—one of the penalties of belonging to the class that toils not nor spins—has discovered a new means of passing an unconventional evening. . . . Nocturnal visits to 'Chinatown' which until recently were the vogue among all those who sought the ultra-Bohemian, have given way to the latest craze—a visit to the Yiddish theater."[14]

Perhaps no one made a farther or more determined slumming expedition to Moskowitz's than did British travel writer Stephen Graham for his titillatingly titled 1927 book *New York Nights*. Graham's homage and vivid depiction of Moskowitz's restaurant was preceded by Moskowitz childhood friend Konrad Bercovici in his 1924 travel book *Around the World in New York*. Moskowitz (whom Graham refers to as "the greatest Jew I ever met") makes repeated appearances throughout Graham's city safari, which starts early (and ends late) at Moskowitz's. "Because of the Saturday night crowd, it is at first difficult to distinguish him. He is not standing behind the elevated table on which his elaborate dulcimer is reposing, but wandering among the swarm of guests, exchanging the local business news and Jewish witticisms."[15] Graham, who was unable to contain his amazement that a restaurant-owning Jew would not station himself in direct proximity to the cash register, allowed that Moskowitz

> is a mellowed easy-going soul, not running "Little Roumania" to make a fortune, but because he loves it (and) does not feel urged to play to the sixty cent audience who are gulping down Roumanian food and hurrying to be in time to Gabel's theater or Houston Street Winter Garden . . .
>
> This first burst of customers is not preferred. When they are gone their places will be taken by those who think they get enough entertainment for the night at Little Roumania . . .
>
> It is most alive after the theater, and becomes thronged with artistic elements of the Lower East Side. It is a marvelous little safety-valve, and its entrance is a trap-door leading away from one of the most commercial regions of the city.[16]

The safety valve was built-in, as Moskowitz was a true humanist, a regular advertiser in progressive publications like the *New Masses*, *Daily Worker*, and *Morgn Freiheit*. In an article about anti-Roma sentiment in New York City, Moskowitz is showcased as their vigorous defender: "The owner of the 'Original Moskowitz Roumanian Restaurant' is always glad to see them in his place, we are told. He stops the orchestra when they come in, gets out his cymbalom and himself plays for their dancing."[17]

After several chapters of visiting other exotic locations, Graham circles back to end the night where he started: at Moskowitz's.

> At ten o'clock the scene in the restaurant is already fine. It is warm and glowing. Moskowitz senior mounts the rostrum and plays his famous dulcimer. He seems to be greatly affected by his music.
>
> Moskowitz playing the dulcimer is a study for an artist. He plays it, head on side like a doctor listening intently to a pulse. His lazy, curved nose sticks out as if scenting music. He is introspective. He rolls his tongue; his lips taste the meager hairs on his moustache. Then suddenly the doctor pose has gone. He is more watchful, vigilant stealthy. He raises one hand with its mallet, like a cat playing with a mouse or pawing at a grappling string. Romanian music, Hungarian music, Russian music, French music—it is all at Moskowitz's command.[18]

Turning his attention to another Moskowitz, Graham wrote:

> The tables are so close and so crowded that it is difficult to move among them, but a popular Jewish soloist manages to do it. He has no platform but zig zags on the floor in the midst of the company, singing from his curious repertoire.
>
> His name is also Moskowitz but he is not related to the proprietor, he is a short slim fellow with a comic-looking bump which attracts the gaze to the head. Music sentimentalizes him. His eyelids hang and his eyes look downward.
>
> He sidesteps jauntily among the tables, singing in a knowing way, but never addressing his song to any one in particular—not concert room singing, not drawing room singing, nor yet street singing—a sort of tavern mode of song not deliberately Jewish, but sufficiently racial to be hypnotic to an imitator.[19]

After two o'clock in the morning, Moskowitz was still taking requests and playing for dancers. Graham concluded that "he and his dulcimer are almost legendary on the East Side. He will never sell out and buy something bigger."[20]

While Graham was right that Moskowitz would never buy anything bigger, he was wrong about Moskowitz not selling out. After the death of his wife, Joseph Moskowitz sold his restaurant and left New York in 1943. Joseph Moskowitz spent the rest of his life, apparently contentedly, playing dinner music in French restaurants in Washington, DC, and, until his passing, demonstrating the still electric musical magnetism that made his glory days so glorious.[21]

Moskowitz and Moskowitz on Record

Through one of the rare convivial coincidences of history, one can hear the cymbalom vocal duets Graham described at Moskowitz's restaurant that night in 1927. The "popular Jewish soloist" was tenor Abe Moskowitz, who began recording in 1921 for Columbia. While there, he became close to fiddler-composer (and fellow Romanian) Abe Schwartz, whose house orchestra would usually accompany the singer. Schwartz had Moskowitz record his own compositions, including the first commercial recording of Schwartz's classic song "Di grine kuzine" ("The Green Cousin") in 1922, still one of the most popular Yiddish American compositions.[1]

In March 1927, they recorded the traditional songs "Vi iz dus gesele" ("Where Is the Street") and "Huliet, huliet kinderlakh" ("Dance, Dance Children").[2] Given that the vast percentage of commercially recorded Yiddish songs were accompanied by muscular fourteen-piece orchestras, this intimate performance, with Abe Moskowitz "singing in a knowing way" and Joseph Moskowitz's spare yet sparkling solo cymbalom, reached back to the oldest strata of Yiddish folk song, a rarity on commercial American Jewish 78s but occurring regularly at Moskowitz's restaurant.

---

1. "Abe Schwartz the Klezmer King," Michael Brooks and Henry Sapoznik, Sony Legacy New York, CD, 2002.

2. "From Avenue A to the Great White Way: Yiddish and American Popular Songs 1914–1950," Michael Brooks and Henry Sapoznik, Sony Legacy, New York, CD, 2002.

Even while Moskowitz gently ruled it, the karnatzlakh circuit was already undergoing a transformational change—a change that not everyone was happy with:

> The East Side has become the tramping ground of the tourist, the slumming-party domain, and it is not unusual to see a group of blasé young gentiles doing the East Side after having had their fill of Chinatown.
>
> The night clubs, all these Itzkowitz's Original Roumanian Inns, Moonlight Lanes, Delancey Rendez-Vous are filled to capacity on Saturday and Sunday night. . . .
>
> Obese manufacturers or insurance brokers on a rampage with or without their wives dance and wipe their brows. It's hot and getting hotter as midnight passes. . . . Toward dawn they break up."[22]

And the mainstream was not far behind, as "Abel," a night club reviewer for *Variety*, noted:

> This hybrid Yiddish-American cabaret belt is a curious study in local color. From effete Second Avenue, the Yiddish rialto, to the Allen and Delancey street dialectaries [*sic*], there have sprung up a string of pretentious restaurants which are dining rooms first and dance-drink adjuncts thereafter. Drawing from a highly concentrated local population, plus a wider radius of taxi trade, these spots have evolved into something of local institutions each with an individual personality equation.
>
> They all give out the same gypsy camp fol-de-rol of "Ah Chichorni" and sobbing violins, plus some further East European. . . . These Roumanian restaurants are of a genus that if one wears a tux, patrons would mistake you for the head waiter.[23]

The Manhattan phone book was full of Romanian restaurants: Heimowitz's Oriental Roumanian (1913), Leibowitz and Tuckeroff Roumanian Village (1917), Hochman's Roumanian Restaurant and Broilings (1919), Shapiro's Little Roumanian Casino (1921), Joe's Roumanian, Greenblatt and Meyers Roumanian Gardens (1923), Garden Restaurant and Broilings (1926),

Vizhnitsky's New Roumanian Paradise (1927), and dozens more. But outside of a Moskowitz-inspired restaurant, the biggest and longest lived was the Old Roumanian.

The Old Roumanian

On July 4, 1929, the recently launched Old Roumanian Restaurant at 169 Allen Street was giving owner Louis Anzelowitz a send-off for his trip to Europe.[24] Anzelowitz was leaving because the Old Roumanian was named in a federal bootlegging indictment and was being padlocked for nine months

Figure 5.2. Advertisement announcing a going away party for Louis Anzelowitz, owner of Old Roumanian, 1929. *Source:* National Library of Israel, Historical Jewish Press website (www.jpress.org.il), founded by the National Library and Tel Aviv University. Used with permission.

starting in June 1929,[25] hence Anzelowitz's hasty going away party, hosted by his brother-in-law (and partner) Jack Silverman.

Jack Silverman (1888–1975) emigrated to the US from Jassi, Romania, around 1905 and began working as a tailor, and later, a quilt manufacturer. By 1925, he owned a squat building at 169 Allen Street whose third floor looked out onto the Second Avenue "el" while its first floor housed a restaurant.[26] Neither a chef nor a musician/singer, Jack Silverman—dubbed "Allen Street's chief exponent of rowdydow"—was a popular front-of-house personality, a press-producing machine, and a shameless showman.[27]

In 1933, the Old Roumanian lost its cabaret license when, during a spot check because of its "bevy of beauties" advertisements, "police found nude women dancing in the cabaret. Arrests were made."[28] Silverman sagaciously built on that salacious notoriety by upping the ante. As *Variety* pointed out, "The Old Roumanian may be the first restaurant on the Lower East Side to feature (risqué) fan and bubble dancers," and noting dryly that "it's the first show of the hotcha type to play this section."[29] Given that bent, an October 1934 Dining and Dancing notice in the *Women's Wear Daily* carried a curious announcement: "In a novel afterpiece to follow the regular presentation of the girl floor revue, [Boris] Thomashefsky will be heard in dramatic readings from the classics, the first of which will be taken from Shakespeare with Regina Zuckerberg assisting the star." This is where Silverman showed himself to be a shrewd showman. This might have been a grotesque sideshow of snickering at the once-reigning Yiddish star who was now reduced to "three shows a night on the cramped floor of a cabaret, where he follows eight scantily dressed chorus girls, a red-haired blues singer and a big blond mistress of ceremonies."[30] Instead, the invitation from Silverman turned into a vest-pocket vindication for the now largely forgotten Thomashefsky: "His dignity, his resonant voice his joint performance with Regina Zukerberg [sic] contrast oddly with the blue smoke haze, the clatter and hum of gossip from the tables, the jazz music of the orchestra. His cabaret efforts rouse steady applause."[31] Another critic noted, "He doesn't want pity. At seventy he is still vigorous, still in possession of the histrionic skill which made him famous. The courage that brought him to the top has not deserted him—yet."[32]

The Old Roumanian brought back Thomashefsky and Zuckerberg the following month. Then the following week. Soon, Thomashefsky was at the core of Silverman's pugnacious programming, such as in a series of "uptown/downtown" mash-ups (one had featured Jewish violinist Rubinoff with Black classical and jazz violinist Eddie South). On October 19, 1934, Thomashefsky split a bill with dancer-singer Bill "Bojangles" Robinson (himself the locality mayor of Harlem), who was on hand to receive a mezuza on behalf of the East Side Friends of Robinson.[33] Over the next two years, Thomashefsky reinvented himself in this new, more intimate setting and did well enough, so that in 1936 he and the loyal Regina Zuckerberg moved up the block to 181 Allen Street and opened Boris Thomashefsky's Roumanian Village. What *Variety* called "a different type of Ghetto-American nocturnal divertissement" which over the last three years of his life that, thanks to the marquee above his popular eatery/cabaret, Boris Thomashefsky went out with his name still in lights on the Lower East Side.[34]

Silverman introduced innovative dining features such as seltzer bottles on each table (which one reviewer called "a sea of blue bottles"). The practice soon became standard operating procedure not only at all Romanian restaurants but throughout the New York Jewish gastronomic world. "Here in America," wrote essayist Joseph Rachin in the *Forverts*,

> we must say we were lucky to have unlimited free seltzer. There was a time, when not one eatery on the east side put out a bottle on the table. First, the *fency* restaurants where a meal would cost a nickel more than in the common places, used to put out a bottle of seltzer out on the table. Then, the common everyday restaurants put out a bottle on every table. Without seltzer water, no restaurant could hope to survive.[35]

As the Old Roumanian shows grew, so did the space: in 1925 it was a 150-seat restaurant; in 1934 he added 200 seats; and, in 1938, another 150.[36] But to fill the big space, Anzelowitz needed a big personality, and he got that in Sadie Banks, who was called "a composite of Sophie Tucker, Mae West and Texas Guinan."[37] One critic described her as "a buxom blonde built along the Mae West pattern of architecture. Miss Banks knows how to handle her crowd and if there are those who in their cups become a bit unruly, she employs imperious and stentorian tones means of effectively improving their decorum. She can also sing a racy song with the proper flavor and innuendo."[38] Another critic noted,

> Almost any evening will find the premises crowded with a colorful and ebullient audience, an audience which believes that mirth should be loud and humor broad. And broad is the word for the declamations of Sadie Banks, the toast of Allen Street,

whose frank songs of advice to husbands and wives might well bring blushes to the cheeks of less hearty folk . . . judging by the volume of guffaws and shrill laughter, [she] is the tour de force of the evening.[39]

However, with the end of World War II, it all unwound. First, the cabaret closed, and the restaurant reverted to occasional banquets, some twenty-fifth wedding anniversaries, and finally, three-dollar deluxe dinners. Then, in 1957, the whole neighborhood was condemned for urban expansion.[40] Silverman, unwilling to read the handwriting on the soon-to-be demolished restaurant wall, moved uptown to Broadway, where he opened the International, whose major shtick was being the only night club with a wedding chapel. The uptown restaurant lasted until 1966. Jack Silverman died on June 17, 1974, the same day as Yiddish theater composer Sholom Secunda.[41]

Louis Anzelowitz: Moskowitz & Lupowitz, Part II

Before Thomashefsky left the Old Roumanian in 1936, there was another, much quieter departure: Jack Silverman's brother-in-law/partner—now brother-in-law/business rival—Louis Anzelowitz. For forty years, of which twenty overlapped, the dominant forces in Lower East Side Romanian restaurants were these brothers-in-law competitors. Just as Jack Silverman's Old Roumanian owned the '30s and '40s, it would be Moskowitz & Lupowitz that owned the '50s and '60s under Louis Anzelowitz.

Louis "Yehuda Leyb" Anzelowitz came from Poland to the US around 1911. On the 1920 census, Anzelowitz listed his profession as "tailor." As Jack Silverman was a quilt manufacturer at the time, that may be how they met. Later, Anzelowitz would marry Jack's sister Rose. By 1925, Anzelowitz was working in eateries (Joe's Restaurant and W&A Roumanian Oriental Restaurant) before settling in at the Old Roumanian in 1929. In 1936, Anzelowitz briefly owned Harry's Chop House and Roumanian Paradise,[42] before making his most important move the following year to Moskowitz & Lupowitz.

With the 1926 departure of popular front-of-house partner Joseph Moskowitz, and with his low-to-no advertising or publicity in the decade after, it is a testament to Samuel Lupowitz that he was even able to keep Moskowitz & Lupowitz afloat. Perhaps his best decision was the 1935 move to 40 Second Avenue on the corner of Second Street, its iconic and best remembered "Second and Second" location. But Lupowitz was no draw, while the dynamic front-of-house personality Louis Anzelowitz, like Joseph Moskowitz, was. "This chubby, kindly host," one paper wrote, "is always around to see that one's visit turns out to be a memorable one, as he is pleasant, ready to offer a suggestion as to what to eat. He flits about and chats with his customers and makes you feel like you are out dining."[43]

Anzelowitz was linked in another way to Joseph Moskowitz, thanks to the former's memorable and virtuosic display of carving and plating meat at the diner's table. One of the historic folkloric names for the cymbalom—Moskowitz's instrument—was "hackbrett" or "cutting board."

Yet in another way, Anzelowitz, the "chubby, kindly host," was nothing like Moskowitz, who cared not for the business end, only for playing tunes.

Figure 5.3. Moskowitz & Lupowitz's Second Avenue and East Second Street location. *Source:* 1940 Tax Photograph Collection, NYC Municipal Archives. Used with permission.

62 | The Tourist's Guide to Lost Yiddish New York City

Anzelowitz, like brother-in-law Jack Silverman, was an astute, aggressive businessman who took over not only the front of house but eventually the rest of the house, too. One example of how quickly he gained control is shown in the advertising he ran not long after his arrival. In October 1937, Anzelowitz went from being listed in small type at the bottom of the ad as managing director[44] to "Louis Anzelowitz is proud to present" at the top of the ad in large type, above the smaller "'Moskowitz & Lupowitz' by December."[45] In the 1940 census, Louis Anzelowitz listed himself as "restaurant partner," while drops in the gossip columns all called him "owner."

While Anzelowitz maintained some of the musical trappings that characterized the founding Moskowitz & Lupowitz (e.g., strolling violins and a Gypsy ensemble), he continued the kind of blunt entertainment that used to pack them in at his brother-in-law's Old Roumanian:

> Moskowitz and Lupowitz is one of the chief magnets in this neighborhood catering to a half Anglicized clientele, it has singers of English as well as Yiddish ballads.
>
> The big blonde girl who sings the heart-rending Yiddish melodies goes from table to table, hoping that some food-sodden customer will respond adequately, either by applauding vociferously at the end or by asking her to join him in something.
>
> Then she sings a favorite "My little city of Belz," which brings back to the diners memories of the little towns that gave them birth, The song has rhythm and a sentimental emotion. It goes over big. And for a short time, the forks stop their swift shuttling between plates and mouths.[46]

In 1955, nearly a year after Samuel Lupowitz's death, Anzelowitz, at a bargain-basement price, bought out his late partner's share from his estate, and for the last few months of Anzelowitz's life, he owned Moskowitz & Lupowitz.[47] Anzelowitz lived long enough to experience the fortuitous opening of television and Broadway rehearsal space at the nearby Central Plaza, next to the old Loew's Commodore, which temporarily stanched the steady decline of local Jewish restaurants.

And while many of the local Jewish eateries benefited from the increased celebrity foot traffic, it was only the savvy Anzelowitz (and his sons after him) who turned it into a PR bonanza by having a photographer on-site (or on-call down the block) to document, among other diners, Charles Laughton, John Garfield, Hans Conried, Basil Rathbone, Fredric March,

Sid Caesar (who had his wedding there), Groucho Marx, Henry Fonda, and many more, whose "grip and grin" photo portraits, with a beaming Anzelowitz, lined the restaurant walls.[48]

Moskowitz & Lupowitz entered its fourth and final period after Anzelowitz's death, when his sons Max and Hyman tag-teamed ownership.[49] And thanks to local television production, Max Anzelowitz (now Robert Anzel), who was a part-time actor, and Moskowitz & Lupowitz itself, played a supporting role in a 1961 episode of the vérité-style detective series *Naked City*.[50] While Moskowitz & Lupowitz enjoyed the last gasp of celebrity drop-ins, and even maintained the old niceties like the strolling violinist, tablecloths, and candles, the grinding rear-guard action to keep the restaurant open saw the brothers try new novelty events, such as the crowning of Miss Gefilte Fish Queen New York and, copying their "uncle" Jack Silverman at the International, opened a wedding chapel. For several years, Moskowitz & Lupowitz hosted gatherings of the Loyal League of Yiddish Sons of Erin, for which the restaurant served traditional Yiddish dishes dyed green.[51]

Clearly, the end was near. In 1965, Moskowitz & Lupowitz declared bankruptcy, and the private school LaSalle Academy bought the block of buildings on its site, which included the old Second and Second restaurant.[52]

And even at the end, a quip accompanied its postmortem. In an article about the disappearing Jewish Lower East Side, when asked why Moskowitz & Lupowitz closed, a former waiter replied, "From too much business, they didn't close."[53] Today, that entire portion of the block is fully razed.

Sammy's Roumanian Steakhouse[54]

In 1975, a curious and wholly unexpected da capo—like a long-delayed burp—occurred nearly a decade after the closing of Moskowitz & Lupowitz, with the opening of Sammy's Roumanian Steakhouse in a cellar at 157 Chrystie Street. Neither a reenactment nor an homage to the golden age of Romanian restaurants, in place of the gas lamps of Joe Moskowitz's wine cellar Sammy's Roumanian Steakhouse featured the harsh florescent lights and dropped acoustical tile ceilings better suited to a check cashing place. Instead of genteel, solicitous, tuxedoed hosts à la Moskowitz & Lupowitz, it featured "servers dressed in Sammy's T-shirts and jeans with a dishrag swinging from one pocket."[55] And instead of readings of Shakespeare in Yiddish or Gypsy violins, as at the Old Roumanian, it featured an overamplified keyboard-wielding ringmaster. Owner and founder Stanley Zimmerman (and later his son, David) created a part fan art, part fever dream deconstructed dinner-theater version of a Romanian restaurant for a new generation.

Sammy's menu included meat items rescued from vanished or faltering Jewish eateries and kitted out his tables with fetish objects, like syrup dispensers of shmaltz, or vodka bottles encased in blocks of ice as if crudely excavated from far-off Siberian glaciers. One tradition Zimmerman included wholly intact was Jack Silverman's ubiquitous seltzer bottles on the tables. It was Sammy's, however, who audaciously repurposed them for another disappearing Jewish delicacy: the egg cream.

Found at all Jewish candy stores, egg creams (milk, chocolate syrup, and seltzer—no eggs) and the recipient of its own overheated and wildly improbable creation myths (i.e., "egg cream" is not a mangled adaption of the Yiddish "ekht krem" [real cream]), egg creams were never restaurant fare (not even in their heyday, and not even at dairy restaurants). In the hands of showman Stanley Zimmerman, the idea of capping off the king of all Jewish meat meals with the queen of all Jewish carbonated dairy drinks—a previously unthinkable, provocatively unkosher move—was brilliantly popular.

Sammy's had already developed a loyal fan base in its first two years when it got a major boost in Mimi Sheraton's rhapsodic 1976 rave *New York Times* review. Sheraton praised its broiled meat dishes served in "staggering proportions," with nothing "to mar the purely monochromatic schemes of beige to brown" of the vegetable-free table. Her two-star review (subsequent references would misidentify it as three) drove new crowds.[56] Even though the *Times* would eventually moderate its zeal (Pete Wells's 2014 review, which crisply characterized it as "a permanent underground bar mitzvah," took back one of Sheraton's stars), it hardly mattered.[57] Sammy's had become a shrine, a pilgrimage, a destination, and surefire filler on the travel pages of regional newspapers giving its readers the lowdown on New York's offbeat experiences, not all that far removed from Stephen Graham's Romanian restaurants in *New York Nights*.

In fact, despite its nearly purposeful crude and blunt delivery, in what might have even made Jack "Rowdydow" Silverman blush, Sammy's had more in common with its Romanian restaurant predecessors than not. The music took a nosedive from the breathtaking heights of Joseph Moskowitz to what longtime Sammy's waiter Mel Brown said of house violinist Ruby Levine: "You name it, he'll play it. Not well, but he'll play it."[58] When Levine passed, replacement MC Dani "Dani Luv" Lubnitzki created his own draw. He provided what the *Daily News* called "so-called music," which, like that in a driven hunt, Luv used to herd the diners into a vodka-fueled evening-ending hora, with one lucky/unlucky patron hoisted into a chair, always in danger of the looming drop tile ceiling.[59] Luv "fired up his keyboard and pumped out his shtick a running monolog of borscht belt insult jokes studded with obscenities and musical matzo-ball soup of Jewish themed tunes and standards and pop songs with ribald or Yiddish lyrics added."[60] How different was that from the legendary and loud Old Roumanian MC, Sadie Banks?

Sammy's Roumanian, long shielded by a protective exoskeleton of schmaltz, survived until succumbing during the Covid-19 pandemic in 2021, but reopened in the spring of 2024 at its new street-level location, 112 Stanton Street.[61]

And finally, in a plot device worthy of the Yiddish theater at its most jaw-droppingly improbable: three mid-twenties identical triplet brothers (Bobby Shafran, David Kellman, and Eddy Galland), who had been given away as babies as part of a twisted social experiment, met in 1980 while working at Sammy's. After leaving what they called "the *S* place" in 1987, the brothers (who were the subject of a film called *Three Identical Strangers*) opened Triplets, a "cleaner, brighter hustle-free clone" of Sammy's, open until 2000.[62]

The Sammy's Before Sammy's

Sammy's Roumanian shares a brash affinity with another Sammy's, which ruled some four blocks uptown for forty years: Sammy's Bowery Follies. Like the restaurant (its previous owner was a Sammy Friedman), the "Sammy" in Sammy's Bowery Follies was an actual Sammy: its founder, high-hatted saloon keeper Sammy Fuchs. Fuchs, who married Bessie Schimmel (older daughter of knish king Yonah Schimmel), in 1937 turned his seedy, skid-row neighborhood dive bar at 267 Bowery into his seedy skid-row destination dive bar. Sammy Fuchs ran it until he died in 1969, after which Bessie ran it until her death the following year. The building was subsequently razed.[1]

Both Sammy's used their gritty, besotted in situ locations to evoke a lost moment in their neighborhood's sepia past: the Bowery Follies of the Gay '90s and the Romanian restaurants of the Jewish Lower East Side. Both were tourist come-ons: the first, for the slumming uptown crowd, and the other, for the bridge-and-tunnel one. While the Bowery's walls were covered with photos of bare-knuckle boxers, Floradora girls, and bewhiskered US presidents, the Roumanian's every surface is covered with years of overlapping, overexposed snapshots of ecstatic eaters in various stages of frantic excess. But most importantly, both Sammy's created an atmosphere in which what happened at Sammy's, stayed at Sammy's.

---

1. I. Jackson, "Der sof fun *semi's bowery folis*," *Forverts*, Sept. 30, 1970, 5.

6

Yiddish Champagne

Seltzer and Dr. Brown's Celery Tonic

In 1929, the St. Louis–based American Beverage Corporation staged a hostile takeover of three New York City soft drink manufacturers: Brownie, a recently launched carbonated chocolate drink, and two venerable—but now deeply enfeebled—manufacturers who were the founding fathers of New York Jewish bubbly beverages.[1]

The first was the carbonation king Carl H. Schultz (1826–1897). Born in Germany, Schultz studied chemistry at the University of Bremen before coming to the US in 1853. It was while working for the government assay office in 1863 that he opened Schultz & Warker's to pursue his interest in producing quality artificial mineral waters.[2] When Schultz went to Europe to study assaying practices, he privately analyzed and documented the mineral waters at the various spas and natural springs. Among the many Schultz visited (Vichy, Kissingen, Carlsbad, and Marienbad) was one from the central German spa town of Selters (and from which the name "seltzer" would derive, though not, as many times declared, through any Yiddish involvement).[3]

Schultz published the results in his 1865 treatise *Mineral Spring Waters: Their Chemical Composition, Physiological Action and Therapeutic Uses*, which was hugely influential. Within three years, Schultz would redesign and patent an improved, more affordable, and safer spigot model, which together with his mastery of recreating spa waters made him New York's big shot of seltzer spigotry for the remainder of the nineteenth century.[4] Among Schultz's enthusiastic fans was actor Edwin Booth (brother of John Wilkes), who in February 1870 wrote a friend suffering "indisposition:" "Get at least six syphons of Schultz & Warker's Seltzer Water drink at your leisure until you're chock full and then fizzle, bang, pop! Your brains will clear, your nerves be stilled & hell be quiet."[5] By 1897, the time of Carl H. Schultz's death, the company was selling a million bottles a year.[6]

Schultz was also interested in spa cures—the "taking of the waters"—then at the height of its pseudoscience popularity. As a self-described "naturalist" and a passionate advocate of science in the service of the greater good, Schultz opened a public artificial mineral springs in Central Park at West Seventy-Sixth street in 1866.[7] In a lavish oriental-ish/Moorish polychrome pavilion designed by the co-creators of Central Park, Schultz evoked and exceeded the great European spas by piping in thirty of his recreated mineral waters, in addition to live band music, making it a mecca for health faddists and a popular tourist attraction.[8] Among its many visitors were immigrant Jews, who brought with them an enthusiasm for mineral spas well-honed back home. (Marienbad, among other regional spas, enjoyed a particular popularity among some Hasidic courts.) A September 14, 1872, illustration in *Harper's Weekly* called "Sunday Morning in Central Park Jews Drinking Mineral Water" illustrated *Harper's* high opinion of Schultz's spa and low opinion of Jews.[9] Schultz's spa thrived until the widespread availability of fresh water from "upstate" reservoirs in Croton (1906) and the Ashokan (1912). The original racehorse quality pavilion would endure decades of dray horse duty as a candy stand starting in 1927 and storage shed into the 1960s before finally being demolished.[10]

Thanks to Schultz's meticulous and easily replicable formulas for carbonated waters and his development of safe and simple siphons (the direct descendant of which is still in use today), the field of carbonated beverages became flooded with competition; by the time the American Beverage Company came calling in 1929, the Carl H. Schultz Company's best days were long behind it.

Dr. Brown's Celery Tonic

One of the many beverages made possible by Carl Schultz's artificial carbonation process was celery tonic. Celery had long been credited with therapeutic and medicinal properties as an antioxidant and anti-inflammatory, but in the realm of late nineteenth-century health claims, it was widely marketed as a nerve tonic.[11] A nationwide cultivation of celery in the 1880s produced the first beverage in 1888, Mayfield's Celery Cola, by James C. Mayfield, a partner of Coca Cola inventor John Pemberton, who himself died before launching his improved cola with celery.[12] By the late 1890s, New York City boasted numerous carbonated celery tonic makers, including William C. Beutel ("celery tonic, a nerve toner"), New York Bottling Company ("celery phosphate, a wholesome beverage"), T. L. Neff and Sons Celery Tonic, and H. W. Pabst (of Blue Ribbon beer fame).[13]

Figure 6.1. Ad for Dr. Brown's Celery Tonic dispenser (1931). Its name would change to Cel-Ray Tonic next year. *Source:* National Library of Israel, Historical Jewish Press website (www.jpress.org.il), founded by the National Library and Tel Aviv University. Used with permission.

And there was Brooklyn's Frederick Schoneberger, who, being mustered out of New York's Twentieth Infantry after the Civil War, went from cider dealer to "soda water maker" by 1870. The 1890 obituary of the leader of downtown Brooklyn's elite noted he had been "engaged in the manufacture of a popular temperance beverage under the name of 'Dr. Brown.' "[14] Upon his death, the business went to Schoneberger's son, Adolph, and to Frederick's former business partner, Robert Noble. By 1896, Schoneberger and Noble was marketing sarsaparilla ("the great blood purifier") and celery tonic "for the nerves." In 1905, not long after moving its factory to the felicitously named Water Street, Schoneberger and Noble began an aggressive campaign of using the courts and charges of patent and trademark infringement to drive other celery tonic makers out of business. The company's "beware of imitators" or "not authentic without this seal" ads all showed its crest: two crossed celery stalks encircled by "one and only one Dr. Brown's" and "celery tonic for the nerves."[15]

After Adolph Schoneberger died in 1912, Noble honed his celery tonic marketing. In addition to its old claim for "nerves," it was now first promoted as "an aid to digestion, to sharpened appetite" and then, by assigning it new healing attributes and veering dangerously close to patent medicine palaver, as "a palliative for the weak, sick and for children and as a blood purifier."[16]

In addition to its health claims, Dr. Brown's founding claims were also heightened. In August 1922, the *Re-Ly-On Bottler* ("a monthly magazine of ideas and ideals for the bottling trade") ran an article called "Dr. Brown's Fame Travels" about how in 1869 Frederick Schoneberger bought the formula for celery tonic from "a kindly old medical practitioner" in Boston, bottling it first there, then in Philadelphia, and finally in Brooklyn. Not surprisingly, it wasn't long after the appearance of the *Re-Ly-On* article that Schoneberger and Noble started using a "since 1869" slogan.[17] This puff piece was probably the singular source for the subsequent creation myth that celery tonic was invented by a "Dr. Brown in Brooklyn in 1869." And yet, despite the long-repeated tale of an actual "Dr. Brown" being eventually pooh-poohed even by the company (in its 1972 trademark renewal, the accompanying product description notes that "the name 'Dr. Brown' is fanciful"), the claim still reappears in newspaper delicatessen articles and Jewish food histories.[18]

While promoting a good health product, the good health of its workers was not as assiduously pursued. Ten-plus-hour shifts and substandard wages drove its employees to seek affiliation with the International Union of United Brewery and Soft Drink Workers of America in 1923. Although the old-line patrician Schoneberger and Noble company negotiated with the union for more than year, these poor conditions would not change until management did in 1928 with the American Beverage Company (ABC) acquisition.[19] By 1933, ABC rebranded its product Dr. Brown's Cel-Ray Tonic ("the original celery tonic") and increased outreach to the Jewish world at a time when other celery tonics (Neff's, Hammer's, Venoz, etc.) were already being marketed there. However, sales of Dr. Brown's soon surpassed all others.[20] ABC acquired Passover certification for Cel-Ray (ads promised that the "clean, fresh drink will help you digest the fat Passover foods").[21] This was followed in 1935 by a series of Yiddish spot ads on Bronx station WBNX, which proved so successful that they launched a fifteen-minute bilingual children's show on WEVD called *Uncle Abe's Mogen Dovid Club*, which played three times a week for thirteen weeks.[22] An August 1, 1936, article in *Broadcast Advertising* marveled at how Dr. Brown's Cel-Ray managed to get ten thousand paying members of the newly formed Twin Triangle Clubs on the Uncle Abe show, resulting in the show's run subsequently extended for the next season.[23] So it was surprising that at the end of that season ABC pulled its show sponsorship, never to advertise on Yiddish radio again, although it continued to buy display ads in the Yiddish papers for non-Jewish shows.

One was a 1938 children's show on station WHN titled *Robinson Crusoe, Jr.* (which had nothing to do with the 1916 Al Jolson musical). A reviewer in *Billboard* was impressed by Cel-Ray's success with the kid target audience, mistakenly thinking "the sponsor's product, a carbonated drink seems more of an adult beverage."[24] In 1939, Cel-Ray sponsored three more shows: a WJZ kiddie quiz show (*Name It and Take It*), adventure show *Buccaneers* on WHN, and a musical variety show on station WOR. (The PR for the WOR variety show, broadcast from the stage of the Brooklyn Paramount Theater, consisted of sending bottles of Cel-Ray to newspaper reviewers. On June 17 *Motion Picture Daily* wryly noted, "The hot pastrami sandwiches are awaited.")[25]

That ABC successfully rebranded and relaunched Dr. Brown's Celery Tonic as Cel-Ray Tonic, brought it to the attention of tens of thousands of new Jewish customers thanks to aggressive and focused marketing, and created original and diverse general radio programming is all the more amazing considering what was going on behind the scenes. E. H. McCullough, the increasingly titular president of ABC, had been quietly ceding control of the company to Brooklyn soft drink distributor Irving Feinberg. As would be revealed in subsequent trials, Feinberg was the finger puppet of Al Capone's former financial mentor, Johnny "Terror" Torrio, and ABC was obtained for its reputation of healthful soft drinks as a cover for an alcohol smuggling operation, for its still active but unused seat on the New York Stock Exchange, and as an elaborate scheme to swindle money from the original ABC investors.[26] When he was convicted and served his two years at Sing Sing, Feinberg relinquished control of ABC in 1985 to Canada Dry Bottling Company owned by Harold Honickman and the Honickman Group.[27] Honickman reinvigorated the inaccurate "since 1869" claim, underscoring it with vivid New Yorkiana–period label designs of the Statue of Liberty (cream soda, its bestseller), the Central Park carousel (black cherry, 30 percent of sales), and the Brooklyn Bridge on Cel-Ray, which accounted 15 percent of all sales.[28]

While Honickman still carries the full line of Dr. Brown's sodas, the addition of high fructose corn syrup means they no longer taste the same.

At the end, several curiosities still endure: How, given celery tonic's close identification with the pure food/vegetarian movement, did it end up being so closely identified with the mortal enemy of "pure food"—meat, and why, given the yawning ubiquity of celery tonics around the country, did only one survive and find such a long and enthusiastic identification in the New York Jewish world? Despite Dr. Brown's being such a powerful cultural Jewish touchstone—everything from comic Jerry Stiller pointing out that his Hibernian wife Anne Meara made Irish Soda bread using Cel-Ray to it getting a shoutout in "Noshville Katz," Bobby Weinstein's 1967 "country and eastern (European)" take-off of John Sebastian's hit "Nashville Cats"—Dr. Brown's is perhaps the only food product so closely identified with Jews in which Jews were not involved in any part of its development, production, ownership, or national distribution.

Celery Tonic Crime

When one thinks about gangsters extorting storekeepers what to sell their thirsty customers, the drink that usually comes to mind is beer, but in the case of hoodlum Max "Kid Twist" Zweifach, it was celery tonic.

Kid Twist (not to be confused with Abe Reles, a later "Kid Twist" who named himself after his childhood hero and who, like his childhood hero, also came to an abrupt end) made his way up the criminal food chain as a vote harvester for Tammany Hall, under whose protection he would efficiently terrorize the Lower East Side as a *shtarker* and torpedo, honing his tough Jew skills under his tough Jew boss, Edward "Monk Eastman" Osterman.[1] Among Kid Twist's many crimes was his "partner" scheme visited upon any new business that had the misfortune to open on his turf. If the partner accepted, their business would hemorrhage profits for months until the place was on the edge of collapse, upon which Twist, "tiring of the business," would ask to be "bought out" for some exorbitant sum. On the other hand, if the mark refused Kid Twist's partnership offer, their place would be boycotted by a troop of Twist's men, to drive off customers. Or the place would be demolished, or the owner beaten or killed, or all of the above.[2]

Among Kid Twist's "partners" was a celery tonic manufacturer, upon whose bottles, in a lovely touch of adding insult to injury, the "hatchet faced Jew" Zweifach put his own profile: "'It's this way,' explained Twist. 'I'm introducing a celery bitters—because there's cush in it. I goes into Baby Flax's an asks him to buy. He hands me out with a 'no!' So, I ups and an' puts his joint on the bum. After this, when I come into a dump, they'll buy me bitters, see. Sure, I cops an order from Flax before I leaves for two cases."[3]

Kid Twist's full nelson on the East Side's celery tonic trade was described by one of his former henchmen in a widely publicized confession of his boss's criminal soft drink empire: "If you roam around the East side go into the different Places You will find his Celery Tonic such as Cigar, Candy Grocery Stores Saloons, Cafes and every Place you think you can go and get a soft drink you would see his Tonic There whether they used it or not they had to buy it."[4]

Yet despite celery tonic's reputation as a health drink, for Zweifach it was anything but. During an ill-advised trip to Coney Island, Kid Twist died in a hail of bullets from the revolver of Louis "Kid" Poggi, in retaliation for Zweifach's reckless expansion to sell celery tonic in Poggi's sphere of influence in the Five Points where, among the Italians, the carbonated coffee soda Manhattan Special held sway.[5]

---

1. George Kibbe Turner, "Tammany's Control of New York By Professional Criminals," *McClure's Magazine*, June 1909, 120.

2. Victor Rousseau, "Lawless New York," *Harper's Weekly*, June 27, 1908, 16.

3. Alfred Henry Lewis, "The Gun Men of New York, The Apaches of the New World," *Salt Lake Telegram*, Sept. 14, 1912, 17.

4. Turner, "Tammany's Control of New York."

However, deceit and celery tonic were not limited to gangsters, as in a headline from November 13, 1924: "Rabbi Held for Larceny, Charged with Turning 670 Bottles of Wine into Celery Tonic." A Rabbi Regensberg was accused of swindling two men who invested $2,800 in his "sacramental champagne" scheme. When they received the shipment, "broke open a bottle, thinking it was champagne, and tasted it. They were disappointed, they said, to find it was nothing but celery tonic." Attempts to recover the investor's money were unsuccessful; when Rabbi Regensberg was captured en route to escaping to Palestine, he explained he'd lost their money to a bootlegger.[6]

---

5. Lewis, "The Gun Men of New York," 17.

6. "Rabbi Held for Larceny, Charged with Turning 670 Bottles of Wine into Celery Tonic," *New York Times*, Nov. 13, 1924, 2.

7

From Adjective to Noun

The Appetizing Store

The transition of "appetizing" from adjective to noun came as a byproduct of the American entry into World War I. The newspaper *New York Sun* launched a campaign to "de-Teutonize" English, eliminating all German borrow words. Its targets included "sauerkraut" ("victory cabbage"), "kindergarten," and the ubiquitous "delicatessen."[1] In response to the campaign, a reader noted that in his Harlem Jewish neighborhood a delicatessen had already put up a sign in its front window with its rough English translation "appetizing."[2] The end of the war returned not only the doughboys but "delicatessen." While some American groceries retained the "appetizing" name, it was in Yiddish New York City that "appetizing store"—a German delicatessen with no meat—was born.

The appetizing store was a cornucopia of candies, coffee beans, dried beans and fruit, halvah, legumes, pickled and smoked vegetables, roasted nuts, and teas. And while technically the meaning of parev is "neither meat nor milk," appetizing stores caucused with the dairy party and so also sold milk, fermented milk, sour milk, buttermilk, cream, sour cream, kefir, and varieties of soft cheeses, including farmer cheese, pot cheese, cottage cheese, and a dozen kinds of cream cheeses.

It is the perplexing, seeming contradiction of how in kashrus, one group of sentient flesh bearing animals (i.e., cow, chicken) is considered "meat" (*fleyshik*), while another sentient flesh bearing animal (i.e., fish) is not, and ends up as "parev."

In the pond of the parev appetizing store, the big fish was fish and fish in all its ready-to-eat permutations: smoked, salted, and pickled, including but not limited to brook trout, butterfish, caviar, chubs, carp, pike, sable, salmon, sardines, sole, sturgeon, and whitefish, not to forget herring (shmaltz, Bismarck, matjes, cream, or wine sauce) slowly pickling in barely covered fifty-five-gallon wooden barrels.

Considering their open layout and close quarters, appetizing stores created a unique dazzling olfactory cornucopia of aromas both foreign and familiar, the closest thing a Jewish neighborhood had to an exotic far-off bazaar.

At their peak between the two World Wars, there were some thirty appetizing stores on the Lower East Side, with Brooklyn not far behind.[3] The numbers declined not only with the change in the Jewish diet but with the widespread postwar availability of many products (nuts, candies, coffee, teas, etc.), now at the cheaper and larger supermarkets. As these products were more critical to the appetizing store's bottom line than the much pricier fish, the availability drove many out of business.[4] In their current streamlined iteration, the surviving appetizing stores have ceded much of the old product territory and circled back to the original star: fish.

Russ & Daughters

Joel Russ (1885–1961), from Strezhov, Poland, came to the US in 1905; his citizenship papers two years later list him as a "peddler." By 1910, Russ owned his own candy shop (unlike a candy store that also sold beverages and newspapers and packaged candy, a candy shop only sold candies loose and in quantity, a standard offering in appetizing stores). From about 1915 to 1918, Joel Russ was at 187 Orchard Street, where the New York directories alternately list him selling fish and, using the prewar nomenclature, as a delicatessen.

Russ's neighbor at 187 Orchard was Isaac Berger, who was known not only for *his* smoked fish but for Chestnut, his delivery horse who, during the summer, would transform from drayhorse to seahorse when Berger took him swimming in the Rockaways. "Berger was the only one of all the bathers," an anonymous reporter for *The New York Times* noted on September 13, 1911, "who had the proud distinction of bresting [*sic*] the waves with a dashing steed."[5]

Joel and Bela Russ, who married in 1909, had three daughters: Hattie (1912–2014), Ida (1915–2001), and Anne (1921–2018). A smoked fish Tevye, Russ dragooned his daughters into the family business so nimbly that what until 1935 had been Russ's Cut-Rate Appetizing Market became Russ & Daughters. Despite people assuming that the traditional, pragmatic, and practical Joel Russ had taken on a partner named Mr. Daughters, Russ did not set out to make a social statement. But in a business world rife with "and Sons," Joel Russ's small but powerful gesture set him apart and did not go unnoticed even in the mainstream press as far away as San Francisco: "As for daughters inheriting the business talent of their fathers and taking part in the conduct of the family business, another example is found in the firm of Russ & Daughters, fish dealers of 179 East Houston Street New York."[6]

However, unlike Tevye, whose daughters dispersed, Russ further solidified his business when his daughters married. (One "Russ-band" referred to himself as "the '&' in 'Russ & Daughters.'") While the rapid loss of matriarch Bella Russ (1958) and three years later patriarch Joel left a hole in the family, it did not leave a hole in the family business, which was wholly self-contained. However, by 1974 its future was not at all assured. "[Daughter] Anne Federman sighed. 'My son is a lawyer, and my girls are into Yoga. Two vegetarian daughters. They're not interested in this humdrum life. It would be a shame if we have to sell this business to someone outside the family.'"[7]

Anne Federman need not have worried. The desire of the third generation of the Russ & Daughters family, to become doctors or lawyers or yoginis, was typical of the transition made by pioneering family retail businesses. Mark Russ Federman, Anne's lawyer son, like dairy restaurant scion Harold Harmatz of the Delancey Street Ratner's, left an unsatisfying law practice to return to the family business and revive it in 1978.[8] When Mark Russ returned, he found a business that had benefited by Joel Russ's solving the two critical continuity problems that plagued other small family businesses: enthusiastic family participation and a familiar, autonomous location.

Around 1923, Russ moved from Orchard Street to the now iconic 179 East Houston Street location as a tenant. But it was Russ's prescient—and gutsy—purchase of the building for $25,000 (about $250,000 today) in the summer of 1949 that ensured the business's survival.[9] Part of the reason the building was "priced to move" was that several floors were boarded up and could not be rented to tenants. In the only part of the building that was habitable, the Russ family let the staff live rent-free.[10] The meticulous maintenance of the store was extended to the rest of the building only in the early 2000s, when the Lower East Side real estate boom increased the building value to finally warrant its first full renovation.[11]

In addition to a book and a short documentary (*The Sturgeon Queens*, dir. Julie Cohen, 1974), Mark Russ Federman's deft rebranding, in a transition from yentas to yuppies, led to the successful handing off of the filleting knife to his daughter Niki Russ Federman and nephew Josh Russ Tupper, who have already instituted changes (satellite locations, a café version) to nimbly start Russ & Daughters second century.

A National Treasure

A mile marker in the arrival of Russ & Daughters as an iconic national institution was its participation at the 2001 Smithsonian Festival of American Folklife's focus on New York City. Among the dozens of the New York–themed exhibitions and presentations that the over one million visitors saw, none elicited a more rapt—and more open-mouthed—response than the workshop and demonstrations by Russ & Daughters' Mark Russ Federman and his decades long employee, Herman Vargas. Calvin Trillin described Vargas's mastery of his craft and customers: "My salmon is still sliced by Herman Vargas the rare Yiddish-speaking Dominican who has worked at Russ & Daughters for more than 30 years; I know him as Herman the Artistic Slicer, although he no longer wears a name badge identifying him as that while waiting for Herman to produce slices thin enough to read *The New York Times* through—not the big-print edition; I'm talking about the regular."[1]

Due to health regulations that forbade the festival from allowing attendees to sample the exhibited food and requiring its proper disposal, all the leftover delicacies were surreptitiously "properly disposed of" at the end of each day by the Smithsonian festival staff, the author (giving presentations nearby on the history of New York City radio) happily included.

---

1. Calvin Trillin and Mark Russ Federman, Russ & Daughters, Reflections and Recipes from the House That Herring Built (New York: Schocken Books, 2013).

Barney Greengrass

"The most aristocratic of smoked foods" was how food writer Craig Clairborne referred to the sturgeon served at the uptown institution Barney Greengrass, named for its founder Berl Gringrass. Berl and his family came to New York from Grajevo Podlaskie in northeastern Poland when he was just three years old, in 1889, by which time sturgeon had stopped being fished in the nearby Hudson River thanks to pollution and depletion.[12] By 1900, the family was on Ludlow Street, where Berl was now "Barnet." By 1910 both father and son were in the food business: the elder Greengrass was the owner of a grocery and twenty-year-old Barnet (now Barney) "owning his own stand" only a few blocks from his Harlem home at 1380 Fifth Avenue.

In 1932, Greengrass moved downtown to the long-standing location on 541 Amsterdam Avenue and Eighty-Sixth Street. Not long after opening, a Thanksgiving publicity stunt helped guarantee the national awareness of smoked sturgeon—and of Greengrass. Learning that one of his regular customers, Judge Samuel Rosenman, was an inner circle confidant of the Roosevelt administration, Greengrass asked him if he thought FDR might enjoy smoked sturgeon at a Thanksgiving meal. When told he might, Greengrass sent a ten-pound slab to the White House. In Walter Winchell's subsequent very widely syndicated column, he related that when Rosenman next came in, Greengrass called out from the back of the store: "Hey, Judge! What goes? It's a whole week, and I ain't heard from that guy yet!"[13]

In 1938, his thirtieth anniversary, Barney Greengrass celebrated with the creation of a "crest," crowning himself "the Sturgeon King" as Neptune holding a trident seated on a rock emblazoned with "1908." A Virginia-based journalist visited Greenglass's establishment, giving it his seal of approval: "Barney Greengrass, the Sturgeon King is a character known to thousands in the vicinity of Amsterdam Avenue and 86th street. Short, fat, baldheaded and baby faced, Barney would do for a very model of Mr. Pickwick. Though he is a Jew born in Russia, his features have little evidence of race or nationality. They're just innocent and agreeable . . . the neon sign across the front of the place carries the name and title for all to admire."[14]

To Hollywood's appetizing deprived Lower East Side expats, smoked sturgeon became a seafood status symbol. In 1938, gossip columnists reported that Eddie Cantor was unwilling to sail to Europe on the *Queen Mary* until he was assured that a complete refrigerated container of Barney Greengrass smoked sturgeon was onboard.[15] George Burns told how Al Jolson would regularly have Barney Greengrass fly him $2,000 (more than $40,000 today) of smoked sturgeon but only share it with those who fawned before him: "So, I'd sit around the table, and tell him how great he was, and I was good for $60 or $70 a month in sturgeon. I liked sturgeon more than I liked Jolson."[16]

> Barney Greengrass the Sturgeon King who died this week, once received a telephone order for sturgeon to be shipped to Hollywood the next day. "Tomorrow is impossible," he said, "Not even for the King of England." "Maybe not for the King of England," said the lady caller, "but would you do it for Mischa Elman? I'm Mrs. Elman." Greengrass asked, "How do I know?" Mrs. Elman called her husband who was practicing nearby. The violinist played "Ave Maria." Greengrass said "OK, where do you want the sturgeon shipped?"[17]

Interestingly, the store's migration out of "appetizing" and back into "delicatessen" with meat—and unkosher meat at that—resulted not only in no drop off in business but in additional press:

> Last week, Mr. and Mrs. William Rhinelander Stewart decided to present an unusual gift to some Long Island friends. Mrs. Stewart therefore telephoned Barney Greengrass, who is famed for his smoked salmon and delicatessen—and ordered two dozen kosher frankfurters. . . . Mr. Greengrass reported that he had excellent frankfurters but no kosher ones. "Sorry, but I want kosher ones," said Mrs. Stewart . . . "But these are just as good," the delicatessen man assured. And so, for ten minutes Mrs. William Rhinelander Stewart repeated her insistence upon kosher frankfurters, while Mr. Barney Greengrass protested that the non-kosher ones were just as good.[18]

By 1940, son Marvin (dubbed "Moe") joined the store and would become the face of the business upon his father's death in 1955.

For Barney Greengrass's fiftieth birthday Moe dropped his menu items to the original opening day prices, leading to lines around the block till closing that night (and would repeat it in 2008 for the one hundredth anniversary). In the 1980s, Moe ceded the store to his son, Gary, and continued to work six days a week until suffering a stroke in 2000, dying two years later.[19]

From 1995 to 2014, Barney Greengrass enjoyed a Hollywood remake of sorts when it returned to the West Coast with an outpost eatery on the roof of the very luxe Barney's New York store in Beverly Hills. This joining was a nod to two departed Jewish Barneys who originally inhabited the very modest rungs of lower-middle-class immigrant shopkeepers: for Barney Greengrass it was fish, and for Barney Pressman (*press/pressl*, Yiddish for "clothes iron") it was his discount men's clothing in Union Square in 1923. Gary Greengrass once described the Beverly Hills Barney Greengrass outpost as "fancy, shmancy" as opposed to the New York store, which was merely "shmancy."[20] Barney Greengrass opened to rapturous reviews ("I had what can only be described as a religious experience," gushed one LA critic), quickly becoming a smoked fish watering hole.[21] The Barney's clothing bankruptcy and sale ended the Barney fish connection in 2014, when the new owners opened their own in-house restaurant instead.[22] (The tone of the split is such that in the historical timeline on the Barney Greengrass website, its nearly twenty-year Beverly Hills sojourn atop Barney's New York is not mentioned.)

Murray's Sturgeon Shop

In a storefront almost as thin as the sturgeon slices they would one day be renowned for selling, Murray Bernstein (1913–2000) and his brother Sam (1905–1977) founded the last of the great appetizing stores while the Sturgeon King still sat on his throne and while Papa Russ was still head of the family.

Born in Lomza, Poland, the brothers came to the US as teens and were longtime food workers. Before their store, Sam was a driver for the Breakstone Dairy company[23] and Murray was a journeyman market clerk, who continued his membership in the Grocery Workers Union long after he owned his own store and had retired to Florida. By 1945, Murray saved enough money to buy a former appetizing store whose deep reserves of dried fruit and nuts sustained the new business for the first few years. By the time the Bernsteins moved a few years later to their sliver-like storefront a mere ten blocks north of Zabar's, they had jettisoned the ancillary appetizing products, focusing instead on sturgeon and its poor cousin, sable.[24]

Where the brothers learned their legendary fish knife skills is unclear. But, in what shows that you can't spell "sturgeon" without the word "surgeon," noted food writer Craig Claiborne, who called their fastidiously clean store "the finest in the city," compared them to Dr. Christiaan Barnard, who had recently performed the world's first heart transplant.[25] Murray's was also a chummy clubhouse with its own cadre of celebrity clients. Zero Mostel and songwriter Sammy Cahn (who, thanks to the store, became a Bernstein brother-in-law) were among the regulars sitting in the back of the postage-sized store nibbling on fish between shots of frozen vodka.[26]

Putting in sixteen hours daily, the brothers ran what *New York Magazine* referred to as "The Tiffany of smoked fish stores" until 1974, when they sold the location and the brand. Sam died in 1977 and Murray in 2002.

8

Eat in Good Health!
Dairy and Vegetarian Restaurants

Seventy-five percent is the conservative estimate of the percentage of Jews who are lactose intolerant, making them unable to properly consume dairy products.[1] Despite that, East European Jews produced a vibrant and popular dairy restaurant culture emanating outward from Shavous, the spring holiday that eschews the eating of meat and for which dairy and parev are the whole show, a voluptuous catalog of dairy dishes like blintzes, latkes, kasha varnishkes (buckwheat groats and bow tie noodles), and kigl (noodle or potato casserole) have graced the traditional Ashkenazic table, and from there, the dairy restaurant menu.

On November 16, 1900, *The Hebrew Standard* reprinted an article from the *New York Sun* that gushed over the new Lower East Side phenomenon: the "blintz . . . a sort of a pancake rolled up and inclosing [sic] curds made savory." It even quotes the unnamed restaurant's signage:

The Time has arrived
When you can be satisfied
By eating blintzes in this place
Two cents apiece; ten cents the plate.

The anonymous writer concluded, "The descent from poetry into mere financial prose is not as satisfying as the blintzes, which are indeed, excellent."[2]

In 1916, *The American Hebrew and Jewish Messenger* lamented the appearance of restaurants selling "latkes and blintzes" on the Lower East Side, harumphing at what they called the "dairy restaurant center." The anonymous correspondent derisively described the decidedly observant diners (i.e., heads covered) to his secular Jewish readers: "These places are filled with diners whose hats wiggle up and down spasmodically while they eat."[3]

One of those places was probably Mrs. J. Kampus' Restaurant ("The only Romanian dairy restaurant on the Lower East Side; 24 years [1892] in the same location at 64 Delancey Street"). The restaurant's *Forverts* ad from May 27, 1916, which reflected the long-held belief that being overweight was healthy, blared "Eat blintzes, get fat!" alongside a drawing of an emaciated man and a portly, and seemingly satisfied, Kampus customer:

> Rumeynishe blintzes frish geshmak
> Gefint ir a seynem stok
> Kreplekh, beygelekh ersht fin eyvin
> Esn megn zey esn der gresten meyvin
> Romanian blintzes, fresh and toothsome
> You'll find here when you come
> Dumplings, bagels hot every day
> Worthy of the greatest gourmet.[4]

Schildkraut's

In the realm of vegetarian restaurants that were equally concerned with what its customers put in their stomachs and in their heads, none exceeded the eponymous chain by vegetarian visionaries/missionaries Sadie and Herman Schildkraut.

Figure 8.1. At its height, over a dozen Schildkraut's vegetarian eateries graced the Big Apple. *Source:* Author's collection.

86 | The Tourist's Guide to Lost Yiddish New York City

Herman was born in Galicia around 1879, coming to America with his parents around 1891. By 1900, the young Schildkraut was peddling ties, and by 1901 he worked as a clerk. Sadie (1886–1937) came from Hungary around 1897, and by 1914 the Schildkrauts opened their first eatery at 198 East Broadway, just a few blocks from the *Forverts* building. By the 1930s, there were some fifteen Schildkraut's Vegetarian Restaurants peppered throughout the Big Apple "for those who are pursuing, or desirous of adopting the 'right way of eating, the right way of living.'"[5]

In the age of raw vegetable diets, Sadie's innovative recipes made her, as her numerous obituaries noted, "the mother of cooked vegetarian dishes," for her Quixotic lifelong quest to create vegetarian food meant to taste like, and have the mouth feel of, meat. Forgotten today, Sadie Schildkraut's personal vision was the true vine from which grew faux-bacon in the 1950s, the Orthodox craze to develop kosher iterations of shrimp (reconstituted cod) in the 1970s, all the way to the recent Impossible Burgers.[6] Sadie's triumph was in taking the gluten-corn starch and flour tabula rasa of Dr. J. H. Kellogg and reimagining it with component elements familiar to their Jewish clients that made her "protose steak" a bedrock staple on all dairy/vegetarian menus.[7]

Healthy Eating, Healthy Living

Even accounting for the diverse and expansive traditional dairy/parev dishes already in service in the Jewish diet, success for the Yiddish dairy/vegetarian restaurants was only possible thanks to the influence of the very non-Jewish Midwest health spas, Utopian societies, and physical culture and wellness movements and their introduction of the slightly mysterious "protose." A portmanteau word cojoining "prot" (from "protein") and "ose" ("abounding in"), the gluten-based invention of Dr. J. H. Kellogg (brother of the inventor of Corn Flakes), whose Battle Creek, Michigan, health spa first introduced it, became one of the sinews that connected the nascent health food movement.[1] While Dr. J. H. Kellogg would move on from his involvement in health food to the promotion of eugenics and enforced sterilization of the "undesirable," it is ironic that his protose would be made even more famous by the very people his subsequent eugenics beliefs would seek to eliminate.

---

1. T. Coraghessan Boyle, *The Road to Wellville* (New York: Viking, 1993), 19.

While Sadie was chef, Herman ran the front of house, identified as the "dietitian [*sic*] and Drugless Physician."⁸ Of equal importance, Herman was the poet laureate of meatless eats, whose vegetarian hot doggerel was affixed to all their printed materials:

We serve food from Nature's own treasure
Thus offering our guests perfect health and pleasure
The sunkist fruits, grains and vegetables are your natural diet
Yours will be perpetual health and happiness, if you try it⁹
Man by nature is of the frugivorous class
His food (should be) fruits, grains and garden sass.¹⁰
and
At Schildkraut's you can eat, and eat your fill
Without the butcher's loathsome bill.¹¹

The Schildkrauts believed that food was an integral part of a higher social equity, advertising in the leading progressive publications, including *Yiddisher Farmer* and the communist *Freiheit*. A 1927 advertisement in the mainstream *Brooklyn Daily Eagle* promoted its ongoing free "luncheon conference for like-minded workers," which on December 12, 1927, featured "Prof. J. C. Chatterji, the greatest Hindu scholar in America."¹² Their success extended into a 1920s chain of health resorts/vegetarian hotels in Lakewood, New Jersey; in Saratoga Springs; on the Hudson; and in the Borscht Belt, "to ensure that vacationers might avoid the usual dietetic risk of the average summer resort of too much of the wrong kind of food."¹³

However, by the early 1930s problems arose, forcing the Schildkrauts to relinquish control of their restaurant chain and most of their hotels, the loss of which possibly led to the untimely death in 1937 of Sadie Schildkraut at the age of fifty-one.¹⁴ Herman continued to run their one remaining vegetarian hotel until his death in 1956, while the founding legacy of the Schildkraut restaurants, though plummeting in number, was assiduously maintained by its new owners.

During World War II, no New York Thanksgiving news story about the meals being offered to servicemembers away from home was complete without a mention of Schildkraut's vegetarian protose turkey.¹⁵ And as late as 1946, in an article profiling the last Schildkraut's on West Twenty-Eighth Street, store manager Maurice Teller (his last name fittingly the Yiddish word for "plate") displayed unflappable optimism in creating vegetarian dishes that mimic meat "without violating our principles" and about their ongoing quest "perfecting a meatless frankfurter."[16] The restaurant closed shortly afterward.

A Tale of Two Ratners

In the mid-1940s, the prolific *Forverts* journalist-at-large Chaim Ehrenreich (1900–1970)—whose beat was everything from the latest Yiddish theater production to rooting out corruption in the handling of postwar Displaced Persons—penned an all-too-brief series about the historic eating habits of American Jews. In one of his first pieces, he featured the Harmatz Brothers: Harry (ca. 1870–1945) and Jacob (ca. 1880–1966) of Ratner's restaurant.[17]

Harry Harmatz came to the US from near Lemberg (today's Lviv) in 1900, followed two years later by his brother Jacob. Both brothers went into the needle trades, but around 1915, inspired by their Tevye-like father who made and sold cheese, butter, and milk, they decided to go into the dairy restaurant business. With a capital of $150, the Harmatz Brothers Restaurant opened at 87 Pitt Street and made a profit the first night.

In 1917, they opened Harmatz Brothers at 107 Second Avenue on the northwest corner of East Sixth Street. By April they were in business with Alex Ratner (1878–1935), who, as the oft repeated forklore relates, won his name on the signage thanks to a coin toss.

But health reasons soon caused Ratner to move to California, and not long after, the Harmatz brothers split Ratners into competing dairy fiefdoms: Harry remained at their original 107 Second Avenue location in the center of the Yiddish theater district, while Jacob, with his new partners the Zankel brothers, moved to the dry goods side of the Lower East Side: 138 Delancey Street off Orchard, at the mouth of the Williamsburg Bridge. In the dairy equivalent of in-laws Jack Silverman and Louis Anzelowitz, the Harmatz brothers maintained a decades-long mutual nonrecognition. The Ratner brother's Yiddish press was written as if the other did not exist, or if he did exist, they were not directly related, or if they were directly related, they were defilers of the family name, as in a 1927 Delancey Street ad that described Jacob as running what was "widely regarded as the true Ratner's restaurant."[18]

The Harmatz brothers also competed on the air. On January 25, 1928, Harry's Second Avenue restaurant sponsored a show on WBNY featuring the Ratner's Dairy Maids, while on October 22, on WABC, Jacob's Delancey

Street restaurant sponsored a Yiddish theater extravaganza featuring Aaron Lebedeff, Betty Simonoff, pianist Abe Ellstein, and Louis Temkin, who was billed as "the cloak maker with the golden voice."[19]

In 1945, when Harry Harmatz died, the Second Avenue restaurant was taken over by his son Abe. Abe's cousin Harold had returned the year before to help run the Delancey Street Ratner's with his father Jacob, who worked there until his death in 1966.[20] For the 1955 fiftieth anniversary, both owners puffed themselves up to their biggest sizes ever. Abe celebrated by investing $150,000 ($1.5 million today) for a recently shuttered cafeteria up the block and instantly tripling his contiguous Second Avenue real estate footprint.[21] Harold, on the other hand, doubled down on the original restaurant by stripping away any and all trace of the burnished wood and matte marble of the immigrant-era aesthetic and replacing it with a triumphalist postwar chrome and leatherette fantasy, which is how his Ratner's is remembered by anyone who remembers it.

Both brothers had the good fortune to open just steps from a popular Loew's movie house, so while the fortunes of the Loews/MGM chain were high, Ratner's benefited by the increased foot traffic. But with the 1948 Paramount Decree and the breakup of the movie studio/theater monopolies, Loew's movie houses were cut adrift and went into steady decline, like Jacob's neighbor, the Loew's Delancey that sputtered and crackled until it finally went dark in 1977.[22]

While Jacob's next door Loew's Commodore had a similar initial trajectory—and did eventually go dark—what gave Ratner's a reprieve was the 1960s neighborhood transformation from the Lower East Side to the East Village. Now instead of blinking out like on Delancey Street, the old Loew's Commodore (recently renamed the Village Theater) would get a temporary high voltage jolt thanks to its acquisition by the Yiddish speaking Holocaust survivor and rock-and-roll impresario Bill Graham for his meteoric and mythic Fillmore East. The frowsy and faded Ratner's, with its cheap prices and twenty-four-hour service, was in perfect antiestablishment harmony with the rhythms of the Aquarian world flowing out of the theater next door. This fusion of "rock and roll" and "onion roll" was a much-needed infusion for the aging eatery. Graham helped by filling the Fillmore's concession with the restaurant's baked goods, and sometimes, following post-show equipment loadouts, he would host a Ratner's feast for the crew on the now empty stage.[23]

That uptick in Ratner's business was so vital that when Graham hung up his spurs on June 27, 1971, Ratner's began a beeline decline, closing on

Figure 8.2. Ratner's restaurant on Delancey Street. *Source:* 1940 Tax Photograph Collection, NYC Municipal Archives. Used with permission.

May 28, 1974, its once sweeping space soon segueing into a series of anonymous, claustrophobic superettes. When the restaurant went under, so did its 115 Second Avenue bakery, whose storefront lay vacant for years. The new building owners (New York University, which housed its film school there) leased it to another kosher baker: Moishe's, where for the next forty years it maintained the neighborhood's long, vernacular Jewish baking tradition, later moving to nearby 504 Grand Street where it is today.

The economic and demographic changes that took down the Second Avenue Ratner's were slower to arrive to the Delancey Street Ratner's, which was still buoyed by the also rapidly disappearing Orchard Street retail traffic. (Harold Harmatz would quip that the money people saved shopping for Orchard Street clothing bargains was spent at Ratner's.) In his own unexpected career coda, Harold, who studied real estate law before going into the family business, would be called back to active legal duty in the 1960s when he and other community leaders successfully beat back Robert Moses's hegemonic vision of slashing an expressway from the Williamsburg Bridge to the Holland Tunnel across their beloved Delancey Street.[24]

In the 1970s, Harold brought out a cookbook (1975) and a retail line of frozen signature dishes, the latter raising the mouth-watering, ironic possibility of their being sold in the frozen food section of one of the "claustrophobic superettes" that once was the Second Avenue Ratner's. A fire closed the Delancey Street Ratner's for the first half of 1991, yet even a full remodel reopening would only slow the restaurant's inevitable closure. Yet, despite the longtime Harmatz borscht-red blood rivalry, the most poignant underscoring of their shared deep spiritual connections to Ratner's came in the aftermath of the restaurants' closings: Abe died the day after his Second Avenue Ratner's was shuttered in 1974, while nephew Harold died in 2004 on the second *yortsayt* (death anniversary) of his Delancey Street Ratner's.[25]

Ratner's Last Gasp: Lansky's Lounge

In 1997, in an attempt to change with the times, Harold Harmatz ceded autonomy to grandchildren Robert and Fred, who opened Lansky Lounge, which traded on its mash-up of both the restaurant's one-time devoted customer Meyer Lansky and the current downtown "punk/gangsta" zeitgeist.[1] The backroom grew to take over the original restaurant so that Ratner's was then only open one day a week. But its demise was also accelerated by its updated menu: for the first time, unkosher shrimp and lobster would join Ratner's celebrated baked whitefish (Meyer Lansky's favorite), driving away remaining old-line customers like Sylvia Fisher, who came to Ratner's for potato pirogen for as long as she could remember: "I don't know about this Lansky-schmansky business . . . I'm not happy about this."[2]

---

1. Corey Kilgannon, "Harold Harmatz, 91, Dies; Owned Ratner's Restaurant," *New York Times*, May 3, 2004, B8.
2. Lukas I. Alpert, "Famous N. Y. Kosher Eatery Fades with Time," *Ithaca Journal*, July 15, 2002, 11A.

Hammer's

While the world rightly celebrates the "I'll have what she's having" appearance of Katz's delicatessen in Rob Reiner's 1989 *When Harry Met Sally*, the equivalent dairy restaurant movie moment fully belongs to the 1976 Martin Ritt Cold War–era drama *The Front*, where a key scene was shot at Hammer's Dairy restaurant on East Fourteenth Street and Second Avenue.

Figure 8.3. Hammer's menu from right before it closed in 1977; its offerings and ownership had not changed in sixty years. *Source:* Author's collection.

Max "Mekhl" Hammer was born in Rohatyn, Poland (now Ukraine), in 1881 and came to New York in 1901; by 1903, he had a restaurant on Brooklyn's Lispenard Street. In 1916, Hammer moved to 243 East Fourteenth Street just off Second Avenue, where the restaurant would remain.

A labor dispute in 1921—caused when a surly waiter was summarily dismissed for insulting a customer about the size of their tip—resulted in aggressive picketing from Waiter's Union Local Number One. One source reported that former employees and union picketers chased away potential customers by "throwing red peppers in their eyes."[26] Hammer responded by bringing in his wife and two sons to continue as a family business.

Hammer's being used for several days of location shooting for *The Front* included a meticulous restoration of the dining room, something that the restaurant had sorely needed for years but that the owners could only dream of doing. Director Martin Ritt, who in the first fifteen minutes of the film had already shown his sweet tooth for setting key dramatic moments around food, opens the scene at Hammer's, with the camera's elegiac panning across its cozy dining room. Settling on a group of four men in a booth, one of whom, Howard (Woody Allen) is arranging "to front" for the assembled blacklisted writers, Ritt caps the moment with vaudevillian comic Joey ("Niagara Falls" and "Floogle Street") Faye as a waiter reciting a perfectly cadenced classic dairy restaurant order readback: "Filet of sole, vegetable cutlet, mushroom omelet, protose steak. Eat in good health."

However, Hammer's new life in the newly restored restaurant would be short-lived. Not long after the grand reopening, the landlord steeply raised the rent and after sixty years drove Hammer's out of business.

B&H

Perhaps the most amazing postscript of the once ubiquitous dairy/vegetarian restaurant story is the hole-in-the-wall, runt-of-the-litter plucky luncheonette, the sole survivor, and its unlikely multicultural cast of Gentile saviors: the B&H.

Co-founder Abraham Bergson (née Berekson) was born in Ostralaka, Poland, in 1910 and arrived with his family in 1920. The Bereksons were already in the food business; his father, Benem Berekson, listed his occupation as "operator" (i.e., sewing machine worker in the garment business) on his 1925 citizenship papers, but he was a *shoykhet* (ritual slaughterer) in the 1930 federal census. On the same census and in 1940, his son Abe is listed as a "restaurant counterman."

> My dad started his business on a handshake. He had worked as a waiter in a store across the street from where the B&H stands. When he decided he wanted to start his own business, he approached many of the restaurant supply merchants on the Bowery. They knew my father to be an honest man, and they all gave him credit with just a handshake.
> The B&H opened in either 1937 or 1938. Originally B&H stood for "Bergson and Heller." Later on, Mr. Heller left the business, and my father's friend Sol Hausman, became his second partner, still B&H. Sol came up with an idea that B&H could also stand for "Better Health."[27]

Ringed by the cries of "Jumbo Jockey" (the counterman's call to indicate that someone had left a tip larger than twenty-five cents), the B&H's concise size and breezy service meant that it was no competition for the larger and luxer Rappoport's or Steinberg's nearby, but pitched across the street from the Public Theater it was the perfect place for play attendees to get a quick bite between acts. It was also perfect for co-founder Abe Bergson, who himself was what was called a *patriyot*—an enthused devotee of the theater:

"Boris Thomashefsky used to come in here," noted longtime counterman Leo Ratnofsky. "Molly Picon. Maurice Schwartz who ran the Yiddish Art Theater. And they'd converse with Abie Bergson over a bowl of soup. I remember Schwartz used to complain that there were more people at the B&H than there were at his theater."[28]

The neighborhood transition was articulated by counterman Ratnofsky, who began there in 1940 and who reminisced on the eve of his retirement in 1978: "These actors and actresses, the hippies, the yippies, the beatniks, the bohemians, people who'd run away from God knows where—I've always felt an attraction to them. Especially the starving ones."[29]

The restaurant continued under the original owners until they sold it in the early 1980s. (Abe Bergson would die in 1986.) The B&H quickly began slipping in quality, leading to increased NYC health violation closings, leading to a series of increasingly inept owners. A 1988 *Daily News* article noted "distraught Bulgarian" owner Nissim Nitzani, who, slapped with yet another extended city health closing, responded by pounding his fist on the counter: "'I'm dead,' moaned Nitzani, "I'm dead. That's all.'"[30] In 1991, *Daily News* restaurant critic Arthur Schwartz, in lambasting Ratner's for its now dependably low-quality food, stated he would still eat there because it was clean, unlike the other remaining dairy restaurants of which, at its perennial bottom listing, was the B&H.[31]

However, despite that ranking the little B&H had its fans, as noted in a poem written by two customers and then long taped to the milk machine:

> Blessings on your counter tops
> Bruchas on your pans and pots
> B&H, the Dairy princes
> Lords of sour cream and blintzes!
> Young and fresh or old and gnarly
> All must slurp your mushroom barley
> Even wealthy uptown fogies
> Grab a cab for your pirogies!
> If we had a dozen wishes
> Never could we find a dish as
> Good as your gefilte fish is!
> Though your premises be narrow
> You have stuffed us to the marrow
> Still, we cannot leave your table
> Till we wheedle or finagle
> One more lox and one more bagel![32]

The fortunes of the vest-pocket vegetarian eatery improved dramatically in 2003 when it was bought by Fawzy Abdelwahad, an Egyptian Muslim (and former B&H counterman) and his Polish Catholic wife Ola Smigielska (who worked across the street at another restaurant). Together with their Latino counter staff they have done something singularly remarkable by accurately evoking a menu with which neither they nor their new enthusiastic customers grew up, yet putting them in direct continuity—in a modest twenty-one-seat kind of way—to the glory days of dairy/vegetarian restaurants.

In 2015, an illegally installed gas line exploded down the block from the B&H, leveling several buildings but, miraculously, not touching the restaurant. However, city red tape shut the restaurant indefinitely, prompting a GoFundMe campaign (with a premium of a bilingual "Challah, por favor!"

T-shirt) that pulled the restaurant out of the hole. When it reopened, the line of relieved loyal customers stretched down Second Avenue.[33]

Despite being swatted yet again during the Covid-19 lockdowns (and having to endure yet another recent protracted city process to repair its storefront), the cry of "Challah, por favor" (alas, no longer "Jumbo Jockey") is still heard at the little B&H that continues to defy all obstacles.

9

Fast, Crowded, and Cheap
The Cafeteria

With their 24/7 open seating, self-service, and anonymous and no-frills style, cafeterias were to eating what the subway was to travel: fast, crowded, and cheap. And like the subway, its users grudgingly ceded space to strangers next to them while enveloping themselves in a culinary cocoon wherein a person could consume an entire meal in nineteen minutes.[1]

Yet also from that laissez-faire environment came crime, and crime in all of its multihued diversity. On the one hand, the cafeteria honor system, with its ticket checkout format, established a low bar for those with weak wills and strong appetites to engage in passive aggressive pilfery by simply misstating the extent of their meal. A May 11, 1926, *New York Times* report on a fire at the "Famous cafeteria" noted that "seventy five patrons departed in the excitement without paying their checks."[2] Just up the crime food chain, as early as 1895 thanks to its highly mobile and ever-changing clientele, gangs of pickpockets—in several cases, women[3]—preyed on the diners, which resulted in ubiquitous "watch your hat and coat signs." A popular Yiddish vaudeville joke told of two men in a cafeteria eating under a "watch your hat and coat" sign. One, Yonah, assiduously obeyed, while Shloime focused on his meal. "Stop looking at our coats," Shloime admonished him. "I'm only watching mine," Yonah answered. "Yours disappeared a while ago."[4]

However, the crime that made cafeterias the ATM of their day were armed robberies. On August 7, 1922, the *New York Tribune* reported on a quartet of well-dressed men who conducted a series of seamlessly coordinated early morning holdups of four Brooklyn cafeterias from "a speedy black and yellow taxi." The four performed so smoothly that "Max Meister, the proprietor standing behind a counter ten feet from the spot where the tall stranger [one of the robbers] was collecting his evening earnings, had no inkling of what was going on until the robbers had departed in their taxicab."[5]

Another crime (abduction) occurred at a Dubrow's cafeteria, where the actual target (robbery) was the nearby Fox's Congress Theater. On February 24, 1931, a group of armed robbers entered the restaurant ("a gathering place for the theater's personnel") and at pistol point rousted the theater manager diner, forcing him back to his office to open its safe.[6]

However, robberies were not the only thing that regularly brought the police to cafeterias. When standard restaurants switched to the cheaper cafeteria format—which allowed them to fire their waitstaff, giving double duty to their remaining workers—union organizers sponsored regular picketing and public actions against the cafeteria owners. There was even fighting among rival cafeteria unions themselves. In 1930, *The New York Times* reported that "17 Communists [were] seized in cafeteria melee" during a demonstration of two thousand people; Zelgreen's Cafeteria was caught between pickets of the AFL's Cafeteria Employees Union and a counterdemonstration by Communist Food Workers Industrial Union.[7]

However, even the Communists had trouble when they opened their own cafeteria in August 1927 at 30 Union Square in a building they shared with the newspapers the Yiddish *Freiheit* and *The Daily Worker*. Cryptically called "Prolectos" (for "proletariat cooperative stores"), this restaurant and cafeteria was funded by six hundred Party shareholders, who, while they got no dividends, did get a 10 percent discount on meals. The restaurant was successful at first, serving five thousand meals a day and even becoming de rigueur on the New York slumming circuit: "The Prolectos Cooperative Cafeteria [is] swarming with the proletariat. If the tables are entirely surrounded by talkative workers, as they are likely to be, he [the visitor] may have an ice cream soda, standing, as he looks at the bold strokes of brawny murals and listens to the tumult of Slavic and Semitic tongues."[8] In what, especially for Communists, was a comically bad misread of capitalism's fiscal underpinnings, Prolectos, after expanding to three times its original size, reopened in the fall of 1929, only weeks before the October Wall Street crash. It closed quickly afterward. While the opening of Prolectos had been carried in the mainstream press (mainly for its novelty value), its closing was nowhere covered except in the pages of longtime arch-enemy the Socialist *Forverts*. In a lengthy four-column article, the paper reveled with lip-smacking glee in every salacious detail of the cafeteria's downfall: "The big Communist cafeteria on Union Square, the pride of the Communist Cooperative Movement, the shmaltz vat of the 'Freiheit' and 'The Daily Worker,' shut down midday last Friday. Those who gathered to eat or to sit for a while were told to leave the cafeteria . . . and go elsewhere to discuss the imminent Communist revolution."[9]

Early Jewish Cafeterias

As with Prolectos, cafeterias were little autonomous regions that catered to specific communal subcategories. The first one started in 1885, the clubby Wall Street's Exchange Buffet, while later cafeterias like the Belmore at Twenty-Eighth Street and Park Avenue catered mainly to cabbies (and thus was a location of the 1976 film *Taxi Driver*), while Kellogg's cafeteria on Forty-Ninth Street (also on the west side) hosted, as its onetime habitué Red Buttons noted, entertainment's "small time guys."[10]

And then there was the parallel universe of Jewish self-service cafeterias anticipated by the Yiddish axiom: "Az men zent nit foyl / hot men in moyl" (If you're not slothful / you'll have a mouthful). This generation of Jewish cafeterias was launched by Max Bernstein, whose Libby's Lunch in Harlem (1916) and on Rutgers Street and East Broadway (1918) offered egalitarian self-service democratic dining for a dime: "'While 10c is ordinarily a small sum, in Libby's it can buy you a nice bite to eat' . . . his ads would read: 'Here all are equal; no rich or poor.' 'Give what you want; a nickel or a dollar . . .' 'No tips! You're the boss! . . . why wait for a waiter to finally get around to you? Put that 5c into another dish!'"[11]

In 1922, Bernstein decided to open a hotel and leave the cafeteria business, creating a vacuum quickly filled. Not surprisingly, given their modest prices, many of the start-up eateries were spare in grim surroundings. This changed when Gross and Lindenboim ("the architects of eating") opened Traffic at 135 Delancey Street. This four-story cafeteria ran boldly designed newspaper ads that bragged about its striking new $100,000 Deco designed home: "This is no basement," assured the ad. "You won't have to crawl in and then clamber your way down . . . all which gold, knowledge, or boundless energy can do has been brought to bear on this cafeteria. Everything is fixed (*upgefixet*) according to the latest methods of modern sanitation procedures."[12]

The policy that made cafeterias the Switzerland of Jewish restaurants was their omnivorous offerings. A ubiquitous mid-1930s jingle on Yiddish radio for Henry Frankel's Parkway Cafeteria in Brooklyn (10 percent discount for Communist Party members) underscored this point:

> If you don't want to quibble
> Where to find a tasty nibble
> It's Parkway cafeteria
> Our homey cooking is the best you've ever seen
> We have meat and milk and everything in between.
> It's Parkway cafeteria
> Parkway cafeteria![13]

Not surprisingly, the cafeteria also proved to be a popular motif in the Yiddish arts. Writer Ossip Dymow's 1927 play *Mentshn Shtoyb* (*Human Dust*) was a hit in Maurice Schwartz's Yiddish Art Theater, in part because of its use of a cafeteria as a setting. The same year composer Joseph Rumshinsky noted how the scores for his latest shows with lyricist Molly Picon (*Molly Dolly*, *Reizele*) were inspired by the dynamics of the cafeteria that he called "the tempo of our generation."[14]

What is perhaps most amazing is that, given the relentless ubiquity of cafeterias and how they directly impacted upon Jewish life, there were not more than a dozen newspaper short stories using cafeterias as a setting/metaphor for contemporary Jewish life, such as in the 1926 feuilleton "The Missouri Jew Declares War on New York":

> Presently, I see a sign "Cafeteria" and it tugs at me . . . but when I went inside I started to tremble, so many people in there. The clatter, the shrieking, the racket just so startles me that I stand stock still in the middle of a packed dining room where, over my head bubbling soup, hot coffee, plates of goulash which give out wafts of steam, glasses of ice cold buttermilk all held aloft by diners each searching for a table on which to put their food.
>
> So, wandering aimlessly in the midst of this chaos, they drag me, too, farther and farther from the food display. And, just as I try to turn to get back to the food, I end up with a cold glass of buttermilk in my face. Having never had a bath like this before, I decided then and there: no more cafeterias.[15]

In Joseph Opatoshu's 1933 serio-comic *In a kafeterye* his foils were two unemployed workers who attempt to get a cafeteria confederate to sneak them full meals for a ten-cent punch of their card. While the workers do get a meal, with their friend exposed, they are both forced to wash dishes to pay their bill.[16] Another *In a kafeterye* (1938) is from author Miriam Raskin, who uses her main character (Miss Heifetz)—a shop worker who luxuriates in the cafeteria's cheap repose—to cast a knowing eye over her fellow diners: an elderly couple whose wife arranges their table as if at home; a pair of double daters where the boys pay attention to only one girl; a woman who waits for a companion who never arrives; and an old music teacher and his young protege.[17] But the cafeteria's lyric poet was Isaac Bashevis Singer, who, in a number of stories—such as in his October–November 1977 serialized *Forverts* novella *Di kafeterye*—created a reverie of overlapping disappearing worlds: of Holocaust survivors, Yiddish, and cafeterias themselves.[18]

Into the mid-1960s, on the Spice Route of Jewish cafeterias, with its northern tip en route to the Catskills on Route 17 near Tuxedo, New York, the fabled—and only recently razed—Red Apple Rest still had over three hundred locations. But a decade later there were only one hundred left, most in Manhattan, with more than 10 percent confined to the area between Columbus Circle and Pennsylvania Station. The last was Dubrow's.[19]

Dubrow's

George F. Dubrow (1903–1956), who at the apogee of his 24/7 cheap eats empire had a half dozen cafeterias, was born in Minsk and arrived with his family in 1915. In the 1920 federal census his father Benjamin is listed as a "keeper" of a restaurant, and by the 1925 census daughter Minnie and son George were both employed there.

In 1929, George Dubrow rented a low-slung, two-story building on the south side of Eastern Parkway and Utica Avenue, opening Dubrow's Pure Food Cafeteria (advertised as "the only fully vegetarian cafeteria in Brownsville") in an area already awash in other eateries, including a half dozen cafeterias such as the Mayflower, Pitkin, Pleasant, Parkway, and Cameo that were bunched on nearby Pitkin Avenue alone: "On Pitkin Avenue the leit-motif was food, and still more food of every variety and description enough to keep the stomach in a perpetual turmoil. Delicatessen stores and cafeterias blazoned forth the most elaborate electrical signs. The delicatessen stores were crowded with women and children, and with the 'younger bloods' of the Avenue. In the cafeterias near the windows sat fat, stodgy men with their buxom wives eating as if their very lives depended on it."

What made Dubrow's (which was called "the big eating place where Murder Mob members occasionally foregathered") was its proximity to the Palooka-circuit Eastern Parkway boxing arena, bookie joints, and half dozen pool halls. It was also walking distance from 779 Saratoga Avenue and the Midnight Rose Candy Store, the headquarters of Murder Inc. In fact, Dubrow's had been the scene of so many robberies, shootings, beatings, abductions, pickets, demonstrations, and street fights that in 1942 the building's landlord embarked on a fruitless years-long attempt to break a twenty-year lease they signed in 1929. Dubrow's would end up staying at that location until 1967.[20]

But Dubrow's not only led all other cafeterias in the number of crimes committed on its premises; it also led all other cafeterias in the number of crimes committed on its premises while its customers (sometimes including police) were busy eating and couldn't even be bothered to look up from their plates. Early morning on September 6, 1938, four robbers made off with over $6,500 in cash and jewelry by lugging a two-hundred-pound ("carelessly covered") safe through the cafeteria as "between 30 and 40 diners breakfasted" unconcernedly nearby. It was only after the night manager, Max Tobin, broke out of the closet in which the robbers had locked him at pistol point and ran into the dining room yelling "Robbery! Robbery!" that the diners first learned of the crime in their midst.[21]

Over the years, night manager Tobin would be the victim of crimes including, but not limited to, armed robbery, detainment, kidnap, intimidation, and being thrown from a speeding car. On June 20, 1946, he suffered all five. When returning home at two-thirty in the morning, Tobin was abducted off the street and threatened by four masked, armed men only to be pushed from their getaway car when they found that the bag he was carrying did not, as they assumed, contain the evenings receipts, but a half dozen onion rolls.[22]

Crime at Dubrow's did not stop at robbery. On September 26, 1941, Dubrow's regular, racketeer and aspiring police informer Abe "Jew Murphy" Babchik sat down in the cafeteria after work where he "toyed leisurely with a Danish pastry" and was gunned down coming out.[23] His assailant, Murder Inc.'s Samuel "Little Kishke" Kovner, made good on his vow to never be taken alive when he died the next month in a running gun battle with police.[24]

Even a new Brooklyn outlet in 1941 at East Sixteenth Street and Kings Highway did not change Dubrow's—or Max Tobin's—luck or the unobservant eating habits of Dubrow's diners. On January 8, 1952, an apparently intoxicated man staggered up to Tobin at one-thirty in the morning in the crowded cafeteria. After asking directions for the men's room (which was near the office) he produced a small automatic pistol, forcing Tobin into his office to open the safe. Then, after binding and gagging him, the crook paid a twenty-cent tab for coffee and, continuing his drunk act, reeled out the front door with $15,000. Tobin later told the press that fifty employees and 450 customers—including four police officers—were unaware of the holdup in the balcony office.[25]

This second Dubrow's (naturally billed as a "cafeteria of refinement") adjacent to the elevated BMT track was followed in 1952 by an outpost in Miami Beach and a garment center satellite on Thirty-Eighth and Seventh Avenue that in less than five months served over five million meals.[26]

Not as successful was his idea of a seafood, steaks, and chops restaurant that opened in May 1946. Dubbed "Dubson" (Dub = Dubrow; son = son, Irwin), replete with a "Hollywood-style opening" and a steady stream of gossip column items, the place managed to attract A-minus-list celebrities for a while. But like the Lansky Lounge later, the unabashedly unkosher eatery failed to attract traditional Jewish diners or Manhattan residents willing to make the forty-minute subway or automobile pilgrimage to Brooklyn's Crown Heights. Dubson's limped along until it was sold to Howard Johnson's in 1949.[27]

With the untimely death of Irwin Dubrow in 1970 at the age of thirty-nine, former dishwasher, short-order cook, and cashier-bookkeeper Leo Martin, who had come to Dubrow's around 1939, bought the Seventh Avenue Dubrow's in 1972.[28] The ebullient Martin (" 'Have a Jewish crepe suzette,' he says, extending a cheese blintz. 'I've got one man who makes 1,500 of these a day' ") oversaw the slow, rear-guard orderly dismantling of the once-popular empire.[29] Dubrow's would get its "ready for my close-up" moment when it was used for Amram Nowak's 1983 public television adaption of Bashevis Singer's 1977 *Forverts* novella *Di kafeterye*.[30] Two years later, this last Dubrow's to open was the last Dubrow's to close.[31]

The Garden Cafeteria

The building that replaced Meyer and Louis Jarmulowsky's bank at 165 East Broadway was a no-nonsense brick structure with small lofts and offices and a ground-floor cafeteria, Fisher's. The restaurant was in the news in 1920 in a photo of a man and woman (he bandaged, she smiling defiantly) both holding signs "On strike for better conditions . . . when they were

Figure 9.1. Ray cafeteria shortly before it changed hands to become the Garden Cafeteria. *Source:* 1940 Tax Photograph Collection, NYC Municipal Archives. Used with permission.

attacked and beaten by strikebreakers who filled their places."³² Fisher's soon went bankrupt and was replaced by the more progressive Ray Cafeteria. Trumpeting that it employed "all union help," the new eatery ran a display ad in the Yiddish anarchist newspaper *Fraye arbeter shtimme*, noting that " 'Publisher's Square' deserves a modern restaurant where journalists, business people, and workers can eat," and concluding with a nod to the concerns of its diners that it maintained a high level of cleanliness: *"sterelyzing mashins* have been repaired [*oyfgefixt*] to wash dishes and utensils in a way human hands cannot."³³ In 1941, Ray was sold to Charles and Beatrice Metzger and renamed Metzger's Garden Cafeteria, or simply "the Garden."

Charles Metzger (1897–1977) came to America from Lemberg (now Lviv) around 1912. By 1925 he was a waiter, and by 1930, a restaurant "proprietor." In its premier ad, Metzger noted not only the addition of a new bakery and air conditioning but *visnshaftlekhe balaykhtung*, which roughly translates somewhere between "latest technological lighting" and "intellectual illumination."[34] Ray previously had improved on the property by installing a two-story illuminated sign. While Metzger eventually took it down, he went one better: he broke through what had been a blank wall onto Rutgers Street, doubling his street frontage and capping the entrance with a new Deco-style neon sign, while its interior was adorned by a WPA-style mural street scene of nearby Orchard Street. Jutting out, the new facade completely dominated the very busy subway station corner. And while other Jewish restaurants closed for Passover, in 1947 the Metzgers had the idea to clean and prepare the Garden to stay open during the holiday, and until the early 1960s it was the only Jewish restaurant offering that.

The Garden, "the self-service Sardi's of the Yiddish intelligensia," oversaw the sunset of Journalism Square.[35] When it opened in 1941, there were still some half dozen publications in the neighborhood; by 1951, two papers (*Tog* and *Morgn Zhurnal*) had become one (*Tog-Morgn Zhurnal*) before ceasing publication entirely in 1971. Then in 1974 the *Forverts* pulled up stakes and moved.[36] And with the *Forverts* gone, writer Bashevis Singer decamped to the Famous dairy restaurant on West Seventy-Second near his home on the Upper West Side.

Toward the end of its run in the early 1970s, it was plagued by the same level of street crime that was rampant in the city. *The New York Times* warned its readers that eating at the cafeteria was "not recommended for those who are already afraid to be out in midtown after dark."[37] And, in a nod to Woody Guthrie's song "Pretty Boy Floyd" ("some men will rob you with a six-gun others with a fountainpen"), the Garden Cafeteria was the victim of both. On March 30, 1965, "a man with his hand in his pocket simulating a pistol" held up the cafeteria for $1,000, and like Dubrow's, "the robbery took place as 10 patrons dined."[38] That had been preceded on April 3, 1963, with the arrest of Lawrence Block, Metzger's longtime accountant, who had over five years quietly swindled over $103,085 ($850,000 today) from the little cafeteria.[39]

Metzger sold the restaurant in 1976 to a Joseph Baumohl. Under his management, the cafeteria endured scathing reviews ("deep dirt, deep grease, and deep disgust are about all you get there these days"[40]) and increasingly frequent Department of Health closings, which validated the scathing reviews. Baumohl cashed out in 1983 with 165 becoming Wing Shoon restaurant,[41] who painted over the cafeteria's celebrated mural. In 2005 the current owners (Wu's Wonton King) discovered that the original crimson-and-cream-colored

Garden Cafeteria signage still existed underneath Wing Shoon's newer sign. It was salvaged for the nearby Eldridge Street Synagogue collection.

Metzger died in 1977, like fellow former dairy restaurateur Harold (Ratner's) Harmatz, on the *yortsayt* of his restaurant's closing.[42]

10

Raisins and Almonds

Chunky Milk Chocolate

Figure 10.1. Phil Silvershein's Top Notch Candy distributorship, a few years before the birth of Chunky Chocolate. *Source:* 1940 Tax Photograph Collection, NYC Municipal Archives. Used with permission.

Phil Silvershein (1894–1982) was born in the Polish Galician town of Buczacz and, along with his older brother William (1891–1961), came to the United States by 1908. The brothers were living with, and working for, an uncle in the confectionary business. (That year's federal census lists them respectively as "shipping clerk" and "errand boy.") By around 1912, the brothers had become "jobbers" (wholesale candy distributors who serviced both candy stores with prepackaged retail candy and appetizing stores with quantity loose candy) and in 1926 founded Top Notch Candy Inc. at 200 Delancey St., which by 1947 was doing $1.5 million annually ($17 million today).[1]

In 1943, right before brother William left to fight in Europe, Phil introduced a new chocolate candy: Chunky. Given the severe home-front shortages of all products, not the least sugar, how he accomplished this feat is unknown. Perhaps it was Silvershein's numerous connections in the national candy distribution network, but it was his long wholesale experience that allowed him to perfect the perfect impulse sales candy. The squat, architecturally shaped chocolate wedge swathed in eye-catching silver wrapping made such a hit that by 1947 Silvershein was able to sell the distribution business and turn attention full-time to Chunky production.[2]

To celebrate, Silvershein took to radio, not mainstream American broadcasting but station WEVD, which revealed his true inspiration for the candy. In the fall of 1947, Silvershein, a lover of Yiddish theater music, sponsored *The Chunky Theater of the Air*, a series of twenty half-hour broadcasts of *Classics Illustrated*-style reductions of Abraham Goldfaden's operas including Bar Kokhba and Akeydes Yitzkhok.[3] The shows were led by Goldfaden legatee Joseph Rumshinsky, who also conducted several of his own musicals such as *Katinka, Goldene Kale*, and *Molly Dolly*.[4]

While there had been isolated broadcasts of portions of Goldfaden operas over the years and while a number of his songs were commercially recorded, the vast majority of Goldfaden's work had not been heard since their earliest stagings. The Chunky shows, then, were a modestly monumental series of broadcasts, with the music interpreted by the last generation skilled and knowledgeable enough to create a sonic bridge between the founding sounds of Yiddish theatrical self-realization and the current state of its self-aware Jewish audience. The inaugural broadcast on June 28, 1947, featured the most popular of all Goldfaden's operettas, *Shulamis*, with its beloved aria "Rozhinkes mit Mandlen" ("Raisins and Almonds"), which were, by design, also Chunky's founding ingredients, a point WEVD announcer Mitchell Levitsky eagerly underscored ("Yes, *those* raisins and almonds"). For a brief moment, Silvershein not only got to bask in the glow of being part of the great flow of Yiddish theater, he also got one of the greatest examples in the canon of Yiddish songs to, in essence, act as a jingle for his product.[5]

Given the show's importance and that it aired on the heels of *The Forverts Hour*, WEVD's signature program, the newspaper radio listings did not note Silvershein's program by name but by generic descriptors like "variety show" or "dramatic sketch." Conversely, Silvershein/Chunky did no advertising in the *Forverts*, reserving show display ads for rival papers, such as the *Tog*.[6]

It would be the tragic, untimely death of his niece Roberta (known as the "chunky baby," the namesake of the product, also born in 1943) that prompted Silvershein to sell Top Notch Candy.[7] A 1948 announcement in *Billboard* noted that Phil Silvershein would no longer have any connection with Chunky but shortly would be producing a new chocolate product. However, he never did and was not heard of again.[8]

The fate of Silvershein's rozhinkes mit mandlen Chunky itself began to change almost immediately after he sold it. While raisins were continued, their Yiddish ingredient mate, almonds—which Silvershein later paired with cheaper filberts, cashews, and Brazil nuts—disappeared when the brand was acquired in 1953 by Ward Foods, under whom it would be memorably hawked on television ("Wotta chunka chocolate") by Jewish comedian Arnold Stang. Chunky was then sold to Nestlé around 1962, who, before selling it in 2018, had replaced all the remaining nut varieties with low-budget peanuts.[9]

Chunky's glory days of being the chocolate candy inspired by a beloved Yiddish song would have been lost to history had not Shereen Silvershein-Willens, Phil Silvershein's niece, heard the 2002 NPR series *The Yiddish Radio Project* and remembered the dozen sixteen-inch radio discs that her uncle had lovingly saved over the years donating them to my Yiddish radio collection at the American Folklife Center of the Library of Congress.

Part 2
Architecture

11

The Rise and Fall of the House of Jarmulowsky

Alexander "Sender" Jarmulowsky, or as he was referred to in the American press, "the Croesus of Canal Street," was born in Grayeve, Poland, in 1841. Together with his wife Rebecca (1842–1915) and their four sons—Albert (1865–1943), Meyer (1868–1947), Louis (1870–1932), and Harry (1878–1947)—he established a vest-pocket Lower East Side "house of Rothschild" banking family.[1]

Despite early rabbinic training, at the age of twenty-six, Jarmulowsky moved to Hamburg to found a bank with his brother-in-law, Solomon Markel, before coming in 1873 to the United States to open a branch at 54 Canal Street.[2] There, Sender Jarmulowsky uninterruptedly conducted his private bank for nearly four decades through numerous runs and, as he would proudly say, no failures. Private banks, unlike those that were state chartered, were run solely on the good word—and practices—of the banker and, if they failed, there was little recourse for recompense.[3] But in the hands of a knowledgeable and ethical banker—which by all accounts Sender Jarmulowsky was—S. Jarmulowsky offered a creative use of the bank platform for the greater good of his community at a time when the community had few other means of American socioeconomic entry.[4] His depositors—about 35,000, which by 1910 amounted to some 3 percent of the New York's Jewish population—trusted Jarmulowsky because he also helped with other things (international bank drafts to send money home, mortgages, ship passages, etc.). Jarmulowsky made his first fortune investing in ships passages, purchasing ship tickets during the lull season and reselling them at a profit during peak travel.

One son would later say that his father made visceral decisions about giving out loans, not worrying about his borrowers' actual financial condition. Jarmulowsky himself took no salary, only drawing that money on which he needed to live.[5] Even in 1890, when the Jarmulowsky family left the Lower East Side and moved to the tony East Sixties, he never lost his downtown street cred thanks to his omnipresence at 54 Canal Street, plus his community ubiquity as a president of several synagogues including the Eldridge Street Synagogue, as one of the founders of Lebanon Hospital (now Bronx Lebanon Hospital), as a founding trustee of the Jewish Theological Seminary, and as head of the United Orthodox Congregation, which was among those responsible for bringing Rabbi Jacob Joseph to New York as Chief Rabbi.

"Jarmulowsky's Tact"

Jarmulowsky's widespread recognized piety enabled him to artfully dodge a potentially fatal 1901 bank run resulting from an unfounded rumor. "Jarmulowsky's Tact" tells how he avoided disaster and managed to pay out all the requested money by buying valuable time:

> The eager-eyed investors in Jarmulowsky's bank at Canal and Orchard Street where a run has been in progress for several days were surprised Saturday morning when a sign appeared on a window of the institution which read:
> "No money will be paid today as it is the Jewish sabbath."
> The depositors though anxious to get their savings read the sign and were reconciled. . . . When they flocked to the bank the next day at daybreak there was a new sign in the window which read:
> "No money will be paid today. It is the Christian sabbath."
> "Jarmulowsky is all right," said one depositor. "A man with a head like that won't fail. Guess I'll leave my money in the bank," and he went home with the crowd.[1]

---

1. "Jarmulowsky's Tact," *Gazette*, Dec. 21, 1901, 20.

Jarmulowsky, who made his wife Rebecca a full partner in his bank (one of very few professional women bankers), leveraged his bank to secure real estate, and soon a day would not go by without real estate notices in the city papers involving S. Jarmulowsky. His influence extended outside of his Lower East Side base to Harlem, Brownsville, the Upper East Side, and other neighborhoods, while the kind of structures he was developing (tenements, factories, hospitals, schools) gave him an outsized influence on the emerging middle-class landscape of pre–World War New York City.

In 1898, sons Meyer and Louis, who had worked for their father, broke with him and went out on their own. (Another son, Harry, was in Germany studying medicine and running the Jarmulowsky Hamburg branch.) An insight into the split between *pere et fils* Jarmulowsky may be seen in that Meyer and Louis secured the mortgages and the properties from their father's banking and real estate competitors. Meyer and Louis opened M&L Jarmulowsky at 173-175 East Broadway (site of the future *Forverts* building) and in 1901 purchased a larger property down the block at 165 (site of the future Garden Cafeteria).[6]

The address 165 East Broadway at the corner of Rutgers Street has a Jewish history stretching back into the 1870s, when its tenants included the Sulamith Lodge No. 167 of the B'nai B'rith (1871) and a Ladies Bikkur Cholim Society Hebrew Industrial School (1883); it was also the site of the convention of Jewish Anarchists (1895) and headquarters of the Dress and Cloak Maker's Union, which in 1901 was the command center of labor leader Joseph Barondess as he led a successful strike of over eight thousand needle trade workers from around New York City.[7] The building also housed Dr. Judah Magnes's anti-pogrom Jewish Defense Fund (1905),[8] and publications like *The Jewish Press Bureau* (the first agency to "furnish the secular English press with correct information on Jewish topics," 1905),[9] the editorial offices of the Yiddish Anarchist magazine *Die Freie Gesellschaft* (*The Free Society*), and the short-lived Yiddish Zionist newspaper *Di Yiddishe Fon* (The Jewish Flag, 1906).[10] Despite its mojo, that building was razed in 1903 to make way for the M&L Jarmulowsky bank.

To date, banks, like government buildings, mainly followed a dependable Greco-Roman template featuring limestone, fluted Corinthian columns, and Carrara marble to denote longevity, dependability. and security. But Meyer Jarmulowsky was having none of that. An architecture student at Columbia University (class of 1891), he had worked as an architect (even designing some updates for his father's bank). Meyer Jarmulowsky's own bank design

Figure 11.1. Meyer and Louis Jarmulowsky's unusual Moorish style bank was razed soon after the bank's failure. *Source:* National Library of Israel, Historical Jewish Press website (www.jpress.org.il), founded by the National Library and Tel Aviv University. Used with permission.

was described by the *New York Tribune* as "something the Sultan of Morocco would get into his head if he wanted to have a tall building in Algiers." The opening of the new seven-story building—one of the biggest on the Lower East Side—attracted thousands of onlookers. The *Tribune* described its careening architectural styles: "The portico being modelled after that of the Palace of Gezireh at Cairo, Egypt. The elaborate vestibule leading to the magnificent counting house is of semi-moresque [*sic*] design, the counting house itself of the French Renaissance."[11] A reporter from the *New York Sun* noted: "The six upper floors are painted a beautiful silver color and in front of each window is a little Moorish balcony. On the ground floor a Moorish arch extends out over the sidewalk supported by columns of gold and silver. On each side of the arch in huge raised letters of gold and silver are the words 'Bank of M. and L. Jarmulowsky.' "[12] "It is a glaring glittering monument to the banking house of M&L," the reporter for the *New York Tribune* dryly noted, "a miracle of white enamel, gold paint of Oriental balconies of brass, and surmounted by a dazzling tower from which the flag of any Sultan might fly with propriety."[13]

And while not a sultan, Jarmulowsky did have a flag of his own design which fluttered from its roof alongside the Stars and Stripes: "A field of white on which a scroll with the name 'Jarmulowsky' was suspended from two trees above which was a stone pyramid and an arch and above that, an American eagle with spread wings against the background of a calm river and a rising sun."[14] This motif was repeated in stained glass in the building's skylight and in all the bank's windows. The amazed reporter for the *New York Sun* concluded he wouldn't be surprised to see "a hooded Arab or a turbaned Turk come sliding out of the door scimitar in hand."

The sons' new bank benefited from the decades-long accrued goodwill of their father's bank. At first, the brothers ran theirs as wholly private, but soon took a charter with the State of New York, giving them additional institutional imprimatur, a decision they would come to regret.[15] Although not as religious as their father, Meyer and Louis maintained the same public community aspects of the building as their father did. In 1905, during the Kishiniev pogroms, the M&L bank opened a large meeting hall under its counting room and provided free stamps, writing materials, and writing assistance for those who had family in the afflicted region.

Meyer Jarmulowsky even demonstrated some progressive tendencies when, as he noted in large 1905 Yiddish splash ads, M&L was "the crossroads where labor and capital meet" and the first bank to recognize the new (and extremely short-lived) Bank and Office Employees Union.[16] On the other hand, Meyer was also president of the Property Owner's Improvement Corporation, white landowners with real estate in Harlem. In seeming to improve Black property values there, the organization was instead attempting to contain African American expansion, or, as a reporter for the *New York Tribune* euphemistically described its aims, that Blacks "will not find it necessary to overspread the district."[17] Jarmulowsky, who in 1912 designed and built Harlem's Lafayette Theater at Seventh Avenue and 132nd Street made history when, soon after its opening (and under duress), it became the first theater in New York to desegregate.[18]

But in 1910, the M&L partnership splintered ("Banker Sues His Brother") when L sued M for $25,000 unpaid profits, and M countersued L, who then returned to S. Jarmulowsky.[19]

Figure 11.2. Sender Jarmulowsky did not live to see the 1912 opening of his beloved bank; today it is a boutique hotel. *Source:* Author's collection.

That same year, Sender Jarmulowsky, who had inhabited the same modest building at 54 Canal Street since first arriving in 1873, planned his own architectural statement and called upon the esteemed architectural firm of Rouse and Goldstone to make it.[20] They in turn produced a classic twelve-story, Beaux Arts building of granite, limestone, and, in its higher sections, ornamental brick. With the bank dominating the ground level and lofts and offices above, the building's distinctive ship's prow frontage is a possible stylistic nod to Jarmulowsky's humble origins dealing in ship passage futures. In addition to all its modern banking features it also had a fully outfitted *beys medresh* (house of prayer), and thanks to its complete electrical wiring and lighting, it was celebrated by inventor (and noted nativist) Thomas Edison in his magazine the *Edison Monthly*.[21] S. Jarmulowsky's bank, five stories higher than his sons', was capped with a distinctive exclamation point tower: a fifty-foot domed *tempietto* encircled by American eagles. Estimated cost of the building: $200,000 ($5 million plus today).[22]

Tragically, the elder Jarmulowsky did not live to see the opening of his bank, dying in August, two months before it was completed. Louis was soon joined by brother Harry, who left his medical practice to join the family banking business. The shock of Sender Jarmulowsky's death was matched by the public release of his will several months later, where it was revealed that due to his extensive charities, the onetime multimillionaire left an estate of only $500,000.[23] Rebecca, who would follow her husband in death two years later, was left an annuity of $10,000 plus 50 percent of all bank profits.[24] Their sons—even rebellious Meyer—were each left $100,000 as a "fund for persons who may then be depositors in case the good-will and assets, when disposed of, should be insufficient to pay all the depositors in full."[25] As goodhearted and solicitous as was this gesture, it was soon revealed to be woefully inadequate to save the house of Jarmulowsky.

It was Meyer's bad luck that two unrelated events combined nearly simultaneously in 1914. First, a change to the state banking laws that strengthened its oversight supervision and against whose implementation Meyer, who at first welcomed the state charter, now vigorously fought.[26] The second was the outbreak of war in August with his and other private ethnic banks being descended upon by thousands of depositors wanting to close their accounts to help families back home in Europe. The run revealed that Meyer owed his depositors tens of times the amount his late father had left him; he had been running M&L like a Ponzi scheme, paying off departing depositors with money from new depositors all the while knowing the bank was insolvent. Meyer's lax legerdemain caught up with him and resulted in the first Jarmulowsky bank to fail and the first Jarmulowsky to be arrested.[27]

The vehement Jewish community response to the M&L failure was immediate and dramatic given that of all the failed private Jewish banks, none was in worse fiscal shape than the M&L, a telling contrast to the late Sender Jarmulowsky whose bank *was* still solvent. On August 30, a *New York Times* headline ran, "5,000 Riot in Front of Closed Banks," and the article reported that thousands marched under a Yiddish banner: "The 60,000 unfortunate depositors of the three private banks demand our money and will not be quiet." The paper noted that "passions were aroused when one of the soapbox orators cried out: 'Let us go over to Jarmulowsky's and make those thieves tell us when they will give us our money,' only to be beaten back by a phalanx of club wielding police encircling the bankrupt bank."[28]

Hundreds stormed Jarmulowsky's Washington Heights home, driving him up over its rooftops where, when he retreated to the street and attempted to escape in a waiting taxicab, had to first run a gantlet of angry depositors. The zeitgeist can be assessed by Jarmulowsky's own landlord having the contents of his tenant's home summarily dumped into the street, while Jarmulowsky's rich neighbors distributed water and sandwiches to the protesters who besieged the banker's home.[29]

On April 3, 1915, after weeks of large demonstrations, a meeting was held with investors and Meyer Jarmulowsky, who promised his creditors full repayment within four years (it would take seven). Suddenly, one angry depositor drew a penknife from his pocket and attempted to drive it into the banker's neck, only to be swiftly thwarted by Jarmulowsky's lawyer, who later acknowledged he had been expecting something like that.[30]

The failure of M&L Jarmulowsky was a foreshadowing of S. Jarmulowsky itself, which had already suffered a wartime seizure of its Hamburg bank assets by the German government. Yet even with a steady attrition (the bank had by then shrunk to only seven thousand depositors) it somehow managed to survive until the United States entered the war in April 1917. With new, more restrictive wartime banking laws—and with new bank runs—S. Jarmulowsky could do nothing but fail.[31] Yet though hundreds turned out to protest its collapse, the demonstrations were short-lived and demonstrably less violent than those against son Meyer, perhaps reflecting the lasting respect in which the Jewish community still held Sender even years after his death.

The 54 Canal Street location soldiered on into 1920 as the North American Bank, of which Harry and Louis Jarmulowsky were listed in the city directory as "clerks" the same year they sold it at a bankruptcy auction.[32] The building would subsequently survive by renting its upper floor lofts (including to H. W. Perlman pianos) to light manufacturing and storage. And like its Lower East Side high-rise rival the *Forverts* building, it subsequently became Nine Orchard, a luxury boutique hotel and condos of today in an area now referred to as "Dime's Square".[33]

In the mid-1920s, brother Louis (now under the name Jarmel) became a shirt manufacturer, and another brother Albert (who also took the name Jarmel) sold insurance.[34] Shortly before the final M&L repayment in March of 1922, Meyer Jarmulowsky and his wife Fanny (possibly to avoid any undue publicity from the required newspaper announcement) were in a Tulsa, Oklahoma, courtroom to legally change their name to Jarmuth, under which they would live in New Rochelle and where Meyer and his son Edwin sold real estate.³⁵ Harry, the only son to retain the Jarmulowsky name, returned to his medical training as a doctor in Paterson, New Jersey, and his numerous obituaries mentioned nothing of his banking family, the once great house of Jarmulowsky.³⁶

12

The *Forverts* Building

From Socialist to Socialite

In 1831, the building at 175 East Broadway ("a street of pleasant residences") was called the Hicks House (the Hicks were related to the Motts of Mott Street fame)¹ and described as "a three-story modern brick building with vault cellar underneath, marble mantles in first and second stories and also in the basement, faithfully built and beautifully finished piazza across the rear, turned columns and balustrade with deck roof overlooking gardens on Rutgers Street. . . . This house is a component part of one of the best blocks in the whole city, in a genteel and fashionable neighborhood."²

At first, 175 East Broadway remained a private residence, but it soon became a boarding house (1852), a forty-person millinery workshop (1859), and back to a boarding house (1887); in 1898, it was acquired by Meyer and Louis Jarmulowsky as their first bank. The Jarmulowskys converted Hicks House to a five-story tenement in 1900, but then three years later sold it to the six-year-old *Forverts*.³ Founder and editor Abraham Cahan took a significant risk acquiring the building and nearly bankrupted the fledgling paper, but its distribution increased enough that, with additional improvements, by 1907, the building was worth $52,000 ($1.5 million today).⁴

In October 1910, when Sender Jarmulowsky announced his intention to build a new twelve-story bank—the highest structure on the East Side—the *Forverts* Association, which in May had already acquired no. 173 next door, adding fifty feet of street frontage, embarked on a building race, which, for all appearances, pit the forces of capital (Jarmulowsky) against the forces of socialism (Cahan). Both, however, represented the forces of capitalism. In January 1911, the *Forverts* Association, through newspaper announcements (though, curiously, not in the *Forverts* itself) invited design and construction bids for the new building.[5] For the architect, the Association chose George Boehm, Columbia University '97 (six years after Meyer Jarmulowsky), for whom this would be one of his first public interest commissions in a half century of design. Despite only a few of his buildings being identified, one can see stylistic elements that link him to his early *Forverts* building.[6]

Architecture historian Shirley Zavin notes the architectural and journalistic connections between the *Forverts* building and its fiery figurehead Abe Cahan, with the still extant 1906 building at 20 Vesey Street built by *The Evening Post* and for whom Cahan was a contributor. Like *The Evening Post* building, the Beaux Arts–Greek Revival *Forverts* building had a seven-story shaft section whose sweeping verticality, emphasized by white-clad, terra cotta edging, "contribut[ing] to the sense of a towering presence."[7] But Boehm's *Forverts* building is also alive with symbolic Socialist stylistic elements, like the torch on the escutcheon above the entryway, and widely festooned (both vertically and horizontally) throughout the building in stone and in stained glass. Although supposedly a retort to Jarmulowsky, the *Forverts* building, a three-minute walk from the bank, mimicked some of its same distinctly non-Jewish conventions (the pretentious use of *V* instead a *U* in Forward Building, etc.).

For the contractor, the *Forverts* turned to construction firm of Dawson and Archer, half century holders of major building achievements (i.e., the Criminal Court building at 100 Centre Street survives). This, however, was not its only track record. While Cahan thought enough of the company to dedicate nearly one-quarter of the paper's celebratory April 22, 1911, front-page article to them, one thing not mentioned was the company's long record of aggressive anti-labor policies going back to the dawn of Unionism in the mid-1880s, with some as recent as two years before.[8]

Only days into digging the foundation and while draining water from the remnant of a canal said to have given Canal Street its name, workers broke into a long-forgotten spring and started pumping out geysers hundreds of feet into the air of very cold, very clean water. In what was called a "Carlsbad spring of the East Side," it produced "long lines of men, women and children [who] waited with buckets, tumblers, pails pitchers, jugs, kettles, and other receptacles to get their share of the ice-cold water which seemed to be as pure as crystal and which was pumped out of the spring below."[9] *The New York Times* noted, "A bent old fellow took a drink of the liquid. 'Yes,' he agreed, smacking his lips like a connoisseur, 'that's the same water. I used to drink it when I was as small as those youngsters are.'"[10]

Figure 12.1. "This will be our new house": Front-page announcement in the *Forverts* about its new building. *Source:* National Library of Israel, Historical Jewish Press website (www.jpress.org.il), founded by the National Library and Tel Aviv University. Used with permission.

The pumping action, which lasted several days, attracted news coverage from most papers, except apparently the *Forverts*. But if the *Forverts* wasn't covering the story, it did turn up in it: "A. Halpern, manager of the Vorwärts Building Association, which owns the ground, was beaming from ear to ear. 'We may make a fortune out of it, yet,' he said. 'If it's really pure spring water, we'll bottle it and run the other water companies out of business.'"[11] Stung by the coarse capitalistic characterization, Cahan took back the story the next day. "Thousands of People Come to Drink Cold, Fresh Water from the *Forverts*'s Foundation," ran the dual-meaning headline above the tabloid-style layout showing beaming neighborhood children romping in the urban waterfalls; it was an ebullient enthusiastic scene of free relief during some of the most brutally hot summer days via nature and the *Forverts*.[12] Despite that mishap, the $300,000 ($8.75 million today) building emerged fully formed on schedule on March 1, 1912.

Upon opening, the *Forverts* building became a kind of Socialist Grand Hotel that counted among its tenants the Arbeter Ring (Workmen's Circle; today the Worker's Circle) and its Folksbeine (amateur Yiddish theater), United Hebrew Trades, Butcher's Union Local 509, the Jewish Socialist Farband, the Naturalization Aid League, and the Yiddish Radio Announcer's Guild, not to mention the site of numerous meetings, plays, rallies, concerts, lectures, and demonstrations in its three-hundred-seat theater.

In 1925, the *Forverts* gained an additional three stories with the erection of a giant thirty-thousand-watt electric sign whose *Jewish Daily Forward* in English (facing south, toward the Manhattan and Brooklyn Bridges) and Yiddish (facing north, toward the Williamsburg Bridge) could be clearly seen all around Lower Manhattan and miles into Brooklyn.[13] It is unclear when that rooftop signage was removed.

After the war, while several of the *Forverts* Jewish East Broadway neighboring organizations with original buildings remained on the Lower East Side (Home of the Sages of Israel at 270 East Broadway, Bialystoker Home for the Aged at 228 East Broadway, etc.), the *Forverts* did not. In 1974, along with its longtime building mate the Arbeter Ring, the *Forverts* moved to a nondescript (now razed) office building at 45 East Thirty-Third after selling its lightly derelict building to the Chinese Alliance Church for just $99,000.[14] A seemingly apocryphal story concerned the new owners and the building's most "revolutionary" elements: the four bas reliefs that frame the carved "Forward Building" above the entryway (showing Karl Marx far left and Fredrich Engels far right, but guesses as to the identities of the other portraits include August Bebel, Kael Liebknecht, Ferdinand Lasalle, and Fredrich Adler). The anti-Communist owners of the church, apparently unaware who adorned their facade, happened to overhear a tour guide describing the bas relief profiles, after which the owners first covered, then removed, the bas reliefs. (They were eventually retrieved and restored.)

In 1977, the building was sold for $316,000 to Mui Hin Lau, who, following the building's landmark listing in 1986, invested some $10 million dollars in the beginnings of a gut renovation to luxury apartments.[15] In the wake of 9/11, the building lay dormant until 2004 when it was purchased by architects/developers Ron Castellano and Chris Hayes for $22 million. The pair realized the building's condo-fication, with the facade faithfully restored and the interior completely gutted to create twenty-nine apartment units with an average price of some $1.5 million, or the 1907 value of the *Forverts* building adjusted for inflation, in its transition from Socialists to socialites.[16]

13

Harrison G. Wiseman
Builder of New York Yiddish Theaters

While Abraham Goldfaden is metaphorically said to have been the "architect" of the Yiddish theater, the man who literally designed and built more New York Yiddish theaters than anyone was Harrison G. Wiseman (1878–1945).

While the first bespoke Yiddish American theater was Jacob P. Adler's 1,700-seat Grand at the corner of Grand and Chrystie Streets in 1903,[1] most troupes were just making do in secondhand theaters that had seen lusher days: Keni Liptzin opened her Irving Place Theater in a former German playhouse off Fourteenth Street, and David Kessler's Thalia on the Bowery was so threadbare that a review of his 1901 Yiddish production of *Uncle Tom's Cabin* sadly noted, "This was once the greatest theater in New York . . . all the finest society of New York [came] here."[2] Boris Thomashefsky's rooftop National Winter Garden on Houston and Second Avenue shared space with a fight arena where "a sign announcing 'The Yankele Litvak' was [adjacent to] Floyd Johnson's name in electric lights as 'the next Heavyweight Champion of the World.'"[3]

It was about when Johnson was going for the title that Harrison G. Wiseman first arrived in New York. Though Wiseman's surname has a familiar Jewish redolence, his first and middle names (Harrison Gahagan) hint that Wiseman, who was born in Toledo, Ohio, in 1877, was probably not Jewish. By 1912, Wiseman advertised "from opera house to masonic hall" and soon accrued a respectable portfolio of apartment buildings, hotels, and private residences. But, by 1922, Wiseman went more fully into theater design most specifically in "dual use" theaters (offering both live performance and movies) and was soon second to none in their design. Wiseman was soon prized for his dazzling neo-orientalist and Deco-styled constructions considered "as magnificent as any in America," although in his writings he professed moderation in design ("Audiences prefer simplicity . . . sharp, drastic colors . . . [that] attract more attention than the play").[6] Wiseman's interest in theater architecture was also focused on acoustics. "There is no bad seat in a Wiseman house," one ad read. His skill in designing performance spaces in which sound is naturally carried would become even more startlingly apparent with the introduction in the next five years of amplification (both in movies and on the live stage).

Within Wiseman's most productive period of theater design were four Yiddish theaters in just about as many years.

The Commodore

In March of 1925, entertainment entrepreneurs Elias Mayer and Louis Schneider, of the M&S Circuit, hired Wiseman to build them a theater.[4] The partners had come up on the Lower East Side and were sleeker and more developed second-generation presenters than pioneering Yiddish showman Frank Seiden's rough-and-tumble exhibition halls. M&S made good coin demonstrating that Seiden's old mixture of movies and vaudeville (both American and Yiddish) was still a viable combination in their twenty-two theaters in Manhattan (with eighteen on the Lower East Side alone).[5] But unlike Seiden, who'd set up shop in any old vacant storefront, Mayer and Schneider wanted to lavish their customers in opulent visual and comfortable surroundings, a Wiseman specialty. He was also one of the first architects to design a theater for use by sound movies. Before signing Wiseman, the partners had already contracted to install the Vitaphone talking picture system in their new house, one of the only ones outside of the Roxy Theater, then showing their first feature, *Don Juan*.

Their brand new $400,000 (more than $7 million today) Commodore flagship vaudeville/movie palace, which, when it opened on September 2, 1926, saw a turnout of 20,000 people for its 3,500 seats, would not, however, remain in Mayer and Schneider's hands for long.[7]

Figure 13.1. Loew's Commodore (later the Fillmore East). Note the original Ratner's on its left. *Source:* 1940 Tax Photograph Collection, NYC Municipal Archives. Used with permission.

Louis N. Jaffe Theater

At the same time as he was working on the Commodore, Wiseman was designing a theater for the theater-less Maurice Schwartz.[8] The idea was willed into existence by lawyer, realtor, and Yiddish culture activist Louis N. Jaffe, who had already been underwriting and producing Schwartz's Yiddish Art troupe in other locations. Jaffe envisioned the L-shaped $350,000 building on East Twelfth Street and Second Avenue as not just a home for the 1,250-seat theater for Schwartz but a center for Yiddish literacy ("in the lounges will be found busts of Abraham Goldfaden, David Kessler, Jacob Adler, Jacob Gordin, Sholem Aleichem, Sigmund Mogulesco and other

Figure 13.2. Built in 1925 for Maurice Schwartz by philanthropist Louis N. Jaffe, the theater is now a multiplex movie house. *Source:* 1940 Tax Photograph Collection, NYC Municipal Archives. Used with permission.

celebrities of the past"), with classrooms, libraries, lecture halls, and space for Yiddish culture organizations in addition to offices and studios of Jaffe's planned Yiddish Zion film company.[9]

Jaffe's additional passionate interest in Zionism influenced the look of "this temple to Jewish Art" via Wiseman's (and co-designer Willy Pogani's) Moorish Revival theme described as "a combination of Palestinian and American architecture." With its smooth, pale sandstone walls, "it has the appearance of an Oriental temple rather than that of a theater," while its ceiling featured innumerable small Stars of David capped with a large star at the apex from which hung the theater's chandelier.[10] It gave the historically literate Jaffe a distinct pleasure that in order to make way for the Jewish theater, a half dozen private houses that had been on the site since Colonial times were all torn down, houses that were owned by descendants of Peter Stuyvesant, the Dutch East India Company head who in the seventeenth century unsuccessfully tried to keep the Jews from landing in New Amsterdam.[11] "I thought a Jewish theater on this very place would be a permanent monument to prove that the Jewish immigrant to this country is a useful citizen and makes a definite contribution to the country." He concluded, "I have answered Peter Stuyvesant 300 years too late, but my answer is none the less conclusive."[12]

With Schwartz leaving after two seasons (apparently never to play there again) the theater had no trouble leasing to nearly every other major Yiddish star (Molly Picon, Menashe Skulnik, and Nellie Casman) for the coming seasons. Despite that, Jaffe was soon bankrupt and was never heard of again.[13] The theater was subsequently acquired by Ludwig Satz for his Folks Teyater, but by the mid-1940s the theater stopped Yiddish shows. What then followed were decades of dizzying transitions to and from movie theaters, bottom-rung Burly-Q (from 1953–1961 it was the Phoenix Theater[14] where greats like Jessica Tandy, Hume Cronyn, Carol Burnett, and Larry Storch worked), and even a brief Yiddish theater revival, before netting a National Register of Historic Places listing in 1985. The theater's thoughtful late 1980s renovation using archival photos and original design references successfully recreated its feel (one popular restoration is the original Star of David in the ceiling's apex). Since 1991, the theater, now owned by Angelika Theaters, has functioned as a destination multiscreen movie house for independent, Hollywood, and revival films.[15]

"The Million Dollar Yiddish Theater"

Shortly after the Jaffe opened, Wiseman was hired by another Yiddish theater benefactor, William Rolland (1887–1960). Rolland came to America at the age of fifteen, working up from a ticket seller at Max Gabel's Bowery Theater[16] to house manager for Jacob Jacobs's Lenox Theater in Harlem. Rolland became a key theatrical player at the age of thirty-seven when, together with the Thomashefsky brothers, he brought the famed Vilna Troupe to New York with its hugely influential production of *The Dybbuk*. Rolland was able to build his own lavish theater only four years later.[17]

While Rolland built the modest Lyric Theater first, his next, the 1,600-seat eponymous Brooklyn playhouse was commonly referred to as "the Million Dollar Theater," which it may well have been, as it was the most lavish and impressive legitimate Yiddish house in New York.[18] For it, Wiseman echoed the round tablet entrance design used in Jaffe's theater. However, as it was situated on a lot of over 15,000 square feet with five time as much street frontage, Wiseman vastly expanded the arched motif as a unifying design feature all down its St. John's Place side. While Jaffe dedicated his theater/temple to Maurice Schwartz, Rolland dedicated *his* temple/theater to the now largely forgotten tenor Michal Michalesco. For the Rolland's second production, "Senorita" Michalesco, who had been a star on the Warsaw stage, played a dual role of both the hero and the title character and was billed as "the first and only successful female impersonator on the Jewish stage today."[19] Like Schwartz at the Jaffe, Michal Michalesco did not last at his own theater and also left after two seasons, only returning after Rolland was gone.

William Rolland was able to steer his theater through five seasons of the Depression by deftly rotating stars and directors thanks to a seemingly inexhaustible supply of new scripts by the house playwright Louis Freiman and house composer Sholom Secunda, whose best-known song with lyricist Jacob Jacobs, "Bei mir bistu sheyn," premiered at the Rolland in the 1932–1933 season.[20] In February of 1934, with promoter Edvin A. Relkin,

Figure 13.3. Harrison Wiseman's signed architectural drawing of the Rolland Theater. *Source:* Joe Fishstein Collection of Yiddish Poetry, Rare Books and Special Collections, McGill University. Public domain.

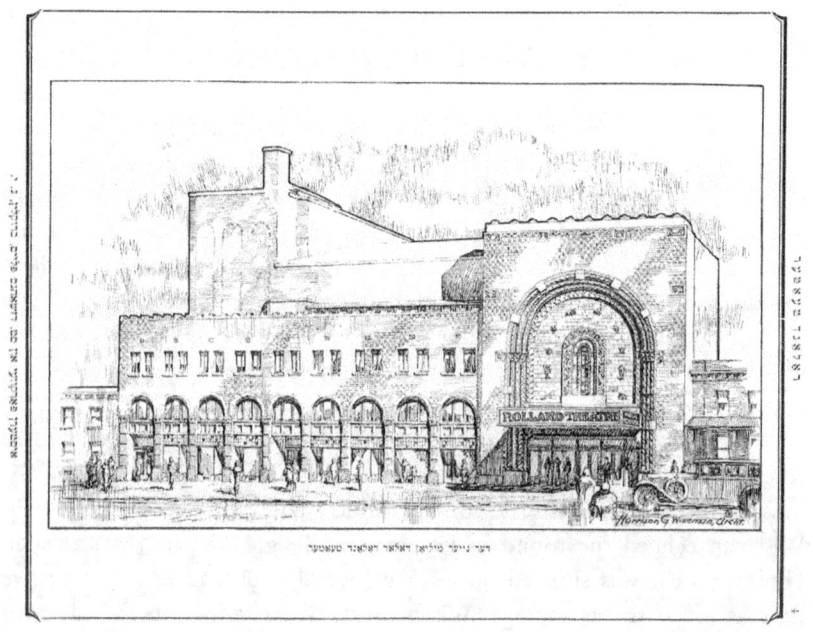

Rolland staged a commercially and critically successful run with Maurice Schwartz's adaptation of I. J. Singer's novel *Yoshe Kalb*. However, on its heels, Rolland abruptly sold his namesake theater and bought the much smaller 1,800-seat Public Theater at 66 Second Avenue (also a Harrison Wiseman design), which opened in December 1926.[21]

In the 1950s, the Public was eventually converted into a street-level retail and an apartment house. Its facade, largely intact above the marquee line, still displays the original stylized theater curtains at its crest.

Back in Brownsville, the Rolland, now under the ownership of Jacob Jacobs and Julius Nathanson, was renamed Parkway Theater and, as the last commercial Yiddish theater, took on surviving acting veterans like a kind of theater lifeboat. But, given the luxe surroundings, the lifeboat was more a kind of Yiddish theater *Titanic*, an ornate wounded vessel sinking in a sea of debt and decay, playing to a dying audience and a disappearing Yiddish. Its submersion would take two lingering decades, with the only revenue coming from periodic Yiddish shows and renting the theater out for school graduations, amateur acting companies, and religious groups, the last in 1956 to the Holy House of Prayer for All People, who still inhabit it.[22]

Wiseman died in 1945 and was universally celebrated for his bold modernization of theaters and literate aesthetic designs. Of the dozens of theaters Harrison G. Wiseman created between 1922 and 1940, only a small number remain in various states of original use. Among those are

- 1923: The Parkview, 188 Prospect Park West, Brooklyn (now the Nitehawk)
- 1926: Louis N. Jaffe Yiddish Art Theater, East Twelfth Street and Second Avenue Theater, NYC (now Village East by Angelika)
- 1926: Rolland Theater/Parkway Theater, 1768 St. John's Place, Brooklyn (now the Holy House of Prayer for All People)
- 1926: Public Theater, 66 Second Avenue (apartment house facade)
- 1927: Loew's Kameo, 530 Eastern Parkway, Brooklyn (now Philadelphia Church of Universal Brotherhood)
- 1927: Loew's Oriental, 1832 Eighty-Sixth Street, Brooklyn (now a Marshall's store)
- 1937: The Waverly, Sixth Avenue and West Fourth Street, NYC (now the IFC Center)

The Second Life of the Commodore

On August 8, 1927, *Variety* announced that Mayer and Schneider's new Commodore theater—on whose walls the paint had barely time to dry—would be sold to competitor Marcus Loew. The quick sale of the diamond in the tiara theater was the beginning of a slow decline of the M&S empire from some forty-four theaters to working as caterers in the once-grand Grand Central Palace hotel in the 1940s.[23]

Marcus Loew upped the offerings at the theater, running it as a "split week" (two headliners a week) vaudeville house and movies. Loew's also continued the Commodore's Yiddish programming when it presented Boris Thomashefsky (whose fortunes continued to wane), appearing in vaudeville only a few blocks from where his own original theater once stood.[24] Loew's theaters were sustained as mixed-use until 1933, when they abandoned vaudeville and switched to showing MGM features and short subjects.

About the only live theater came in the late 1930s with the arrival of station WLTH from Brooklyn that opened offices/studios in the adjacent Broadway Central building. Poet, actor, and director (and the driving force of WLTH Yiddish programming) Victor Packer would periodically have broadcasts on the Commodore's stage before a live theater audience of his adaptations of Yiddish novels and plays until the station was forced off the air in 1942.[25]

The 1948 antitrust rulings against movie studios owning their own theaters meant that all Loew's theaters (including the Commodore and the Delancey) were cut loose from the studio system and had to fend for themselves. The Loew's Commodore name stayed until around 1968 when it became the Village Theater, whose management paid the bills between presenting neighborhood theater groups, foreign films, and short-run seasonal leases. One of the "short-run/local theater group/foreign language" leases was to Polish-born Yiddish actor Ben Bonus.

Bonus (1920–1984) came to the US in 1929 and, like most applicants, was denied membership in the Hebrew Actor's Union, so toured the country in his so-called Jewish Mobile Theater ("a limousine with scenery tied on the roof and six actors huddled inside"). His road work, along the remnant of Edvin A. Relkin's regional Yiddish circuit, led him to be a kind of Yiddish theater Johnny Appleseed championing the higher works of Goldfaden, Sholem Asch, and Mendele Moykher Sforim. In 1964, Bonus and producer/partner Sol Dickstein started leasing the Village Theater, running what ads described as "a musical revue with American and Yiddish stars and revivals of Yiddish film classics"; in other words, the successful 1900s "mixed-use" policy of Frank Seiden and of Mayer and Schneider in the 1920s. Together with his wife, the late Yiddish actress Mina Bern, their shows like *Let's Sing Yiddish* (and its tie-in LP), when matched to their unspooling of old Yiddish talkies, drew in crowds. For a while, and only with judicious scheduling, Bonus attracted an audience for a few weekends a month.[26]

But external changes were already in place at the theater; a November 11, 1965, press release touts a "folk rock" concert starring Chuck Berry.[27] An even more stark harbinger of change was the weekly Tuesday night Religious Psychedelic Celebration of the League for Spiritual Discovery led by Dr. Timothy Leary. In a 1966 image, Leary appeared puckishly posed beneath the Loew's Commodore marquee, on which he is billed as the "reincarnation of Jesus Christ," photobombed by both the banner for Bonus's Yiddish American vaudeville theater and the entrance of Ratner's restaurant.[28] By 1968, Ben Bonus had moved out and the theater's next Yiddish-speaking Holocaust survivor occupant moved in.

The Fillmore East

The Berlin-born Bill Graham (Wulf Grajonca) was rescued in a "kinder transport" out of Germany to France from where, subsequently, he grew up in the Bronx.[29] Despite neutralizing his childhood German accent, changing his name, and moving to California where he became the über-promoter for bands like the Grateful Dead, Jefferson Airplane, and Big Brother and the Holding Company/Janis Joplin, Graham maintained an active link with his Yiddishkayt. He was the first underwriter of Chabad San Francisco's giant Chanukah menorah, the first of its kind outside of Israel. His older sister, the late Esther Chichinsky, was known to be a fluent Yiddish speaker.[30]

It is impossible not to think that Graham—educated, clear-eyed, and intuitive—would be unaware of the irony of what he was doing. Graham, like a smoked salmon swimming back upstream, returned in 1968 to the New York of his middle youth to open a "church of rock and roll" in a former Jewish theater. His all-too-brief tenure running the Fillmore East led to the building's further transformations, including a short time as a disco. It is now fully debased and disemboweled—first, one of a herd of redundant and anonymous neighborhood ATMs and then an apartment house, assuring that Graham would be the last of the flamboyant Jewish impresarios to make its walls ring.

Thanks to Graham, the old theater still had one secret to reveal. Fillmore East sound engineer John Chester, who knew he was mixing music in a space not designed for anywhere that amount of volume, was surprised by how little amplification was needed before the hall's natural acoustics took over. In most old theaters, that amount of volume would not have filled the space, but, conversely, raising the volume to overcome the hall's natural acoustics would result in ringing feedback. However, Wiseman's theaters used an innovative ceiling design that consisted of a series of compound elliptical arches at the front and sides with, like the Jaffe theater, a shallow dome at the center that acted as a kind of resonator, while the lowered ceiling above the proscenium provided a sonic reflection for the balcony seating.[31] It appears that Wiseman's theories on amplified theater acoustics were, in a word, sound.

14

Hotel Herzl
Max Bernstein and the Libby's Hotel and Baths

The history of New York's Jewish hotels is dominated by the rural Catskills, while New York City's Jewish hotels are all but forgotten. Libby's, the world's first bespoke urban Jewish hotel and Russo-Turkish baths, was poised to usher in a new golden era for the Jewish Lower East side but instead ended up a victim of greed, betrayal, destruction, and forgetting.

Early Jewish Hotels

Classified and small display ads for boarding houses, hotels, rooms, and services available to Jews were the fiscal backbone of the early Anglo-Jewish publications in America. In an era rife with resorts that blandly brandished "No Hebrews" signs, the appearance of these ads in Jewish publications around the country established a kind of underground railroad for Jews seeking a safe haven away from home. As early as 1849, on the same page that the newspaper *The Asmonean* had its traveler's directory, which gave the general comings and goings of ships and trains, it also carried some of the earliest notices for urban rooming houses and hotels friendly to Jews (such as Mme. Levy's Mosaic Accommodations and Boardinghouse, Misses Palache's Boarding and Day School for Young Ladies of the Jewish Persuasion, and Hebrew Hotel and Baths, etc.).[1] A February 18, 1881, ad in *The Hebrew Leader* by kosher Harlem hotelier Jacob Cohen offered facilities that included "a concert hall, billiard room, ten pin alley, a saloon and a rifle range."[2] These decades would see the transition of Jewish boarding houses' supper rooms en route to the first generation of "eating houses" en route to the first generation of modern Jewish restaurants.

In 1916, the seven-year-old *Yiddisher Farmer*, with offices at the decidedly unbucolic 174 Second Avenue, gathered all the diverse national Jewish boarding houses and kosher hotels ads into a single volume, *The Jewish Vacation Guide Hotels, Boarding Houses and Rooming Houses Where Jews Are Welcome*.[3] The guide, which ran through several editions (and was no doubt the model for Victor H. Green's 1936 publication *The Negro Motorist Green Book*), reflected the nascent rise of leisure and commercial culture. In New York, it focused on hotels in otherwise restricted rural Ulster and Sullivan counties and not Jewish identified hostels in New York City, the greatest of which would be the Libby's.

The Birth of Libby's

Max Bernstein was born Moishe (later Morris and finally Max) Bernstein in the Belarus city of Minsk on August 10, 1889, arriving with his family in United States in 1900. Tragedy struck the next year when Bernstein's mother Leah (whose nickname, Libe [Lovey], was Americanized as Libby) unexpectedly died at the age of thirty-seven. Her loss would deeply affect the young Max and inspire him to memorialize her, when in 1915 Bernstein opened his first Libby's Lunch budget cafeteria in Harlem with another branch at Rutgers Street and East Broadway in 1918 and Delancey Street the next year. For his Libby's restaurant, Bernstein borrowed the distinctive Spencerian script logo of the Midwest canned food company of the same name whose products Bernstein most likely used. Yet despite the obvious lift, Libby's apparently never objected and Bernstein also used it later for his hotel.

What altered Bernstein's trajectory from restaurateur to hotelier was finding his customers asleep at their table, saying they had no other place to stay.[4] Starting early in 1921, Bernstein ran a series of small Yiddish newspaper ads disguised as articles provocatively asking why, in the greatest Jewish city in America (and thus, the world) there was not a hotel where visiting Jews could feel at home. Why didn't Jews, who were unwelcomed in Gentile hotels, have a place where they would be treated with respect and consideration and be among their own?[5] The answer was what he called *der unternemung* ("the undertaking"), the building of the world's largest Jewish hotel. Bernstein, equal parts visionary, showman, and urban planner, was a Herzl with a hotel, who single-handedly willed into existence an awe-inspiring and majestic iconic building on the Lower East Side, the Yiddish Times Square.[6]

Now, the quotidian "article-like" ads blossomed into lavish full-page display ads as chic and eye-catching as the hotel he was hawking. Bernstein's penchant for self-promotion led him to ads that usually included his picture, like some benevolent deity, hovering near the top while others offered dramatic "before and after" pictures of the crumbling tenements on the northeast corner of Chrystie and Delancey Streets being demolished to build the modern mammoth hotel.[7] In typical third-person grandiosity, an April 12, 1925, advertisement declared "Mr. Max Bernstein president and founder of Libby's Hotel and Baths who, in this great undertaking has shown a vision that will forever be part of the New York story."[8] The ballyhoo was rife with enthusiastic endorsements from Orthodox rabbis, lawmakers and politicians, celebrity cantors, and theater stars, all lining out with Talmudic-like presentation the powerful efficacy of the Jewish hotel.

By the spring, Bernstein launched Libby's Baths Inc., and bolstered by a $1.5 million loan from American Bond and Mortgage (AB&M), he went in search of investors.

While Bernstein had several high-profile backers (George Jessel, Yossele Rosenblatt, and David Belasco, etc.), his public stock offerings at $10 a share ($140 today) netted over four thousand small local investors, the equivalent of 10 percent of the Jewish population of the Lower East Side.[9] The stock offering surged as a heady mix for all strata of the Jewish world: for the traditional Jews, a "heymish" welcoming hotel; for the capitalists, a solid investment with a good projected return; for the socialists, collective ownership; and for all, a $2.5 million dollar, super-sized modern hotel and baths, their own neighborhood clubhouse: "Der shtoltz fin der east *sayd*" (The pride of the East Side).[10]

Time magazine, which characterized Bernstein as "a Manhattan Jew whose fine necktie bore witness to his shrewdness," featured a glowing review of the new structure:

> Mr. Bernstein has introduced a magnificence that could be the inspiration only of an able Jew. There are telephones at every turn, express elevators that fly up like harnessed rockets and drop down like oiled meteors. Lounge rooms gorgeously decorated, allure business weary-limbs with divans and sofas and curving love-chairs; while upstairs, opening upon corridors carpeted

with rugs into which feet sink as into perfumed snow, bridal suites, and grand suites and super suites await their imminent occupants with tapestries of many various colors and furnitures [sic] beyond Park Avenue.[11]

Figure 14.1. Bernstein's full page ads for his hotel were as dramatic and exciting as the hotel would prove to be. Source: National Library of Israel, Historical Jewish Press website (www.jpress.org.il), founded by the National Library and Tel Aviv University. Used with permission.

Libby's was impossible to miss, rising thirteen-plus stories above the Lower East Side's low rooftops. It surpassed the iconic *Forverts* building by three floors (even with the newspaper's massive rooftop electric sign) and squeaked past Sender Jarmulowsky's bank building by one floor. Bernstein trumped Jarmulowsky's two-story tempietto with a two-story enclosure for a trio of twenty-thousand-gallon water tanks: one with city water and two with water from the hotel's own specially dug artesian well. At night, the sprawling theater-like horizontal marquee that jutted out onto Chrystie Street, illuminated by hundreds of bulbs along with an eleven-story illuminated vertical sign, bathed the busy neighborhood in an omnipresent, insistent glow.

The hotel's entrance was a grand carpeted stairway leading to a lobby whose ceilings swept up two stories; a vast room framed by fluted Corinthian columns abutting a subway-car-length check-in desk. Public spaces alternated marble with warm burnished quarter-sawn English oak, while walls and ceilings were interspersed with ornamental carving and wood inlaid marquetry. Upper floors displayed Bernstein's tiered hotel accessibility and was divided among a variety of nightly room types (floor four: dormitories; floors five to seven: cubicles; floors eight to twelve: 235 full bedrooms and baths), all enough for one thousand guests.[12] The third-story mezzanine that overlooked the vast lobby offered every conceivable amenity for Jewish travelers: tailor, barber, business offices with public stenographers, a link to the New York Stock exchange, a telegraph office, dentist, chiropractors, doctors and nurses, a newsstand, and hat blocking and cleaner, making Libby's a kind of vertical shtetl.[13]

To make Libby's a central place in Jewish life, Bernstein opened Libby's facilities to all Jewish communal, social service, and political organizations. He also had a policy where any Jew—whether they were registered at the hotel or not—could receive their mail there. During the High Holidays, Bernstein transformed the hotel's grand ballroom into a synagogue, creating one of the city's largest holiday services.[14]

But for Bernstein, the hotel's raison d'être was its baths, whose centrality he characterized in advertising, placing it deep within the great panorama of Jewish life: from the ritual *mikve* to the Turkish baths, a remnant of Roman-era Jewish captivity to the *banyas* of the Jewish diaspora, and finally to his world's largest Russian and Turkish baths.[15]

Libby's designers, the Jewish architects Gronenberg and Leuchtag, had been building hotels and baths since 1910. They had just recently designed a $250,000 Russian and Turkish bathhouse in the heart of the Lower East Side at the corner of Second Avenue and East First Street in the old Florentine Building, one of the first cast-iron front structures in that part of town, and one of the last of the luxury buildings from when the so-called old families still lived in the area.[16] The Libby baths, however, were larger and included an Olympic-sized pool, a bank of steam rooms, and massage areas each appointed in different kinds of marble. The walls and ceilings of the adjoining bathers' lounge had Oriental/exotic red-and-green-painted terra cotta tiles, overlooking a room generous with leather Mission-style easy chairs and couches abutting an informal dining room with marble-topped tables.[17]

Time magazine described it as "a square of water as blue as a banner, a liquid panel like a window into star space, it dreams, moveless, in the white tile floor. Drawn up against walls patterned less purely with tiles of ochre and green and ruby, naked attendants in breech clouts wait to knead and oil the bathers in hot rooms. Steam rooms, medicated rooms, therapeutic rooms beyond. All the builders of Babylon could do no more."[18]

Mac Levy and Jewish Physical Culture

To head the baths, Bernstein tapped one of the Jewish pioneers of the physical culture movement: Max "Mac" Levy (1873–1934) or, as in his professional billing, "Professor" Mac Levy. The son of a Brooklyn lawyer, Levy made a name for himself in his teens through his amazing strength and gymnastic and boxing abilities as a Jew in a world that saw Jews as weak, mincing, and fearful. He traded on this popular misperception in crafting his creation myth—a scenario kept popular into our own era through the comic book display ads of strongman Charles Atlas—in his miraculous transformation from a dyspeptic ninety-eight-pound weakling to "man on the flying trapeze" robustness. An 1895 performance review described Levy's gymnastic partner jumping off a chair from several feet away onto Levy's stomach, and with "the reboundings like rubber, threw the young man off."[1]

In 1900, during a time when most posh hotels in New York were restricted against Jews, Captain William Tumbridge's St. George Hotel (now "The St. George Towers") at 111 Hicks Street in Brooklyn Heights bucked the trend and hired Levy to run its new gymnasium and Russian and Turkish baths with its Olympic sized salt water pool, its mirrored ceilings and waterfalls. The Mac Levy Institute of Physical Culture was soon *the* New York City health destination for the monied classes.[2]

---

1. "Heavy Lifting Remarkable Feats of Two South Brooklyn Amateurs," *Standard Union*, June 25, 1895, 1.
2. *Brooklyn Daily Eagle*, Mar. 15, 1900, 14.

Levy was also an inventor. To ease the anxiety of new swimmers, Levy fabricated a "trolley system" (a harness attached to a swimmer in the pool to keep them from sinking). Its success led him to design additional gym equipment, including one of the earliest indoor rowing machines, whose fundamental design is still used today. Levy was no stranger to printer's ink, with over a half dozen newspaper accounts between 1888 and 1898 describing him clocking a variety of holdup men, drunk assailants, and intemperate braggarts. He met his future bride, Lillian Edna Frank, in 1899 while rescuing her from drowning at Brooklyn's Bath Beach. Both the rescue and their subsequent wedding were covered.[3]

In 1902, Levy was a key character witness for the defense in a grisly murder case concerning his former employee William Hooper Young, grandson of Mormon leader Brigham Young. When the fleeing Young was finally located he would only surrender to Levy, who subsequently professed his former employee's innocence. Young, who was quickly convicted of murdering and dismembering his pregnant girlfriend, served eighteen years in Sing Sing before being released and subsequently disappearing.[4]

Levy next offered an aggressive—and slightly sketchy—stock offering for a state-of-the-art gymnasium/Russian and Turkish baths. Levy's picture-radiating chesty good looks, with a thick tract of black hair and bristling mustachios, saturated the pages of hundreds of popular magazines and newspapers across the country with his high-pressure offer to invest in his planned luxury enterprise.[5] It did not go well. Trade magazines, like *Printer's Ink*, ran harsh editorials decrying Levy's scheme and celebrated its crash and burn.[6] The failed offering (and subsequent bankruptcy) only temporarily took some of the luster off Mac Levy, who soon rebranded himself as the owner of a rural health farm, a newspaper columnist ("the Health Farmer"), an author (he penned two books, one a 1916 energetic jeremiad against smoking), a radio commentator, and

---

3. "Romance of the Seashore," *Brooklyn Daily Eagle*, Dec. 8, 1899, 18.

4. "Hooper Young Caught in Connecticut Admits Guilt," *St. Louis Post Dispatch*, Sept. 23, 1902, 9.

5. "The Mac Levy Institute for Physical Development," *New York Daily Tribune*, July 30, 1905, 8.

6. "End of a Questionable Campaign," *Printer's Ink: A Journal for Advertisers*, Sept. 6, 1905, 80.

the owner of a namesake gym at Madison Square Garden used by all the boxers who fought at the storied arena.[7]

In 1926, Max Bernstein, in another demonstration of the underlying Jewishness of Libby's, hired Mac Levy and provided him with both ends of the hotel: the basement/ground floor baths and a penthouse gymnasium replete with a regulation twenty-four-foot boxing ring, two handball courts, and Mac Levy's personally designed and manufactured workout equipment all with an unimpeded 360-degree view of lower Manhattan, the East River, and Brooklyn beyond.[8] Levy underscored Bernstein's Jewish branding by encouraging young Jews to study boxing while also arranging for the popular former Jewish welterweight champion Benny "the Ghetto Wizard" Leonard to train at Libby's for an unprecedented—and unrealized—return to the ring.[9]

Mac Levy remained with the hotel until its closing, after which he returned to his gymnasium equipment manufacturing and, after several more bankruptcies, died in 1934.

The Mac Levy name lived on with his son, Montague "Monty" now calling himself "MacLevy" in a kind of Scottish meets Yiddish mashup. MacLevy redirected his father's legacy from transforming weaklings into physical health to exploiting women's body image anxiety with a successful chain of "slenderizing parlors." In the 1940s and 1950s, MacLevy opened a modest empire of dance and children's talent studios in the early days of television, and although the studios quickly faded, MacLevy kept the slenderizing/gymnasium equipment company going until his death in 1980.

---

7. "With the Leather Punchers at Mac Levy's Gym," *Daily News*, Oct. 26, 1922, 24.
8. *Architecture and Building*, Aug. 1926, 154–59.
9. "Believe It or Not, Benny Is Training," *Daily News*, May 27, 1926, 34.

Opening Night

"Come, Look and Be Dazzled" read the headline of the full-page Yiddish ads in New York's Jewish papers. The invitation to inspect the new hotel drew over 15,000 people over the course of a day, including its over 3,500 investors.[19] May 17, 1926, opening night, was a crush of betuxed and begowned guests who descended upon the hotel. Uptowners like New York mayor "Gentleman" Jimmy Walker, hotel investor and star of Broadway's *The Jazz Singer* George Jessel, Eddie Cantor, and comedienne Fanny Brice mingled with downtown Yiddish theater stars Molly Picon, Maurice Schwartz, Yossele Rosenblatt, and Muni Weisenfreund (Hollywood would dub him "Paul Muni"). A garrulous bunch calling itself the Cheese Club (cartoonists Milt Gross, Harry Hirshfield, Max and Dave Fleischer, and Rube Goldberg) occupied a table alongside Morris and Rose, parents of George and Ira Gershwin.[20]

Figure 14.2. Sheet music commemorating the opening of Libby's Hotel by largely forgotten Solomon Smulewitz. *Source:* Library of Congress, Music. Public domain.

The show featured house orchestra Joseph Cherniavsky's twenty-two-piece Hasidic American Jazz Band performing the newly composed "Libby's March" by Solomon "A brivele der mamen" Smulewitz. The crowd all joined in on the chorus:

Libby's Baths Hotel is a zitadel
Mechtig, prechtig un dreist
Dos zeigt dem yidishen geist
Der unternemung iz grois, yidelach s'iz ayer hoyz
S'vet brengen groyse nuzen schnell
Libby's baths un hotel.

Libby's Baths Hotel is a citadel
Grand and gorgeous, bold and bluff
It's where Jews can strut their stuff
The task was great, so Jews don't wait
Its great value time will tell
Libby's Baths Hotel.[21]

Shortly after midnight, the guests were led to the lobby, where, to rapturous applause, Max Bernstein unveiled, overlooking the check-in desk, a giant oil painting of his mother.[22] However, had his departed mother been alive, she wouldn't have been able to take advantage of the hotels' most desirous attractions, that Libby's made no accommodation for women: "There is no great bathroom for women. The wives of the guests, whether of those who sleep in the super suites or the cheap beds in the dormitories, wash themselves in tubs, eat at ordinary tables."[23] Even more puzzling was that, unlike the policy of most every Russian or Turkish bath house, Libby's does not appear to have even offered a segregated ladies night.

It is not surprising that the very Jewish identified Libby's would be characterized as "kosher," which seemed self-evident by the lyric in a verse of Smulewitz's "Libby's March":

Kosher meals are served to order
By our chefs who are the best
A taste of home you can afford here
For each and every Libby's guest.[24]

However, in none of the dozens of newspaper ads or in the detailed descriptions of the hotel stock offerings was Libby's characterized as "kosher." His ads, which boasted "heymishe multsaytn mit a yiddishn tam" (Homey dishes with a Jewish taste), were code for "kosher style."[25] The closest Bernstein came was an oblique reference to "kosher" in a 1922 comic strip ad in the Yiddish satirical magazine *Groyser Kundes* (*The Big Stick*), where one panel depicted an out-of-town Jew obliged to stay at a Gentile hotel, gawping at the hotel restaurant's arcane and relentlessly treyf bill of fare.[26] When it came time for a banquet on April 28, 1926, to celebrate the opening of Libby's, it was not held at any of the kosher eateries such as the Manischewitz-owned Broadway Central or at Trotzky's midtown restaurant, but at the decidedly unkosher Biltmore Hotel.[27]

Theater and Radio at the Hotel

Before his hotel—even before his cafeteria—Max Bernstein's first passion was the Yiddish theater. In 1908, the stage-struck young Bernstein, together with actor Jacob Sheikowitz (who, along with his wife would later run a Yiddish vaudeville house in the Bronx), published *Yiddisher Dilettante* (*The Hebrew Amateur*) a short-lived magazine billed as "a monthly theater journal filled with witticisms, humor and criticism." Yet despite amateur theatrics enjoying the same widespread grassroots popularity as professional Yiddish theater (the Folksbeine was still seven years away from its founding), the magazine did not last long.[28] Bernstein's ongoing passion for the Yiddish theater was clear in a stunning full-page ad in the October 25, 1925, *Forverts*, which placed Libby's (and Bernstein pictured above it) as the sun around which rotated a solar system of Manhattan Yiddish theaters and the walking time from the hotel to each of them.[29]

One of the de rigueur amenities of modern, deluxe hotels was an in-house radio station. It was Bernstein's luck to join recently launched station WFBH, which was headquartered at the Hotel Majestic at West Seventy-Second Street and Central Park West. Despite the lavish studios *The Voice of Central Park* enjoyed at its upscale uptown hostelry, WFBH agreed to install equipment for remote broadcasts from the Libby's ballroom, which Bernstein would exaggeratedly claim as "the first Yiddish radio station in the world." His ads for the hotel had fancifully drawn transmitting towers atop it with bold lightning-like typography that read "Libby's Yiddish radio station."[30]

To run his programs, Bernstein hired veteran Yiddish impresario Harry Gotti (b. Hershel Gottleib) and who, along with Joseph Cherniavksy, produced a weekly one-hour Sunday night broadcast of cantorial music and Yiddish theater and art songs, a programming structure that would be assiduously followed for decades by subsequent stations such WABC, WLTH, and on WEVD's *Forverts Hour*. Not all the radio programming was high art. Gotti scheduled a radio wedding on June 6, 1926.[31] Though clearly aimed at the Jewish community, non-Jews also tuned in: "WFBH was set up at Libby's Hotel to transmit the appearance of Cantor Joseph Rosenblatt tenor assisted by his son, Henry. Personally, a little bit of real Jewish music goes a long way with us, but making the statement is no attempt to belittle the capability of the two singers heard last night. Both are extremely capable."[32] However, WFBH's management style was chaotic: the station seemed indifferent to providing accurate or consistent program listings to the newspapers and often did not air the scheduled shows when it did list them. WFBH's state-of-the-art studios belied their rocky relationship with their upscale hotel hosts, which became so bad that in the face of WFBH not paying its rent, the hotel would periodically cut off their power, finally driving the station off the air in January 1927.[33]

Libby's would resurface on WHN from September 1926 until March 1927, but it is unclear whether the music by the "Libby's Hotel Dance Orchestra" was Jewish or mainstream potted palm dance music.

"For the first time in the careers of show business and Turkish baths, both are being mated with a continuous vaudeville show as an entertainment adjunct to the baths."[34] When radio foundered, Bernstein redirected his theatrical impulses and unveiled Libby's Music Hall, a three-hundred-seat theater set in his Turkish baths where, every night from nine o'clock until three o'clock in the morning, togaed and toweled patrons would see a heady mix of variety, vaudeville, and Yiddish theater. "Why not?" asked Bernstein. "You enjoy music with your meals, don't you? The bath is just another step in the direction of complete relaxation for tired businessmen."[35] Over the coming months, the music hall featured, among other acts, child star Seymour Rechtzeit (who would nightly perform his Libby's theme composition "Swim-Music-Swim"), Black cantors Thomas LaRue Jones and David Kohl, and a revue called *A nakht in gan eyden* (*A Night in the Garden of Eden*) (fortified by a "troupe of cabaret girls") accompanied by Cherniavsky's Hasidic Jazz Band and MC'd by *kuplet* and rhymester Sam Lowenwirth.[36]

One the last acts the music hall featured before it closed the following year at the end of 1928 was its most fantastic: "a Hindu fakir, a student of Thurston, the magician goes into suspend [sic] animation and is lowered into a glass-topped coffin into the swimming pool, blissfully cataleptic for hours, while the hotel guests splashed around him."[37]

Katz in a Shvitz

Fifty years after it closed, a "review" of the hotel appeared in the pages of comedian Mickey Katz's 1977 "as-told-to" memoir, *Papa, Play for Me*. In a well-polished and "strictly for a gag" anecdote, Katz recounted coming to New York as an aspiring musician when, on his father's advice (gleaned from seeing Libby's ads in the Cleveland edition of the *Forverts*), he stayed there.

> [Libby's] was at Delancey and Essex in the center of the Lower East Side. The next morning, I was awakened by the loudest cacophony I have ever heard in my life. I looked out the window and below in the street there must have been five hundred pushcarts, with the peddlers all yelling, "BAGELS! COATS! DRESSES! UMBRELLAS! SAFETY PINS!" It was a sight never to be forgotten. It was the heyday of the Lower East Side.
>
> Libby's wasn't primarily a hotel, it was essentially a concrete *shvitz* [bathhouse]. When I'd checked in the night before, I thought the rate seemed high—$2.50 a day—but the clerk proudly explained that this included "the baths."
>
> So, on my first morning I wrapped a sheet around me, took the elevator down to the basement, and tried "the baths." This feature of the hotel consisted of huge Russians laying you on a marble slab and beating the hell out of you with their big hands and with brooms soaked in hot soapy water.
>
> After my first battering in the bathhouse, I decided that I didn't need being that clean. Surviving Libby's baths was, in two words "tzum-possible."[1]

---

1. Mickey Katz, *Papa, Play For Me*, with Hannibal Coons (New York: Simon and Shuster, 1977), 46–47.

Early Triumph, Early Defeat

Despite Bernstein's penchant for novelty and theatrics, neither his press about the opulence of the hotel nor his prognostications that the construction of Libby's would lead to a rise in the value of local real estate and Jewish community uplift were overstated. On the contrary, on the heels of its opening, Yiddish- and even major English-language publications—including the largely sniffy *New York Times*—enthusiastically reported the budding signs of the Lower East Side's ascending economic advancement brought about by Libby's.[38] Industry publication *Architecture and Building* concurred in a lavish six-page spread including detailed floor plans and fashion photos of the interior: "A great step in the improvement of the Lower East Side is the completion of the Libby's hotel . . . the scheme of this hotel is unusual and differs from anything else in this country. Combined with the hotel accommodation which is complete in every way are baths which are extensive and completely appointed."[39] Even entertainment journal *Variety* saw the positive efficacy of the Jewish hotel and observed that "the enterprise is a community movement, and its success is accordingly assured."[40]

However, the triumphant opening and the hotel's heady honeymoon period was shattered by another untimely death in Bernstein's life: his wife Sarah on October 19, 1926, at the age of thirty, no doubt reminiscent of his mother who also died in her thirties, and an evil portent of the imminent untimely end for the hotel itself.[41]

Before Bernstein took the plunge with his dream hotel, he had already tested the realty waters when he purchased the building that housed his first Libby's Luncheonette in Harlem. So enamored was Bernstein of owning property that in 1925, at the height of his hotel, on the census he listed his profession as "real estate." Yet, although he had succeeded in his early property ventures, Bernstein would soon learn a tragic reality of realty.

American Bond and Mortgage (AB&M), which provided Bernstein's underwriting, was founded by William J. Moore in Chicago in 1920. At first, it racked up an impressive track record of successful private and public mortgagees with underlying bonds. A 1921 newspaper profile on Moore characterized him as a modern real estate Horace Greely with his admonition "Go in debt young man. Debt is the beginning of fortune. No man ever got rich who was afraid to go in debt."[42] It was this kind of economic chicanery that was the DNA of the coming Depression.

Soon, Moore and his sons perfected a hazardous hat trick of predatory mortgages, aggressive extralegal no-notice foreclosures, and quick property purchases at a fraction of the original value, giving pennies on the dollar to its swindled investors.

The Moore family's scam could not have succeeded without the active collusion of local and state legislators and their hand-picked judicial co-conspirators. For this, New York's Tammany Hall was wide open for business, on down from the state's popular Democratic governor Alfred E. Smith. To carry out the state-approved malfeasance, a suave, urbane, and wholly corrupt lawyer named Joseph Force Crater was tapped as a receivership judge, a plum assignment, which, in addition to its guaranteed per-transaction fee of $10,000 ($150,000 today), offered land-rush potential for subsequent graft.[43]

On May 10, 1928, at a meeting of the City Council, the fix was instigated by Mayor Walker (who not long before had been a guest carousing at Libby's opening festivities) to erect model housing and widen Chrystie and Forsyth Streets from East Broadway to Houston Street through "excess land condemnation." To everyone's surprise, the city's plan did not build on the good will and economic uplift Libby's had already brought to the area but instead called for tearing it down.[44]

Although Bernstein successfully made his first interest payment, it quickly became clear he could never make enough money to cover the following one. He requested a lower payment, which was refused. By missing the next payment, the foreclosure procedure was triggered. Judge Joseph Force Crater now smoothly facilitated the proceedings. First, most hotel depositions were routinely denied, such as owing to misspellings or typos. ("An apostrophe and the letter *s* was omitted. The text read 'Libby' hotel, instead of 'Libby's hotel,' and for that reason, was invalidated."[45]) Then, the property value was critically downgraded, leading to a hastily convened behind-closed-doors sale, where the $2.5 million dollar hotel was sold for just its $75,000 unpaid mortgage interest to a woman later revealed as an agent of the AB&M.[46]

Bernstein, robbed of his hotel, and in a grief response, raged through its corridors turning out the registered guests and turning off the heat and hot water, until the police arrived and returned the guests, heat, and hot water, but not Bernstein. As non-Jewish newspapers characterized it, "If he couldn't have his hotel, nobody else could."[47]

Libby's was not the only local victim of the AB&M scam: in leafy Brooklyn Heights, the $5 million Leverich Towers Hotel at 21 Clark Street was also resisting efforts to have its own mortgage called and forced into bankruptcy. While the Leverich Towers escaped being torn down, its foreclosure and acquisition by the Moores led to the subsequent suicide of hotel owner Augustus Leverich.[48] The restored building today survives as "The Watermark at Brooklyn Heights," a luxury senior assisted living facility.

Bernstein's lawyers mounted a stepped-up grassroots fight to redress the fictive low valuation that the city had put upon the building and the mass swindle of its investors.[49] One of the few municipal voices raised in defense of Libby's and the Lower East Side community was Republican mayoral candidate Fiorello LaGuardia. In public meetings, LaGuardia (in both English and Yiddish) accurately called the Tammany scheme to condemn and raze the hotel and replace it with never-to-be-delivered affordable housing and a street widening a "typical steal."[50] LaGuardia's only victory was foiling a plan to rent the seized hotel in the months before its destruction to a Tammany *apparatchik*, but instead got it turned it over to a group of the hotel's small investors to try to recoup their losses. Yet even there, they were still being soaked by the Moore family: 60 percent of the hotel gross would first revert to AB&M before the swindled investors even saw a penny.[51]

Following this, Crater then re-reassessed the property for its actual $2.75 million worth, which the city promptly paid Moore and sons.[52]

Then, in one of the most famous of all "disappearances," Judge Joseph Force Crater was last seen on August 6, 1930, entering a taxi en route to Grand Central, and he vanished without a trace. When his apartment was subsequently searched, a note to his wife in his own hand was found, which read: "Libby's Hotel—there will be a very large sum due me when the city pays the $2,750,00 in condemnation. Martin Lippman will attend to it. Keep in touch with him."[53]

Yet even as the AB&M was raking in the spoils from their scheme, its extralegal exploits were being exposed. The wheels came off the AB&M wagon in 1931 thanks to revelations of yet more Moore family real estate crimes, reaching all the way up to the White House and resulting in Department of Justice hearings.[54] In sometimes turbulent testimony, Charles S. Craig—who as the former New York City controller stood by helplessly and watched AB&M strip-mine the city—characterized the family as "a ring of realty racketeers."[55] But despite overwhelming evidence pointing to the vehement criminality of AB&M, which would drive the company into receivership and Moore to prison, Bernstein and his thousands of hotel investors were routinely rebuffed in subsequent court appeals.[56]

When it came time to raze Libby's Hotel in the fall of 1930, the Walker administration turned to a young protégé of Governor Al Smith, Robert Moses, in one of the first of his many large-scale urban deconstruction projects. Whereas biblical Moses led the Jews to the promised land, municipal Moses bulldozed Bernstein's fledgling Jewish promised land.

On March 13, 1932, *The New York Times* ran a breathlessly upbeat article on the future economics of the Lower East Side illustrated with a sweeping photo of the neighborhood from the vantage point of where Libby's had only recently stood.[57]

In 1934, four years after the razing of the hotel and the neighborhood, now-mayor LaGuardia—once a fierce opponent of that very razing but now attempting to cover the gaping scar on the corner of Chrystie and Forsythe—turned again to Robert Moses. The irony of having the same person who oversaw the hotel's demolition now tasked with replacing it is matched only by the new park, like Libby's, also being named to honor a mother, in this case Sara D. Roosevelt, mother of President Franklin Roosevelt.[58]

The final transaction of Libby's money came in 1939, when the courts officially ruled Joseph Crater dead, allowing his widow to receive accrued monies from the estate, the majority composed of the legal fee of $10,000 that the judge had obtained for handling the Libby's deal.[59]

After the destruction of the hotel, Bernstein quickly faded from public view and went into the real estate business along with sons Leonard and Bernard. Yet even into the 1940s, in newspaper advertisements Bernstein billed himself as "the founder and president of Libby's Hotel." Bernstein died in 1946, his passing unremarked in the Yiddish papers that once regularly lauded him. Perhaps the most heartbreaking—and wholly unexplainable—irony is that Bernstein, who was deeply devoted to his mother and wife and assiduously made sure his wife's final resting place was adjacent to his mother's in Brooklyn's Washington Cemetery, is himself not buried in Washington Cemetery or even in the same borough. More so, Bernstein's grave has no headstone but only a modest footer.

Libby's Hotel and Baths, however, was not yet out of the news. In the spring of 2001, a sinkhole twenty-feet wide and six-feet deep opened in Sara Roosevelt Park, alarming many at a senior center on the site. When city engineers who came to investigate lowered a camera twenty-two feet down, they were astounded to discover "a cinderblock room the size of a tenement apartment with bookcases, rubble and a locked door" that turned out to be Libby's sub-basement, now revealed thanks to a collapsed hotel elevator shaft. After determining its provenance, the city decided to fill "the space with grout to bind loose material and prevent future settling, or visitors," and burying the hotel for its second and final time.[60]

Part 3

Music

15

"To Hear..."

The First Yiddish Records

Figure 15.1. Advertisement for Dr. Lando's combination optometrist office and studios of earliest known Yiddish record label Standard, 1901. *Source:* National Library of Israel, Historical Jewish Press website (www.jpress.org.il), founded by the National Library and Tel Aviv University. Used with permission.

Standard Records

The father of American recording of Jewish music was optician Dr. George Lando. In March of 1900, the recently graduated Dr. Lando, a dealer in eyeglasses ("eyes examined free") and opera glasses invested $1,500 (about

$50,000 today) in the establishment of the Standard Phonograph Company of New York City.[1] By 1901, he opened a dual-purpose store on Grand Street selling both optical supplies and Edison and Columbia cylinder machines.[2]

Dr. Lando (who used "all the latest scientific knowledge") was running ads in the Yiddish press under the headline "To Hear and to See," with a cylinder phonograph and pair of Pince Nez glasses side by side.

Lando advertised only in Yiddish papers including the socialist *Forverts* and the *Fraye Arbeter Shtimme*, the newspaper of the Jewish anarchists.[3] No surprise then that 451 Grand Street, the building in which George Lando hung his "To Hear and to See" shingle, brimmed with radical and labor activity from the offices of the Painters, Decorators, and Paperhangers Union, the Progressive Dramatic League (the forerunner of Maurice Schwartz's Yiddish Art Theater), and the Radical Reading Room.[4] Lando also ran phonograph concerts of Yiddish music and opera for radical Jewish and labor groups, including one for guest of honor Emma Goldman.[5]

Lando was also offering the "latest Yiddish records" at a time when established labels (Edison, Columbia, and Victor) had barely—if at all—gotten into making those themselves.[6] That Lando was selling Yiddish records possibly means he was recording them himself, a relatively easy proposition. Cylinder machines, unlike later pressed disc machines, could convert from playback to record by reversing the stylus used to play the cylinder and by using the horn as a microphone, turning out one first-generation recording after another.

By early 1903, his Standard Phonograph Company ran aground (Lando had recently added "sporting goods" to his store's product line), and with debts of over $4,420 ($125,000 today) he liquidated all his assets.[7] Dr. George Lando and the Standard records he made disappeared without a trace. Or not.

"Stenderd Rekords"

Between 1900 and 1905, Lambert cylinders—known for their clear sound and rugged construction as well as their eye-popping pink, fuchsia, and/or purple colors—issued some thirteen hundred respectable but quotidian titles of contemporary pop materials: "coon" songs, banjo solos, ragtime anthems, paeans to the mythic Dixie, and lachrymose ballads of mother and home.[1] But tucked away in the middle of Lambert's

---

1. *Attractive Hebrews: The Lambert Yiddish Cylinders 1901–1905*, co-produced/liner notes by Henry Sapoznik, Archeophone 8001, 2016 CD.

1903 catalog (pages 15–17) are some fifty Yiddish and Hebrew recordings—only fifteen of which have ever surfaced—lost gems from the earliest days of Yiddish operatic arias, cantorial hymns, time-worn folk songs, and newly crafted broadside ballads.[2]

But their appearance in the Lambert catalog is a puzzle. These records—Lambert's only foreign-language offerings—were made by New York Yiddish theater stars, not something the small Midwest Lambert company could afford to bring out.[3] It was unclear just how these New York recordings ended up on the Chicago label. It was only after collector David Giovannoni provided me with copies that, as probably the first native Yiddish speaker to listen to these recordings in over a century, the answer was quickly revealed.

From the earliest days of commercial sound recording, in an attempt to thwart mechanical piracy, most performances were preceded by a spoken announcement of the names of the song, performer, and/or record label. Already familiar with other Lambert cylinders and expecting introductions crediting either the Lambert Indestructible Record Company or the Lambert Company of Chicago, I clearly heard, however, "Standard Records" (or, given the accent of the speaker/singer, "Stenderd Rekords"), exactly as in Lando's Yiddish newspaper ads. As they are the only known Lambert recordings with a different label name announcement, could these be the missing Standards? It is quite possible that Lando (the doctor who used "all the latest scientific knowledge") was attracted by the superior Lambert system and ordered the cylinders. However, in his subsequent bankruptcy, and liquidation of his assets, the finished recordings may have remained with Lambert as default stock that Lambert issued to fill out his catalog and to make back some of his production expenses.[4]

The Lambert label would come to an end in 1906 thanks to its predatorially litigious competitor, Thomas Edison, Lambert's resilient brilliant sounding-molded celluloid cylinders, was a major improvement over Edison's soft and easily damaged brown wax recordings. But as was a favored business model, Edison badgered the small company with endless frivolous lawsuits, ultimately driving it out of business and acquiring Lambert's patent as his own.

---

2. Lambert Company catalog, Sept. 1903.
3. Chicago had a vibrant and popular theater headed by the charismatic Ellis Glickman, and if Lambert really wanted Yiddish theater music, Glickman could have provided it. Alas, no one in Glickman's theater company ever commercially recorded.
4. *Attractive Hebrews*, 11.

> In 2019, the National Recording Registry of the Library of Congress, tasked with bringing awareness and celebrating unjustly forgotten or overlooked important historical sound recordings, listed the cylinders on the Lambert Yiddish reissue.

United Hebrew Disc and Cylinder Record Company/H. W. Perlman Pianos

Almost as soon as Dr. George Lando shuttered Standard Phonograph in 1904, another Jewish-owned/Jewish-content record label rose to take its place. On July 8, 1904, Louis Rosansky (1874–1931) registered a small record label with a big name: United Hebrew Disc and Cylinder Record Company of New York (eventually shortened to United Hebrew Record or UHD&C) with a big starting capital of $20,000 (over a half million dollars today).[8] Louis Rosansky's partner was pianist Harry Wolf Perlman (1874–1966). Both Rosansky and Perlman were born in Russia and arrived in the US in 1890, and both initially worked as tailors.[9] However, they would both soon swap sewing machine needles for phonograph needles. By 1902, Perlman and Rosansky opened a piano store at 460 Grand Street, a stretch of Grand Street already alive with piano dealers. For the first two years, that's all Perlman and Rosansky carried, but in 1904 they offered "the wonder of the 20th century," Victor's Victrola.[10] It's not hard to understand why pianos and phonographs were sold together under the new-fangled policy of paying in installments, a popular device for cash-strapped immigrant households. The Perlman and Rosansky ads offered pianos at $1 a week, plus free "tuning, polishing, moving, teachers and music books."[11]

Yet like Lando (and unlike most phonographs dealers), Perlman and Rosansky also offered their own recordings. The earliest known UHD&C record (no. 79, *Hashkiveynu*) is also the earliest known piracy of another Jewish recording. The anonymous label credit of "Cantor" fails to mask the unmistakable voice of Gershon Sirota, then the world's most famous cantor. The UHD&C piracy even preserved the delicate sound of the needle going into the groove of the record being copied![12]

By May of 1905, UHD&C had amassed a catalog of over fifty titles (about a third of all they would release) including singers who were already veteran recording artists such as Solomon Smulewitz, Regina Prager, and Kalmen Juvelier. As most UHD&C records were of solo singers, the small piano used to accompany them was—presumably—a Perlman and Rosansky spinet, played by Perlman himself. While the performances were as good as those made by these artists for Victor, Edison, and Columbia, UHD&C discs did not compare technically with those of the larger companies.

On the eve of record no. 199, the UHD&C company president and treasurer suddenly quit, only to set up shop a few blocks away selling pianos, phonographs, and records stolen from Perlman and Rosansky.[13] That was shortly followed by a falling out between Perlman and Rosansky themselves. Louis Rosansky moved a few streets away to sell pianos and run United Hebrew Records for a few more months. And, while UHD&C was technically still "active" into 1915, Rosansky never issued another recording. After selling pianos for a few more years, Louis Rosansky died in 1931.[14] UHD&C would be the last Jewish-owned/Jewish-content record label for nearly half a century in America.

With Rosansky's departure, the house instrument was rebranded as the H. W. Perlman piano. And though Perlman left the recording business, it did not leave him. For one brief, wild moment in 1919, Perlman introduced the Perlton line of player pianos and talking machines, at a time when one (the player piano) was on its way out and the other (the talking machine) was in far better hands at Victor and Columbia. Perlton did not last the year.[15] Perlman did well enough though, and subsequently bought his own building at 345-347 Grand Street, allowing him to better withstand the Depression by also selling furniture and radios. He even sponsored a show on station WLTH of—not surprisingly—his piano playing.[16]

During World War II, Perlman's factory was repurposed for making walnut stocks for Thompson submachine guns and M1 Garand rifles. H. W. Perlman pianos continued into 1964, with Perlman dying two years later. Curiously, while his brief obituary in the April 2, 1966, "paper of record" (his passing was noted in no Jewish publication) correctly identified him as a piano magnate, it conflated him with an entirely different Harry Perlman (and one without a *W* middle initial) who died the same day, a movie pioneer who worked with Mary Pickford, Clara Bow, and B. P. Schulberg.[17]

Perhaps Perlman's greatest New York City legacy was one long in plain sight. A fire at the Perlman factory in 1914 forced the company to seek other facilities, which turned out to be a floor at the S. Jarmulowsky Bank Building at 54-58 Canal Street.[18] While Perlman's actual stay at the Jarmulowsky building only lasted a year, he got generations of visibility by turning the tabula rasa of the building's west-facing exterior wall, painting a five-story ad, "H. W. Perlman Corp. manufacturer of grand and spinet

Figure 15.2. H. W. Perlman advertisement on the Jarmulowsky Bank Building. The ghost sign was visible to scores of subway riders decades after the factory went out of business. *Source:* Walter Grutchfield. Used with permission.

pianos" and "Showrooms 345 Grand Street NYC," that soared above the Lower East Side for decades. Even after Perlman was long gone, the ad was plainly visible to hundreds of thousands of straphangers crossing the Manhattan Bridge. It's unclear exactly when the ghost sign was finally removed.

Post–World War II Labels

Just as America was processing the attack on Pearl Harbor on December 7, 1941, America was attacked a second time in 1942. James C. Petrillo, president of the American Federation of Musicians, in a dispute with record labels over royalties, called for a recording ban, which lasted for the War. While mainstream labels had sufficient popular music backlog to keep issuing records, smaller genres (like Yiddish) did not and quickly ground to a halt. When the War (and the strike) ended, what also ended was record labels' longtime proactive development of their ethnic/foreign catalogs. For the first time—and in a policy that was also reflected in national radio programming—ethnic/foreign content was no longer pursued, and even more (as with Jewish content), all but eliminated. The nail in the coffin was upstart labels, like Capitol, who initiated the new paradigm policy of producing ethnic/foreign music for export and not domestic release, and even getting the longtime vaunted foreign music head at Columbia (and onetime protégé of David Nodiff), Sandor Porges, to do it.[19]

David Nodiff: The Artist and Repertoire Man

During the first decades of sound recording, the recording of Jewish music was solidly centered in Europe, which had the world's largest percentage of Jews and where most of the great cantors, singers, actors and actresses, and klezmer bandleaders lived and performed. A myriad of record labels large and small sprang up within easy reach of the still fertile homelands that spawned these powerful outlets of Jewish creativity.[1]

World War I ended Europe's dominance and shifted the action to the United States, which would dominate recorded Jewish music until World War II.[2] For nearly half of the twentieth century, major American record labels operated under the belief that because they were in the business of making sound recordings, they should make all manner of sound recordings regardless of genre, function, or audience. And for nearly the first half of the twentieth century, American record labels came perilously close to acting like ethnomusicologists with their artist and repertoire (A&R) agents, working within ethnic/foreign-language communities and locating, developing, and directing representative talent to the record label.

One of the best-known A&R men focusing on Jewish music worked for Columbia Records. David Nodiff (1892–1946) was born

---

1. Although a near definitive list of pre-Petrillo ban American Yiddish and Hebrew records was compiled by historian Richard Spottswood, no comparable discography for Euro-Yiddish records has yet been assembled.
2. Richard Spottswood, *Ethnic Music on Records: A Discography of Ethnic Recordings Produced in the United States, 1893–1942* (Urbana: University of Illinois Press, 1990).

in Odessa and in 1910 came to the United States, where he worked as a salesman. He was also a bit of a composer, and two songs he wrote in 1922—"Baym Rebin's Tish" ("At the Rabbi's Table") and "Di Babe Ligt in Kimpet" ("Grandma's Pregnant")—both had music by Romanian fiddler Abe Schwartz (1881–1943),[3] the versatile and prolific Jewish orchestra leader. Schwartz was the go-to in-house Jewish bandleader at Columbia starting in 1917 and was most certainly Nodiff's entrée to the label somewhere around 1923. Nodiff used his sales skills and expanded the Columbia office taking out classified ads seeking a "*ofis* girls good with *typeraytn* and can write and read Yiddish."[4]

In 1925, Nodiff summoned the up-and-coming klezmer clarinetist Dave Tarras to the Columbia studios. Even decades later, Tarras, who would still refer to the one-time Columbia A&R man as "Mr. Nodiff," recalled the life changing encounter: "Nodiff calls me up and books me to play a record . . . four sides, two recordings. He says 'Mr. Tarras, I'm giving you $40 and make me a session. And then, if it's alright, I'll give you more.' . . . I was making a record."[5]

During his tenure, Nodiff brought some dozen Yiddish artists to record, but with the Depression, Columbia quickly eliminated the smaller catalogs (such as Yiddish) and the people who ran them. By 1930 David Nodiff had gone back to sales in the parallel world of radio. He died in 1946.

---

3. Heskes, op. cit., 197.

4. Advertisement, *Forverts*, Sept. 2, 1927, 7.

5. Henry Sapoznik, "Dave Tarras Yiddish-American Klezmer Music 1925–1956," Yazoo Records, 1992.

Banner Records

While Capitol did sign new Jewish acts (Mickey Katz, Bas Sheva, etc.) and the majors did keep some of their former Yiddish artists, a number of new labels rushed to fill the void. The best known and most successful was Banner Records. Banner was founded by Sam Selsman, Pete Doraine, and Vincent Beck, names not native to the Yiddish culture world, who were noted in *Variety* as being of the genus/specie "Broadway music staffer and plugger," with offices overlooking Broadway at Fifty-First Street. Their "show biz" background got the entertainment trade publications (like *Variety*) to take notice and give them press.[20]

But what got the label's Yiddish cachet (and cash) was signing the popular composer-accompanist Abe Ellstein as musical director.[21] Banner was a budget label, and so Ellstein did what he could with modest settings for organ or small ensembles. The sound was intimate and knowing, and while not exciting (excitement was reserved for the too-few Dave Tarras 78s), it was recognizable, cozy, and distinct as a "label sound." Ellstein also encouraged Banner to sign all the reigning—and now label-less—Yiddish performing royalty: Moishe Oysher, Molly Picon, Menashe Skulnik, Leibele Waldman, and the one who gave Banner a hit almost immediately: comic, actor, dialectician, and character/character actor Michel Rosenberg (1901–1972).

Born in Warsaw, Rosenberg came to New York in his twenties as a longtime member of Maurice Schwartz's Yiddish Art Theater, famous for his amazing dramatic and comedic stretch and seemingly limitless array of dialects, characters, and voices.[22] Rosenberg's first Banner record was *Getzl Bay a Football Game*, his frantic retelling of greenhorn Getzl's first uncomprehending encounter with football and his increasingly frenzied reaction to it. The record was a huge hit (its royalties would bankroll Rosenberg's Romanian restaurant in Miami Beach) and sold so well it may have been the inspiration for an English-language version recorded six years later that follows the same story concept, called *What It Was, Was Football*, which jumpstarted the career of actor Andy Griffith.[23]

In 1948, Banner's next hit was completely unexpected—*Der Shirtz*, a Yiddish translation of the Gilbert and Sullivan operetta *HMS Pinafore*. Written by schoolteacher Miriam Walowit (1907–1988), it was staged as a fundraiser at Brooklyn's Kadima chapter of Hadassah and was such a success that the show was repeated a dozen more times (and raised tens of thousands of dollars). Jerry Morse, president of Banner, heard it in 1950 and signed up a *Reader's Digest* version of the operetta for a two-disc deal.[24] The record's cheerful, amateur feel with its pinch-your-cheek closeness, perky organ, and Sunday school English narration sold over one hundred thousand copies, leading to Kadima coming back in 1952 with a three-record set of *Die Yam Banditten (The Pirates of Penzance)*, which sold almost as well.[25] After Walowit moved to Florida, a staging of both operettas was held in 1987, the year before her death.[26]

In order to give the *Pinafore* additional run time (without releasing it on a longer and more expensive twelve-inch disc) the recordings were issued using the new microgroove process not yet common on 78s. Banner was already phasing out its ten-inch discs in preparation for the transition to vinyl 45s and LP.[27]

A Surprise Encore

In 1981, the recording came back to life (in a way) when a group called the Yiddish Gilbert and Sullivan Light Opera Company revived *Der Shirtz* (now renamed *The Yiddish Pinafore*) for what was, curiously, a return to the original Yiddish translation's function as a fundraiser. As one of its members explained, "We don't sell our own tickets . . . we sell the show to a library or an organization like a charity or a temple . . . and the group has the headache of filling the house." The show was now credited to an Al Grand, who "discovered a Yiddish version of the operetta on an old recording" without ever acknowledging the still very much alive Miriam Walowit whose name was clearly on the label of the "old recording" Al Grand "discovered."

Yet, at the height of these and other successes, the original owners sold out. "Banner Reactivates to Do Jewish Disks" was the headline in *Variety* at the end of December 1950 announcing the new Banner headed by "the former controller of a textile firm," Gerald J. Morse. The other change was replacing Ellstein as musical director with a popular Yiddish singer who had not been on the original Banner, "warbler-actor" Seymour Rechtzeit.[28]

Seymour Rechtzeit (1912–2002) was already a wunderkind cantor and singer in Poland when he and his father came to the US in 1920. Possessed of a sweet tenor and an ethereal falsetto, Rechtzeit almost immediately made national headlines when he sang before President Calvin Coolidge to loosen the immigration quota numbers so to allow his mother and siblings entry to the US. It worked. Despite Rechtzeit's start in recording at the age of thirteen, it wasn't until 1940 that he recorded for RCA Victor some of his most iconic titles ("Mayn Shtetele Belz," "Ikh Hob Dikh Tsufil Lib," etc.), issuing a baker's dozen titles leading up to the 1942 Petrillo ban. Rechtzeit celebrated his first Banner record with a quick Yiddish cover of Phil Harris's novelty song "The Thing," translated by Louis Markowitz, who also penned "Getzl Bay a Football Game."[29] Rechtzeit would end up owning the label.

In the early 1960s, with the continued passing of old Yiddish performers and no new recordings, Banner became a 78 reissue label. Unlike the contemporary aficionado reissues for jazz and folk fans accompanied by voluminous historical or discographic notes, Banner's were being produced solely for nostalgia with next to no notes. Banner indulged in the latest gimmick gadgetry to lessen the old 78 surface noise and either issued the records with a faint echo or, later when stereo came in, remastered the old mono records out of phase to create a "stereo effect," in both cases to their sonic ruination, unlike specialty reissue labels with carefully remastered sound like Folkways and Collector's Guild.[30]

Benedict and Helen Stambler: The Patron Saints of Jewish Recording

The standard by which all other Jewish record labels in the 1950s and 1960s can be judged was established by the Collector's Guild label founded by Benedict and Helen Stambler.

Benedict Stambler (1904–1967) was born in Pennsylvania and grew up in Brooklyn. Though he received a law degree in 1930, Stambler spent most of his professional life teaching English at Brooklyn's Tilden High School, while indulging his hobby as an armchair ethnomusicologist. Helen (née Huddisman, 1919–2016) was born in Brooklyn and became a high school English teacher. They married in 1938.

Stambler, a passionate packrat of thousands of Yiddish 78s (that at one point threatened to displace the couple from their home and were in danger of being thrown out by his wife) in the mold of jazz, blues, and traditional country music reissue labels, he and Helen founded Collector's Guild in 1959.[1]

Collector's Guild, the first solely Jewish reissue label, focused on cantorial and later Yiddish theater, setting a very high standard characterized by Benedict's clean 78s, meticulous remastering by recording engineer David Hancock, and Helen's informative notes and discographic details.[2]

Collector's Guild skirted the edges of record piracy with its 78 reissues from major labels. At one point, RCA threatened a quarter-million-dollar infringement suit for Collector's Guild reissue of Cantor

---

1. Helen Stambler Latner, interview by Hankus Netsky, June 5, 2015, https://www.yiddishbookcenter.org/collections/oral-histories/interviews/woh-fi-0000704/helen-stambler-latner-2015.

2. Klezmer reissues would have to wait until 1981 when Folkways issued my "Klezmer Music 1910–1942".

Zavel Kwartin recordings ca. 1930. Stambler, reaching back into his long-disused legal training, determined that RCA only had rights to a single issue of those sides and had illegally kept the titles in print for years, without Kwartin's permission. Case dismissed.[3]

By the early 1960s, the Stamblers boldly expanded into ethnographic field and studio recordings of Hasidic and Ladino music, new recordings of classic cantors, and several LPs of wedding music, by the then-reigning king of Hasidic bandstands, clarinetist Rudy Tepel.

By 1967, with nearly two hundred titles, Benedict Stambler died.

In 1971, Helen Stambler Latner made important bequests of the Collector's Guild collection to Columbia University and the Library of Congress. She also donated over four thousand 78s to the Rodgers and Hammerstein Archives of Recorded Sound at the New York Public Library at Lincoln Center. There, Chief archivist David Hall's easy access catalog/listening protocol would become the model of the YIVO Institute when I founded its sound archives in 1982.

Helen Stambler Latner would go on to become a book author and newspaper columnist.

The legacy of Collector's Guild is that despite all the subsequent major advances in digital sound and remastering technology, just how well the records still sound and read, a half century on.

---

3. Helen Stambler Latner, Interview by Hankus Netsky, June 5, 2015.

Party Records

During Banner's peak, Yinglish party records became another trend in Jewish American music—slightly ribald, lightly suggestive—made by and for an American-born audience for whom Yiddish was less their "mother tongue" than their "other tongue." Despite the label holding aloft its banner of old-time Yiddish popular culture, it quietly founded a subsidiary "Carnival" label to release the edgier material, starting with what amounts to the national anthem of the Borscht Belt: "Essen" ("Eating") by Billy Hodes and Ray Carter's Catskill Cowboys.[31]

Essen

Billy Hodes started in the early 1930s in burlesque as a "song and dance juvenile" (an October 20, 1934, gig at Max Kroll's Orpheum Theater in Paterson, New Jersey, had him splitting a bill with "eccentric comic" Lou Costello, still two years away from partnering with Bud Abbott).[32] In 1935, Hodes began a decade-long tenure in the Catskills at the Flagler Hotel in South Fallsburg, one of the largest Borscht Belt resorts, as the social director/MC ("tummler"). In this in situ role, he perfected the "Essen" catalog of the pleasures of Catskills hotel living—boating, golf, and swimming are bypassed in a breathless machine gun litany of menu options: "orangejuiceprunejuice tomatojuicepineapplejuicesomebakedapplesstewedprunes!"[33]

Almost immediately, a competing version of "Essen" by comedian Lee Tully came out on the new Jubilee label.[34] Tully was from Chicago and had come to New York during World War II working as an MC in midtown clubs and theaters.[35] While the Tully version uses some of the same component parts of the Hodes version (its title, rapid-fire delineation of the dining room menu, and a catchy chorus), it's quite a different song: Hodes opens with Bernie Share's tight, small band driven by a propulsive tuba and does his routine with a heavy Jewish accent, while Tully fronts a piano trio with a muted trumpet in unaccented English. Even the choruses are different, with Hodes leading a chant of "Essen! Essen! Essen!" while Tully's sung version is in Yiddish he can't quite pronounce.

The market for the record is made clear in a Jubilee *Billboard* ad, where "Essen" is touted as "a sure nickel grabber," indicating that in addition to home ("party") use, it would also generate good jukebox play.[36] Jubilee's owner Herb Abramson (who later co-founded Atlantic Records with Ahmet Ertegun) navigated the label into R&B and pop releases and away from Yiddish party records.

Joe and Paul

However, the best known of all Yiddish party records did not come from these labels but from one already known for its doo-wop, blues, and gospel: Apollo Records. "Joe and Paul" is ostensibly an ad on a fictional Jewish radio station (WBVD, a reference to an underwear manufacturer) whose increasingly racy and suggestive program interludes are punctuated by the sponsor's infectious theme song:

Joe and Paul, a farganign
Joe and Paul men ken a bargain krign
A suit, a coat a gaberdine
Brengt arayn dayn kleynem zin
Joe and Paul, a pleasure
Joe and Paul, you'll get a bargain
A suit, a coat a gabardine
Bring in your young son.[37]

Figure 15.3. The original Joe and Paul store on Stanton Street, a block once famous for men's and boy's discount clothing. *Source:* 1940 Tax Photograph Collection, NYC Municipal Archives. Used with permission.

Apollo Records

The Apollo label goes back to partners Phil Sturtz and Louis Falk, who by 1921 ran the Savoy Music shop on Second Avenue and 107th Street specializing in cantorial records.[1] By 1938, Sturtz and Falk moved to 102 West 125th and changed not only their address but their name (now The Rainbow Music and Gift Shop) and also their specialty—from cantorial

---

1. Advertisement, *Forverts*, Dec. 11, 1921, 10.

to blues, gospel, and jazz. By the following year, New York's African American *Amsterdam News* called it "Harlem's greatest record store."[2] By 1946, the shop's in-house Apollo label (quite likely named for its across-the-street neighbor the Apollo Theater) booked a broad swath of African American artists.

In 1948, the owners sold out to former employee Bess Berman who was more than equal to the task of the rough-and-tumble world of cutthroat indie labels and headed Apollo until its demise in the early 1960s. When the African American *Pittsburgh Courier* launched a campaign "against wax race tags" (segregating "race record" identifiers in marketing Black music), Apollo, whose majority artists were Black, was one of the first labels to sign on. "Apollo Records never has used these terms," Mrs. Berman related, "and disapproves of the practice strongly."[3] Berman signed gospel pioneer Mahalia Jackson, who at first was unwilling to sing sacred music to a secular audience until Berman pointed out, "That's where all the sinners are.[4] In the spring of 1948, Bess Berman issued side-by-side releases of her two incongruous new finds: Mahalia Jackson's simple and moving *I Want to Rest / He Knows My Heart* next to the lightly leering Yinglish party record *Joe and Paul*. Both sold tremendously well.

Berman also had quixotic tastes in music: she hired tenor banjo virtuoso Harry Reser to head the planned "novelty" line of records, and in the faint early days of what would become the folk music craze, the label recorded Black songster Josh White and with an Apollo musical director making like Alan Lomax and "waxing a bunch of songs in South America and Tennessee."[5] Berman even won a high-visibility breach of contract case against Dean Martin, who, right after signing with Apollo in 1947, teamed with Jerry Lewis and jumped ship for Capitol Records.[6]

---

2. "Hot Music," *New York Amsterdam News*, Feb. 19, 1938, 19.

3. George F. Brown, "King, Apollo Denounce Wax Race Tags," *Pittsburgh Courier*, May 14, 1949, 19.

4. "Religioso Upbeat Sees More DJs Hop on Spiritual-Gospel Bandwagon," *Variety*, Oct. 6, 1954, 55.

5. "Music Notes," *Variety*, June 11, 1947, 44.

6. "Apollo Awarded $3,500 Dean Martin Judgement," *Variety*, May 24, 1950, 53.

Paul Emanuel Kofsky was born in 1900 in Kiev and came to the US in 1920. By the next year, when he applied for citizenship, Kofsky was already a "clothing dealer." Described as an immaculately groomed man with a penchant for paper neckties, in 1926 Paul Kofsky opened his Stanton Street store, naming it Joe & Paul, believing that customers would trust him more if they thought he had a partner. Kofsky had been advertising on the radio for five years when he opened his second store in September 1936 on Pitkin Avenue in Brownsville, Brooklyn.

It's not surprising why the Joe & Paul jingle would become an earworm: during the mid-1930s, Kofsky was sponsoring three shows that aired three times a week on three different stations: WBNX in the Bronx, WBBC in Brooklyn, and WLTH in Manhattan. Curiously, of all the stations that Kofsky sponsored, the one on which the Joe & Paul jingle was never heard was WEVD (the object of its underwear reference).

The jingle was born at WLTH, whose musical director Sholom Secunda composed the melody and accompanied Kofsky when he sang his own Yiddish lyrics:

> Joe un Paul a stor a farganign
> Joe un Paul men ken a bargain krign
> A suit, a coat a gitn, ales perfekt
> Ikh zug aykh, darft ir koyfen nor by Joe un Paul
> Joe and Paul, a store, a pleasure
> Joe and Paul, you'll find a bargain
> A suit, a coat, everything's good and perfect
> I tell you, you should only shop at Joe and Paul.[38]

The birth of the subsequent skit was described by comedian-actor Aaron "Red Buttons" Chwat:

> We used to hang around the cafeterias in the thirties, there was Kellogg's cafeteria on 49th street. It was a cafeteria for the small-time guys. So, we'd sit around the table, Jewish kids we were first generation Americans, and we'd follow up with "Joe & Paul a farganign . . ." Number one: it was funny. Number two it was musical. You know, it was catchy, it was a very, very catchy refrain . . . there was something about it that had a little "*kheyn*," you know, a little heart to it. So, we used to tap it off

on the tables . . . and I just started to play around with it and it caught on immediately.³⁹

Chwat introduced the bit in the Catskills before he left in 1942 to go to war, but he never revived it when he returned. Claims of authorship also come from Eddie Barton, one half of the Barton Brothers, who recorded it. Barton spoke no Yiddish but broke into Yiddish radio as a child by singing on station WMCA (he learned all the latest songs when his family lived above a Lower East Side record store that played the records "morning, noon and night").⁴⁰ Barton did a Jewish dialect act at Catskills hotels (one of the hotel bands with whom he worked was led by a violinist named Henny Youngman). Barton then formed a duo with Murray Nestor—as their agent said, "Brother acts were hot." They became the Barton Brothers, and with the Yiddish-speaking Murray, they performed the skit.⁴¹

The *Joe & Paul* recording session was headed by Irv Carrol (born Irving Gellers in Brooklyn) and anchored by klezmer trumpeter Willie Epstein of the esteemed klezmer Epstein Brothers. Barton recalled the session went so fast they made both sides of the 78 in an afternoon: "We recorded it and we got $250 and we ran out of town; we thought we stole $250."⁴²

"We're out of town five or six months," Barton said, "and I get a call from the agent and he said, 'Listen, what are you doing out of town? You've sold about three quarter of a million records.' And I said, 'What records?' and he said, 'The records you made!' "⁴³

Paul Kofsky, who had once given the Bartons permission to use the song at a charity function, was shocked to learn of the party record it had become. Kofsky sued the Barton Brothers and Apollo Records for "corrupting his tune with obscene and suggestive lyrics," asking for damages of $225,000, the amount he said he invested in radio promotion since he started advertising his store on the radio in 1931.⁴⁴ In the legal dustup that followed, Apollo filed a countersuit against Kofsky ("not a real party to the action") and even against the Bartons themselves for "breach of warranty." The ten-car pileup never made it to court and was settled for an undisclosed sum. Eddie Barton would later contend that thanks to the lawsuit, Kofsky made more money from the record than the Barton Brothers.⁴⁵

How many actual copies of *Joe & Paul* were sold will never be known. And while it was most likely not "three quarters of a million records," sales were such that, by a very wide margin, no Jewish 78 turns up more often in thrift stores, in flea markets, or on vintage record lists than *Joe & Paul*. A farganign.

Although Apollo was clearly rooted in doo-wop, blues, and gospel, for the most part it released only a few Jewish records: the novelty/comedy records by the Barton Brothers and schoolteacher turned stand-up comic Sam Levenson, several cantorial sides, and some actual Yiddish cuts.

The one Apollo issue that aesthetically reflected the peak of prewar Yiddish American pop music was its 1949 "Ich Bin a Boarder By Mein Weib" ("I Am My Wife's Boarder").[46] The release marked the final recording of bandleader-composer Abe Schwartz, who had, coincidentally, provided the orchestral accompaniment for the song's first recording in 1923. This also marked the first recording of Yiddish comic Fyvush Finkel, who would later win Emmy awards for TV shows like *Picket Fences*. Finkel recreated his Apollo performance for the 1995 PBS Itzhak Perlman program *In the Fiddler's House* when he sang the original Yiddish version (with my English translation) accompanied by my klezmer group Kapelye.[47]

Savoy Records

"Two Yiddlekh from Newark" was how klezmer clarinetist Dave Tarras described the owners of the Savoy record label when they contacted him to do some "Yiddish swing" 78s in 1946.[48] The "Yiddlekh" were Herman Lubinsky and Fred Mendelsohn.

If Hyman "Herman" Lubinsky (1896–1974) is known for anything, it is for being the central casting idea of a pugilistic, avaricious, parsimonious, and equal parts hated, feared, and admired independent jazz record label owner. Lubinsky was born in Connecticut into an observant Jewish family who moved to Newark when he was a child. Lubinsky's early interest in radio blossomed so quickly that with the outbreak of World War I he was hired by the US Army right out of high school to teach broadcasting and radio repair.[49] After the War, the twenty-three-year-old (now "Herman") opened the Radio Shop of Newark, selling radios and, by 1923, airing his own fifty-watt radio station, WRAZ.[50] In 1924, its call letters were changed to WNJ (Wireless New Jersey), and the station that called itself "the voice of Newark" had become a bedrock in New York City–area broadcasting.

While focusing on quotidian radio shows (news, children's programming, music) Lubinsky already showed his interest in diversity with foreign language offerings (Greek, Polish, etc.) and African American shows. Lubinsky aired regular Jewish shows in Yiddish and English, and WNJ was the first station to feature local Newark African American cantor Thomas LaRue Jones, who appeared several times.[51]

When the station was forced off the air in 1933, Lubinsky returned to retail, and in 1943, at the height of the Petrillo AFM recording ban, Lubinsky successfully launched a record label, as the recording musicians were not members of the AFM, thus untouched by its union prohibition. His Savoy label partner Fred Mendelsohn was the musical director at Bronx station WBNX, where he had come up playing accordion, piano, and organ for its many ethnic, Yiddish, and African American programs.

Considering the seismic effect the independent label brought to postwar jazz, R&B, and gospel, Savoy's earliest 1943 issues alternated among less successful genres such as country western and novelty: "The Savoy Record Co, in Newark, releases a new 10-inch single on which the Savoy-Musette Quintet can be heard playing two compositions by H. Lubinsky 'Johnny Doughboy Polka,' and 'Gay Vienna.'" The anonymous writer is quick to assure his readers: "These are better than their titles would indicate. They are sprightly and well played, particularly the polka."[52]

The label would straighten up and fly right by the time "the two Yiddlekh from Newark" contacted Dave Tarras in early 1946. Dave Tarras was then the reigning master of all things klezmer clarinet on stage, records, and radio. He was the featured soloist of the popular WHN show *Your American Jewish Hour: Yiddish Melodies in Swing*, inspired by the 1938 crossover Yiddish hit "Bei mir bistu sheyn." The show's orchestra was led by Sam Medoff, the son of Yiddish theater royalty David and Raisa Medoff. The younger Medoff was a pianist and arranger with a sweet tooth for contemporary swing, and over the course of the show's nearly fifteen years, crafted knowing and inventive swing arrangements of Yiddish music for vocalists the Barry Sisters and tenor Jan Bart, all deftly woven around the smoothly mellifluous soloing of Tarras, who could not play a single note of swing.

It's unclear why Lubinsky didn't go with the proven formula of the musicians and arrangements of the WHN show for Tarras. Perhaps the station or the show's sponsor B. Manischewitz would not give permission, or perhaps Lubinsky—never one to pay what a service is worth—wanted to bypass the rights involved and issue something he himself owned. (The label of the two discs features the unusual proprietary credit, "Direction H. Lubinsky.") On the positive side, Savoy used the excellent arrangements by Tarras's son-in-law, clarinetist Sammy Musiker (misspelled as "Musica"). Musiker—whose name means what it appears to mean—was a brilliant klezmer player who, just before the war, had also been the number one clarinet/sax chair for the Gene Krupa Orchestra, a vaunted position in the world of swing.

Unfortunately for the Savoy session, Lubinsky didn't use Musiker to play his own arrangements. For a label renowned for having the most representative musicians of their genre, the "Yiddish swing" orchestra was pluperfect awful. Trumpet player Lou Lockett, whose only other claim to fame (tellingly, perhaps) was as director of the orchestra on the ill-fated SS *Normandie*, could not convincingly realize Musiker's smart charts, which was evident even to the *Billboard* critic for whom this was probably his first klezmer review: "Long identified with the playing of Jewish folk music, Dave Tarras adds four such sides to the label's catalog . . . it's the winning clarinet that carries each spin. As a matter of fact, it's only the clarinet that displays a true concept of this type of folk music. And since that instrument counts most, even the feeble trumpeting can be forgiven."[53] Dave Tarras noted, "The stores said, 'It's a good record, it's beautiful, but if jazz we want, we got Benny Goodman.' It's not Jewish 'cause it's mixing in too much jazz, and it's not jazz 'cause it's mixing in too much Jewish. It's what killed it: too much jazz. They had a contract with me for more records, but they stopped it, and they paid me a lump of money to get out of the contract. I really loved the records, but I let them out of the contract."[54]

Even with a couple more desultory Jewish-themed titles, Lubinsky and Mendelsohn's dalliance with Yiddish music was over, and they returned Savoy to being an R&B, gospel, country and western, and jazz indie label.

16

The First Yiddish Recording Artists

Frank Seiden: The Fire King

The first two Jewish recording stars in 1900 revealed Yiddish theater's direct line to *badkhones*, the improvisatory wedding poet/MC and stand-up comic entertainer central to Ashkenazic tradition. One was Frank Seiden (ca. 1861–1931), who stands at the makeshift juncture of traditional East European folk culture and Yiddish American pop culture en route to American mass culture.[1]

Efraim "Frank" Seiden was born in Galicia and came to America in about 1880, where, by the end of the decade, he was "Prof." Seiden, a "First Class Magician, Fire King, and Punch and Judy Man."[2] In 1889, Seiden appeared on the modest dime museum circuit: "Magic, Mirth and Mystery Monopolized by the Magician Monarch" alliterated the headline for his turn at Austin and Stone's Museum in Boston.[3] Reviewers marveled at "the humorist and magician" whose strategically flawed, accented English ("malapropistic misdirection") cleverly distracted his audiences while executing his up-close-and-personal parlor prestidigitations. "Professor Seiden," wrote the *Boston Post*, "presented a new programme of magical illusions and interspersed his performances with humorous ideas that provoked unrestrained laughter"—something a *badkhn* would also be used to doing.[4]

In 1889, the New York City directory lists Seiden at 122 Attorney Street, a six-story tenement, with his business given as "beer," which supports anecdotes about Seiden winning a saloon in a poker game. (Who would play poker with a magician skilled in card tricks?)

Max Malini: King of Magicians

At one point, Seiden hired teenager Mendel "Max" Katz (1873–1942) to work around the saloon. Katz, who was fascinated by Seiden's intimate sleight of hand magic, got the older man to agree to teach him. From this, Katz (as "Mailini") would become the father of modern sleight of hand magic. Katz was born in Yaroslav, Galicia, and in a lengthy interview in the *Forverts* on February 21, 1926, explained that his family name was derived from the initials for Cohen/Tzaddik (K'Tz). While the portly and stubby-fingered Katz might have seemed ill-equipped to take to up-close, nimble legerdemain, Katz's natural dexterity enabled him to master not only Seiden's sleight of hand but also his "malapropistic misdirection." (Malini's English was also said to be barely rudimentary, which, as the writer in the 1926 *Forverts* noted, was—as with Seiden—just part of his stage *shtick*.[1])

Student soon surpassed teacher, with Malini becoming one of the world's great sleight of hand magicians as the "Last of the Mountebanks," whose fans included Theodore Roosevelt, Al Capone, King Edward II, and Morris "Two Gun" Cohen.[2] Prof. Seiden's magic legacy remains, as some of the tricks he taught Malini—and Malini popularized—are still in active sleight of hand magic use.

---

1. Ben Zion, "Der vunderbarster shvartz-kinstler: an *east-sayder* yid," *Forverts*, Feb. 24, 1926, 13.
2. Zion, 13.

In addition to his mastery of card tricks, Seiden had perfected a series of fire-based tricks and was widely popular as the "Fire King." An article in the *American Hebrew* describes a "Prof. Seiden" performance at the Educational Alliance on the Lower East Side where the students enjoyed his sleight of hand but truly came alive "when the Professor appeared as the 'Fire King,' and ate balls of flaming cotton, and blew flames from his mouth and lighted lamps by breathing on them."[5] In a bitter irony, on July 25, 1893, the Fire King's own toddler daughter died in a blaze at their Attorney Street apartment, caused by her playing with matches.[6] Yet despite this tragic loss, Seiden continued to appear as the Fire King.

By 1900, Seiden wholly abandoned legerdemain and was now into a new kind of magic, as one of about forty phonograph dealers in New

York City.⁷ The next year Seiden moved from behind the horn to in front of it when he recorded for Berliner, Monarch, Victor, Columbia, and the little known "American" label.⁸ It is in the grooves of the over two hundred cylinders and discs that Frank Seiden made between 1901 and 1905 that his sonic autobiography emerges.

Frank Seiden was not blessed with a mellifluous voice but a loud one, a critical skill in the noisy venues in which he first performed and in the early recording days, when singers who projected into a large horn to make a record found that a leather lung meant as much as a golden throat. Add to that, Seiden's modest harmonic range and raspy, gruff tone were nearly indistinguishable from the record's own surface noise. But just beneath those seemingly fatal flaws there is a tremendous artistry and a seemingly bottomless source of folk and early theater compositions undocumented anywhere else. From his first recording (Abraham Goldfaden's already beloved "Rozhinkes Mit Mandlen" ["Raisins and Almonds"]) Seiden went on to record songs from a dozen other early, now wholly forgotten Yiddish operas, songs that he could very easily have learned as a member of a traveling Yiddish theater troupe. Among the operatic arias, Seiden recorded several event songs (broadsides) like "Kapitan Dreifuss," "Spanish-American Schlacht," and "Chorbn Kishiniev" ("Kishiniev Disaster"), all of which, with their sense of on-the-spot reportage, invoke the nineteenth-century street-smart *shtetl griot*—the *Broder Zinger*—whose immediacy and rough-and-tumble visceral performances were their stock in trade. Seiden could very well have been one of them too.

However, it is in the precious fewest of Seiden's records where he reveals his truest self: in spoken introductions, Seiden identifies himself as *der balibter badkhn* (the beloved wedding poet) and launches into deeply nuanced, time-honored wedding rhymes, invocations, and witticisms, the kinds for which old country *badkhonim/marshalikim* were renowned. Seiden's poetic flights, meant to make wedding family and friends laugh and cry, and his ability to direct the correct ritual sequence of the wedding, were only some of the skills with which *badkhonim* entertained the guests, which also included sleight of hand, fire tricks, and juggling, those very skills that turned Efraim Seiden into Prof. Seiden.

After he finished recording in 1905, Seiden went back to running phonograph nickelodeons. When the nickelodeon craze shifted from recordings to movies, Seiden shifted too. In 1908, Seiden, along with William Fox (the Fox in 20th Century Fox) and Marcus Loew (MGM), was a founding member of one of New York's earliest movie distribution/exhibition organizations, the guts of what imminently was to be the standard Hollywood lifeline.⁹

He also opened a mixed-use theater at 66 Columbia Street. "Mr. Seiden" and his Columbia Street theater make a guest appearance in the 1955 George Burns memoir *I Love Her, That's Why: An Autobiography*:

> This was a picture house which ran vaudeville acts as well. There was a pool hall downstairs and it was difficult to hear either the vaudeville acts before the movie or the music accompanying the picture—the noise of the pool balls drowned out almost all other sounds. The movies were made as silent pictures, but by the time the Seidens, father and sons got through with them they were anything but. . . . So the three of them, Mr. Seiden, Joe, and Jack, stood behind the screen and talked for the actors. They had a few regular parts. Joe was always the girl, although he played other parts as well. . . .
>
> The theater ran two vaudeville acts—one in Yiddish and one in English. The Burns Brothers job was to handle the curtain. This took a bit of doing, because the curtain rolled up from the bottom on a heavy wooden pole which was controlled by ropes on either side of the stage, Burns and Burns together weighed about 120 pounds and the pole weighed half again as much. We were able to get the curtain up twice without staggering, but if the act went over big and they took more than two curtain calls we were dead. One week Seiden booked a Yiddish sketch called "Religion Versus Love." The plot involved a Gentile girl who wanted her Jewish lover to give up his religion and marry her. The smash finish of this act was when the boy cried: "No! A Jew I was born and a Jew I shall die!" Well, this was good for about fifteen curtain calls, and with each we got weaker and the curtain got lower. For the last bow the actors were lying on their stomachs.[10]

Outsinging a Mob

"Sang to Save His Life from a Mob," a 1908 article, tells that while singing at the theater to illustrated magic lantern slides, Seiden learned about a new "Sunday law" that made it illegal. Despite announcing to the full house that he could no longer sing on Sunday without fear of arrest, "many and various things were thrown at him by the audience." To quell the crowd, Seiden began singing when, after only a few bars, "detectives

> took him out the rear entrance and hustled him to the station house." In court, Zeiden [*sic*] showed the marks on his body where missiles struck him, which the detectives corroborated, to which the judge ruled, "Your violation of the law was a case of necessity, I guess." Case dismissed.

Seiden's theater would move several times (including to 58 Willett Street around 1914) before giving it up in 1916, when he and his son Joseph (1892–1974) opened a short-lived movie production studio (Teeandess Film Co.). In the 1920 and 1930 census, Frank Seiden lists "none" under "profession."

Frank Seiden died in 1931, and while small notices of his passing in the movie and theater trade magazines remarked on his place in magic, movies, and vaudeville, none noted his role as a pioneering recording artist.[11] Worse still, no Yiddish paper noted his passing, nor did Zalmen Zilbercweig include him in his otherwise exhaustive *Lexikon of Yiddish Theater*.

Figure 16.1. Frank Seiden (with hat and cane) at his Yiddish and English Willett Street Theater, 1913. *Source:* Courtesy of the National Center for Jewish Film. Used with permission.

Seiden's son Joseph, in his Judea Films, would go on to produce and direct over two dozen budget Yiddish films including *Kol Nidre* (1939), *Motl der Operator* (1940), *Got, Mentsh un Tayvl*, and *Monticello, Here We Come* (1950), and Black musicals *Paradise in Harlem* (1939) and *Stars on Parade* (1946), together with his in-law, sound recordist Murray Dichter.[12] Dichter's son, Lee (b. 1944), mixed sound on over three hundred films for directors including Woody Allen, Sidney Lumet, Barry Sonnenfeld, Sally Heckel, Tim Robbins, and Josh Waletzky.[13]

Solomon Smulewitz/Small

Seiden's contemporary was fiddler, badkhn, cantor, rabbi, poet, composer, publisher, singer, and entrepreneur Shloime "Solomon" Smulewitz. Smulewitz (1868–1943) was born in Pinsk, where at the age of five his cantor father taught him cantorial singing and entered him in a yeshiva where he learned to read and write. Smulewitz was later apprenticed to the great cantor Nisi Belzer, who would teach him to read and write music. With the death of his father, Smulewitz began singing songs of his own composition, and supplementing his income with a traveling Yiddish theater troupe or a cantor's choir for his so-called *esn teg* (eating days gigs that came with meals). In 1881 in Vilna, Smulewitz learned the fiddle, and in Minsk, badkhones, at which he soon became so adept that he was writing rhymes for other more established badkhonim. Smulewitz would publish several poems and a book before coming to America in about 1893.[14]

While there is no trace of what Smulewitz did in New York in his earliest years, it is possible he earned his living as a tailor, a craft he learned in his teens. Smulewitz also obtained his *smikhe* (rabbinic ordination) and became a rabbi. But, blessed with a pleasant and resonant tenor voice and a renewable resource of his own compositions, Smulewitz began giving concerts in vaudeville houses, making his first record in 1901 and continuing until 1920; about 150 records for every label, including Standard, Zonophone, United Hebrew Record, Edison, Columbia, and Victor.[15] And Smulewitz, like Seiden, made it clear in the spoken introduction to his recordings how he wanted to be known: *dikhter* Smulewitz (poet Smulewitz).

While Smulewitz concentrated on his own songs (he recorded a number of them several times), he also sang the compositions of others and was an effortless collaborator as the lyricist in some, the composer in others. It's unclear exactly how many songs Smulewitz wrote. Irene Heskes in her *Yiddish American Popular Songs, 1895–1950* documents over three hundred published songs and manuscripts registered with the copyright office.[16] Zalmen Zilbercweig (the Boswell of the Yiddish theater) estimates over five hundred.[17] However, given Smulewitz's prolific output in other venues (newspapers, his *Teyater Zinger* [*Theater Singer*] magazine, private commissioned compositions, etc.), Zilbercweig and Heskes combined numbers might be closer.

Smulewitz's earliest known published American song is the odd "Er Hot Gelakht" ("He Laughed," 1903), Yiddish in title only, rendered in a clumsy, tortured English.

> At the ball he chanced to meet her
> a flow'r she was, lovely and pure
> He courted, with humor and wit, her
> To him, married she was, to be sure
> He swore to be faithful and true her
> But she was not aware of his craft!
> What delighted her most in her suer [sic]
> Is the smiling, and he, well, he laughed!
> But in the laughing there is chaffing
> Sorts there are a score!
> It may happen that this weapon
> Pierce may, very sore.[18]

Yet with its setting at a ball, a bouncy waltz time signature, and the subject of tragic misdirected love, it was nothing less than his homage to Milwaukee's Jewish Charles K. Harris, the composer of the megahit "After the Ball." In 1907, Smulewitz wrote his own megahit, "A Brivele der Mamen" ("A Little Letter to Mother"), a teary mixed-time ballad (verse in three, chorus in two). The song, about a mother back home fruitlessly awaiting a letter from her son in America, dramatically captured that moment of peak Jewish emigration, starting a cottage industry of other *Brivele* compositions, of which Smulewitz produced not a few.[19]

These two songs, and a surprising number of others, were written either from a woman's point of view or in the woman's voice in which Smulewitz portrayed women positively and showed himself to be keenly aware of the societal double standards that victimized them. One of those songs was also the first known recorded Yiddish parody of an English language song: "The Honeysuckle and the Bee" (1901).

On his "Tsu Gefellen Mener" ("Getting Men to Fall for You") Smulewitz turns the earlier treacly English music hall romantic love song on its ear, and in the woman's voice coolly redresses the question of gender inequality:

With both grace and charm I'm blessed
Everyone is quite impressed
When they see me, they are all struck
I've got strength and I've got looks
Nothing you can get from books
I'm blessed with both good fortune
And good luck
Men all love me so they say
I just take their breath away
Just like straw I mow their poor hearts down
Swains all fall upon their knees
I'm so wearied by their pleas
And I laugh at them
Just as you would a clown
But to get men to fall for you
You must be smart
And my plan will really do
Just for a start
I know my looks are key
Vengeance is my plan
Men just lay down for me
And don't get up again
Men are guilty to be sure
When women are made impure
Men are guiltless, avoiding blame
All their lovey dovey chatter
Meant to fool and meant to flatter
And the phony tears they well up without shame
It's so hard to figure out
We're just human there's no doubt
So, we fall for it and we pay the price
But in no time flat you'll see
That the kind of man is he
Who'll grow distant from his wife
And turn to ice.[20]

Starting in 1905, Smulewitz published an annual *Teyater Zinger*, a collection of his latest songs (words, no music), poems, witticisms, and popular song parodies. Though *Teyater Zinger* lasted for five issues, it was clearly not easy (each edition had a different mailing address, possibly pointing to Smulewitz having to move for financial reasons). Smulewitz's ideas about self-promotion were original and proactive, and he anticipated cross-marketing platforms years ahead of its time. Perhaps too far: for all his marketing prescience, his enterprises failed.[21]

In 1912, in a move usually associated with someone crossing out of the Jewish world, Solomon Smulewitz changed his name to Small (something the corpulent singer was not) and so toggled uneasily between the two surnames for the rest of his life. That same year, on the first sheet with both names, Smulewitz composed, published, and recorded another timely ballad, "Khurbn titanik oder der naser keyver" ("The Titanic Disaster or the Watery Grave") only weeks after the sea catastrophe. While the world was awash with other Titanic songs that also pointed out the underlying tragic hubris of the mighty vessel, only Smulewitz's song called out the love and bravery of passengers Isador Straus (he of Macy's fame) and his wife Ida, who decided to die together, an image splashed on the cover of Smulewitz's Hebrew Publishing sheet music.[22]

The post–World War I era saw a dramatic change in Yiddish popular music away from the folk autodidactic "singer songwriters" like Smulewitz. Now, jazz-influenced Yiddish theater music by Joseph Rumshinsky and Alexander Olshanetsky made Smulewitz's songs seem even older than they were, and the bottom gave out with a sudden unforgiving ferocity. Smulewitz would make his last record in 1920, while his last published song would be a commission from Max Bernstein in 1927 for the opening of his Libby's Hotel and Baths, a distinctly old fashioned march for the otherwise ultra-modern Libby's. Smulewitz became the embodiment of the wandering Jew, reduced to a grueling tour of provincial Jewish communities usually in the company of his daughter Dorothy (herself a fine singer), performing in a series of benefits (i.e., fundraising concerts closing with a description of his present dire circumstances).[23] Yet even in his health decline and in poverty, Smulewitz continued to be productive and creative. In 1938, he self-published *Origienele retenishn in ritm un raym* (*Original Riddles in Rhythm and Rhyme*), a collection of puzzles and riddles in macaronic Yiddish and English with an ingenious answer code, whose extreme rarity points to just how badly it sold.[24]

Without end, Smulewitz struggled against his "forgotten but not gone" status. In an October 23, 1941, *Forverts* column "Fun folk tsu folk" (From People to People), Smulewitz wrote a letter to comment about a previous article that referred to "A brivele der mamen" "as old and forgotten" (a description that also fit Smulewitz). "I would like to thank the writer,"

Smulewitz wrote, "but the song is not forgotten. It's heard in concerts and on the radio," he noted. "It was even recently the subject of an entire film in which the song was the movie's *light motif*."[25] Smulewitz ended his letter with the rhetorical question: "Who is the author, is he still alive? And if not, his name should still be mentioned. His name? Solomon Smulewitz, old and broken but he still lives and writes new songs!"[26] When Solomon Smulewitz died on January 1, 1943, a brief obituary appeared in the pages of *The New York Times*, but his passing, like that of Frank Seiden before him, went unreported in the Yiddish press.[27]

Smulewitz's zeal to be "the poet of the people" came at a steep price. His dizzying prolific output made his work omnipresent, and with it, a kind of "folk" anonymity set in, making him—but not his songs—invisible even to his greatest fans. In this way, Smulewitz was very much like the father of the Yiddish theater, Abraham Goldfaden, whose critical success and influence was vast but whose financial success was not. At the end of his life, Goldfaden, broken and broke, approached New York's Jewish poohbahs and begged them for the equivalent of the cost of the monument they would erect to him after his death so he could comfortably see out his last days doing his work. Goldfaden was refused, and as predicted, he died in poverty and the monument that was erected to him in Brooklyn's Washington Cemetery is impressive.

In this one way, however, Smulewitz had the last word by composing his own headstone elegy, a Yiddish acrostic (one of his favorite poetic devices) spelling out his name in a quatrain testifying to his lush literary legacy:

> **S**ilently, a life passes
> **O**f poems written for the masses
> **L**ife's tenor through his lyre
> **O**f skits and humor and satire
> **M**uch like an illusion, lost, diffuse
> **O** Where is he? Where is his muse?
> **N**ow dead! But his song will still be heard
> **S**o time creates, there's no last word
> **M**elodies, gazettes, and songs
> **U**nstinting poems for the throngs
> **L**oving heartfelt, the sweetest sound
> **E**arnest awareness, true, profound
> **W**it and humor, each word bespoke
> **I**n the service of his folk
> **T**alks and writings, with loving regard
> **Z**ion's singer, Israel's Bard.[28]

Figure 16.2. Solomon Smulewitz's headstone with his own acrostic quatrain epitaph. *Source:* Photograph by David H. Wieder. Used with permission.

Benny Bell

Musician and singer Benny Bell represents a variant on the trajectory of performers who go from Jewish into mainstream performing. Born Benjamin Samberg (1906–1999) in Brooklyn, he founded a small label that carried mostly Jewish recordings but would gain fame decades later for his one decidedly un-Jewish disc.

By 1930 Samberg was already using the professional name Benny Bell playing dance band trumpet. A November 14, 1936, review in *Billboard* of Allen Leafer and Orchestra at New York's swanky Continental Room already called out Bell's attention-grabbing tendencies: "In an orchestra which stays away from all novelty effects and instrumentations, one of the trumpets, (Benny) Bell, does, however, step forth to hit high C and a fifth above the high C."[29]

By 1941, Samberg left playing music to start the Radio Record Company, in whose ads he billed himself as "the burlesque song king . . . where each one is a lulu."[30] In 1943, Benny changed the company's name to Bell Novelty and made his "nom de label" Bell too. From his studio/warehouse redoubt on Pitkin Avenue in Brownsville, Bell released his first comedy record: a brawling Hibernian ditty "McCarthy and McGinnis" set to the tune of "The Irish Washerwoman," and a flip side of the turn-of-the-century comedy song "I Had but 50 Cents" that *Billboard* believed would "find wide circulation . . . in the tap and tavern locations."[31]

But it was the 1946 Jewsy-bluesy "Pincus the Peddler" novelty disc that changed his direction. "New York went wild," read the trade publication ads run by Empire Coin Machine Sales on Coney Island Avenue: "Bell recordings which took New York by storm . . . played and sung by the inimitable Bell."[32] In his batch of 1946 discs, Samberg remakes his own versions of old Yiddish songs. One ("Blessing the Bride") was a comedy parody badkhones replete with crying women, a onetime staple in early Yiddish 78s. Bell's Brooklyn accent betrays which side of the Atlantic he's from, but his arch and comedic lyrics and modal references recall an older performance source. So too does the accompaniment, whose close-to-the-bone sound reveals Bell's deep love for old-time Yiddish dance music.[33]

Bell's records featured members of New York's klezmer world from the already illustrious Epstein Brothers (Max, clarinet; Chizik, drums; and Willie, trumpet) to a young up-and-coming reed player Rudy Tepel, all of which give his records a feel somewhere between studio and field recordings. The label was dominated by Yiddish- and Jewish-themed records, comedy take-offs, badkhones, and a few instrumentals even using Yiddish orthography label copy. Yet Samberg did not market Bell Novelty records in the Yiddish or Jewish press, only in the mainstream English language entertainment trade publications. In 1952, Bell would come as close as ever to selling a song to a major label and artist. That year, for Mercury Records, he penned "Ship Ahoy" for former child star Baby Rose Marie (later, as Rose Marie, she co-starred as Sally Rogers on television's *The Dick Van Dyke Show*). The record did not do well.[34]

By 1955, Samberg's novelty records were wearing out their welcome. The review for "In 1492 (What Did Columbus Do?)" concedes it's "typical Benny Bell novelty . . . general potential is small."[35] By 1962 (six records later) *Billboard* began listing his records (i.e., *Kosher Twist*) under its "limited sales potential" category.[36] It was the Jewish records that kept him afloat. Around 1959, Samberg began mining his back catalog and cobbled together an LP reissue as The Brownsville Klezmers, tracking a contemporary sequential catering hall wedding band repertoire replete with Bell as badkhn/MC. It, and his next reissue, *Kosher Comedy* (1961), did unexpectedly well.

However, Stamberg's lifelong wish of writing a bestselling song was about to come true decades after the fact. In the mid-1940s, Samberg penned "Shaving Cream" for what was most likely his own sub-rosa "under the counter" blue label *Cocktail Party Songs*. The waltz-time ditty, accompanied by Rudy Tepel's kazoo-ish tenor sax, was sung by Brooklyn bandleader Phil "Paul Wynn" Weinstein, who makes Samberg's blunt device clear right away:

> I have a sad story to tell you
> it may hurt your feelings, a bit
> Last night when I walked into my bathroom
> I stepped in a thick pile of
> Shaving Cream!
> Be nice and clean
> Shave every day and you'll
> Always look keen.[37]

In 1974, Samberg brought a copy of "Shaving Cream" to popular WNBC disc jockey Cousin Bruce Morrow (born Meyerowitz) to play on his upcoming New Year's Eve show.[38] The reaction was so positive that by March, Vanguard Records (famous for its folk and jazz lines) licensed "Shaving Cream" from Samberg both as an LP bundled with his other Jewish 78s and also as a general release 45, going out to nearly every radio station in America. For a few weeks in the spring of 1975, when "Shaving Cream" peaked at number 37 on the *Billboard Top 100*, it was getting airplay alongside David Bowie, Freddy Fender, John Denver, and Kraftwerk, among others.[39] This one record was heard by more people and made more money than all of Samberg's previous recordings combined. And it still had an unexpected third act.

A few years later, Barret Eugene Hansen (better known as Dr. Demento) played "Shaving Cream" on his popular syndicated radio show and Samberg found yet another enthusiastic audience. At one live event, when Samberg had finished singing "Shaving Cream," the crowd demanded more verses, "so Dr. Demento came out on stage and together they created some."[40] In the end, Sholom ben Gedalye Leyb Ha' Cohen (a.k.a. Benjamin Samberg DBA Benny Bell) died uniquely secure in the knowledge that his long effort to create successful entertainment and memorable music was right all along.

17

Jews and Jazz

From Before the Beginning

When you think of Jews and jazz, the names that come to mind include Benny Goodman, Artie Shaw, Stan Getz, and Mezz Mezzrow: American-born all. But what of the earlier generation of European-born Jewish musicians—klezmorim—who, upon arrival, were obliged to learn two new languages: English and jazz. How did they navigate through a new challenging soundscape to become viable parts of their new land?

While New Orleans is rightly called the birthplace of jazz, New York is one of the playpens in which it grew up. In New York, there was initially no place more essential than the Clef Club in Harlem, along with its co-founder—composer, bandleader, war hero, murder victim—James Reese Europe.[1] Born in Mobile, Alabama, but raised in a middle-class family in Washington, DC, Europe was trained on the violin as a child and came to New York around 1903. Along with other pioneering African American musicians/composers like Ernest Hogan, Will Marion Cook, and James Rosemond Johnson, he was central to the creation of a freestanding Black music community, which came in the form of the Clef Club.

Harlem of that time was home to the second-largest American Jewish community after the Lower East Side and so had a substantial amount of its cultural infrastructure in place (theaters, synagogues, social organizations), which acted as a model for the African American community. While some Jews did take some part in the late 1890s ragtime craze (e.g., composer Sadie Koninsky from Troy, New York, who, among her hundreds of published pieces, penned the very popular rag "Eli Green's Cakewalk" [1898], and New York–born pianist Rube Bloom, who began his long career as the one of the greatest exponents of the "novelty rag" craze), it would be nothing like the Jewish involvement with jazz.[2]

While it's unclear if immigrant Jews encountered jazz at African American clubs or concerts, one form of jazz was widely available outside of the Black community by 1917. It was in that year that Reisenweber's Restaurant, on Fourteenth Street, brought in the white New Orleans jazz quintet the Original Dixie Jazz Band (ODJB), who had recently scored a major recording success with "Livery Stable Blues." When the ODJB left, they were replaced by Earl Fuller's Jazz Band, two of whose members were among the first Jews making the tenuous steps at playing professional jazz. One was Theodore "Ted Lewis" Leopold Freedman (1890–1971), the clarinet player from Circleville, Ohio. As the "high hatted tragedian of jazz," Lewis would ride to fame on the catchphrase "Is everybody happy?"

The other Jewish member was Harry Raderman (ca. 1883–1940), a trombonist credited with developing a playing and band style ("rag-a-jazz") that bridged the late ragtime and early jazz eras but who faded away when the more refined trombone styles of Miff Mole and Tommy Dorsey became popular.[3] Raderman, who was born near Odessa along with his two other brothers (musicians Elias, who worked in hotel bands, and Max, who played in theater orchestras), migrated in the mid-1890s. While Raderman's inaugural records in 1917 were with Earl Fuller, it was at the first session under his own name for OKeh in February 1920 that he had a major success with the novelty composition "Make That Trombone Laugh."

Another recording from that session was probably the first recording to mix traditional Jewish music and jazz. "Song of Omar" by Tin Pan Alley stalwart Leo Edwards is a nondescript "orientale"-themed melody, which anticipated the craze for those melodies that would follow the film *The Sheik* (1921) and the discovery of "King Tut" the following year.[4] However, it was halfway into the arrangement that, during a solo built on a repeated minor chord, Raderman migrates away from the pale, potted-palm construct of the "orientale" and lays into a full-throated unmistakable and flawless free metered modal semi-improvisational Yiddish-style *doina*. Raderman then trades phrases with the clarinet (possibly Ted Lewis or Nathan Glantz), and to shouts of "Tekiah," "Tekiah gedoylah" (commands in the blowing of the shofar), mimics them effortlessly. This earliest-known recording of an attempt to meld authentic Jewish music with a form of popular music is all the more interesting in that, in a few years' time, Raderman would also be making klezmer records with his fellow Bronx neighbor Shloimke Beckerman. (Beckerman at that time also had a hand in transitional jazz as a member of Paul Whiteman's orchestra at New York's Little Club.) The Raderman klezmer discs would be clarinet-driven, with Raderman only playing backup, so in the entire canon of golden age klezmer records, the only authentic klezmer trombone solo was on the pop record *Song of Omar*.[5]

Klezmorim were not the only ones excited by jazz. Yiddish poet Zishe Vaynper's modernist 1924 "Jazz" reads like he himself attended a jam session or two. The poet introduced his readers to their newest musical neighbors (banjo, saxophone) while he intuited and translated for them the creative process of jazz:

> In the cozy night café
> Tea or coffee, either way
> Bass, banjo and saxophone
> Lost in talk as if they're one.
> And that band does swing and sway!
> In the cozy night café
> Strutting, strumming
> The banjo
> Hippity-hop! Get up and go!
> And to the dazzling saxophone
> All are dancing, everyone
> Giddyap and wiggle waggle
> Like a wild and untamed gaggle
> Unbound from its sonic snaggle
> Giddyap and wiggle waggle!
> And two paws upon the piano
> Brash and brusque have their say so
> Hotsy totsy hot cha cha
> And the people ha, ha, ha!
> In the cozy night café
> Wiggle waggle, swing and sway.[6]

When "jazz" (דזשעז transliterated *dzhez*) begins turning up in the pages of the Yiddish press by 1919, it spanned the spectrum from perennially perplexing puzzlement to full-out fear. One of the earliest references was a letter to the *Forverts* editor asking what happened to the once common German "ooom-pah" bands that would play in the streets of New York. The unnamed editor replied that while World War I did nothing to enhance anything with a German affiliation, it was jazz that gave the coup de grâce to these once quaint street ensembles.[7]

Other questions were from worried parents, for example, "a mother who is very concerned about the new crazy dances" (i.e., jazz), and another mother terrified about her daughter's matrimonial prospects after she had taken up the banjo. A satirical advice column by Regina Frishvasser, who under the headline "Marrying Young or Old Men" advised young girls not to wed old men as "they will not understand your wanting to leave the house at night to go hear a jazz band."[8] Cautionary warnings about the effects of jazz popped up regularly as in a June 12, 1924, report: "Due to corsets, dancing, automobiles and jazz, women get doubles chins." On March 3, 1925, the *Tog* countered with "Radio, Jazz and Bad Schnaaps Bring On Madness, Says Doctor."

The *Morgn Freiheit* called out the Memphis, Tennessee, musicians union (whom the writer derisively calls "klezmer") for not allowing the playing of jazz. In the February 1, 1922, issue of the *Forverts*, the writer responds to a recent church sermon that assailed the popularity of jazz by saying it would soon become the "national anthem of America." The writer wondered how this would affect the Jews:

> Just picture, an old Jew, a pants operator arrives to get his citizenship papers.
> "Do you know jazz?" asks the judge.
> "No, I had no time to go learn it," answers the little Jew in broken English. "I work long hours during the day."
> "Bad," and the judge bangs his gavel on the table. "Go home and have your children teach you jazz, or there is no way you will become an American."[9]

However, if jazz was a conflicted subject in the front of the newspaper, it was in the back with the display and classified ads that showed just how much the Jewish audiences craved it. One of the prime directives of *landsmanshaftn* (i.e., fraternal/social help organizations of Jews from the same Old Country region), was the celebration, perpetuation, and mutual support of social/cultural institutions/traditions related to their hometowns. One would then think that these expatriate Jewish groups, longing to hear their language with their own accent and dishes prepared the way they liked them, would also want to hear their own music too. So it is telling

Figure 17.1. Early 1920s ads for *landsmanshaftn*, who, when it came time to book dance music, chose jazz. *Source:* National Library of Israel, Historical Jewish Press website (www.jpress.org.il), founded by the National Library and Tel Aviv University. Used with permission.

that starting around 1921, the annual balls sponsored by the dozens of New York landsmanshaftn featured not old-time klezmer bands playing the latest songs from the Yiddish theater but jazz bands headed by a Slutsky, a Greenberg, or a Fogelman, or even a trio of competing professors (Prof. Schiller's Jazz Band, Prof. Schulman's Jazz Band, and Prof. Nodelman's Union Double Jazz Band).[10] As ubiquitous as were these groups (and a dozen more like them), we will never know what they sounded like as none recorded.

Joseph Cherniavsky

However, during that small but enthusiastic mid-1920s mini boom of Yiddish bands exploring "jazz," some did record, like Art Shryer's Modern Jewish Orchestra, which brought the "wah-wah" trumpet style to Yiddish music and Philadelphia's Harry Kandel (as Kandel's Jazz Orchestra). But the best known was Joseph Cherniavsky and his Hasidic American Jazz Band. The cello-playing Cherniavsky (1891–1955), who was descended from klezmer on both sides of his family, studied at the Petersburg Conservatory before becoming part of the Zimro Ensemble, a Soviet Yiddish art sextette. In 1919, the ensemble came to the US, when Cherniavsky jumped ship along with fellow member Simeon Bellison (who would go on to become first chair of the New York Philharmonic).[11]

In 1921, Cherniavsky penned a score for Maurice Schwartz's production of the *Dybbuk*. The jazz-tinged music proved so popular that the next year when Cherniavsky was hired by actor Boris Thomashefsky to compose music for several of his shows, the showman also spun off a vaudeville revue built around the band.

Dressed alternately as Hasidim or Cossacks, the orchestra was a true star-studded baker's dozen of the top Jewish musicians, including Cherniavsky's wife Lara on piano and the brilliant but volatile clarinetist-saxophonist Naftule Brandwein (whose offstage antics later caused his banishment from the group and replacement by young gun Dave Tarras). Also on clarinet and sax was Shloimke "Sam" Beckerman.[12]

Of the ten sides Cherniavsky recorded, nine were of his own *Dybbuk* compositions, but it was the tenth, "Oi Vey Titina," that gives the best idea of his conception of modern American music.[13] Written in 1917, the original French chanson "Je cherche après Titine" came across the Atlantic in the stage revue *Daniderf's Puzzles of 1925*. Renamed "Titina," it is perhaps

Figure 17.2. Joseph Cherniavsky's Hasidic American Jazz Band would perform in vaudeville either dressed as Cossacks or, as here, Hasidim, ca. 1923. *Source:* Author's collection.

best known when a dancing Charlie Chaplin sings nonsense lyrics to it in his first talking picture, *Modern Times* (1936).

Cherniavsky's clever and crisp 1925 arrangement opens with the bedrock favorite "Khusen, kale mazel tov" ("Congratulations Bride and Groom"), the ubiquitous Yiddish theater melody played upon the completion of the wedding ceremony, but here a sly fake out with the song's Yiddish lyrics that tell of a heartbroken swain. In a smoothly programmatic arrangement with pinpoint accuracy, Cherniavsky's nod to "jazz" contains all of poet Zishe Vaynper's instruments, with banjo and saxes in front, where, like any other modern dance orchestra, their propulsive qualities are harnessed and showcased. But when Dave Tarras's sax gets four clear measures, he plays it in straight Yiddish style, as if klezmer had been invented for it.

Cherniavsky's concept of "jazz" is not a structurally musical one but one that intuited the zeitgeist of jazz (i.e., modern, American). Outside of some superficial stylistic elements, his "jazz" was more about arrival and the well-being that comes with a secure sense of place (what the Yiddish *Bundists* would call *do'ekayt* ["hereness"]). But his lack of jazz structural literacy made no difference to Cherniavsky's audience or critics, who had no way of parsing the authenticity of his "jazz," never having experienced the real thing. In fact, for much of his audience, the stage Hasidim/Cossacks

Jews and Jazz | 199

the orchestra portrayed were as exotic as the jazz they played, as described by Cherniavsky's drummer, Joe Helfenbein: "We had a number—Jewish—a beautiful number, the lights got dim, everybody wore kapotes, peyes, I'd give a roll on the big tom-toms and the fiddle started, you know. We had another Jewish number, good, like a bulgar, then an English number. We opened up in the Manhattan Center and most of the Jews were there. They used to love it, they used to eat it up."[14] The press agreed: "They licked their fingers," was how a critic for the *Forverts* described the Cherniavsky audience. "They made such a racket, stamped their feet with repeated ovations. You'd have thought it was some world-famous musicians."[15]

Cherniavsky took a six-month victory lap up and down the East Coast (without his drummer, eighteen-year-old Helfenbein, whose mother wouldn't let him go). When he returned, it was as the orchestra director at the new, lavish Libby's Hotel and Baths, replete with a regular radio slot. For a brief moment, Cherniavsky floated weightlessly above the Jewish music world when a nod from Carl Laemmle at Universal Studios seemed to offer him a glittering Hollywood ending.

Cherniavsky first led the orchestra at a Universal-affiliated movie theater, then was swiftly kicked upstairs and given a five-year contract to lead the orchestra for Universal musicals and shipped out to Hollywood to make his first film.

In the panicked post–*Jazz Singer* upheaval, "All talking, all singing" became a chimeric mantra of movie studios. And Universal, having just licensed the sophisticated Movietone sound on film system, needed its own *Jazz Singer*, so it secured the film rights to Edna Ferber's *Show Boat*, which was then breaking all records on Broadway.[16]

However, the shooting script, developed by producer Carl Laemmle Jr., was derived from the *Show Boat* book, not the show, and so made no place for the music of Jerome Kern and lyrics of Oscar Hammerstein and P. G. Wodehouse. So now Universal needed new music, and plenty of it.[17] In a way, Cherniavksy was a good choice for this thankless and hopeless task. Because of his brush with African American music and support of jazz, Cherniavksy was enthusiastic about having Black singing voices in film.[18] And while it was no "Can't Help Lovin' Dat Man," Cherniavsky even produced a romantic ballad, "Love Sings a Song in My Heart" (with lyrics by Clarence J. Marks), which would, for a time, be a member of the *Great American Songbook*. After messy and costly negotiations with Ziegfeld, Universal finally got the rights to use several of the best known songs as part of a now partially lost prelude. Directed by Will Vodery, Florenz Ziegfeld's African American arranger, it featured all the original stage stars, including Jules Bledsoe and chorus singing "Old Man River."

Despite Universal's *Show Boat* scoring good reviews and nice houses, it was not their predicted blockbuster and considered a financial studio disaster. And, as such, somebody's head had to roll. So, on September 29—just one year into a five-year contract, and already at work on a half dozen new film scores—Joseph Cherniavsky was now reported in the trade press "considering an offer to head the musical department of another studio."[19]

Cherniavsky's banishment from Hollywood led to a slow downward spiral, conducting second string orchestras at lightly frowsy hotels or serving as music director at lower-wattage radio stations in Chicago (1935), Cincinnati (1940), and New York (1953). He finally moved to Saginaw, Michigan, where he worked as the music director of the City Recreation Department until he died in 1959.[20]

The first tangible transition from "Jewish" to "jazz" happened with the unprecedented rebirth of the 1933 Yiddish theater love song "Bei mir bistu sheyn" and its 1938 crossover success.

Jewish Melodies in Jazztime

While there was a longstanding tradition of mainstream and art performance covers of "Kol Nidre" and "Eli, Eli," none of these songs crossed over to take on lives of their own quite like "Bei mir bistu sheyn." It was additionally unusual to have music from a long-closed show flame back into life years later as a major hit for a brand new record label (Decca) by brand new performers (the Andrews Sisters) in a new language. Yet when it first came out, the song was nothing special. Period reviews in the Yiddish press did not mention the song any more than any of the dozen other Sholom Secunda/Jacob Jacobs offerings in the show.

One of the ad nauseum tales of the Yiddish theater was of Sholom Secunda selling the rights to "Bei mir bistu sheyn" for $30, a sadly normal transaction for music to a show that has just closed.[21] Now rechristened the Teutonic "Bei mir bistu sheyn," with new words by Saul Chaplin and Sammy Cahn, its sudden success even surprised Decca, sending the production team back to the moribund Yiddish theater catalog to revive other long in the tooth, one-time hits like Nellie Casman and Joseph Steinberg's

1922 classic "Yosl, Yosl," refitted for the Andrews Sisters as "Joseph, Joseph." Now, a full-fledged "there's gold in them thar Goldbergs" rush for the next Jewish crossover hit produced songs like Benny Goodman's "My Little Cousin" (from Abe Schwartz's 1922 "Grine kuzine"), Al Jolson's reworking of Alexander Olshanetsky's "Mayn shtetele belz" as "That Wonderful Girl of Mine," and Xavier Cugat's "Wedding Samba" (remade from Abe Ellstein's "Der nayer sher").[22]

However, the record that most bridged what had until then been an unbreachable chasm between Yiddish music that sounded like jazz and vice versa was not drawn from Yiddish popular music but from old-time klezmer music. On December 29, 1938, trumpet player Harry "Ziggy Elman" Finkelman brought seven of his Benny Goodman bandmates to his first session at the RCA budget label Bluebird. Elman did not choose from a catalog of music he had played since joining Goodman in 1936 but instead reached back to his Philadelphia childhood to reimagine two standards from the deep Jewish bandstand. One was "Bublitchki," popular in Yiddish as "Beigelakh" ("Little Bagels") and featured Elman's Jewish ornamented trumpet dancing above the smooth-tempoed swing fox trot, opening and closing with a vest-pocket *doina*, its surefire klezmer signifier.[23]

The flip side was "And the Angels Sing," which, though Elman claimed composer credit, was actually the workhorse klezmer tune "Der Shtiller Bulgar" ("The Quiet Bulgar"). It had competing recorded versions going back to 1917 by Abe Schwartz and Harry Kandel (the Philly-born Elman may have even learned it from the playing of the local Kandel). "And the Angels Sing" is arranged as a triptych. In the first section, in a fox trot tempo slightly brighter than "Bublitchki," Elman plays the major key melody clearly, neither jazzy nor Jewish, a pleasant yet not particularly distinguished dance tune. The drums announce the change from a swing tempo to the syncopated, traditional eight beat *bulgar* backbeat of three-three-two, over which Elman launches into a high-octane reading of the melody that, now placed within its original klezmer dance band context, explodes outward. Elman's clipped and precise notes with their vocal-like ornaments drive the melody on the downbeats, landing like the dancer's feet for whom it was originally intended. Yet it's when the tempo slows for the final third section that "And the Angels Sing" really takes off. With the melody carried by the reeds and horns, Elman swoops high above them, now ignoring the downbeats, his screaming, high-register jazz improvisation a statement of arrival with its ineffable sense of easy, unashamed, and unquestioned ownership of both jazz and Jewish: its true biculturality.

Both pieces enjoyed their own afterlives with the big Goodman orchestra: "Bublitchki" as an instrumental, and "Freilach in Swing: And the Angels Sing" with words by Johnny Mercer and sung by Martha Tilton. Goodman featured it with his big band on the big label (RCA Victor), where it commanded the top of the charts.[24] Ellman's arrangement, cleverly combining and alternating klezmer and swing harmonizations, found its own reprise when he joined Mickey Katz's band, where it became the template standard Katz arrangement.

The collective result of the Andrews' hits and the Ellman disc came in 1939 in the form of a radio show called *Yiddish Melodies in Swing*, which, as the title implies, attempted to plug into this almost unheard-of interest in Jewish music by mainstream audiences. Pianist-arranger Sam Medoff was the musical director of the show that station WHN, part of the Loew's system, broadcast from the chain's 3,200-seat State Theater in midtown Manhattan. Although the trade reviews were ghastly ("There's little in the half hour of professional caliber"[25]), the weekly cast settled down to sisters Claire and Merna Bagelman (here called "Pert" and "Gaye"—the Jewish answer to the Andrews Sisters), tenor Jan Bart, and David Medoff, leading an orchestra whose highlight was the most popular klezmer clarinetist of the day, Dave Tarras. However, Tarras could not—nor ever did learn how to—play jazz, so Medoff created solid swing orchestrations of popular and Yiddish folk songs during which Tarras sat out or played fills (in the first or A section), leaving him thirty-two measures in the middle to play a breathtaking klezmer-style solo (B) before returning to swing closing (A). Despite shrinking it from a twelve-piece orchestra playing an hour and broadcasting from a 3,200-seat auditorium to a quintet playing fifteen minutes in a small studio, Manischewitz Matzos continued to sponsor the show on WHN into the mid-1950s, long after both swing and Yiddish had any marquee value.[26]

The Year of Jewish Jazz Hybrids

In rapid succession during 1962, three LPs by three drummers-percussionists using jazz to interpret Jewish music were all released. But despite the similar concept, the recordings could not be more different. The title of Shelly Manne's *My Son the Jazz Drummer!* (Contemporary, 1962) is a gag riff on the recent hit LP by Jewish parodist Allan (*My Son, the Folksinger*) Sherman, but whose subtitle (*Modern Jazz Versions of Jewish and Israeli Songs*) is not a gag. The LP is a serious ingathering of great contemporary jazz musicians playing industrial-strength modern jazz arrangements of Yiddish and Israeli tunes.

Manne's family were Jewish and musicians, but were not "Jewish musicians," so his record lacks any intuitive Jewish musical center from which to depart. And while there are moments that nearly align the disparate musics (Al Viola's guitar on "Mayn Yiddishe Mame" faintly echoes a mandolin), the arrangements by Lennie Niehaus, who had previously written for Stan Kenton, mainly consisted of numbers like the theme to the film *Exodus* played as a bossa nova. The liner notes, while discursive and seemingly extensive, don't mention how thousands of years of Jewish music heritage are here served by a quintet of unquestionably great musicians who, until this recording session, had apparently never before played Jewish music. The record garnered reviews ranging from "This could have been a schnorr of an album" to acknowledging its Los Angeles provenance as "More Hermosa Beach than Red Sea."[27]

The second record was made by music store owner-klezmer trumpet player Shimele Blank's son, Manny. When *Manny Blanc Plays Jewish Jazz* was made, Blanc, who swapped the C into his last name, was transitioning from a life as a musician-arranger to that of an abstract painter, bringing the same challenging and jagged techniques to vinyl that he was bringing to canvas.[28] While more original source music survives in Blanc's farewell music project, this album was primarily a showcase for his skills as novelty arranger: old klezmer tunes played on an assortment of aggressively anachronistic instruments (marimba, electric guitar, duck call, bass clarinet, etc.), with them all given cranky food titles ("Jazzy Borscht," "Matzo Ball Bounce," and "Heartburn Heartburn Heartburn"). Although Blanc brought aboard klezmer clarinet giant Sammy Musiker, he is ultimately buried and isolated in the potpourri arrangements and in the final mix. Blanc's music is currently getting second attention thanks to clarinetist Matt Darriau, who has been presenting in concert his interpretations of the Blanc arrangements.[29]

But of the three LPs, the "Goldilocks third" (i.e., "just right") is *Terry Gibbs Plays Jewish Melodies in Jazztime*. Gibbs (b. 1924, Julius Gubenko)—whose stage first name was his homage to a local boxing idol, while his last name was the result of an inhospitable marquee that would not fit all of "Gubenko"—was born in Brooklyn. His father, fiddler Abe Gubenko (1880–1976), was born in Ekaterinoslav, Ukraine, and came to the US in 1922. He and his three younger brothers all played music. By

Figure 17.3. Klezmer fiddler Abe Gubenko's son, vibraphonist Terry Gibbs, would have a profound effect on postwar jazz. *Source:* Author.

the early 1930s, the elder Gubenko led a variety of bands (Abe Gubenko's Radio Novelty Orchestra, the Abe Gubenko Little Symphony Orchestra, and Gubenko's Balalaika Serenaders) playing weddings, banquets, and on radio. When his son Julius was seven, Abe Gubenko brought him into his ensemble on drums and xylophone, which were taught to him by his older brother, Sol.

Two 1936 Gibbs radio broadcasts (both of which have astoundingly survived) offer a perspective on the quantum leap from Julius Gubkeno to "Terry Gibbs." One was a regular slot-playing old-time klezmer tunes on low-power Brooklyn station WCNW with his father on fiddle and possibly clarinetist Max Epstein, while the other was his blazing forty-five-second xylophone solo of Monti's "Czardas" on the nationally syndicated NBC show *Major Bowes Amateur Hour*, which brought him the championship and a national tour. The young Gibbs then joined several big bands (notably those led by Buddy Rich and Woody Herman).[30] It was while Gibbs rode the crest of his modern jazz fame (he had been recently voted best jazz vibes player in polls in *Downbeat* and *Metronome* magazines) that he too conceived a Jewish jazz album inspired by a spate of LPs devoted to popular music played in Latin style. Gibbs convinced his label, Mercury, to allow him to cut *Terry Gibbs Plays Jewish Melodies in Jazztime*, along with longtime producer the late Quincy Jones, who famously showed up on the first day of recording wearing a yarmulka.[31]

Unlike the Manne record (which Gibbs likes very much, and not just because they were Woody Herman Second Herd alums from the late '40s), Gibbs's Jewish music would not be buried under an Orthodox modern jazz arrangement any more than it would be under goofy novelty orchestrations as on the Blanc album. What set the Gibbs project apart was his judicious creation of a fusion band whose core players included Yiddish music veterans clarinetist Ray Musiker (brother of Sammy) and Sammy Kutcher on trombone, wisely securing the ensemble's important top and middle layers to create a discernable and fundamental Jewish dance band sound. The rest of the band were deep-dish jazz players such as pianist Alice McLeod, for whom this was both her first recording date and her first time playing Jewish modal music. Thanks to Gibbs's intervention as a *shadkhn* (matchmaker), McLeod would soon be better known as Alice Coltrane.[32]

Given this collection of musicians, Gibbs did not use one music to disassemble and obscure the other. Like Sam Medoff did for *Yiddish Melodies in Swing*, Gibbs created a transparent sonic environment where the essential presence of both musics was accessible and that at no point let you forget you are listening to a jazz record—and a Jewish one. But, of course, when Gibbs played the finished the LP for his mother (herself a musician), she said, "I like it, but there's not enough Jewish."[33]

What is perhaps most amazing is that despite both Gibbs and Manny Blanc being contemporaneous drum-playing children of professional klezmorim in New York City, and despite both spending time in the Tommy Dorsey orchestra, and despite both coming out with Jewish jazz records at the same time using one each of the famed Musiker brothers—Terry Gibbs did not know, or had even ever heard of, Manny Blanc.[34]

18

Sam Ash and Shimele Blank

Two Music Stores

Shimele Blank

The scion of what would become the American branch of the Blank family was Yankl Shimen "Shimele" Blankleder. Born in 1889 in eastern Lomazy, Lubelskie, Poland, Shimen was already a professional musician when he came to the United States in 1907. By 1920, he was Samuel Blank, a musician, music teacher, and dealer in musical instruments.[1] By 1925, Blank moved into his longtime store at 190 East Second Street, when the neighborhood was still the epicenter of New York's professional Jewish musicians. It was just a few blocks east of the big theaters, restaurants and catering halls, and nightclubs that all offered live music. Blank's store was not only selling and repairing instruments but would serve as a kind of "union floor" where musicians would stop by to find out about a call for jobs.[2]

Shimele Blank's store even figures into the creation myth about the great Jewish crossover hit "Bei mir bistu sheyn" by its English lyricist Sammy Cahn. In his memoir, Cahn tried to convince Tommy Dorsey about the potential of a "Bei mir bistu sheyn" co-lyricist English version after having just heard the Yiddish original performed by the Black duo Johnnie and George in Harlem:

> He stared at me and he kept saying: "You're out of your God-damn mind."

I couldn't convince him.

On Second Avenue there used to be a little music store, the kind where you saw dozens of instruments hanging in the window. It was called S. Blank, Shimele Blank. This man came from a whole family of musicians. As a matter of fact, his claim to fame was that his nephew was the trombonist who used to make the trombone laugh. When Ted Lewis would ask "Is everybody happy?" Shimele Blank's nephew's trombone would go "Wah-wah-wah!"

So, I walked into this music store, and I asked: "Do you have a copy of a song called 'Bei Mir Bist Du Schön' [sic]?"

He said "Sure" and I bought the copy for 35 cents.

Now I take this copy and I go back to Dorsey. You know me—relentless. He throws me out and the copy out. He couldn't comprehend why I would want him to do this Jewish song.[3]

Figure 18.1. Trumpet player and music store owner Shimele Blank's self-published "Doina," 1922. *Source:* Author's collection.

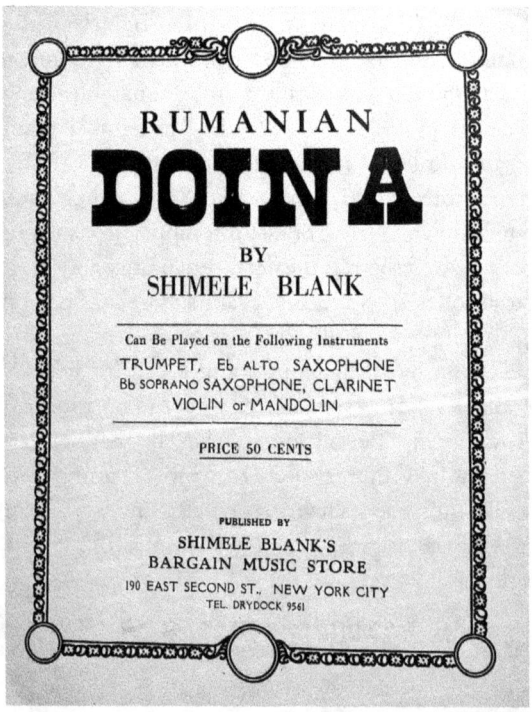

While Shimele continued to play Jewish jobs and even publish some of his own compositions on the Blank's Bargain Music Store imprint, his sons, while having played their share of weddings, navigated outward. By the age of nineteen, Menashe "Manny" (1914–1984) fronted his own American dance band. In 1940 (now spelling his name Blanc), he was recruited for the Army's 186 Field Artillery Band, a unit created to attract former members of professional big bands. (Blanc appears to have played with the Tommy Dorsey Orchestra, though he did not record with them.)[4] Manny's slightly younger trumpet-playing brother, Morris "Murray" (1916–1992), also had his own little mainstream dance band when in 1944 he was hired by the comic novelty orchestra of trombonist Walter "Mousy" Powell. Not only was Murray a good musician (reviews note his excellent upper register command, a talent he shared with his father, an uncommon brass skill in that performance era), but the funny Blank also weighed 350 pounds and played off it as "Blimpy." A critic noted: "Murray Blank, the 'Fat Boy,' who plays the trumpet holds much of the spotlight being a natural born comic."[5]

In 1943, when Manny returned from the service, he too joined Mousie Powell's low-rent Spike Jones act. The brothers recorded several "soundies" (short films played on a jukebox-like machine), some of which ("I Like Mountain Music," "Slap Happy," etc.) featured Murray on vocals and trumpet solo.[6] Mousie's band also featured the song "I Was Only a Sailor's Sweetheart" sung by Manny dressed as Shirley Temple in a blond wig. The act went over so well it became Manny's featured stooge and drag act.

After leaving Powell, Manny stayed a music arranger, and for a while even opened a competing music store cheek by jowl to his father and brother. Haranguing customers from their doorways, loudly cajoling them with offers of better bargains and predicting dire consequences if they patronized the other, the Blank/Blanc brothers effectively chased away as much business as they generated. Manny left the business; Murray stayed.[7] In the late 1950s, while recovering from an injury, Manny was given a painting set, which changed his life. After studying with Charles Seide at the art school of the Brooklyn Museum, Blanc subsequently became a minor noted abstract painter, among whose subjects, not surprisingly, were musicians.[8]

The last nightclub at which Murray played with Mousey Powell was owned by comedian-cellist Morey Amsterdam. Later, when the DuMont television network offered Amsterdam a regular weekly comedy/variety show, he invited Manny—in all his high-pitched screaming trumpet, little girl dresses, blond wig, and cigar-chomping corpulent comic overabundance—to be in the featured cast. The premise of the show, about a second-rate nightclub struggling to stay open, unfortunately mirrored the series, which was canceled at the end of the year. While Morey Amsterdam would later gain fame as the wise-cracking comedy writer Buddy Sorrell on TVs *The Dick Van Dyke Show*, Amsterdam's other DuMont co-star, Art Carney, was luckier quicker, transitioning to Jackie Gleason's *Cavalcade of Stars* en route to his role as "Ed Norton" in *The Honeymooners*. Blimpy, however, wasn't that lucky. The time for novelty bands had passed, and the last reviewers noted that he continued to "contribute gags that have outlived their time." The gags—and the gigs—ran out by the end of the year.[9]

Murray retreated to Blank's Bargain Music Store, whose own irrelevance was in full swing: an old Jewish business in a neighborhood of junkies. In a musical twist on a Yiddish curse, Blank was selling fiddles and clarinets when everyone was buying guitars and drums. Tragically, the neighborhood caught up with Shimele: in 1971, he died of wounds received when resisting a robber who turned on him when he gave chase.

Yet Murray remained. A onetime neighbor recalled, "When we moved here in 1977, the Lower East Side was rife with junkies and heroin. An unusual outpost was the music store run by Murray 'Blimpy' Blank, his wife Sylvia and their glacially moving poorly named geriatric, arthritic shepherd named 'Fleet.' Murray was a trip; extremely rotund . . . he told tales of riding the trains in Russia at the age of 13, sleeping between the cars and hustling tips by singing and playing the trumpet."[10] Another memoir from a decade later involved pianist Pete Sokolow, an acquaintance of Murray's:

> Among all this chaos and decay was Blank's. Barely able to see the storefront beneath the spray-painted graffiti on its gates, we went in. Upon entering the stuffy, cramped store my eye immediately fell upon a framed picture near the counter. A child's drawing, it showed the outside of Blank's store, but instead of the grim post-apocalyptic scene that existed, it was now a large, airy house, surrounded by trees, grass and a smiley face sun—a sad and ironic image given the reality.
>
> Then there was Blank himself. Old and tired, he still proffered clear explanation of his well-worn nickname: Blimpy was enormously fat.
>
> The store's shelves were a farrago of broken fiddles, fraying violin bows and empty instrument cases covered in Eisenhower-era dust. While Pete rummaged around trying to find enough clarinet parts to make a single workable instrument, he asked

Blank how he managed to stay in business. For some reason, Blank told us, the local junkies and other detritus took a liking to him and protected his store. It was true. Unaccustomed to seeing customers when we were there, Blank's "neighbors" would periodically poke their heads in and ask, "Everything okay, Mr. Blimpy?" It was obvious someone was looking out for him; his was the only sign of retail life in this downtown lunar landscape.[11]

Murray Blank died in 1992.

Sam Ash

Like Yonah Schimmel, his knish corollary, most people only know the name Sam Ash from ubiquitous advertising and, not as a flesh-and-blood person. Sam Ash was born Shmuel Ashkynasye (1897–1956) in Yanov (now Yaniv), Ukraine, and came to the United States with his parents in 1910. Ashkynasye worked in the needle trades as a fabric cutter until around 1918, but he preferred fiddle playing, which he learned in childhood and soon started moonlighting in small wedding bands.[12] In 1924, Ashkynasye made three important decisions: he married Rose Dinin (who would eventually run the store), applied for citizenship, and joined American Federation of Musicians Local 802, to whom he continued to pay dues long after he stopped performing music. Ashkenasye also changed his name to Sam Ash, a curious choice as it was concurrently the name of a popular musical comedy tenor and—even more confusingly—a prolific recording violinist.

Ash's transition from sideman to leader at the modest Brooklyn catering hall the Hopkinson Manor meant that he now picked the musicians. One of the newcomers he hired—and one with whom he would enjoy a lifelong friendship—was clarinetist Dave Tarras. Ash saw himself in Tarras, from when he too was desperate to escape the needle trades. Tarras impressed Ash on the bandstand, but it was during a break, when he picked up and flawlessly played Ash's fiddle, that he said to Tarras in Yiddish: "Young man, you work in a shop? Why not do what I do? Give lessons; make Mischa Elmans of little Jewish boys . . . I teach the boy for a year, the mother says the teacher is no good, I say that the boy is not talented. She gets another teacher and I get another sucker."[13]

By 1924, Rose Ash parlayed the income from her husband's teaching (and some from pawning her wedding ring, which she got back) into their

Figure 18.2. Sam Ash's original Brooklyn store opened in 1924, with the franchise closing a century later. *Source:* 1940 Tax Photograph Collection, NYC Municipal Archives. Used with permission.

eponymous store at 410 Saratoga Avenue on the corner of Park Place. By focusing on children's lessons, Ash consolidated a connection with the New York Board of Education, renting and servicing instruments and providing music scores for school bands and orchestras, a vital unbroken income stream. But Ash continued playing with his little Club Society Orchestra, mostly at ethnic parties usually held in someone's home:

> "Once they put us in the kitchen of a three-room apartment," he said grinning. "We were jammed near the stove, and sweating rivers. Waiters were trying to carry trays of food out, and every now and then soup would flop into the sax and a pickle would bounce on my violin strings! Then, a tray of soup fell all over

one of my players, and the waiter, an excitable guy, yelled, 'I'm going to sue you, I burned my pinky!' "[14]

Ash was thus able to withstand the Depression and by 1949 exchanged his rental store for even larger newly purchased quarters a few blocks west at 242 Utica Avenue. Unlike Blimpy Blank, Ash, thanks to his sons Jerry and Paul, understood the influence of rock and roll and added guitars to his store inventory. He even created a record department, which at one time accounted for half of the store's revenues. But Ash, while never a great musician, still preferred playing fiddle to tending the store and resisted all efforts to expand.[15]

After Ash's death in 1956, his sons embarked on a policy of growth and expansion: in addition to opening another Brooklyn store on Coney Island Avenue and Kings Highway, they opened several branches on Long Island, which turned out to be even bigger money makers.

It was their 1969 move to West Forty-Eighth Street's illustrious "Music Row" that gave Sam Ash "city" street cred and propelled it to international prominence, eventually opening over forty national locations. By 2010, Music Row had ceased being a destination, and the store moved to Thirty-Forth Street, where it lasted four years before Sam Ash declared bankruptcy, closing after a century.[16]

19

*Khaznte*s

Women Cantors of the Stage

One of the most unique performance traditions to come out of Yiddish American popular entertainment were the *khazntes*. The term's original meaning was simply "wife of the cantor," just as *rebetzin* was the "wife of the rabbi." But its transformation into a nearly half-century phenomenon of women mastering *khazones*, the difficult and venerated synagogue liturgy ordinarily sung solely by men, is an American, and primarily New York, one.[1]

The word gained significant popular visibility thanks to Yiddish composer Joseph Rumshinsky's 1918 stage hit *Di khaznte* about a free-spirited cantor's wife. One reviewer prophetically noted star Regina Prager's signature performance (where a key aria, in which she reminisces about her late cantor husband, has her sing extended sections of bedrock cantorial performances): "If last season's hit show *Di khaznte* proved anything was that if you took what was a traditional *khaznte*, gave her a voice and set her centerstage as did Rumshinsky, young and old would run to hear her sing."[2]

The khaznte emerged in an era that venerated great singing and great voices, such as prolific recording *khazonim* Yossele Rosenblatt and Gershon Sirota. The khazntes not only perfected and internalized the *khazonish* repertoire and style but also took to donning its accoutrements (*rase* [robe], yarmulke, tallis) and even using the time-honored honorific of referring to a cantor with a diminutive endearment of their first name (Yossele, Berele, Chatskele, etc.) in the form of Freidele, Sheindele, and Breindele. The khazntes who took on the repertoire and style of the male khazonim all shared similar alto voices, whose pitch was reminiscent of an adolescent *meshoyrer* (choir boy), and so quite familiar and not as shocking.

The khazntes were not, however, revolutionaries attempting to redress the received Orthodox gender-religious arrangement, to shatter the sonic *mekhitze* (separation) between the men's and women's section that kept them from performing this music in its proper place and time. Jewish religious and educational outlets only took notice of khazntes to treat them with dismissive disdain, as did cantorial composer and professor at the Jewish Theological Seminary Max Wohlberg in a speech in 1951: "A variety show is on its way to Broadway wherein an actress dons a cap and talis and intones prayers from our sacred service. . . . It is also high time to put a stop to the shameful phenomenon, the so-called professional 'hazzente.'"[3]

Despite no official recognition, the popularity of khazntes rose thanks to the explosions of variety/vaudeville in both the Jewish and Gentile worlds, with concerts in the synagogue/Jewish community, Jewish resorts, records, and radio.

By the mid-1950s khazntes had become far more common in Jewish community programming, not only in New York (with performers like Perele Feig, Evelyn Selniker, Ruchele Finkle, Rosa Krauss, etc.) but radiating outside the Northeast (southern California's Malkeleh and Mirele Friedman in Milwaukee, among others).[4]

The khaznte phenomenon nearly lasted until the Jewish sacred world finally discovered what the Jewish secular world had long known and offered ordination to women cantors: first in 1975 to Barbara Jean Ostfeld through the Reform Hebrew Union College-Jewish Institute of Religion, and then in 1987 to Erica Lippitz and Marla Rosenfeld Barugel through the Jewish Theological Seminary of the Conservative Synagogue.[5]

However, this coincided with the disappearance of the dominant prewar Ashkenazic cantillation styles in modern American congregations. The old repertoire and sound was being replaced by more "sing-along" melodies of Shlomo Carlebach, whose folkie bona fides found him featured, alongside Bob Dylan, Joan Baez, Pete Seeger, and many other icons, in the seminal 1968 book *The Face of Folk Music*.[6] The ripples of the folk singer-songwriter tradition led to the next generation: composer Debbie Friedman, who more than anyone has come to be "the de facto norm of the synagogue sound."[7] Women now make up a commanding percentage of the cantorial practitioners of contemporary Reform and Conservative congregations, yet do not celebrate the "founding mother" khazntes as icons for having blazed the trail of women singing liturgical music.

There are whisps of evidence that the earliest days of the twentieth century saw women already as khazntes. (A Feb. 20, 1916, Brooklyn concert ad lists "cantorial melodies from the renowned *khaznte*, Miss Rabinowitz."[8]) But the first woman to properly exploit this new American tradition only first arrived in 1917: Madame Sophie Kurtzer.

Madame Sophie Kurtzer (1897–1973)

Sophie Kurtzer was born Khaye Sore Kanefsky in Poltava, Ukraine, four hundred miles northeast of Odessa, to a long line of *khazonim*. She and her younger brother Yossele were the fourth generation of singers, and Yossele's daughter, Bernice, as Bas Sheva, would be the last.[9] To come to America, the family followed a circuitous concert/emigration route through Europe to Palestine; Alexandria, Egypt; and finally to Piraeus, Greece, from where the Kanefskys sailed to America in 1915. In 1917, Kanefsky married part-time *khazn* Aaron "Arnold" Kurtzer, the newlyweds settling for a time in Rhode Island before coming to New York.

Figure 19.1. Madame Sophie Kurtzer (*left*) and her mother, ca. 1920. *Source:* Author's collection.

By 1920, Khaye Sore Kanefsky Kurtzer emerged as "Madame Sophia Kurtzer: the Odesser Khaznte" and "the Only Woman Cantor in the World"—this last title to be claimed by all subsequent khazntes.[10] Kurtzer's rollout wasn't in a synagogue, the Yiddish theater, or even a Jewish forum but at New York's prestigious Great Hall of Cooper Union on December 13, 1920, accompanied by a twenty-seven-voice mixed choir. Kurtzer's arrival was heightened by running "open letters" in Yiddish newspapers:

> To the Women of New York and everywhere and to the men, too . . .
>
> I appeal to the women of New York—who all know that when it comes to the physical and the spiritual, women do things better than men . . . come to the concert and bring their husbands because if their husband is an expert on *khazones* (and whose isn't?) they will have to agree that they have never before heard anything like this . . . come with your husbands, let them be convinced that women can attain the highest level in everything.[11]

Another endorsement also encouraged women to attend: "If you are a fan of heart, soul and great feeling, even more than in a man. In fact, women: bring your men and see if they themselves don't agree that no male cantor has this kind of sweet, deeply felt and heavenly tinged singing . . . women should say a '*shehekhiyonu*' (prayer of gratitude) that they live in a day of such a woman cantor."[12] Yet, despite the suffragist/feminist tone, Kurtzer offered a curious bifurcated profile: on the one hand, she was traditionally religious and the concerts she gave (many with her brother, Yossele) were for philanthropic, charity, or religious groups. In one 1920 ad, she reaches to "societies" (*landsmanshaftn*) who were collecting money for those still suffering the effects of the war and the ongoing postwar anti-Jewish violence.[13] But despite her adherence to the Orthodox world, Kurtzer actively pursued a career, hiring a manager and forming a booking agency, with her "act" listing in the bible of vaudeville, *Variety*.[14]

At an April 1921 concert outside of Chicago, Kurtzer learned shortly before going onstage that the local promoter had absconded with the gate receipts and the crowd of two thousand was getting unruly. Kurtzer (who was owed $500—$7,000 today) eventually agreed to continue with some of her performance to quell the crowd, during which time, the promoter was caught (with all the cash) attempting to board a westbound train.[15]

Kurtzer's reputation now grew through the Yiddish theater world. In January 1922, B. Kovner (born Jacob Adler)—author of the wildly popular *Yente Telebende* newspaper series that was currently a major stage hit—wrote and starred in *Shayke fin bronzvil* (*Shayke from Brownsville*), a comedy-drama that asked the question "Does a wife have the right to take part in a man's business?" Kovner's unequivocal answer at the play's end was for the curtain to part, revealing Kurtzer and a twenty-voice choir singing "Hallelujah" and bringing the house to its feet. *Yiddishes Togesblatt* theater reviewer Z. Rubinzohn (who also wrote about Black cantors) suggested the managers get structural engineers to examine the theater after the audience's tumultuous response.[16]

In 1924–1925, Sophie Kurtzer recorded for Pathé, whose Jewish roster was like its recording quality: small. Pathé's thin, narrow sonics did not suit singers such as Kurtzer, whom reviews noted for a sweet yet powerful sound. It's also a shame that her records, like most cantorial 78s, used an ahistorical instrumental accompaniment—despite one session being led by the legendary klezmer Israel J. Hochman—and not her regularly advertised mixed-voice choir.

Kurtzer's cache of recordings comprise a concise practical toolkit of a working khazn: some High Holidays prayers, some prayers for Shabbos, and an industrial-strength kiddush for wine. Kurtzer's performances are solid and centered, with phrasing both elegant and knowing. Her mastery of tone production is such that on "Kiddush," it is only at the two-minute-plus mark, when Kurtzer goes to a falsetto, that we hear that it is a woman, a reveal that continues to amaze listeners to this day.

Kurzter stopped performing in 1926 to raise a family (in the 1920, 1925, and 1930 census—the first two during the height of her performing popularity—she listed herself either with "no profession" or as a "housewife"). Sophie Kurtzer died in 1976. Her headstone reads:

> Our dear mother, modest in her ways
> And glorified in her actions
> cherishes her wealth to give to the poor
> She devoted herself to raising and cherishing her children.[17]

Despite a vigorous 1950s and 1960s whirlwind of cantorial LP reissues, no women cantors were included. Kurtzer had to wait until my 1994 Yazoo anthology *Mysteries of the Sabbath* to become both the first khaznte to record and the first khaznte to be reissued.[18] Kurtzer would again make history the following year as the first khaznte whose performance would be replicated as part of the Yiddish/klezmer revival as a track sung by the late Adrienne Cooper on the 1995 Kapelye CD *On the Air*.[19]

Bas Sheva (Bernice Kanefsky 1926–1960)

The daughter of Sophie Kurtzer's older brother, Cantor Yossele Kanefsky, Bernice was born in Brooklyn in 1929, moving several times as her father changed congregations to Philadelphia and then to the Boston area. In 1943, Bernice made her performing debut with her father, using her Jewish name, Bas Sheva.[20] Over the next few years father and daughter gave live and radio concerts throughout New England, returning to New York in 1946.

Bas Sheva, as her aunt Sophie Kurtzer had done before her, appeared as the *ekstra etrekshn* between the acts in a string of Yiddish plays: *Ir ershte libe* (*Her First Love*) playing at Brooklyn's Parkway Theater, followed by *Vik-end* (*Weekend*) at Manhattan's National Theater, and in Chaim Tauber's melodramatic *Motl der opreyter* (*Motl the Sewing Machine Operator*), all in which she sang both khazones and Yiddish songs.[21]

The year 1950 was a peak for Bas Sheva, as she co-starred in the kitschy, catchy Yiddish musical film *Catskill Honeymoon* with Julius Adler, Jan Bart, and the Feder sisters, among others. The movie, which garnered some surprisingly nice reviews in the mainstream press, became a hit not only in the dwindling live stage show and Yiddish movie theaters but also at Catskills hotel movie nights screened by itinerant projectionists.[22]

In addition, Bas Sheva came into the orbit of Jewish American star Mickey Katz and his annual *Borscht Capades* revue. Started in 1948 in Los Angeles, the Yiddish-ish music and comedy revue started touring nationally when Bas Sheva was hired in 1950 (she appeared in the revue and its offshoots until 1959).[23] During 1951–1952, Bas Sheva took a brief break as lounge singer Beth Hunter ("the nation's most talked about singing discovery") and sang at Miami Beach's Copa City as part of a comedy act with the Ritz Brothers.[24]

Bas Sheva on Record

In 1953, Bas Sheva was signed to an extended contract with Capitol Records at the insistence of Mickey Katz, who had recently come to the label from RCA Victor. Bas Sheva's first issue was a 45 featuring a curious semi-Semitic arrangement of Duke Ellington's "Caravan" and "My Mother's Lullaby," a dependably derivative "My Yiddishe Mame."[1]

---

1. "Popular Records," *Kansas City Star*, Apr. 5, 1953, 97.

Record labels, when introducing new playback or recording formats, did not risk using a star artist and so would usually feature an offbeat or upcoming performer in a work created specifically to showcase the new format. So Capitol's January 1954 rollout for its new "Full Dimensional Sound Hi-Fi" LPs featured Bas Sheva in perhaps her best-known recording: *The Passions*, composed and conducted by Les Baxter. Baxter, who had previously discovered and developed Yma Sumac, was probably grooming Bas Sheva as Sumac's replacement, right down to the unusual singing style and offbeat stage name.[2] His suite of wordless songs about despair, ecstasy, hate, lust, terror, jealousy, and joy interpreted by Bas Sheva's grunts, moans, cackles, growls, and shrieks, got the same kind of reviews. One critic for Dayton Ohio's *Daily News* rhapsodized, "Bas Sheva is the vocalist who contrives to set your hair on end. Here is a voice with seemingly limitless scope. And an amazingly fine musician she must be too to make such a fine recording."[3] However, another reviewer at the *Ft. Worth Star-Telegram* curtly described her singing as "positively terrifying in primordial abandon."[4] Capitol had her drop another 45 in yet another direction: two Roaring Twenties pop songs—Rudy Vallee's "Deep Night" and Al Jolson's "Rock a Bye Your Baby with a Dixie Melody." Unlike the mixed reviews of *The Passions*, this got only bad ones.[5]

With the fourth time seemingly being the charm, Capitol released her cantorial debut *Soul of a People* in the spring of 1954. While burdened with overbearing theatrical orchestrations by Harold Mooney, and anonymous liner notes that maddeningly only refer to cantors as "he," Bas Sheva's LP included arrangements by her father and piano scores by her husband, Al Houseman. The record received uniformly good reviews. (*Variety*, in its classical Longhair Disc Reviews, gave it a thumbs-up: "A cantor's daughter in rich, expressive synagog [sic] chants; some gay but most sad and filled with longing.") This, however, would be her last recording.[6]

---

2. *Variety*, Jan. 12, 1954, 46.
3. Betty A. Dietz, "Study in Sounds Test Hi-Fi Sets and Ears, too," *Dayton Daily News*, Feb. 7, 1954, 26.
4. "News on the Turntable," *Ft. Worth Star-Telegram*, Feb. 28, 1954, 38.
5. Roger Beck, "Off the Records," *Los Angeles Mirror*, June 26, 1954, 5.
6. "Longhair Disc Reviews," *Variety*, Sept. 29, 1954, 46.

On March 24, 1956, Bas Sheva appeared on the Ed Sullivan show singing several songs including one cantorial (*Variety* noted that she gave "an impressive delivery of a Hebrew number"), and thanks to an enthusiastic audience response, she was quickly invited back.[25] However, again, Jewish organizations such as the Cantor's Assembly protested her khazones, calling it "objectionable," and successfully scuttled her return appearance.[26]

Bas Sheva continued touring Yiddish American variety shows, as in the 1957 Sholom Secunda vaudeville revue *Bagels and Yox*, appearing with the Barton Brothers (of "Joe and Paul" fame) and Black Yiddish singer Napoleon Reed, while Mickey Katz continued to feature her in ongoing stage revues, culminating with the tenth anniversary edition of *Borscht Capades*. Bas Sheva died tragically young, just like her mother and from the same disease: diabetes. Already losing her eyesight, it was while performing on a cruise ship that Bas Sheva was inadvertently given an injection for sea sickness to which she had a fatal reaction; she was only thirty-four years old.[27]

Frieidele Oysher (1913–2004)

The last European-born *khaznte*, Freidele, from the Romanian-Bessarabian culture divide, was a multi-generational descendant of *khazonim* along with her older brother, who has probably the most euphonious name in all Jewish entertainment, Moishe Oysher. Their cantor father had preceded them to the New World: "Mama, Moishe and I came later . . . my father was in America. My mother had six other sons, then five sons, then four . . . then one was left, Moyshe was left, four had died poverty, disease, destruction, you know, hunger, you know."[28] The family shuttled through a series of hardscrabble homes first in Montreal, then Brooklyn and then Philadelphia, where Freidele's earliest musical ear training began. She eavesdropped on her father teaching cantorial stylings to her brother Moishe. When her father found out—and heard what a marvelous singer she was—he began to teach her too.[29] After three and half years of study at the Curtis Institute of Music, Freidele was championed by Philadelphia's Workmen's Circle music educator Michl Gelbart, who introduced her to composer Lipa Feingold in New York. (Freidele was desperate to leave Philadelphia, where she was working in a pretzel factory and had been begging Moishe, who was already performing there, to bring her up.[30])

Feingold was music director for S. P. Mogelewsky, president of the World Clothing Exchange, whose sponsored shows flooded the Yiddish air-

Figure 19.2. During Passover c. 1954, Freidele Oysher with her daughter "Toni Michel" (Marilyn Michaels) entertained at the Borscht Belt Normandie Hotel, alongside my father, Cantor Zindel Sapoznik (*right*), who conducted services and seders. *Source:* Author's collection.

waves. Feingold penned Oysher's first radio hit, the bar mitzvah song "Der nayer yid" ("The New Jew") in 1934, establishing her local popularity.[31] When she premiered onstage, she was deemed too small and too flat, so Freidele declined the romantic soubrette role, and instead parlayed her mischievous temperament and paint-peeling voice in pants roles like her petite pal Molly Picon, who "loaned me my first dress to wear for a role. I had

Khazntes | 223

no dresses," and Nellie Casman, who was also inspired to try being a stage khaznte.³² Freidele's fame expanded the next year when composer Sholom Secunda (who created the piano sheet music arrangement of "Der nayer yid") and playwright Louis Freiman collaborated on her showcase musical *Freidele's khasene* (*Freidele's Wedding*) at Brooklyn's Hopkinson Theater. The show gave her a chance to display both her command of theater songs and her "famous kiddush which, when those audience members who went in the lobby to catch a smoke, heard it, quickly returned."³³

Freidele's khasene was the template for all subsequent shows built around her unique cantorial-inflected Yiddish singing and riveting khazones like *A malke af peysakh* (*The Passover Queen*, 1945), *A khazind'l af shabbos* (*A Cantor for Shabbos*, 1947), *Der khazn's tokhter* (*The Cantor's Daughter*, 1948), and *Zing, freidele zing* (*Sing, Freidele Sing*, 1952), with which she successfully toured the provinces throughout the 1940s and 1950s.³⁴

Unlike the other well-known khazntes, Freidele, who was not observant and could not read Hebrew, did not see khazones as an extension of religious beliefs but as her fundamental birthright musical identity. Her brother Moishe took a different path, as she recalled: "Moishe's heart was in the theater, but his soul was in the synagogue."³⁵

Freidele came to recording in the late 1940s on the Banner label, making just two 78s, the first commercial recordings of a khaznte since Sophie Kurtzer's 1923 Pathé discs. Accompanied on organ by Abe Ellstein, the records show her warm, powerful, and knowing mastery of the style at the height of her power and sounding, not coincidentally, like her brother Moishe.

In 1955, Freidele and Moishe opened their first co-starring show at Second Avenue's National Theater called *Lomir Beyde Zingn* (*Let's Both Sing*). The uniqueness of the pairing resulted in the advertisements guaranteeing that "both would appear on the same stage and sing together." This led to a series of concerts (*Oysherik un yoysherik* [*Wholly Oysherish*]),³⁶ which featured Moishe, Freidele, and her daughter, future Broadway star Marilyn Michaels. Freidele died in 2004.

Goldele and Gittele Malavsky

Of all the professional khazntes, only the Malavsky sisters (Gertrude/Gittele, 1922–2006, and Gloria/Goldele, 1924–1995) were to the manor born. Along with their father Shmuel, and brothers Abraham (Albert) and Morton, the Malavsky family was to cantorial music what the Carter family was to country music, a powerful reaffirmation of unbroken generational of faith and continuity wrapped in really great singing.

Shmuel "Samuel" Malavsky (1894–1985) was born near Kiev, having been a *meshoyrer* (chorister) and child cantor before coming to the US in 1913.[37] Possessed of a "rich and warm wide-ranging lyric tenor with phenomenally genuinely fluid coloratura,"[38] Malavsky worked as a butcher until he was championed by the reigning King of Cantors (and fellow Ukrainian) Yossele Rosenblatt, who took the young émigré under his wing as his full-time protégé.[39] Rosenblatt not only concertized with Malavsky, he featured him on several duet recordings in 1915, 1919, and 1926 (something he did not do for anyone else, including his own son Henry), and Rosenblatt even provided the piano accompaniment for Malavsky's now lost 1918 Victor test recording.[40] Malavsky eventually signed with Columbia, who honored him by issuing his recordings not on the quotidian (and cheaper) three-plus-minute ten-inch discs but on the prestigious, one-minute-longer (and one-dollar-pricier) twelve-inch discs.

Malavsky held so many national synagogue postings that none of his five children were born in the same city.[41] Starting in 1932, Malavsky stopped taking yearly synagogue posts and became a freelance cantor, giving concerts and conducting High Holiday and Passover services around the country. In 1935, when Malavsky returned to New York, he began building his family choir by taking his second-oldest daughter Goldele (billed as the "ten-year singer of Hebrew folk songs") on his national tours.[42] In 1938, Malavsky included his four oldest children and conducted services at Reform temples and synagogue concerts until the war broke out and his sons enlisted leaving Malavsky to soldier on with Goldele and Gittele.[43]

However, Malavsky was not merely marking time until his sons returned. As he had previously done by including Goldele onstage, Malavsky was proactively putting forward his daughters—and by extension, all women—as legitimate and valid carriers of the cantorial heritage. In a quiet way, Samuel Malavsky, while providing traditional synagogue services, was able to introduce his daughters as part of the cantorials and choir, thus challenging the Orthodox *kol isha* restriction against women's voices (public singing for women was only possible in the more lenient Reform temples). Another indication of Malavsky's success in breeching the walls of Orthodoxy and introducing women's voices to the traditional synagogue was that most advertisements and overwhelmingly positive reviews of Malavsky concerts and recordings occurred in the pages of the conservative religious paper the *Morgn Zhurnal*.

In 1946, Malavsky self-produced an album of four 78s on the vanity Zion Records label, which featured several solos by his daughters—Malavsky's own setting of the Chanukah prayer "Mi sheoso nisim" and "Zion, Zion," an aria from one of the earliest Yiddish operas—and performed in a way its first audiences would have recognized thanks to Malavsky's insistence his daughters sing in their natural voices and not shadow a male-influenced vocal sound. The set even included a duet by Gittele and Goldele singing a wartime Yiddish song, "Victory Tantz."[44] Unlike the Rosie the Riveters, who were replaced when the men returned from war, when the Malavsky sons came home the entire choir was reunited and even augmented with daughters Ruth and Minnie.

In 1946, on a three-record set on Moe Asch's eponymous label, Malavsky steps back, allowing his daughters more front presence while displaying his own skills as a choir leader and arranger with this now wider vocal palette.[45] Yet despite having made inroads in normalizing women's voices in the synagogue, Malavsky abandoned synagogue-based services with his family for synagogue-based concerts, hotel Passover seders, and the twilight of the Yiddish vaudeville circuit.

In 1948, inspired by the success of the Barry Sisters on their long-running *Yiddish Melodies in Swing* WHN radio show, Gittele and Goldele Malavsky reimagined themselves as the Marlin Sisters. Replete with pensive, pouty, bare-shouldered publicity photos, they premiered at Little Romania, Yiddish comedian Michl Rosenberg's Miami Beach club, splitting a bill with Rosenberg and theater veteran Aaron Lebedeff. The Yiddish newspapers lauded their premier: "The English press praises them to the skies calling them 'the Songbirds of Swing' but we call them 'a credit to the Jewish community of Miami.'" English-language publications noted, "The Marlin sisters are a nice pair of thrushes, who, though sticking strictly to the Yiddish (with occasional English lyrics) hit with their swing versions of folk songs."[46]

The Marlin Sisters premiered on a major label in 1949 with a cover of the Andrews Sisters' "Toolie Ooolie Doolie," but better known for its flip side "You Can't Be True, Dear," the first recording of a twenty-year-old Eddie Fisher. Like Capitol with Bas Sheva, Columbia did not seem to know exactly what to do with the Marlin Sisters, platooning them as the Polka Debs on Gay '90s songs with the Ted Steele Orchestra, with tenor Vaughn Horton, though also a very good pairing with polka king Frankie Yankovic on "Rosalinda Waltz," "Charlie Was a Boxer," and "The Blue Skirt Waltz," a big seller for Yankovic.[47]

Around 1950 the Marlin Sisters went from London Records to Coral (1953), where, with the electric mandolin/accordion-based Pinetoppers, turned out a redolent performance with a country western-ish cover of the 1952 Georgia Gibbs hit "Seven Lonely Days." They would fold the Marlin Sisters act a few years later.

In the 1950s, the Malavsky family appeared on the big screen in several charming two-reel shorts for Joseph Seiden's Cinema Service Corp and on the small screen on March 22, 1953, on *The Kate Smith Hour*, doing an abbreviated seder service.[48]

Cantor Samuel Malavsky would die in 1985. The only Malavsky to continue in music in the later years was Goldele, who would become choir director for her synagogue Congregation Ahavat Shalom in Lakewood, New Jersey.

The obituary in her hometown paper condensed her historic and wide-ranging career to simply, "She was a singer and entertainer many years ago, performing with her sisters."[49]

Sheindele di Khaznte (1916–1981)

Born in Philadelphia, Jean Gornish was the first of the professional American khazntes not descended from a line of khazonim. There were also no music professionals in her Orthodox family. Despite her parents' objections ("Our father never really approved of a woman singing," she later recalled),[50] by her mid-teens Gornish was performing locally for Philadelphia Jewish philanthropic organizations and community programs, and on local low-power radio stations.[51]

Gornish emerged in 1936, bedecked in full cantorial attire and inaccurately billing herself as "Sheindele, the world's only woman cantor."[52] (A possible sideways nod to Gornish came in 1941 when Yiddish composer Joseph Rumshinsky penned a new musical called *Sheindele: The Cantor's Daughter*, which ran at Ludwig Satz's Folks Theater.[53])

During the war years, Max Malamut, owner of the kosher hotels the Astor and the Breakers in Atlantic City, hit on the idea to have Sheindele co-lead (with a male cantor) the High Holiday services in the hotel's synagogue as a perk for its guests.[54] Its success led to her returning the following Passover to lead the synagogue services and seders and again the following High Holiday. Sheindele continued to co-lead Passover seders into the early 1950s.

By this time, Gornish's father had come around and wholly approved of his daughter's career, "He'd hear her on the radio and sit and cry."⁵⁵ Her radio sponsor, Planters Hi-Hat Peanut Oil, underwrote Gornish on every Philadelphia station that carried Yiddish shows, an unusual amount of coverage for any performer. In 1943, Planters expanded Sheindele's radio congregation to include Chicago's WSBC, and then in 1947, New York station WEVD, until 1960. Sheindele's on-air ubiquity was such that on her 1950 census report she listed her profession as "radio singer."

In 1953, at the height of her popularity, Jean Gornish married Robert Siegel and soon left performing, joining her husband in the health care business.⁵⁶ Sheindele enjoyed a brief coda a decade later in 1963 with an LP on the indie Margot label, *Sheindele Sings the Songs of Her People*.⁵⁷ Despite being in full command of a warm and resonant sound, interpreting cantorial, classic, and popular Yiddish songs, the record's stiff and scripted feel is not surprising given that the oversized orchestral accompaniment by Abe Ellstein and magniloquent English narration by Zvee Scooler were her colleagues at station WEVD and may have been intended as a broadcast.

Outside of this LP, there is virtually no other quality example of her singing, for, despite Sheindele's decades on radio in three cities, no original broadcasts are known to exist.

Breindele: Bernice Zuckerberg Gordon (b. 1937)

Bernice "Bryna" Zuckerberg was born in Brooklyn, where her father, Israel Zuckerberg (1901–1983) was cantor at the Manhattan Beach Jewish Center.⁵⁸ In her 2012 short story "The Chazzen's Daughter," Zuckerberg Gordon recalls when, as a child of four, she first accompanied *Tati* (father) Israel to *shul* and, amazed, notes his transformation to *sheliakh tzibur* ("messenger of the people"), a signal moment in her own Jewish musical identity.

> When I was really very young, my father and G-d got mushed together in my head. It's not that I didn't know who was who; I understood that there was G-d and that Father was Father. I think that's a part of how I inwardly functioned. I didn't think out loud about this. But it was a comfortable feeling I had when I was very young.⁵⁹

Figure 19.3. Publicity picture of Breindele di khaznte, ca. 1945. *Source:* Bernice Zuckerberg Gordon. Used with permission.

Cantor Zuckerberg enthusiastically taught his daughter traditional cantorial repertoire and style so that by the age of ten Bernice was performing as Breindele, the world's youngest khaznte, one of the very few claims in the otherwise overheated universe of *khaznte* ballyhoo that was accurate. Says Breindele:

> When I first learned cantorial music from my father, it was cantorial duets. I imitated what I heard, but it came out in my voice as I pulled it into myself.
>
> Later, I began to do solo cantorial pieces at concerts and on the radio. I really had to understand which prayers I was doing. It was a big deal that my father felt finally that I could handle these things. When I was five or six, I used to sing

the Adon Olam in shul, and the congregation sang with me. I understood it, and that it was a major piece of devotion to G-d. I'm still singing it.[60]

For a decade starting in the late 1940s, father and daughter performed as "Israel Zuckerberg and his talented daughter 'Breindele'" on what was left of the circuit of synagogue concerts, Yiddish variety stage shows, and Catskills hotels. A May 1949 Yiddish display ad for the coming summer season featuring a fresh-faced Breindele with braided hair was headlined "Of great importance for the hotel *kippers* in the *montens* (mountains)."[61] There was also Israel Rosenberg's slot on WEVD he'd had, off and on, since 1939.

Breindele came to the attention of Yiddish composer Sholom Secunda, who at the time was musical director at the prestigious Brooklyn Jewish Center on Eastern Parkway (today a Lubavitch school). Impressed, Secunda mentored and accompanied Breindele while also composing songs showcasing her cantorial skills, including "V'chol Ma'aminim," with lyrics by Isidore Lillian, in 1950. Secunda made the young singer a featured soloist for several seasons when he was musical director at the Concord Hotel in Kiamesha Lake.[62]

In 1962, Bernice married Sheldon "Shelley" Gordon, one of New York's top klezmer trumpet players. Not suffering the fate of Jean Gornish when she married, Bernice continued performing into the 1970s at private parties and premier hotels, such as the Waldorf Astoria, the Plaza, and the Pierre, as well as in the Catskills. Bernice lives in Seattle, near her children and grandchildren, where she writes her memoirs.

20

Thomas LaRue Jones, Gladys Mae Sellers, and the Lost World of Black Cantors

While the history of Black-Jewish cultural interaction has always focused on how Jews adopted and adapted Black music—including ragtime, jazz, swing, R&B, and blues—as performers, promoters, managers, and record label operators, what has never before been explored are the Black performers of Yiddish and cantorial music in the Jewish community, in theaters, on record, and on radio between the World Wars as the so-called *shvartze khazonim* (Black cantors). (Today, the Yiddish word "shvartze/shvartzer" [black], when in reference to a person, is considered a racist and pejorative term. However, this was not so when African American singers were billed as "shvartze khazonim," so was not used in a demeaning or dismissive way in marketing, reviewing, promoting, or referring to these performers. Its use here is in that historical context.)

African American Synagogues

The rise of African American synagogues drew inspiration from Jewish tradition and a Black worldview. What accounts for this rise is manyfold: Jim Crow laws that supplanted Reconstruction in the South drove a northern migration, a demographic shift to New York and to the already established Jewish community in Harlem. Blacks were now encountering Jews as neighbors, employers, allies, customers, rivals, friends, and enemies. Simultaneously, Black national aspirations grew and drew inspiration from

Zionism—itself a kind of "back to Africa movement"—as a model in the development of the Harlem Renaissance.¹

Unaffiliated and unaccepted by the Jewish religious establishment, Black congregations were small and poor. Meeting in a storefront or a house—what similarly sized Ashkenazi Orthodox congregations would call a *shtibl* (a little house)—they constructed a plethora of traditional Jewish practices (life cycle events, modesty of dress, *kashrus*, and separate seating) while services were for the most part in Hebrew and English with some Yiddish. Today, one of the most active congregations is Chicago's prestigious Beth Shalom B'nai Zaken Ethiopian Hebrew Congregation under the leadership of Rabbi Capers Funnye, cousin of Michelle Obama, and the only African American rabbi to have *smikhe* (accreditation) from the Conservative synagogue.²

Some Black Jews claimed Abyssinian descent, with its unbroken historic identification with Old Testament Hebrews. One of those was Rabbi Mordechai Herman of the Moorish Zionist Temple, who claimed direct Ethiopian lineage for himself and his congregants and was a member of the Marcus Garvey movement.³

A surprisingly large percentage of Caribbean Blacks were in these congregations, which might point to Jewish slaveholders who, like Christians, had servants who converted to the household religion.⁴ There was the Commandment Keepers Ethiopian Hebrew Congregation founded in 1919 by Rabbi Wentworth Arthur Matthew, a West Indian immigrant who would establish a network of synagogues in the US and the Caribbean based on traditional Orthodox Ashkenazi traditions.⁵ There was also Congregation Beth B'nai Abraham, founded in 1929 by the Barbados-born Rabbi Arnold Josiah Ford as an outgrowth of his right-hand work with Marcus Garvey. Matthew came to Harlem in 1909 and, given his interest in music and social uplift, joined the progressive Black music organization the Clef Club, run by James Reese Europe. Ford's hymnals, which he privately published, were a lively mix of Christian, Jewish, and Islamic music prayer traditions.⁶

The Yiddish press was alternately fascinated, suspicious, and puzzled by the interest of African Americans in Jewish life and customs. One who was all three—and through whom we know about the earliest Black cantors in 1920s—was journalist and essayist Z. Rubinzohn of the *Yiddishes Togblatt* (*The Jewish Daily News*). In his weekly column Fun groys nu york (From Big New York), Rubinzohn produced a series of pithy feuilletons, well-observed portraits of local Jewish life. In his column on June 28, 1920, Rubinzohn tells of arriving in his office to a young Black man waiting to speak to him.⁷

The man introduced himself as a press agent for Kessler's theater, looking for a plug in Rubinzohn's column for their new show featuring his specialty: Yiddish songs and cantorial prayers.

Asked for a demonstration, Mendel launched into the industrial-strength Yiddish showstopper "A khazndl af shabes" ("A Cantor on the Sabbath"), a demanding pyrotechnical mix of ornate cantorial melismas and snappy barn-burning theatricality. "He sings with a real Yiddish turn," Rubinzohn marveled, "with a real Yiddish moan and sigh. The old time Jewish trope is there and really Jewish. . . . Make no mistake," he assures his readers, "until now we've only had a Jewish Black—Al Jolson—a cantor's son who makes believe he is Black. But here is a Black man who is a cantor who calls himself 'Mendel the shvartzer khazn.' " Rubinzohn comments on Mendel's *reyner yiddish* (a clean Yiddish) and tells the story of his life from his birth in Barbados, coming to America around 1910, and eventual migration to the Yiddish theater, concluding: "Here is Mendel the Black cantor: a non-Jew, a Black who offers up no name other than 'Mendele' but who is a real cantor, here in Big New York."

Figure 20.1. "Mendel, der shvartzer khazn" (1922). *Source:* National Library of Israel, Historical Jewish Press website (www.jpress.org.il), founded by the National Library and Tel Aviv University. Used with permission.

"The Lion"

Figure 20.1. Willie "The Lion" Smith's business card in Yiddish and English. *Source*: Author's collection.

> AUdubon 6-1660
>
> **WILLIE THE LION SMITH**
>
> MODERN PIANO TEACHING
>
> SWING, MIKE TRAINING, VOICE COACHING
>
> The Hebrew Cantor   1674 Broadway, Room 507
>
> דער אידישער חזן   NEW YORK

Another member of the Clef Club connected to Jewish music was Harlem stride pianist Willie "The Lion" Smith (b. William Henry Joseph Bonaparte Bertholoff, 1897–1973), who throughout his life actively proclaimed his Jewish connection. In the opening of his 1964 memoir *Music on My Mind*, Smith pays homage to his Jewish father; and youthful years in Newark, New Jersey; with Jewish neighbors, the Rothschilds. In a story that mirrors the childhood experience of Louis Armstrong (i.e., the early intervention of a local supportive Jewish family), not only did the Rothschilds allow Smith to receive religious instruction from a local rabbi alongside their own children, but the rabbi took great pains, when he saw how receptive Smith was in preparation for his bar mitzvah, to introduce him to the literature of cantorial modes, tropes, and articulations.[1] "You could say I am Jewish partly by origin and partly by association," Smith wrote. "As it turned out I favored the Jewish religion all my life and at one time served as a Hebrew cantor in a Harlem congregation." This last claim is hazy despite Smith's business card, which had emblazoned on it דער אידישער חזן (The Hebrew Cantor).

Jazz historian Dan Morgenstern offered a perspective on Smith's cantorial claims:

> While I got to know Willie quite well, he was evasive about the extent of his cantorial activities and I never heard him sing

---

1. Willie The Lion Smith and George Hoefer, *Music on My Mind: The Memoirs of an American Pianist* (New York: Doubleday) 1964), 8.

anything approaching it or say or sing anything in Hebrew. His Yiddish, however, was fluent and he set witty lyrics to "I've Found a New Baby" that I wish he had recorded. His sing-song vocalizing had a definite Jewish tinge. I'm no authority on Yiddish though my father was. And so was my little trumpeter friend Nat Lorber who certified the Lion's (Yiddish) to me. They sometimes conversed.[2]

While The Lion did not record his Yiddish "I've Found a New Baby," he did wax a puckishly suggestive version of the folk song "Nokh a bisl" ("A Little More"), which more than validates his Yiddish lingo claims.[3]

---

2. Correspondence with Dan Morgenstern, Mar. 21, 2021.
3. "The Memoirs of Willie The Lion Smith," Willie The Lion Smith, *RCA Victor LSP-6016, 1968.*

Dovid Kollscritta: The Falasha Polyglot

"Happy holiday," trumpets Rubinzohn in a column a few months later on September 20, "we have another Black cantor in New York!"[8] Named "Dovid, di kollscritta, ha'koen der falash" (1893–1944), Kollscritta (which Rubinzohn translates as a "calligrapher") was born in the Ethiopian port city of Masawa and claimed direct descendance from the Queen of Sheba. In a wide-ranging conversation that toggled effortlessly between Yiddish and Hebrew (Kollscritta spoke twenty-nine languages, fourteen fluently) he offered a whirlwind narrative about being educated in Paris and Palestine, studying under a cantor in Russia as a *meshoyrer*, marrying a woman named Rukhl in Pinsk, and fathering two children before leaving for America shortly before the outbreak of World War I. Kollscritta lived in Milwaukee, Wisconsin, where he joined the US Army, first as an interpreter but finally in the Medical Corps, and later filed for American citizenship based on his military service. Rubinzohn was curious: What did Kollscritta's parents say about his marriage? "They were horrified and thought that it was a *shande* (a disgrace). The real Jews of old were all brown or black," his parents said. "White Jews are not real Jews; they're just fakers."[9]

A notice a couple of months later in *Variety* notes that "David Kohl" has embarked on the vaudeville stage, singing Yiddish songs and cantorial hymns and demonstrating his linguistic skills (he'd invite members of the audience up to try and stump him in a language he could not speak).[10] Kollscritta sang on March 17, 1934, at a Gala Proletarian Revel for the Communist *The Daily Worker* (admission: forty-nine cents). On November 18, he was the subject of a *Brooklyn Times Union* headline: "Colored Borough Rabbi Testifies to Aid Woman." Regarding his appearance on behalf of the plaintiff, he was described as "wearing a skullcap and a traditional black beard . . . and as dark skinned as Othello."[11] We hear of David Kollscritta one last time in 1944 as cantor at Pittsburgh's Universal Ancient Ethiopian Spiritual Church of Christ, whose congregation he led in Hebrew prayer, and as dean of the Pittsburgh Afro-American Language School.[12]

Another Black cantor was Abraham Ben Benjamin Franklin. Franklin also claimed an Abyssinian rabbinic lineage (although he was born in Missouri and lived in Windsor, Ontario). Like Kollscritta, Franklin had prodigious multilingual skills and would deliver trilingual sermons (in Hebrew, Yiddish, and English) with titles such as "Comfort for the Jews"[13] From 1930 to 1942, Franklin crisscrossed the US as a *maggid* (an itinerant preacher) and appears to have been the only Black cantor who was not only endorsed by the white rabbinical authorities but also conducted synagogue services for their congregations.[14]

There was Sam Wilson, billing himself as "The only colored entertainer singing Hebrew songs and telling stories," whose specialty was "singing ragtime songs in Yiddish with a negro accent." From 1919 to 1925, Wilson toured vaudeville, as a February 1920 *Variety* review marveled: "Sam Wilson is as black as the ace of spades and opens with Dardanella a moment later he makes the house gasp repeating the vocal offering in Yiddish. He also impersonates a couple of Hebrew actors and does a short monolog in dialect. . . . In New York and other cities with Hebraic populations Wilson will stop things cold."[15] The *Amerikaner familyen magazin un gazetn* (*The American Family Magazine and Gazette*) radio show on New York station WOV, during the month of November 1929, featured Milton Grossman, "the 9-year-old Black cantorial wunderkind."[16]

But only one—billed simply as *Der shvartzer khazn*—would be instantly identifiable to Yiddish theater audiences in America and Europe in the 1920s and 1930s.

Thomas LaRue Jones (1894–1954)

In the April 8, 1922, issue of the African American newspaper *The New York Age*, columnist Lucien H. White introduces his readers to Thomas LaRue Jones as "a young Negro born 20 years ago whose mother accepted the religious beliefs of the Hebrews and raised up her son in that way." White quoted LaRue saying: "It began with my mother. She lived in Newark where she found race prejudice to be very strong. She could make friends only with Jewish women preferring the company of Jews to Christians."[17] LaRue's mother insisted he receive a traditional Jewish primary school education (Talmud Torah), and that he and his sister should both be able to pray from a *siddur* (prayer book). While LaRue Jones's later press provided variations of this narrative, the official paper trail tells a wholly different story.

Thomas LaRue Jones was born in 1894 in Nanesmond County, Virginia, one of four children, and by the age of six he was living in Newark, New Jersey,[18] in and adjacent to Newark's Jewish neighborhoods at a time when Newark was one of strongest Yiddish cultural communities in the metropolitan area.[19] La Rue's mother died when he was four years old, too young to have been the influence attested to in many of his interviews. LaRue Jones's involvement in Jewish music did not extend to anyone else in his family: his older brother Demosthanes ("Demos") was a song and dance man on the Black vaudeville circuit, while a younger brother Herbert Socrates ("HS") wrote songs for both Black and white stages. Both brothers died tragically young, just as their popularity was growing.

By his early twenties, LaRue Jones was part of Newark's Jewish community life cycle entertainments, singing at weddings, synagogue concerts, and community fundraising and charity events. Some of his earliest performance affiliations were with Ahavath Zion, one of Newark's largest Orthodox congregations, a testament to LaRue Jones's early successfully internalizing both the sacred and secular Jewish languages and music.

LaRue Jones was already performing by 1912, and in 1918–1919 the *Forverts* sponsored a series of salons (musicians, declaimers, poets) featuring LaRue Jones singing what would become his standard mix of cantorial, Yiddish, and Russian songs.[20] The next year, under the management of Yiddish theater impresario Edvin A. Relkin, LaRue Jones toured the provincial Jewish circuit (including Kansas City, Cincinnati, Omaha, Denver, Sioux City) as "Reb Toyve," an African cantor. LaRue's act is described in a *Harrisburg*

Telegraph review, on September 15, 1921, where he and the local synagogue's cantor "between the acts, will have a challenge," the "challenge" being a cantorial version of the jazz "trading eights" in which increasingly ornate and dazzling improvised vocal riffs are passed back and forth.[21] LaRue's popularity was such that a January 30, 1921, item in *Variety* quoted Eddie Cantor, who upon being told about Thomas LaRue Jones quipped, "And here I thought I was the only colored Cantor living."[22]

Figure 20.2. Poster for *Dos khupe kleyd* (*The Wedding Dress*) featuring Thomas LaRue Jones, 1922. *Source:* YIVO Institute for Jewish Research. Used with permission.

Back in New York, Edvin A. Relkin booked LaRue Jones as an *ekstre etrekshin* ("extra attraction"), a showstopping specialty of the Yiddish musical *Dos khupe kleyd* (*The Wedding Dress*) at Nathan Goldberg and Jacob Jacobs's Lenox Theater at the corner of Lenox Avenue and 111th Street in the heart of Harlem. In posters for *Dos khupe kleyd*, a photo of a robed Thomas LaRue Jones with a fourteen-voice boys choir is in the lower half, with text: "A giant concert by the world renowned Black Cantor with a large Newark-based choir under the leadership of the renowned Jewish choir director Joseph Germansky. LaRue will astound Harlem with his amazing singing of the finest compositions from R' Yossele Rosenblatt, Gershon Sirota and Kwartin."[23] These composer/cantors represented the apex of contemporary liturgical singing, which few cantors could hope to emulate. But with LaRue Jones, it was not ballyhoo. Two occasions—one being a benefit concert for LaRue Jones—were attended by Yossele Rosenblatt.

LaRue was catnip to the Yiddish press. Theater scribe Z. Karnblit of the *Morgn Zhurnal* (*The Morning Journal*) in a November 4, 1921, feature called "Have You Heard of the Famous Cantor Reb' Toyvele?" describes how he sat slack-jawed through LaRue's performance:

> There he was: a slender, Black youth in a black frock coat and vest under which he wore a crisp white shirt, who came out singing a Yiddish song, a song beginning even before he stepped out on stage. I could not believe my eyes or ears.
>
> When I hear at a concert that someone will sing "Eli, Eli"—it could be the best singer in the world—I run in the opposite direction as if cornered by a well-known pest dragging a steamer trunk full of oft-heard and exhausted moth-eaten anecdotes from decades past . . .
>
> This, however, was a new "Eli, Eli" by a Black cantor which was so very heartfelt, and which drew so deeply from Jewish martyrdom, the Jewish cry, begging God why he has forsaken him, and producing from this song what even the greatest opera singers could not. Every person in the theater was transfixed by the Black cantor's powerful poetic harmony.[24]

After the concert, Karnblit sat with LaRue and spoke about Jones's recent provincial Jewish experience "billed as one of the Black Jews of India, while no one suspected he was simply an American Negro." The Anglo-Jewish press was equally amazed: "Thomas LaRue Jones, the colored chazan. Not only is he black but he has a white heart and a fine Jewish soul. If some of our natural Jews could have some of his fine Jewish spirit, the problem of Judaism in this country would not be a serious one."25 "Thomas LaRue and Co. the world's wonder cantor . . . never before has there appeared on the theatrical stage or any other platform a man who could vocally impersonate a cantor in the manner that this colored gentleman does. He turns the entire audience into a house of worship."

Yet other Jewish outlets were not as generous. *The American Israelite*, already no fan of Yiddish popular culture, on December 27, 1923, sniffed: "There can exist no doubt as to the catholicity of the Yiddish public. For some time, as is well-known, the singing of a negro chazan has been something of a rage in Yiddish circles. This colored cantor is now singing synagogual [*sic*] melodies for the phonograph companies."

Thomas LaRue Jones made the only known recording of a period Black cantor for the OKeh label. While labels like Columbia and Victor had much larger Jewish catalogs, OKeh's much more modest Jewish catalog only started in 1921 and continued just into mid-1923, right after LaRue recorded for them. OKeh led in recording African Americans on their so-called race records (i.e., Black records). (Some of LaRue's label mates were Louis Armstrong, Alberta Hunter, Duke Ellington, Victoria Spivey, Clarence Williams, and Lonnie Johnson.) Because of his repertoire, Thomas LaRue Jones may have been the only African American artist on OKeh whose records were not released in its segregated race catalog.

For the Yiddish side of the disc, LaRue Jones recorded a song he copyrighted in October 1920, composed for him by the up-and-coming twenty-three-year-old Sholom Secunda, whose "Bie mir bistu sheyn" was still over a decade away. "Farlir nor nit dein hofenung reb yid" (Don't give up hope, Mr. Jew) was published by Newark Yiddish music dealer M. Mansky and pictures a serious LaRue Jones in the only publicity picture in which he does not wear cantorial raiment.

For his recording, LaRue Jones could have easily chosen current Yiddish pop songs to show off his seamless and polished Yiddish, or a love ballad to transmit his passionate delivery. Instead, his powerful 1920 Zionist song features the most unapologetic listing of historic tormentors of the Jews and the violence against the Jews. It is simultaneously a throwback to the earliest seedling days of the Yiddish theater a half century before, with the street singing shtetl griot—the Broder Zinger—and also a leap ahead as a

Yiddish corollary to another Jewish composition against racist violence with a powerful African American association: Abel Meeropol's 1937 "Strange Fruit" and its unforgettable Billie Holiday interpretation.

The connection to "Strange Fruit" is chilling given the 1920 backdrop when Thomas LaRue's song was written. That year saw both the continuation of the murders of African Americans (with over fifty lynchings) and in Poland—called out in the song for its deadly pogroms—the most recent anti-Jewish violence in the city of Zamość with multiple killings.

> God long ago made a pledge to the Jews
> That he would never allow them to lose
> They'll grow in number like sand on the shore
> Like stars in the heavens and then, even more
> So, what has become of the Jew today
> The Gentiles, the monsters, their pogroms carried out
> Make Jewish blood gush as if from a spout
> His life is embittered, a constant ordeal
> As Gentiles take all they can steal
> The monster, will slay your children his prey
> Jews dream of the God who in Egypt once saved them
> "Next year in Jerusalem"
> Don't give up hope yet, Mr. Jew
> One day it will all work out for you
> Pharaoh, Haman and Amolek taught a bitter lesson
> But those days are through
> Czar Nikolai, has met his destiny
> And from Poland, you'll soon be free
> Don't give up hope yet, Mr. Jew
> You'll be brought with pride to save it
> Into the land of the Star of David.[26]

For the cantorial side of the recording, LaRue again chose not to go with one of the barn burners like "Kol Nidre" from the High Holiday service, or even "Eli, Eli," for which he was renowned, but a modest prayer of supplication from the daily morning *shakhris* services: "Misratzeh berach'mim" ("Become favorable through compassion"). Like the flip side, it is a reminder, a reaffirmation of an historic bond: "Don't forget us, you are our guardian, we are the people you said were so unique."

> Become favorable through compassion
> and become appeased through supplication
> Become favorable and appeased to the poor generations for
>   there is no helper
> Our Father our King be gracious with us and answer us
> Though we have no worthy deeds
> Treat us with charity and kindness and save us.

Among the popular stories about LaRue Jones was how he learned his khazones. One of the most common is about a young LaRue attending a local synagogue, enamored of the music, and when the cantor falls ill he takes to the *omid* (pulpit) to finish the services. However, in other articles—and in interviews with LaRue himself—he blithely admits to the common practice of learning from commercial recordings.

Such is the case with "Misratzeh berach'mim," which was first recorded in March 1921 for Columbia by Bessarabian cantor Shloimele Rothstein. While Rothstein has the more finely attuned coloratura and intricate knowledge of the critical ornamental melismatic *shtiklekh* (pieces) that organically bind the musical segments together, LaRue Jones is the superior singer, who more accurately transmits the underlying textual meaning through his artistic command. On "Misratzeh berach'mim," LaRue begins meekly in the quieter head tone but switches into his resonant chest voice midway on the significant words *Ovinu malkeynu* ("Our Father, Our King"), a dramatic transition melding messenger and message and catapulting the quotidian prayer to its powerful conclusion.

Great care was apparently taken in the coupling of the songs for LaRue's record. Both call for the welfare and security of the Jewish people, one from a time immemorial text and the other, a Zionist call ripped from the day's headlines. Taken together, LaRue's performances are passionate and buoyed by his strong command of the languages and his sure touch of familiar cantorial tonalities. This seamless command imbued his singing with a powerful and instant veracity. Music historian Dick Spottswood offers the keen observation that on record, LaRue Jones could say things as a Black man in Yiddish that he couldn't say as a Black man in English.

LaRue's 1923 release is both a great recording and an important one. It is great because it stands on its own merits when compared to other better-known period Jewish recordings of white cantors, even to the record from which one side was copied. And it is important because it success-

Figure 20.3. Thomas LaRue Jones is only identified as the black cantor in Yiddish, 1923. *Source:* Author's collection. Used with permission.

fully and triumphantly stands in for the muted voices of the other shvartze khazonim who were once part of a fully formed, freestanding phenomenon but who never stood before a recording microphone.

On September 19, 1930, Jewish newspapers around the world ran this item from the *Jewish Telegraphic Agency*: "*Cairo: En route to Europe, a concert was given here by the Black Cantor from New York where he is known as 'Toyve the Black Cantor.' The Black cantor's program of cantorial hymns and Yiddish folk songs elicited great interest and his large audiences had many non-Jews.*"²⁷ The historic tour was the result of three years of Edvin A. Relkin's planning, with Thomas LaRue Jones singing where Jews had historically lived: Palestine, Egypt, Germany, and Poland. The audacity (*khutzpe*) of the tour came in the form of an African American billed as "Toyve Ha'Cohen," who not only claimed to have mastered speaking and singing Yiddish and Hebrew but, as a priestly Cohen, placed a Black man in continuity with the foundation of the Temple: Holy of Holies.

Gone was the story of the inner-city child of a single mother who favored the company of Jews (let alone the actual truth). LaRue Jones was now reinvented with a more colorful creation myth, which toggled between "a Jew descended from generations of the Ten Lost Tribes in the city of Bet

El Set between Abyssinia and Arabia" (*Ilustrowana Republika*, Lodz) and "a *Shabtis* [a descendant of the followers of the seventeenth-century false messiah, Shabbtai Zvi], with a father who was a healer and made herbal elixirs as did Toyve himself in New York" (*Dos Naye Lebn*, Bialystok).[28] In *Unzer Grodner Moment*, Ha'Cohen's father was said to be "named Petrosi, a very cultured man who was a high official in local Abyssinian government, while his mother Alia, died when he was young." And in order to explain (however improbably) LaRue's New Jersey residence, it was noted that his father "wanted him to be a fully realized Jew, so he was sent to study with a Russian rabbi in Newark."[29] Clearly, if LaRue Jones was a press magnet in the US, where Blacks were a common sight for urban Jews, in Europe, where Jews had rarely ever seen a Black person let alone one who spoke and sang like a native, the press could not get enough of him. His defenders and detractors—many and well distributed—were defined long before he set foot there.

The European portion of the tour would start and end in Warsaw, the international center of great cantorial singing, with him performing in the shadow of the great Tlomackie synagogue, the revered home to one of world's greatest cantors—and one of Jones's idols—Gershon Sirota. Warsaw Jewish audiences were tough; their enthusiastic devotion to cantorial singing split the difference between it about spiritual/aesthetic uplift and being an aggressive blood sport. It was the latter that LaRue would experience at his premier. In an unsigned *Unzer Express* concert review, the author makes clear at the outset (and at the close too, for good measure) that the concert's two Polish promoters were "shady characters" who had earlier produced a show where the only thing the cantor they presented had in common with the cantor they advertised was his name, leaving very angry attendees demanding refunds from the organizers, who were nowhere to be found. Now these same impresarios were back, and the Warsaw community (and *Unzer Express*), knowing that they had previously been conned by these "shady characters," naturally figured that the "Black Cantor" too was a scam.[30]

When LaRue stepped onto the stage, Conservatory Hall was largely empty but for some comped guests, a handful of intrepid and curious listeners, and the ubiquitous confrontational hecklers in the gallery (at one point, they derisively called out "Sing 'Sonny Boy,'" Al Jolson's hit of the previous season).[31] *Unzer Express* described in delighted detail LaRue Jones's "deer in the headlights" response—he was reduced to begging the audience in Yiddish to give him a chance. In the end, he gave a truncated fifty-minute concert, with what little audience remained streaming out as he sang. LaRue was chastised for everything from his doubtful lineage to his stage mannerisms to his cantorial singing being influenced by 78s. The coup de grâce was an accompanying cartoon of a minstrel-like Toyvele standing at a pulpit holding his *siddur* upside down (thus questioning his very basic literacy) and being told to turn it right side up by a little man behind the pulpit labeled "impresario," one of the "shady characters."[32]

His next stop was entirely different. "Toyvele, the Black cantor demonstrated here that the defamation he faced in the pages of a well-known Warsaw newspaper was completely without merit." So ran the lead in the review of LaRue's Bialystok concert. The paper, *Naye Leben* (*The New Life*), had been a fan of LaRue's since even before his arrival, having run a story about LaRue Jones in 1921. *Naye Leben* rolled out the red carpet for LaRue, including a preconcert sit-down interview with their editor ("He is a genial young man of not just looks but his speech makes it seem as if the waters of the Jewish Diaspora have cascaded down upon him"). In its review, the paper also deftly deflated the charge in the Warsaw press about LaRue's reliance on commercial sound recordings by simply acknowledging it: "True, his cantorial prayers sound as if he learned them off phonograph records and lack the burning immediacy of traditional cantorial improvisation, but the same can be said for a hundred percent of modern cantors even those who are currently practicing." It concluded with an ecstatic concert review: "The audience gave him several standing ovations not allowing him to go on with the rest of the concert. . . . He is an unrivaled master worthy of the kind of praise heaped upon opera singers. In his bestowing sincerity, honesty and artistic heart in each of his songs, you experience his true artistry."[33]

From there LaRue Jones went to Lodz, Leipzig, and Berlin. The Grodno papers excitedly reported on this previous stop:

> The Black cantor arrives here direct from Berlin where his concerts in their largest concert hall generated such a colossal response that he had to increase to 12 his scheduled three concerts. . . . The Berlin music critics were effusive in their praise of the Black cantor in the *Berliner Tageblatt*, *Vossische Zeitung*, *Morgen Post* and many others. Reviewers were captivated by the concerts so it would stand to reason that here in Grodno—where we know a thing or two about khazones—his imminent arrival has generated so much interest.[34]

Jones ended his first European tour on December 20 where it started, in Warsaw, but was now the scene of his comeback triumph. LaRue Jones broadcast nationwide on the Polish state radio and included cantorial, Yiddish songs, and even jazz. LaRue had had the last word.

LaRue Jones would return to Europe several more times, but the treatment he received was starting to deteriorate. A return concert in Berlin was upended when the German Cantor's Association called out the "undignified manner in which foreign Jewish cantors—particularly a negro cantor from America have recently been advertising their concerts and charges about an illicit affair with an unnamed noblewoman."[35] Perhaps the most shameful treatment occurred in 1935. In his memoir *Theatrical Caravans*, theater empresario Sh. Harendorf wrote of vacationing in Bratislava, when he was invited to attend a LaRue Jones concert in a small town outside the city.[36] Harendorf met with LaRue, who told him (in yet another origin story variation) that he was born in Harlem to Abyssinian Jewish parents, studied in an African American Talmud Torah, and didn't learn khazones from a cantor but from 78s. LaRue Jones shared with Harendorf that, despite the great acclaim for his performances, his audiences were split—some believed he was a Jew, and others did not.

Hardendorf, who believed he was Jewish, described such a demonstration by several hundred outside LaRue's theater. Some claimed LaRue was not a Jew and simply learned a few cantorial pieces, while others believed he was Jewish and that it was against all tenets of Jewish ethics to humiliate him. A provocateur then called out that in order to prove it, LaRue Jones should be taken to the *mikve* (ritual bath) and undressed, to see if he was circumcised. Despite LaRue's tearful protestations, the mob took up the chant and demanded he expose himself before they would let him perform. LaRue refused and left the country, never to return.[37]

Back in Newark, LaRue Jones returned to his insider/outsider status, being a part of and apart from the adjacent Jewish world. LaRue participated in helping orphaned boys learn their bar mitzvah *haftorah* that were far beyond the scope of an "entertainer," which points to LaRue's deeper and complex connectivity with the Jewish community.[38] An eyewitness recalled some half century later,

> I recall a political meeting at the old Hebrew Democratic Club he sang a Yiddish song. The hall was filled with politicians and Third Ward mob . . . all the *shtarkers*. Tommy sang (he had a sad voice when he needed it) about a boy in the cemetery, *shtain shtain tayere shtain* (dear stone you were once my mother) . . .
> Believe it or not these "tough" guys were crying . . . ever Yiddish *shtarkers* in their hearts.[39]

Yet for his dependable longtime proximity, utility, and ubiquity, LaRue endured serial racism, intended or not. A notice in the *Newark Evening Star*, from January 1, 1916, states that a Jewish social group hired LaRue Jones to sing and "to give cakewalks," while nearly two decades later on December 12, 1933, Temple Sharey Tefillo, despite having worked with him before, offered mangled inaccurate ballyhoo for his appearance at the East Orange congregation: "The music will be of the same high quality as last year's and will be furnished by the same orchestra the 'Bumble Bee Radio Broadcast Orchestra.' Thomas LaRue, a negro musical director of Newark who is said to be a Negro Jew born in Afghanistan will be in personal charge of the orchestra. It is planned to have a midnight minstrel show duplicating the success of last year, and starring Mr. LaRue."[40]

LaRue Jones enjoyed a one-off coda on the Yiddish stage in 1937 as a *speshl etrekshn* for old employer Jacob Jacobs in the Bronx McKinley Square Theater production of *Falshe tokhter* (*False Daughter*) and a brief tour of the provincial Yiddish circuit with concerts in Chicago, Baltimore, and Pittsburgh.

During the war years, LaRue Jones worked for the Brewster Aeronautical Company in Newark airport, manufacturing dive bombers and pursuit planes for the US Navy, including the infamous F-2A Buffalo.[41] While it is unclear what war work LaRue Jones did, he had experience in design, manufacturing, and mechanical technology: on January 18, 1927, after seven years of work, Thomas LaRue Jones was awarded US patent no. 1,614, 675 for his "elevator safety appliance," an automatic braking system.[42] LaRue Jones's last known musical performance occurred only a year before his death in 1954 for the same Orthodox synagogue, Ahavath Zion, with whom he had been affiliated in the 1920s.[43]

The question of whether LaRue Jones was actually Jewish continues to be unanswered. He was not buried in a Jewish cemetery, but in an unmarked grave in a former potter's field of a nonsectarian cemetery. More tellingly, despite the cemetery having a Jewish section, LaRue Jones is not in it. Cemetery burial records do not indicate the involvement of any religious institution in his funeral, only of LaRue Jones's destitute, widowed sister with whom the lifelong bachelor LaRue Jones lived.

In July 2021, after a brief fundraising effort, a headstone was erected on Thomas LaRue Jones's unmarked grave and a small ceremony of about a dozen attendees was held, at which I spoke and played LaRue Jones' record of "Don't Give Up Hope, Mr. Jew."[44]

Figure 20.4. Gladys Mae Sellers as Goldye Di Shvartze Khaznte ca. 1928. *Source:* YIVO Institute for Jewish Research. Used with permission.

Gladys Mae Sellers: Goldye, Di Shvartze Khaznte

As improbable as were the Black men who mastered Yiddish and cantorial singing, even more astounding was the woman, first introduced in the promo for a 1925 Pittsburgh Jewish community concert:

The life of this artist is interesting. It reads like a story from a thousand and one nights. Goldye, the colored cantor, one of the most beautiful women in Africa, was born in Abyssinia, Africa, twenty-eight years ago. Once a tribal chief met her at the mines, and after hearing her sing his interest was so great that he sent her to Milan, Italy, to cultivate her voice.

Goldye is a member of the Jewish tribe known as "Sheba of Gza." They are a tribe of colored Jews in Africa. When Goldye returned from her studies in Italy she sang on a concert stage in Africa, as well as in the synagogue of her own people. Goldye sings in six languages—Hebrew, Yiddish, Russian, German, French and English, and is fluent in all of them. Goldye is a linguist, a poet and a composer. She is now visiting America for the first time in concerts that were never heard.

She is a cantor, a singer of Jewish folksongs, and her singing touches the strings of the human heart.[45]

This "biography" was actually the plot of a play that she had written for her, but as with Thomas LaRue Jones, the true story is far more astounding and amazing.

Gladys Mae Sellers (alternately "Sellars," 1890–1960) was born in Illinois and grew up in Milwaukee's Black community, where, starting in her teens, she was giving highly acclaimed concerts through the city's various African American churches and for its philanthropic organizations.[46] A 1915 marriage to Albert Smack (described as a "silver toned tenor") introduced her to the Black Midwest vaudeville circuit, a distinct shift from her church and art music repertoires. A review of their Chicago concert had Sellers following up arias from *Tales of Hoffman* with "Mighty Lak a Rose," which the paper said she rendered "with ease and feeling."[47] By 1917, Sellers studied with Chicago's Black doyenne Mme. E. Azalia Hackley, who pioneered teaching Western art music and African American traditional vernacular song to Black women as part of their societal cultural uplift.[48]

Appreciation of Gladys Sellers's singing came early and often, as newspapers in her adolescence were already using terms like "electrical," "unforgettable," and "spellbinding." At a the end of a 1919 Milwaukee concert by the pioneering African American composer Will Marion Cook, "Director Cook asked to hear one of the little colored usher girls of the Pabst, Gladys Sellers, sing. He was so pleased with the girls' voice that he at once made her an offer to join his orchestra as a vocalist and the offer was accepted."⁴⁹ In another abrupt transition in her singing styles, for most of 1922 Gladys Sellers was a member of drummer John H. Wickliffe's Famous Ginger Band. Since 1916, it was Chicago's pioneering rag-a-jazz orchestra, prior to the arrival of King Oliver and Louis Armstrong.⁵⁰

From her earliest years, Sellers was keen on creating new identities; early clippings alternately describe her as the Bronze Melba (after white lyric coloratura soprano Nellie Melba), the Race's Dramatic Soprano Nightingale, the Cream City Coloratura, and the Wisconsin Nightingale, among others.⁵¹ So, after nothing is heard from or about her until 1924, like Athena springing fully formed from the head of Zeus, Gladys Mae Sellers emerges fully formed as the polyglot poet/princess Goldye, di shvartze khaznte.⁵² And despite her previous stylistic reinventions, from church music to opera to Tin Pan Alley and then-nascent jazz (all genres within reach in her Black Milwaukee world), Sellers—unlike Thomas LaRue Jones in Newark—had no connections to a Jewish community soundscape from which to learn.

How she learned her Yiddish and cantorial repertoire to join the traveling Yiddish theater troupes could have been, like LaRue Jones, from Jewish 78s. (A review for a benefit concert at a Hebrew day school noted that she sang "Sorea Zedokos" ["God plants the seeds, so we can give"], which was a bestselling disc for Yossele Rosenblatt in 1916 and found many imitators.)⁵³ Yet even with that, the question of how Gladys Mae Sellers apparently mastered these two Jewish music forms in under two years is unclear.

Yet putting aside the formidable task of constructing a deep, culturally resonant repertoire (and the parallel language skills), how could Sellers have even conceived of such a performance character as a "Black woman cantor"? As noted, both khazntes and shvartze khazonim were relatively new inventions on their own terms. But a combination—a Black woman cantor—was, and remains, wholly without precedent.⁵⁴ How could Sellers have understood and navigated the subtle cultural and gender issues underlying the promotion of her character, Goldye, to the very community for whom those sociocultural lines were clearly articulated and inviolable?

Could Sellers have even known about shvartze khazonim? Thomas LaRue Jones had already started in New York by 1916 and toured the Midwest in the years immediately after that; perhaps she saw him there. David Kollscritta was living down the block from Sellers in Milwaukee in 1918, perhaps he and Sellers met. Is it possible that Sellers attended (heard about?) Sophie Kurtzer's ill-fated, semi-aborted Chicago-area 1921 concert? In creating "Goldye," Sellers appears to have drawn from the Sophie Kurzter playbook. First, Goldye too adopted the prefix "Madame," imbuing herself with a matronly and settled persona. And Goldye, like the physically full Sophie Kurtzer, wore the full regulation cantorial gown and a miter yarmulka.

However, what Sellers could not borrow from Sophie Kurtzer was the latter's Eastern European backstory. So she went one better by transforming herself from a Milwaukee Baptist church attending, Black vaudeville touring, jazz band singing "Cream City Coloratura" into the exotic, proud, Abyssinian-born multilingual singing Jewish poet/princess: Goldye, di Shvartze Khaznte.

Gladys Mae Sellers's transformation into the Ethiopian/Queen of Sheba descendant Goldye the Shvartze Khaznte may have been engineered by her Yiddish circuit tour impresario Edvin A. Relkin given its similarity to Relkin's later transformation of Thomas LaRue Jones into the Abyssinian-born Toyve, Ha'Cohen on his 1930 European tour.

Goldye arrived in New York City in 1924 and lived at 228 Eldridge Street on the Lower East Side, which no doubt helped her Yiddish, before moving to Morningside Heights for the next twenty years. Goldye's New York Yiddish bow at Harlem's Mount Morris vaudeville house (a year after LaRue played there) was immortalized in a January 23, 1925, pan review in the anarchist Yiddish newspaper *Fraye Arbeter Shtimme*. Under the banner "Vaudeville—Russian, American and Yiddish," author L. Krishtal elevates Nikita Balief's very popular Chauve-Souris variety troupe by trashing Goldye as "being the best that American Yiddish vaudeville can provide": "Here today in 1925, we have 'Golda [sic] the Black Cantor,' a 'star' in the vaudeville theater among banal, coarse couplets and duets and foolish acts which are standard for Jews in all vaudeville presentations."[55]

On the other hand, the *Forverts* lauded her Harlem show: "She is one of the most beautiful singers and her wonderful appearances featuring cantorial and folk songs has brought her wide audience admiration."[56] "Baltimore Awaits with Impatience the 17th of June" was another *Forverts* headline for an appearance in which Goldye split the bill with "Samuel Zimbalist, the 'Jascha Heifetz of the Cymbalom.'"[57] The African American press also took notice, as the March 7, 1925, *Pittsburgh Courier* previewed an upcoming concert of hers: "This is a real novelty; hearing a Negro singing Hebrew, Jewish, German and French. The talent of this artist proves that we as a race are taking our place in the realm of the higher arts."[58]

Lulu Belle on Broadway

Goldye's breakout appearance in New York would not, however, be in the Yiddish world but on Broadway. Goldye had long longed to be a stage actress; on her 1910 federal census, even before taking any theater work, she listed her profession as "actress" in the industry of "theater." On Broadway, she rechristened herself yet again; while retaining the moniker Goldye and her birth middle name, she changed her last name to Steiner. The show in which "Goldye Mae Steiner" appeared was David Belasco's controversial *Lulu Belle*, a lavish, lascivious mixed-race *Carmen in Harlem* that opened in fall 1926.

The play's salacious staging had what one reviewer called "a brazen cabaret scene of howling sex and saxophones." It was performed by a white cast in blackface and a segregated Black cast, causing Sylvester Russell of the African American newspaper *The Pittsburgh Courier* to peg it as featuring "a white playwright's version of free common racial slander to be depicted in stage usage to blaspheme, slander and lower rate a weaker minority race for the glory of an ignorant, prejudiced white majority."[1]

Despite the general revulsion of the play in the Black community, Goldye's appearance opened her entry to the Harlem Renaissance. A December 4, 1926, article about a lavish party thrown by pioneering blues recording artist Lucille Hegamin included, in addition to Goldye and the cast of *Lulu Belle*, composer-poet Andy "Ain't Misbehavin'" Razaf, J. C. "the Joint Is Jumpin'" Johnson, and many others.[2] Thanks to the play's controversy, *Lulu Belle* would run for more than a year and give more than 429 performances. When it closed, Goldye, di Shvartze Khaznte reappeared on the provincial Yiddish circuit.

---

1. Sylvester Russell, "Connotation Script Jeopardized Belasco Publicity Interests," *Pittsburgh Courier*, Feb. 13, 1926, 10.

2. "Lucille Hegamin Record Star Gives 'Too Bad' Party," *Pittsburgh Courier*, Dec. 4, 1926, 11.

Goldye Mae Steiner returned to the English-language stage on April 8, 1928, in a play called *Him* by poet e. e. cummings. Staged by the Provincetown Playhouse in Greenwich Village, the modernist experimental play was met with devastatingly bad reviews ("weird and unusual drama," snorted *The New York Times*) and somehow staggered through twenty-seven performances. The *Daily News* reviewer (who walked out after the second act) panned the show but celebrated Goldye: "Miss Steiner sang the Frankie and Johnny legend with excellent effect."[59] The song brought down the curtain (and the house) at the end of act two, the first time this quintessential African American murder ballad was performed on a major stage.

The moment was immortalized by artist John French Sloan, one of the founders of the so-called Ashcan School. Sloan, who caught one of the twenty-seven performances, rendered an electrifying etching of Goldye's enraptured performance surrounded by "a masked corps of assistants who sing and dance."[60]

With the abrupt closing of *Him*, Goldye's next gig was at the McKinley Square Theater in the Bronx in a Yiddish vaudeville revue, *Yente af brodvey* with wunderkind Seymour Rechtzeit, Hirsh Gross and his Famous Yiddish-English Jazz Band, and Jacob and Nina Sheikowitz (the latter billed as "the Volcano of Joy").[61]

Now armed with significant, legitimate stage experience, Goldye returned to the out-of-town Yiddish circuit with her own show. The play,

Figure 20.5. John Sloan's etching of Goldye Mae Steiner singing "Frankie and Johnny" in the e. e. cummings play *Him*, 1928. *Source:* Library of Congress Prints and Photographs division. Public domain.

The Daughter of a Lost Tribe by a Dr. S. Brody, concretized Goldye's faux backstory across "18 numbers of Oriental and Yiddish Music" and toured the Yiddish hinterlands for months.[62] There was even talk, early in 1929, of a Broadway production, but it never materialized.

Goldye returned to New York by March 1932 with a fifteen-minute cantorial show on WNYC and WEVD, but it would be broadcasts on a different station—and in a completely different religious context—that would show her amazing versatility and adaptability. In late April of 1933, the article "The Day in New York," described the Easter services of Bowery hooligan turned colorful Christian evangelical preacher Tom Noonan (the self-proclaimed "Bishop of Chinatown"), at his rescue mission the "Cathedral of the Underworld" in a former Doyers Street opium den. The article describes the colorful scene: "Behind Tom Noonan on the stage they saw a jazz orchestra, a volunteer choir, a portly Negress, a Japanese, a Jew, three cornet players and a song leader and stooge. The Negress turned out to be Goldye Mae Steiner, student of Hebrew and the only colored woman cantor in America. She sang the great Jewish lament ['Eli, Eli'] then sat down and joined lustily in 'Onward Christian Soldiers.' "[63] Starting in 1933 until the show went off the air in 1938, Goldye Mae Steiner was the Jewish music regular on Noonan's WMCA Sunday afternoon *Cathedral of the Underworld*. Despite the overtly Christian context of the show, Goldye's regular khazones segment explains why it was included in the broadcast listings of Yiddish and Anglo-Jewish papers like *The Brooklyn Jewish Examiner*.[64]

Goldye's final concerts show her tremendous biracial and bicultural stretch, her presence in both Black and Jewish, and her seemingly unending plethora of stage names. On May 8, 1938, in what was possibly a model for the later Benny Goodman Carnegie Hall Spirituals to Swing concert, the Urban League staged Swing to Opera at the Brooklyn Academy of Music featuring many top African American performers like Duke Ellington, Noble Sissle, Fats Waller, and Hazel Scott, and including Gladys Sellers. Yet here she is billed as "Goldye Steiner, the only colored cantor in the world," choosing a Jewish performance identity and repertoire for a distinctly African American context and audience.[65]

Conversely, the following year she appeared in her final known Yiddish stage shows. In the first, *Der poylisher rebbe* (*The Polish Rabbi*), a musical comedy by the dean of Yiddish composers Alexander Olshanetsky, starring Leo Fuchs, she is billed as "Gladys Mae Sellers," her birth name that she had not used onstage in decades. The anonymous *Daily News* reviewer on March 21, 1939, marveled: "The cast also is aided by the presence of Miss

Gladys Mae Sellers a colored entertainer of generous proportions who adds some novel, if startling, touches to the proceedings."[66] What those "startling touches" were is a mystery.

When *Der poylisher rebbe* closed, star Itzik Feld opened another musical comedy at the Clinton Theater (*Der rebetzin's dzhigalo* [Mrs. Rabbi's Gigolo]), along with Gladys Mae Sellers, here billed as "Goldye, di Shvartze Khaznte."[67] As a sort of unintentional race counterpoint, playing at the same time at the nearby National Theater was Israel Rosenberg's Yiddish adaptation of *Imitation of Life* (*Shvartze mame* [Black Mother]), a musical melodrama dealing with issues of miscegenation and racism and with actress Gertie Stein as Delilah Johnson, presumably in blackface.[68]

In 1941, Gladys married Richard Armstead and, in the closure of her long life arc, moved back to Milwaukee around 1950 where she lived until her death in 1960. In 2022, Milwaukee native Shahanna McKinney Baldon (inspired by my research and who performs as Goldye), located her long-forgotten unmarked grave, and echoing the headstone campaign for Thomas LaRue Jones, raised money to place a marker in 2024.

Unlike Thomas LaRue Jones, who left behind a recording, and despite Gladys's years of radio appearances and close proximity to New York's recording center, no example of her singing appears to exist. Perhaps what is most curious about LaRue Jones and Gladys Mae Sellers is that, despite the fact that both were the best-known exponents of Black cantorial singing, toured the same regional Yiddish circuit, headlined the Mt. Morris theater in the Bronx, were managed by Edvin A. Relkin, and lived in the New York metropolitan area, there is nothing to indicate they ever performed together or that they even met.

Part 4
Theater

21

Yente Telebende

The Woman with the Wallop

Of all the words that have migrated from Yiddish to English, one of the best known, "Yenta" ("gossip" or "busybody"), was made popular by a character in the show/film *Fiddler on the Roof*. But this fictional Yenta (with an *a*) obscures an earlier fictional Yente (with an *e*), who was nothing like her: a strong, loud woman whose seemingly endless stream of colorful, full throttle take-no-prisoners invective deeply endeared her to tens of thousands of immigrant Jews: Yente Telebende.

Yente's roots go back to the Latin *Gentilis*, and in old Italian meaning "refined," "noble," "highborn," and perhaps most ironically, "Gentile." The word became the Yiddish name Yente (and Yentl) as both a first and middle name (Tzipe Yente, Beyle Yente Khaye Yente, etc.). Yente turns up in folk axioms (e.g., "Mayn yente" [my gal], "Di zelbe yente nor andersh geshlayert" [The same girl in a different getup]), and in Alexander Harkavy's 1928 Yiddish-Hebrew-English dictionary it appears as both a name and defined as "an old fashioned woman."[1]

And Telebende? In linguist-broadcaster Nahum Stutchkoff's magisterial language lexicon *Der oytser fun der yiddisher sprakh* (*The Treasure of the Yiddish Language*, 1950), among the nearly 1,200 synonyms for the word "hit" (*khmalye, patsh, frask, tuze,* etc.) are a subset of "tele" prefix words, less "hit" than "wallop," "smash," or "whoop ass," which include *telemertshe, telepetshe, telemetshe,* and *telebende*.[2]

The "old fashioned whoop ass woman" was the invention of poet, memoirist, humorist, and playwright Jacob "Yankev" Adler (1874–1974), who wrote under a dizzying number of noms de plume in an equally dizzying number of publications.[3] Adler was born in Dinov, Galicia, and grew up with a religious education. At the age of sixteen he came to US, where he worked in a factory. Around 1897, Adler began submitting poems to Yiddish workers' newspapers including the *Forverts*. Editor Abe Cahan soon took a shine to Adler and not only brought him on as a columnist on the same page as his editorials but also anointed him his pen name (B. Kovner) to avoid confusion with Yiddish actor Jacob P. Adler.

On May 17, 1913, Kovner published the column Mayn *peyper* un mayn yente. While ostensibly about Mendel Telebende reading the day's news, readers had an immediate and enthusiastic reaction to the salty, sassy, heat-seeking, sharp-eyed, sharp-tongued deconstructive and destructive reactions of his wife, Yente. So every Saturday night readers eagerly awaited the thousand words about the rough-and-tumble, hardscrabble, rambunctious, and dysfunctional Telebendes, including hapless husband Mendel, their children (referred to breezily as "*di mamzeyrim*" [the bastards])—son Pinye "the Candy Kid" (a Yiddish Bart Simpson) and his sister Malke (a female Bart)—and the Telebende's colorful neighbors, Moishe Kapoyer ([head upside down]his name derived from the *kapoyre hindl*/sacrificial poultry), Fishl Dovid, the Teacher, Payshe der Farmer, and Sammy der Big Bluffer, plus doctors, boarders, landlords, and friends. But mostly readers loved the fire-breathing, curse-spewing Yente.

Yente Telebende did not come out of nowhere. Kovner, like Cahan, was a keen observer of American popular culture and actively incorporated its successful elements into his work.

In January 1913, King Features rolled out the new comic strip *Bringing Up Father* by George McManus. The strip, about a nouveau riche, shanty Irish couple, with husband (Jiggs) beleaguered by Maggie, his battling, belting and belittling, rolling-pin-wielding wife, would run for almost ninety years. So when Yente Telebende bowed that spring, she was transformed from "Hibernian" to "Hebrew," and Maggie's famous rolling pin became Yente's omnipresent "valgerholtz." ("In one hand she carries a rolling pin, while in the other she leads Pinye, a scamp of eleven years with a twisted cap and a fresh black eye."[4]) Very quickly, Yente stories were as popular in Yiddish-speaking homes as McManus's *Bringing Up Father* comic strip was in the mainstream.

Not being a comic, readers were curious what she looked like. Kovner described Yente as "a big, heavy old married woman with a wide nose and thin blue lips, given to cursing, with a wrinkled, unwashed dress, dirty neck and eyes." She was first visualized on November 25, 1914, when the *Forverts* staged a "lightning sketches" night, featuring staff cartoonists Joseph Branin and Peter Neago, who drew "Pinye, Mendel Telebende, Fishl Duvid the teacher, Nukhem Knish the poet, and more" before a live audience. (But it was cartoonist/puppeteer Zuni Maud, who, when Yente Telebende became a stage show, created its visual images as shown in the ads and reviews featuring his drawings.)[5]

In the fall of 1917, the production of *Yente Telebende* came out at Thomashefsky's National Theater at Houston and Second Avenue with a score by Joseph Rumshinsky and directed by Thomashefsky. The title role went to Bina Abramovitch (later called "the mother of the American Yiddish theater" because, at one time or another, she played everyone's mother); Julius Nathanson played Yente's ne'er-do-well, long-suffering Mendel; and Thomashefsky played a new character specially written for him as Yente's brother. Cahan let loose his top-gun culture writer Hillel Rogoff to pen a first night review from the aisle.

"This is an entirely new thing for the Yiddish stage," Rogoff noted of what was no doubt the first "spin off" in Yiddish popular culture, while "on Broadway American audiences are long used to such things."[6] The play ran at Thomashefsky's National for its full season.

Despite the musical's success, no commercial recordings were made. But coincidentally, 1917 saw the release of a dozen of what would be more than one hundred *Yente Telebende* records over the next four decades. Although none were written by Kovner, all accurately reflected and amplified his original Telebende characters while greatly extending the parameters and distribution of their popularity. During the 1920s—when more than half of the records were issued—Yente and Mendel Telebende appeared on virtually every major record label (Victor, Columbia, Emerson, Cardinal, Pathé, OKeh, etc.) in an equally large number of new contexts:

Mendel Telebende vert president (*Mendel Telebende Becomes President*, 1917)
Yente vert a djanitor (*Yente Becomes a Janitor*, 1919)
Yente fregt di fir kashes (*Yente Asks the Four Questions*, 1920)
Yente khulemt fin a luftshif (*Yente Dreams of an Airship*, 1921)
Yente hot faint di mener (*Yente Hates the Men*, 1921)
Mendel vert a polisman (*Mendel Becomes a Policeman*, 1922)

Yente blaybt a yente (*Yente Remains a Yente*, 1923)
Mendel vert a prayz fayter (*Mendel Becomes a Prize Fighter*, 1924)

The recordings all followed the same tried-and-true structure of a vaudeville turn (something the actual stage Yente never was): an eight-bar musical intro preceded a short comic skit setting up the subsequent verse/chorus song that, with repeats and a quick reprise of the entrance music, all fit very neatly on a three-ish-minute ten-inch disc.

One of the first records, a patriotic wartime entry recorded by the Telebende Quartet (Clara Gold, Gus Goldstein, Miss Poline, and Mr. Gittleman) for Columbia on May 22, 1917, reflects the up-front adversarial, dysfunctional Telebende family that readers—now also listeners—loved:

MENDEL: Yente Telebende my wife, Sadie, my daughter, Pinye my son, gather around I have something to tell you all.

ALL: What?

MENDEL: I want to tell you that I have decided to become a *soldjer*. And not just I became a *soldjer*: Reb Gedalye, Tall Moishe, Chaim the Crip and Redheaded Fayvl and Getsl the Gimp have also become *soldjers*. And we will all of us scream *hooray for America* we will cry out *three cheers for America* and we will *fight* until we will win.

PINYE: Hooray for my father and even more for my mother who will be a widow! (Singsong) "And I'll recite the Kaddish, And I'll recite the Kaddish!"

SADIE: And I'll have a new father! And when you die, we'll make you such a nice funeral so I can say: "my dead father, Mendel Telebende, was buried just like a general!"

YENTE: Aha, Mendele, you're going to be a *soldjer* and think you'll be rid of me? I understand what's in your little mind. I certainly want America to win the war but I also want you to lose an eye. The Americans should catch a German submarine and you should catch a Romanian head cold! Oh, but maybe you have a little tootsie socked away somewhere, where is your tootsie?

MENDEL: Me? What are you talking about? Who has a tootsie?

ALL: Who is your tootsie?[7]

A popular Yente interpreter was contralto Anna Hoffman, who, from 1916 to 1926, recorded over 150 Yiddish 78s mainly for Columbia and Victor. On June 21, 1917, two months after America entered the war (and

Figure 21.1. Every performance of the 1922 *Yente Telebende* production also featured a showstopping appearance by Thomas LaRue Jones (Der shvartzer khazn). *Source:* National Library of Israel, Historical Jewish Press website (www.jpress.org.il), founded by the National Library and Tel Aviv University. Used with permission.

nearly a half year before the Thomashefsky Yente stage production opened) Hoffman recorded her own patriotic "Yente Gait Zech Registin" ("Yente Registers for the Draft") with actor and lyricist Jacob Jacobs (as Mendel) in whose theater troupe she was a member.

It would be Jacob Jacobs's subsequent 1922 *Telebende* production that pulled off a rarity on the professional New York stage: taking a recently successful musical comedy with one cast, book, and score and remounting it just a few years later with a new cast, book, and score and outperforming the original. The new show was described as a burlesque, a kind of French bedroom farce with the Telebendes trying to marry off their daughter to unsuspecting suitors before they learn that she has her mother's same foul-tempered, invective-spewing predisposition. It opened on New Year's Eve at Jacobs and Goldberg's Harlem-based Lenox Theater with Abe Cahan giving a talk on humor and Kovner reading from his feuilletons. *Yente Telebende* played to packed houses for a solid year.

Unlike in 1917, some of the show's thirty songs by Jacobs and composer L. Cohen were commercially recorded, including the title song sung by Anna Hoffman:

> I don't have to introduce myself, it's really no conceit
> I'm Yente Telebende
> All the kids call out when they see me in the *strit*
> "Hey! Yente Telebende!"
> No one dares to cross me as you wouldn't take the risk
> The cops will never stop me, as they're too afraid to frisk
> If I curse you in New York, they will hear it back in Brisk
> I'm Yente Telebende
> CHORUS
> Yente Telebende, Yente Telebende
> Everything by me is good and fine
> I'm red hot, tell 'em Yente sent ya
> Telebende, Yente Yente is alright!
> My Mendel hasn't seen the dentist in a year or more
> I am Yente Telebende
> Because I knocked his teeth out and they're laying on the floor
> Me, Yente Telebende
> I know this from deep within my heart
> That the Angel of death fears me so he'd better not start
> And if he does, like Mendel, I will tear him right apart
> I'm Yente Telebende.[8]

Not everyone was amused by Yente-mania. The *Tog* commented: "From time to time, we do battle with the *Forverts*, perhaps because they are socialists? The *Forverts* itself knows that is not true. We struggle against the *Forverts* not about Socialism, but 'Yente Telebende,' the fact that everything which passes through his [Cahan's] hands he makes vulgar, so crude, so brutish."[9]

"This degradation of the Jewish woman has been going on for too long already," thundered essayist Reuven Brinan. "It's become a tradition to denigrate and laugh at Jewish women, [Yente] in a series of cutting curses, a never ending, living well, Yente herself becomes engulfed, reduced and degraded without heart by these curses now a kind of horror, full of holes and who is now beneath, and made to look more foolish than, the man, the 'wise one.' "[10] Another *Tog* columnist, A. Drashner, in his column teyater feuillitonen, sniped that Cahan honored Yente by putting it cheek by jowl with his beloved editorials. "It now appears that 'Yente Telebende,' is thank God, more popular than Karl Marx despite both being very popular with Abe Cahan. However, Marx was doing nothing for circulation so was replaced on the editorial page by Yente Telebende."[11] And when it came to the new play, the paper's theater critic was also quick and unsparing:

> If the intention of this production was to make people forget about the previous production a mere five years ago by Boris Thomashefsky, in this, they did not succeed. . . . Given the vast invective that he [Mendel] receives I'd like to see a production where the man gives her back the same because she is wholly deserving of it. Then, I would like to see them both concentrate their bile at the creator of this show because *he* is wholly deserving of it.[12]

Not surprisingly, the *Forverts'* arch enemy, the *Freiheit*, also hated the show, inspiring its staff cartoonist William Gropper to portray Cahan as a Yente-ish, spitting, skillet-wielding, scold looming over the *Forverts*.[13]

Despite, the incessant razzing from the *Tog* (which may have spilled more ink discussing the show than the *Forverts*), *Yente Telebende* was a license to print money.

However, as much as the public loved Yente, what was really driving packed houses night after night for a solid year was the showstopper at the end of act three, as noted by the theater critic from the *Morgn Zhurnal*: "Yes, it has great music, humor, dancing, but above all is the wonderful 'Black Cantor,' and it is due to solely to him that this show is worth seeing again and again."[14]

Figure 21.2. "And he talks . . ." *Forverts* editor Abe Cahan depicted as Yente Telebende by William Gropper. *Source:* National Yiddish Book Center/Annice Jacoby. Used with permission.

A Black character had already been part of Kovner's column for years. In 1916, among the other members of his Yente repertory company, Adler introduced scalawag Pinye's best friend and partner in crime, identified as "Dos Niger'l." Kovner imbued the boys with a kind of rough, urban, interracial interaction as would become popular in only a few years in Hal Roach's *Our Gang* shorts. Kovner's readers clamored for more about him, as Kovner noted in the January 17, 1920, column Pinye's khaver, Dos Niger'l:

> "Wow! Dos Niger'l! What didn't he do with Pinye?
> He helped him in all his undertakings.
> If Pinye wanted to break windows, pull long Jewish beards, throw *snoubols* at Jewish girls, not allow others to pass on the

street, or on *Sukkas*, deliver *esrogs* to synagogues, or on Purim bring *shalakh mones* (food gifts), or on Chanukah eat all the latkes which Yente made.

In these, and all undertakings, was Dos Niger'l Pinye's pal and partner.

Kovner imbued Dos Niger'l with a depth even beyond his Jewish characters as when Pinye brings home a flyer:

ASTOUNDING! ASTOUNDING! ASTOUNDING!

A real Black man will sing folk songs in a downhome Yiddish and also cantorial pieces. Come hear him next Friday night at Scheur Hall, first floor you will literally be overwhelmed the profits go to help victims of the recent war.

Tickets are 35c including a hat check.

Come in mass.

First he sang, "Oyfn Pripetshik," followed by a cantorial solo "Odom Yesodo Meofor" then he conducted the Rosh Chodesh blessings, sang "A brivele der mamen," "Di mezinke oysgegebn," "Eli, Eli" . . . all mouths shut and all ears opened and the hall became still . . . in short, he took the audience by storm.

The concept of a Black man mastering Yiddish and Hebrew music no doubt surprised Kovner's tens of thousands of readers. As Yente said, "Our own children don't speak Yiddish and he, a Black child, can sing Yiddish songs."[15]

Given the detail, Kovner was probably describing one of Thomas LaRue Jones's 1918 *Forverts* salons.[16] Kovner then created an amazing staging platform to see the "actual" grown-up Niger'l project a powerful sense of veracity when LaRue Jones was added to the cast in his bring-down-the-house show closing scene.

Even in the running gun battle between the *Tog* and the *Forverts*, the only thing about which the two papers could agree was Thomas LaRue Jones. The *Tog* noted: "And we would be remiss not to point out the Black cantor who mimics Yossele Rosenblatt perfectly and sings Yiddish and Russian songs with a deep heart feeling."[17] And Cahan, in the *Forverts*, agreed: "In the last act [at Payshe's farm] out steps the Black Cantor and sings cantorial songs, Yiddish, Russian . . . and he has wholly earned the wildly enthusiastic applause of his audiences. If at all possible, it is important to come see this."[18]

The producers drove attendance with the guarantee in their ads that "the Black Cantor will sing all new Yiddish, Hebrew and Russian songs at each show."

Yet this breakthrough casting idea was counterbalanced by a wholly regressive casting decision. In his 1900s staging of *Uncle Tom's Cabin*, Boris Thomashefsky challenged social and stage conventions by not requiring his Black actors to don burnt cork. However, for his 1917 *Telebende* production, Thomashefsky not only brought back burnt cork but also had the Dos Niger'l part played by a Miss Winters, a white actress. "Vashington, linken un moyshe rabeynu" ["Washington, Lincoln and Moses, Our Teacher"], the only song example from the show that survives, ridicules racial boundaries and opens startlingly with the coarse children's rhyme "Eeny Meeny Minie Moe" then offers a duet of both Jewish and Black racial stereotypes as Dos Niger'l sings:

> Why am I black
> Because my mother drank ink
> while she carried me
> Negroes can dance and
> Negroes can eat watermelon
> And shoot craps with dice
> And make goo goo eyes.[19]

As regressive as was Thomashefsky's retrograde burnt-cork casting, at the time there was no known pool of Yiddish-literate Black actors for him to draw upon. As Thomas LaRue Jones makes clear, that was not the case when it came time to cast the 1922 production but Dos Niger'l was continued as a cork/pants role, this time by ingenue Diana Goldberg.[20] Even before the original Yente show closed, it spun off several Yente road companies that toured the provincial Yiddish circuit in one form or another throughout the 1930s.

In December, Kovner and company launched a new play *Yente oyf yener velt* (*Yente from Beyond*), where Yente, now dead, returns to earth to haunt all her old characters. The *Forverts* declared it "a terrific success which opens with Yente in Heaven trading barbs with [matriarchs] Sarah, Leah, Rivke and Rukhl, to the final scene of the Black Cantor singing out of a siddur, the audience is in enraptured delight."[21]

However, the next time Kovner killed off Yente Telebende, she stayed dead. On March 21, 1931, he published "Yente Telebende is Dead" underscoring the seriousness of the title by changing the column's longstanding subhead "a shtiferay" ("a playful spoof") to "nisht kayn shtiferay" ("not a playful spoof"). After eighteen years, nearly a thousand entries, and over 930,000 words, Kovner set the final column around Yente Telebende's grave, where all the characters in the series reflect on her legacy and with no deus ex machina, as in "Yente af yener velt."[22] Except for one column in 1966 ("Yente Telebende's shvester"/"Yente Telebende's Sister"), Kovner stayed true to his decision and returned to writing poetry, observational essays, and humorous columns.

It actually didn't matter because Yente's decades of mass popularity meant she had her own trajectory as a kind of folk character kept alive by among others, Jacob Jacobs and the star of his 1922 Yente show, his wife Betty Jacobs who took their now exceedingly well-honed Mendel and Yente act to hotels and clubs and synagogue concerts. As Jacob Jacobs made one of the first Yente records in 1917, he and Betty would make the last around 1953 for Banner. Like the earlier Yente records that were mirrors of their time, this last 78 (*Gin Rummy*) also reflects its modern cultural markers with the popularity of the card game and a vogue for Latin types, but still retained the original vaudeville turn structure and more than a spark of the combativeness of the old franchise:

YT: Men-DEL!

MT: What is it, Yente Telebende?

YT: Listen to what I've decided!

MT: What is it, my little Yente?

YT: I want to be stylish. I want to change my name I don't want to be "Yente Telebende" any more. No matter where I go that name follows me around, from today forward Yente is dead!

MT: Dead? Who knew?

YT: Mendel, don't be a wiseguy. I'll make sure your meathead will fit in a dairy pot.

MT: Your name you're changing? How about your mouth?

YT: Men-DEL! Shut your kishke hole. I'm changing my name. No more Yente Telebende.

MT: So what will you be called?

YT: I'll be called Vonsya Chiquita Marcita Margarita Telebende.

MT: You can change what you want but Yente remains Yente and that's all.

YT: I wanna be stylish, you get me?

MT: Oy, I got you I got you and I'm trying to get rid of you.

YT: I wanna play Gin Rummy like all the stylish ladies

MT: Rummy? What sort of illness is that?

YT: It's not a sickness it's a game.

MT: A game? I know! I can play pinochle a whole day. Mishe peyshe a whole afternoon and a whole night, poker . . .

YT: I'll make you a poker on the head! That's for greenhorns. I want gin rummy. Look, here's a deck of cards. I'll give you the first lesson. You take ten cards. And give me eleven cards.

MT: Wait: why do you get more cards than me?

YT: That's the way it's played and sha-DAP! So, if I have five, six seven I have a—

MT: And if I have eight, nine, ten do I have a—

YT: And if I have good cards, I knock.

MT: Knock knock? Who's there? And what if I have bad cards and have nothing?

YT: If you have nothing then I knock you.

MT: Oy, you always do! I don't like it. Leave me alone with your gin rummy.

YT: That's only the first lesson! I will make you a box.

MT: Oh, she's preparing a box for me burying me together with gin rummy.

Gin Rummy Gin Rummy no matter where you roam
Gin Rummy Gin Rummy is played in every home
Mendel and Yente play most every day
She gives him a cuffing and he yells out oy vey
Gin Rummy Gin Rummy Gin Rummy Gin Rummy
Gin Rummy Gin Rummy folks play it all their lives
The baker the butcher they play it with their wives
The women who shop there say he can't be beat
He gets all their money, and they get all his meat.[23]

At the height of the 1922 Yente-mania, excited Yiddish journalists asked if Yente was destined for Broadway.[24] One answer to that was a short-lived pirate play, *Yente af brodvey*, at the Hopkinson Theater (in Yente's beloved Brownsville), which even had Lucille Rogers, a Black singer, at the show's end.[25] But no one could imagine how Yente would eventually come to Broadway.

Though found nowhere in Sholem Aleichem's "Tevye" stories from which the 1964 musical *Fiddler On the Roof* was derived, Jerry Bock and Sheldon Harnick invented the gossipy matchmaker character named Yenta and spelled with an A.

The snoopy character was introduced in act two in the song "The Rumor/I Just Heard" by its original actress Bea Arthur.

And just as in the film, where Zero Mostel's Maurice Schwartz influenced Tevye was eliminated in favor of Topol's Tevye-lite version, Bea Arthur, who would go on to portray a classic Kovner Yente (strong willed/fiery temperament) on TV as Maude was cut (together with her song), by Molly Picon who put an even greater indelible stamp on the mincing, busybody/gossipy Yenta.

The phenomenal success of *Fiddler On the Roof* would also be reflected in Leo Rosten's 1968 paean to Yinglish *The Joys of Yiddish* where the *Fiddler* definition of a "Yenta" as a scandal spreader, rumormonger, would first be in print.[26]

Four years later Yenta was first included in an American dictionary the eighth edition of Merriam Webster as "one who meddles, blabbermouth, gossip," codifying its acceptance.[27]

A pithy, accurate description that avoided the revisionist definition came from the unknown scribe in the 1975 *New York Times* B. Kovner obit, describing "Yenta" as "a loquacious battle-ax." (The inculcation of *Fiddler On the Roof*'s characterization of Yenta was so immersive that even today Microsoft Word will autocorrect "yente" to "yenta.")

The Yiddish world was also reckoning with a "naye Yente."

The Uriel Weinreich 1968 dictionary (published the same year as *The Joys of Yiddish*) echoes Harkavy's "vulgar, sentimental woman," as does the 2013 Beinfeld-Bochner *The Comprehensive Yiddish-English Dictionary*'s repeat of Harkavy's, but adds "gossip" for the first time in a Yiddish dictionary.[28]

Surprisingly, though it offers definitions for "busybody" (*kibitzer/kokhleff*) and gossip (*loshnhorenik, pliatkenik*, etc.), "yente" does not appear in the 2016 Schaechter-Viswanath-l *Glasser Comprehensive English-Yiddish Dictionary*.[29]

This transition from a woman who would get up in your face into one who would talk behind your back resulted from the weakening signal from the original Yiddish source but as shown, Kovner's pugnacious, combative, and colorful Yente was no yenta.

22

Uncle Thomashefsky's Cabin

The 1900s Yiddish Uncle Tom Shows

Despite the rural/agrarian context of blackface minstrelsy and its debased funhouse mirror reflection of African Americans, its formative performance history is solidly in the city, and most specifically, New York City. It was in New York, for example, which had abolished slavery in 1837, that the first strains of "Dixie" were sung and played on the banjo and fiddle by the blackface Bryant's Minstrels in April of 1859.[1] New York would be the center of the concentric circle for burnt-cork entertainment and the subsequent meth lab for the visualization of "the other," buffoonish ethnic depictions—"Dutch," Irish, Chinese, Italians, Jews—that would be part of American variety theater for the next century.

The cultural counterpoint to minstrelsy was Harriet Beecher Stowe's 1852 *Uncle Tom's Cabin or, Life Among the Lowly*, an unprecedented literary success that, even before the ink on its newly published pages was dry, spawned scores of Uncle Tom theatrical troupes crisscrossing the country bringing the story to life. And while the "Tom shows" were putatively seen as a rejoinder to the grotesquery of minstrelsy, they came to propagate their own stage stereotypes (i.e., the Mammy character) that, when taken together with minstrelsy, would be how millions of Americans would experience theater and perceive race.

The gains made under Reconstruction were rolled back in the 1880s rise of Jim Crow (the term itself borrowed from a blackface stage character) and introduced a new, grander form of minstrel show. In reflecting the tone of the Gilded Age, these were more lavish, louder, and larger than the previous folksy banjo-and-fiddle-driven bands and offered even more degraded characterizations than before. Ironically, it was only then that African American performers were first allowed to take to the stage, provided they fulfilled the minstrel stage conventions centered on the obligatory wearing of burnt cork and speaking in fractured English.

It was into this socio-theatrical foment that Yiddish-speaking Jews first arrived with their "still under construction" theater in tow. In the same way new immigrants move into a previous community's residences, houses of worship, and theaters, so too did these new emigres move into the previous community's theatrical conventions, in this case adopting blackface: the long-proven, surefire method of making one's way up the socioeconomic ladder by portraying someone farther down it.

Jewish interest in *Uncle Tom's Cabin* arose even before the first Yiddish speakers landed on these shores. Translations of the book started coming out in the 1860s with two published in Vilna by Isaac Myer Dik (1868 and 1887) one by a Mendel Rippel. By 1896, the first American-published Yiddish version was printed in New York by Kantrowitz and Katzenelenbogen (quite possibly a translation of a Hebrew edition published in Warsaw).[2] A December 1900 serial translation called *Di shvartze shklafn* (*The Black Slaves*) ran for four months in the *Arbeter Tsaytung* (*The Worker's Newspaper*) by B. Goren.[3]

In 1901, William A. Brady, a popular showman of spectacles and prize fights, staged a lavish *Uncle Tom's Cabin* revival, featuring "400 people in the plantation scene," at the Academy of Music on East Fourteenth Street and Irving Place on the northern border of the Lower East Side.[4] The show, which would run for months, sent excited ripples through the nearby Yiddish cultural world. Simultaneously, dueling Tom productions by two of New York's three major Yiddish theaters sprang up: actor-manager David Kessler's Thalia Theater, and Boris Thomashefsky—who had gotten his start at Kessler's Thalia and who was not above "improving" Kessler's plays—at the People's Theater.[5] While both productions offered newly written music (Kessler hired composer Joseph Brody, and Thomashefsky hired Sigmund Mogulesco and Louis Friedsel), what really reached across the footlights and grabbed the audiences by the ears were the Yiddish/English versions of songs drawn from minstrelsy, such as "Suwanee River," "Shoo Fly Don't Bother Me," "My Money Never Gives Out," and "Oh, Dem Golden Slippers," these last two by African American composers Irving Jones (1900) and James A. Bland (1879).

A remarkable firsthand account of the Kessler production appeared in *The New York Sun* on May 26, 1901, credited to a "Colonel Carrots of Atlanta," an unrepentant Confederate (he describes the play as "iniquitous"). After the article's brief obligatory prelude in which the Jewish box office agent, upon seeing how easily the Colonel is willing to pay for good house seats, immediately doubles the price, Carrots settles in to give a sympathetic eyewitness account of the show: "There were mothers with babies at their breast, and aged crones hobbling between the support of a young woman's arm and a wabbly [sic] cane. Squads of alert-eyed and sharp-faced young men, collarless and gabbling [sic] whispered words in one another's ears and bumped into squads of girls in gayly colored waist and hat; like flower gardens, who seemed to be moving up and down the steps merely for the sake of moving." Carrots describes Mrs. Wilensky, the actress who played Topsy, as making "a highly creditable effort to sing coon songs in Yiddish, with some retention of the broader tokens of the negro dialect." His article reproduced her macaronic version of "Oh, Dem Golden Slippers," which closely follows the lyrics and rhyming pattern of Bland's original:

> Meine goldene Slipers bin ich bereit
> Ich well nicht trugen sei bis mein Hochzeit
> Und mein langer Mantel, was ist elegant
> Ihm onthün well wen der Cariage steht gespannt
> Oh dem golden slippers
> Oh dem golden slippers
> Mine Slipers vel ich dan geyn
> Sei fiten mir ganz schön!⁶

Both Yiddish productions, like the Brady revival, employed a corps of African American performers. Yet while all the cast members—including the Black ones—in the mainstream *Uncle Tom's Cabin* followed the era's norm in using burnt cork, in the Yiddish productions the Black cast members did not, years ahead of Broadway. (Even when African American comedy star Bert Williams broke the color bar to join the 1910 *Ziegfeld Follies*, he did so in blackface.⁷) A reviewer for the *Indianapolis Star* noted a discrepancy in a scene between husband and wife Boris and Bessie Thomashefsky and an African American child actor playing their son: "The pickaninny . . . was a rich chocolate in hue, while it's papa and mama were orange-colored and this contrast was awkward."⁸

Not surprisingly, the Jewish press engaged around these productions. In *The American Hebrew* on May 24, a writer cheers on these cultural efforts and points out that the Jewish audience would more quickly respond to the character George Harris "and the combative spirit of the slave, willing to fight for his freedom as opposed to the other, the non-resisting, suffering spirit" of Uncle Tom.⁹ The next month *The American Israelite* retorted, expressing distaste for Yiddish by using the dismissive "jargon": "The New Yiddish theater company has staged 'Uncle Tom's Cabin' and now one is inclined to wonder how the Negro dialect sounds in Jargon. A Yiddish 'Topsy' should certainly be a curiosity. Too bad that Harriet Beecher Stowe has not lived to see the day."¹⁰

Figure 22.1. Cartoon in mainstream press defaming the mixed-race Yiddish *Uncle Tom's Cabin*. *Source:* National Library of Israel, Historical Jewish Press website (www.jpress.org.il), founded by the National Library and Tel Aviv University. Used with permission.

In the American press, however, it was the norm to lambaste these Yiddish theatrical pretentions. And to do so and also get in a dig at Blacks was a bonus. A May 9 article in the *Democrat and Chronicle* (Rochester), headlined: "Simon Le Greesky Arrested for Failing to Support His Wife" described the interracial Thomashefsky company that came to court to support their fellow actor: "The benches were crowded with a number of the pickaninskys [*sic*] and Hebrew black-face specialists who take part in the production."[11] "The limit has been reached," bleated the *Topeka State Journal* on May 18. "Will some Medium call the shade of Harriet Beecher Stowe to the protection of her own? 'Uncle Tom's Cabin' is to be given on the Bowery in Yiddish. Think of this."[12] Others gleefully pointed out flaws in the production: "To add to the realism, the blood hounds proved their fierceness by snapping at several members of the company."[13]

But non-Jewish papers were also dazzled by Thomashefsky's Tom, with several comparing him positively to the then-reigning Tom actor Wilton Lackaye: "Herr Thomashefsky, who takes the part of Uncle Tom, is truly a wonderful performer. His rendering of the title role may well cause Wilton Lackeye who is the Uncle Tom of the Brady production [and who was later famous for his Jewish portrayal of Svengali in the play *Trilby*] to thank his lucky stars that his Hebrew rival's repertoire is essentially Yiddish and that Thomashefsky is not ambitious to take the English role."[14] The Wilton Lackeye performance inspired yet another Yiddish Uncle Tom production in Chicago by the self-made theater impresario Edvin A. Relkin (née Avrohom Arnold).[15] Born in New York in 1880, Relkin ran away to Chicago as a child. In the 1890s, he worked his way up from being a candy butcher (selling candy in a theater) to become the manager of the theater owned by the father of Chicago's Yiddish stage, Ellis S. Glickman. Relkin, knowing that Glickman had seen the Academy of Music *Uncle Tom's Cabin* production—and having obtained a Yiddish script from New York—convinced Glickman to stage his own version, which was a huge success.[16]

After being hired away by Thomashefsky to manage his New York theater, Relkin, who spoke no Yiddish, became the wunderkind darling of the aging royalty of the Yiddish stage (Keni Liptzin, Bertha Kalisch, Kalman Juvelier, Jacob P. Adler, etc.), managing their performances and tours and inheriting their list of venues. Upon his return to Chicago around 1905, it was from these connections that Relkin stitched together a crazy quilt of theaters, synagogues, and opera houses into a national Yiddish theater network, both bringing it to cities that ordinarily did not feature Yiddish acts while giving the entire New York Yiddish theater community additional work. Relkin's formula for a successful play was "Give me a good story, lots of rabbis and lots of good Jewish music and I'll make the world come see it!"—but also he created a parallel variety/vaudeville circuit for more popular tastes. Relkin, thanks to a freakish ability to memorize national rail schedules, smoothly choreographed a number of theater companies around the country. At one point, no Yiddish performer who played outside of New York City could do so without being on some part of Relkin's circuit, as over his career Edvin A. Relkin booked Yiddish theater in more than eighty cities across the United States and Canada.

Ellis Glickman revived *Uncle Tom's Cabin* in 1903 to even better reviews than before. "Members of one persecuted race portrayed the wrongs of another" ran the lead line in a lavish illustrated spread in the February 28 edition of the *Chicago Daily Tribune*. Interestingly, the *Tribune* reviewer echoed the opinion of *The American Hebrew* reviewer of two years before in how the Jewish audience's favorite was not Uncle Tom but Harris, the mixed-race character struggling for his freedom. As "he delivered his Yiddish lines upon the wrongs of life in bondage, a murmur of emotion ran through the audience." The reviewer also noted that the cast member playing Topsy both "brought tears to the eyes of the audience with her 'pathetic Yiddish variations'" and then "sang coon songs in Yiddish and did cakewalks."[17]

Boris Thomashefsky revived his show in 1906 to solid reviews: "It is doubtful that the old play with its slave drivers, its suffering heroine, its blood hounds its floating ice was ever given a more vigorous treatment." The *Indianapolis Star* pointed out the normal visceral reaction of the audience (i.e., hissing at the villain) was significantly heightened when an actor, appearing as one of Eliza's dogged pursuers, "donned a Cossack cap and blouse, which he wore with great swagger."[18]

A 1911 Thomashefsky revival was not by Boris but by his younger brother Max "Mike" Thomashefsky, the beloved star and manager of Philadelphia's Arch Street Theater. In its review, *The Jewish Exponent* swooned over Thomashefsky's "sympathetic and true performance," while in its penultimate paragraph noted a twelve-year-old actress who "is also deserving of especial credit for the manner in which she played Little Eva. Mollie Picon."[19] Picon's first performance was in this last of the Yiddish Uncle Tom shows.

23

Before Jolson

The Jazz Singer, Jessel, and the Jews

Perhaps the most important New York Yiddish play of the years between the two World Wars was not in Yiddish, but in English: *The Jazz Singer*. While wholly eclipsed by the film adaptation, the play and the short story before it reveal the levels of Jewish self-identity and doubt and how Jews (only if temporarily) triumphed over the powerful assimilation engine of popular and mass culture. But what for the Jewish world made the play so important more than the film (which changed a critical plot point) was it's vital, resonant, and unexpectedly powerful, positive Jewish portrayal at a time when "Jewish" in mass popular culture was of the pushy, socially inept Hebe, the "Jewface" comic sporting oversized derbies and spouting laughably garbled malaprops.

Played against the backdrop of a glittering Broadway and shabby Lower East Side, the story of a Jewish boy who must choose between his family and tradition to become a "jazz singer" (later an "entertainer," "comic," or "rock star") has, in its over one-hundred-year history, revealed itself as a game of telephone where its initial modest message of Jewish identity continuity becomes wholly mangled by its final iteration. (Yiddish music historian Ron Robboy observed that what was Jolson's *tallis* in the original film has, by the 1980 Neil Diamond remake, become his scarf.) In its wake, the film not only serves as a flashpoint of Jewish identity but lies at a critical juncture of American film, technology, and race history.

The powerful level of Jewish identity set against the irresistible lure of popular culture that *The Jazz Singer* revealed was a story with which Yiddish-speaking Jews were already long familiar. On March 30, 1898, at Kessler's Thalia Theater on the Bowery, a benefit performance for the magazine *Naye Tsayt* (*New Times*) presented a play by a B. Goren (a.k.a. Yitzkok Goida-Hoida) a writer for the *Arbeter Tsaytung* (*The Workman's Paper*).[1] The play, "based on true facts from Jewish life in four acts," starred and was directed by David Kessler with "honest Jewish sweet music" by Peretz Sandler (who was still eight years away from writing his greatest hit, "Eli, Eli"). The story was of Joel David Levensohn (1816–1850), a brilliant child singer whose father was the Vilna city cantor. Upon his father's death, the teenaged Levensohn successfully assumes the cantor's position and secures his Ashkenaz-wide reputation. Sometime in his twenties, beguiled by opera, its glittering promises (and a beautiful Polish prima donna), Levensohn abandons his cantorial position and his world, and, unprepared for this new setting, is soon broken and unmoored and returns to his home synagogue on Yom Kippur in time to sing *Kol Nidre* and die. Curtain.[2]

Called *Der vilner balabesl* (*The Little Vilna Boss*), the nickname given Levensohn by his passionate adherents, the story is better known through the later 1908 Mark Arnshteyn play of the same name, which would reach the screen in 1940 as *Overture to Glory*, directed by Max Nosseck and starring cantor/Yiddish actor Moishe Oysher.[3] But in a modest confluence of sorts, Goren's March 30, 1898, opening coincided with the second birthday of a neighborhood boy. And while there is no definitive proof that the child, Samson Raphaelson, was taken to see the play for his birthday, the same *Der vilner balabesl* story arc (son of a cantor torn between tradition and assimilation and a beautiful love interest, with a boffo Yom Kippur/Kol Nidre denouement) appears first in his short story *The Day of Atonement* and then as the drama *The Jazz Singer*.[4]

Raphaelson, who was said to have disliked the confining life on the Lower East Side, enrolled in the University of Illinois Chicago in 1913, working his way through college waiting tables.[5] He swiftly attained BMOC status despite being the skinny Jewish kid with glasses who could not play football. He was, instead, the skinny Jewish kid with glasses who would write the football team's popular theme song "Fight Illian." By 1916, Raphaelson was editor of the campus humor magazine, *The Siren*.[6] He published a half dozen fiction pieces in papers around the country in 1917, all while trying out different signatures like "S. M. Raphaelson" and "Sampson Raphaelson."[7] Light, bright, and glib, Raphaelson's short stories showed flashes of the kind of writing for which he would soon be famous.

The Short Story: "The Day of Atonement"

When Raphaelson left Chicago for New York in 1921, he had already sold his first national piece to *Hearst's Magazine*. By the end of the year, and while working a day job in advertising, *Everybody's Magazine* published his "The Day of Atonement" in its January 1922 issue. While Raphaelson may have disliked his East Side upbringing and previously shown no interest in Jewish culture, "The Day of Atonement" generously drew upon that world with an insider's view, delivering the reader into a lively and embattled Jewish universe. By putting valid Yiddish and Hebrew into the mouths of his characters, Raphaelson humanized them and afforded the reader a vicarious sense of eavesdropping.

Raphaelson provided other resonant cultural markers to enhance the story's context. For example, the name he chose for Jakie's cantor father, Yossele "Little Joe" was the instantly very recognizable nickname of the great cantor Yossele Rosenblatt. When Yossele Rabinowitz objected to his son's life as an actor, calling actors "loafers," his wife Rivka countered by invoking the Yiddish stage's most popular idol: "Every actor, he ain't a loafer, Yossele," she would say. "Look—is Jacob Adler a loafer? A finer man you couldn't find it if you should search a whole lifetime."[8] By also invoking substantive Jewish locations, Raphaelson girded his story in a strong sense of place by calling out the important Lower East Side Orthodox synagogue Beys Hamedresh Ha'Godol while also locating the ten generations of Rabinowitz cantors in the Lithuanian city of Vilna, a knowing nod to *Der vilner balabesl*.

The Jakie Rabinowitz character that Raphaelson introduces at the opening of "The Day of Atonement" is not a singer but a tough and defiant "sheeny" on the East Side, fighting off "micks" with equal defiance of the "rebi" in the "Chaidar" whom he hates and desperately wishes to escape and his teeter board relationship with popular culture:

> "I'll sing in the choir every Sabbath," he said then, "But honest pa *honest* I'd quicker die than go every day to a *Chaidar*."

His father had to find comfort during the several years that followed in hearing the liquid golden tones of Jakie's alto voice in the choir only on Sabbath and on holy days.

The rest of the time

people came hours early to the Great Alcazar Palace to stand in line 20 deep to see Jakie, now Jack Robin, sing "Lovey Joe," and "When Dat Midnight Choo-Choo Leaves For Alabam'."

A vaudeville agent hears him perform and notes that he has a "swifter, more potent tunefulness than a certain black-face comedian whom he was paying a thousand dollars a week for singing the same song on Broadway." Promising Jakie to "place you on Broadway in electric lights," the agent sends him on the vaudeville circuit where he meets (and is smitten with) Amy Prentiss, the "World-Famous Dancer of Joyous Dances." When Jack asks why, his confidant in "Mooney's Ballet" Henrietta Mooney (born Sadie Rudnick), explains it: "You wonder why? She's a Shiksa; that's why! I've seen Jewish boys fall that way before. It ain't new to me! You come from the Ghetto, and she studied fancy dancing in a private school. You're the son of a poor old *Chazon*, and she's the daughter of a Boston lawyer. You're—Aw, you make me sick!" (Among its twenty or so Yiddish/Hebrewisms, the word *shiksa* appears a half dozen times.)

Raphaelson explores Jack's deep ambiguity, not only about his devotion to his parents but to the rituals and traditions with which he grew up, by having him stay in New York between vaudeville tours to sing in his father's choir:

He took a month's vacation and spent two weeks of it in New York. For two consecutive Sabbath days he attended the synagogue and the old cantor singing from the pulpit, exulted in the conviction that his son was returning to his God.

Jack himself found a certain solace in it. As he sat on the old familiar wooden bench, clothed in the silk *Talis*—the prayer-shawl which his father had so solemnly presented to him on his *Bar Mitzvah*—with good old Yudelson, the cobbler, on one side of him and Lupinsky, the red-haired butcher on the other, he felt a singular warmth and sweetness. And the voice of his father, still clear and lyric, rising in the intricacies of the familiar old lamenting prayers—prayers which he remembered perfectly, which he would never forget—the dissonant rumble of response from the congregation, the restive shufflings of youngsters—all these were to him blessedly familiar and blissful.

But now the push and pull heats up his inner conflict: Jack begins drinking and missing curtain calls, jeopardizing his career until the "World-Famous Dancer of Joyous Dances" reappears, rekindling their relationship and agreeing to marry him. The news, however, which heartens the Broadway producer, gives Jack's cantor father a fatal heart attack. Now consumed with guilt over his father's death, Jack agrees to perform "Kol Nidre" at his tiny synagogue—instead of appearing as planned in the debut of his new Broadway show. As word got out, Jews, many of whom had already bought tickets to fancier, pricier, and more comfortable synagogues, abandoned them and the shul quickly filled beyond capacity.

At the story's close, Jack is rewarded with a double redemption: one with his family and tradition and one with the Broadway producer whom he had let down. The last scene, which points irresistibly to a sequel, finds the producer at the East Side synagogue to hear Jack sing and, when he hears "Kol Nidre," ducks into a drug store and phones his partner: "Do you want to hear the greatest ragtime singer in America in the making? A wonder, Harry a wonder! . . . Come down right away. It's a dirty little hole on the East Side called the Hester Street synagogue."

The Play: The Jazz Singer

Just as Jakie's future on the stage was assured, so too was Raphaelson's. The subhead that appeared with publication of "The Day of Atonement" reads: "So sound and dramatic is this tale that a manager plans to make a play of it."[9] Actually, three managers approached Raphaelson about a stage version: Albert Lewis and Max Gordon, who, along with Sam Harris (the one-time partner of George M. Cohan) had since 1921 produced a baker's dozen of successful frothy Broadway musical comedies and farces. However, none of them had experience staging or marketing a drama. So it was unexpected that not only did they mount the play, but Albert Lewis, whose theater experience was as an actor and producer, decided to direct ("staged by"). Lewis was so instrumental in the transformation of "The Day of Atonement" that Raphaelson dedicated the subsequent published script to him, describing Lewis as "a gentleman from the East Side and a scholar from Broadway."[10] On the one hand, "the gentleman from the East Side," Polish-born, Yiddish-speaking Lewis, was sympathetic to the humanized Jewish characterization found in "The Day of Atonement" and crafted an extended opening scene (not in the story) depicting a warm and intimate Cantor Yossele (described in the stage directions as a "holy man among a humane people") teaching "V'ani Tsefilosee" ("I, My Prayer"), a cantorial solo, to Moey, a member of his choir: "Sing it with a sigh. Do you understand, my child? With a sigh! You are praying to God."

Yudelson (in the original story only a name mentioned in passing) became the story's moral center as a reliable, steadfast peacemaker whose thoughtful loyalty to the family was delivered via the heavily accented, malapropistic comic-relief stage Hebe. Yudelson is used to set up a clever running gag to lighten the otherwise dense dramatic context, in which all the guests at the Cantor's surprise sixtieth birthday have brought him the same gift (a tallis), a bit repeated in the film.

However, Lewis (as "the scholar from Broadway") knew that too much of that kind of Jewish humanization would be box office poison, so toned down the story's Jewish language and imagery. This would be Raphaelson's first encounter with Jews in popular culture who were terrified of representing Jews in popular culture, and his first taste of preemptive Jewish deracination.

Gone now are the story's numerous Semiticisms that gave the reader a sonic entry to the character's world. Where "The Day of Atonement" used "siddur," "bar mitzvah," and "tallis," *The Jazz Singer* used "prayer book," "confirmation," and the creepily discordant "praying shawl." Raphaelson's more authentic bilingual tonalities were replaced with the ruptured syntax of the stereotypical stage "Hebe." ("Why are you asking me like these questions?") Gone too are the more subtle—but more fundamental—character nuances; "Day of Atonement" Jakie loved popular songs but also found "solace" in singing synagogue music, while *Jazz Singer* Jakie did not: "I don't want to sing this stuff that I don't understand—to a God whose meaning I don't get."

Jazz Singer Jakie's immersion in the Gentile world is so deep that it seeps into the play's stage directions, which note he "carries a large pig-skin English bag." Raphaelson even has him point that out to his astounded mother (now "Sara") now a two-dimensional character who bears a closer resemblance to then Yiddish theater actresses Jennie Goldstein, Esther Field, and Madame Bertha Hart, playing the long-suffering, hand-wringing "Yiddishe Mame" roles.

Act 1 ends in a clever theatrical musical device that underscores the inevitable intrusion of modernity. Earlier, Jack's father returns to hear him serenading his mother with "Red Hot Mama" (a Raphaelson original). After a brief confrontation with his father, Jack is thrown out. But the song is soon insidiously reprised:

> *The Cantor now hears the singing, which is coming closer. He raises his hand. His face is suddenly the face of a corpse, as the door opens and Moey enters, blithely singing "Every time I look at you, I want to hotter Hot Tamales."*

In what may be the first Broadway show featuring the now all-too-familiar backstage Broadway opening night, the brisk and breathless pacing of act two has Albert Lewis's fingerprints all over it. Yet as Lewis's influence informed the show's backstage action, Raphaelson's insistence that this was *not* a "musical" but a "drama with songs," the director innovatively and counterintuitively set the show's half dozen musical numbers (including the show-ending "Kol Nidre") either offstage or with the actor's back to the house, a gamble that paid tremendous dramatic and critical dividends. For a play with music that was not a musical, great care was taken with the music. And like 1927's *Showboat* (which usually garners credit as the first Broadway musical whose songs were meant to advance the plot), *The Jazz Singer* too integrated its songs into the action.

The closing scene features Jack, whose mother has come to beg him to return home, going offstage to belt out the curtain-dropping end of Act 2 with another Raphaelson blackface song, "Dixie Mammy," which the stage directions note:

> *His rendition is excellent jazz—that is, it has an evangelical fervor a fanatical frenzy; it wallows in plaintiveness and has moments of staggering dramatic intensity, despite the obvious shoddiness of the words and the music. We are listening to a Cantor in blackface, to a ritual supplication on the stage, to religion cheapened and intensified by the trappings of Broadway.*

> I—want—you—to—understand
> That—it's—my—mammy
> My—mammy—I—tell—you
> And—my—daddy
> You—bet

    Your—life
    It's—my—mammy—and—daddy, I—tell—you
    I'm—going—back—
    I'm—going—back—down—South—
    Down—South,—I—tell—you

In this one stanza, Raphaelson not only juxtaposes the "Black Mammy" and the "Yiddishe Mame" but even slyly repurposes the moth-eaten "down south" trope to mean the Lower East Side, which in fact is "down south" from Forty-Sixth and Broadway.

Throughout, Raphaelson uses the familiar to offset the foreign. To demonstrate Jack's idea of connection between the Jewish and jazz musics, he sings the Sabbath prayer "Eyn Keloheynu" ("There Is None Like Our God"):

> *He sings four bars of it, swiftly with feeling. And then, suddenly, to the same tune and with the same plaintiveness but with a new rhythm and shaking his shoulders, he sings a popular song*
>
> Nothing ever hurries me
> Nothing ever worries me.
> Easy come, easy go
> It's all the same to me.

The song that really anchors the play—as it had *Der vilner balabesl*—is "Kol Nidre." It's not surprising that Raphaelson hinged his story, and the play's popular and critical success, on the magnetism of "Kol Nidre," one of the most important and dramatic prayer settings in Jewish liturgy. By this time, the piece was already quite well known outside the Jewish community. With the rise of variety theater and commercial recordings, "Kol Nidre" (usually paired with Peretz Sandler's 1896 "Eli, Eli") became the most widely performed and recorded Jewish song by non-Jews, from opera singer Alma Gluck (mother of Efrem Zimbalist Jr.) to Pablo Casals, Harry James, and later Perry Como and Johnny Mathis.

In the wake of the play's success, Raphaelson began producing skewed Talmudic commentary about his characters and the world they—and he—inhabited, such as in his introduction to the 1926 edition of *The Jazz Singer*:

> In seeking a symbol of the vital chaos of America's soul, I find no more adequate one than jazz. Here you have the rhythm of

frenzy staggering against a symphonic background—a background composed of lewdness, heart's delight, soul-racked madness, monumental boldness, exquisite humility, but principally prayer. I hear jazz, and I am given a vision of cathedrals and temples collapsing and silhouetted against the setting sun, a solitary figure, a lost soul, dancing grotesquely on the ruins. . . . Thus, do I see the jazz singer.

Jazz is prayer. It is too passionate to be anything else. It is prayer distorted, sick, unconscious of its destination. The singer of jazz is what Matthew Arnold said of the Jew, "lost between two worlds, one dead, the other powerless to be born." In this, my first play, I have tried to crystallize the ironic truth that one of the Americas of 1925—that one which pack to overflowing our cabarets, musical revues, and dance halls—is praying with a fervor as intense as that of the America which goes sedately to church and synagogue. The jazz American is different from the dancing dervish, from the Zulu medicine man, from the negro evangelist only in that he doesn't know he is praying.

Raphaelson then expounds on his belief in the Manifest Destiny of the Jewish assumption of Black musical culture:

I have used a Jewish youth as my protagonist because the Jews are determining the nature and scope of jazz more than any other race—more than the negroes, from whom they have stolen jazz and given it a new color and meaning. Jazz is Irving Berlin, Al Jolson, George Gershwin, Sophie Tucker. These are Jews with their roots in the synagogue. And these are expressing in evangelical terms the nature of our chaos today.

You find the soul of a people in the songs they sing. You find the meaning of the songs in the souls of the minstrels who create and interpret them. In "The Jazz Singer" I have attempted an exploration of the soul of one of these minstrels.

Raphaelson's sensitivity to the nuances of Jewish tradition and continuity that drove his story stops short when it comes to ragtime and jazz and the community that created it. For example, Raphaelson's willing misperception of minstrel stage characters as representative of the world they claimed to represent, and his associating jazz with Jolson and Tucker (though less with Gershwin, who *could* play jazz) as proper legatees of the music solely because they were Jews. His interchangeable description of Jack as a "ragtime singer" and a "jazz singer" as an avatar of cutting-edge popularity in the mid-1920s is a case in point: Ragtime, the revolutionary syncopated Black instrumental music, burst upon the world in 1897 with the success of Scott Joplin's *Maple Leaf Rag* and held sway into the late teens when it was unceremoniously and unalterably displaced by jazz. And while there was a brief rococo period ("rag-a-jazz") where the two terms comingled, it had ended long before the action of *The Jazz Singer* takes place. Raphaelson's fans and critics allowed him this poetic license.

Another poetic license, not in the original story but upon which the play (and later film) is vitally hinged—is the time conflict between the two opening nights: Kol Nidre services and showtime, which, given Jewish law, theater protocol, and actual travel time, is no conflict. Broadway shows of the era had 8:30 curtains, while Yom Kippur, on September 27, 1925 (a week after the actual show bowed) began about 6:45, almost two hours before curtain. Kol Nidre is a roughly half-hour service and the four-mile distance from Orchard Street (where the synagogue is supposed to have been) to the theater district (the location of the Winter Garden) is approximately a half-hour drive or subway ride, leaving roughly an hour in which to go on.

George Jessel

With a completed play, a star was required. Here again, Albert Lewis "the scholar from Broadway" came through, with an atypical choice: comedian George Jessel.

In his 1944 autobiography *So Help Me*, Jessel—named for illustrious British ancestor Sir George Jessel—talked about growing up poor in the Bronx. His mother, Charlotte, was a ticket taker at a local movie house and ferried him around to sing to magic lantern slides (not unlike what George Burns did at Seiden's theater on the Lower East Side).[11] Jessel eventually joined famed songwriter ("By the Light of the Silvery Moon") Gus Edwards (née Schmelowsky) in his popular "Kiddie Kabaret" specializing in "Hebe" characters; other Lower East Side strivers who were company members were tenor Walter Winchell (later one of the most important newscasters—and then notorious right-wing gossip columnists—of the day) and Eddie "Banjo Eyes" Cantor. An August 26, 1913, review describes Cantor as portraying

"'Jefferson' a black butler who sustains most of the fun of the piece" and "George Jessel a close second as Mutky, jolly little Jew."[12] Cantor would shortly join the prestigious *Ziegfeld Follies*, where as Sonny he partnered with the African American comedian/singer Bert Williams (as Pappy) in a burnt-cork comedy act.

After leaving Gus Edwards, Jessel worked with George "Honey Boy" Evan's minstrel troupe. However, blackface wasn't Jessel's primary bread and butter, unlike Jolson and Cantor. Jessel was noted for his strong (though not always accurate) singing voice, "calisthenic ad-libbing," and rapid-fire patter. When he joined Loew's vaudeville circuit in the early 1920s, he was billed as the "Court Jester of the American People" and was soon producing his own shows, including the now largely forgotten hit 1923 George S. Kaufman and Bert Kalmar and Harry Ruby musical comedy *Helen of Troy, New York*.

At the same time, down the block Jessel was starring in the Jolson-style Shubert Brothers's *Passing Show of 1923* where he introduced one of his most enduring stage performances. In the sketch "Mama at a French Play," Jessel played a boy accompanying his Yiddish-speaking "Mommer" to a show in a language she could not understand. Jessel's wise-cracky English translations (for the Gentile audience) and his improvised Yiddishisms (for "Mommer" and his growing Yiddish language fans) was a big hit. He soon spun this routine into his better known "Hello, Mama" telephone bit.[13]

Jessel's route from the variety to the legitimate stage was facilitated by Albert Lewis, who cowrote the book for Jessel's first musical comedy revue, *Troubles of 1920*. Lewis became Jessel's manager, and after *The Jazz Singer* (whose title Jessel is said to have come up with to replace "The Day of Atonement,") produced and directed Jessel's unsuccessful 1928 Broadway show *The War Song*.

Though brimming with stage craft, *The Jazz Singer* would be Jessel's first time speaking memorized lines, and although he initially turned down the part, he soon relented.[14]

Another inspired bit of Lewis's casting was Sam Jaffe as Yudelson. Jaffe, whose mother Ida was a Yiddish theater chorine, was, by the time of *The Jazz Singer*, already a tested stage Jew, having appeared as Reb Eli in Sholem Asch's controversial 1922 play *God of Vengeance* about a Jewish bordello owner. Jaffe, best known for his later screen roles as Gunga Din, and TV's Dr. Zorba on *Ben Casey*, would stay with *The Jazz Singer* company for over two years both in New York and on the road. Despite ecstatic out-of-town reviews, Broadway held its breath about the new show by an unknown playwright, staged by its producer who had never directed and featuring a star who had never acted in a drama.

The Critics

One of the things that made *The Jazz Singer* stand out were two other shows currently running on Broadway: *Kosher Kitty Kelly*, recently opened, and *Abie's Irish Rose*, already 1,500 performances into its five-year run. Both plays traded on the familiar stereotype of Jewish-Irish interaction and championed assimilation and intermarriage, a sore point for the Yiddish press: "It is a notorious fact that all some know about Jewish life has been gained from such 'scientific' documents as 'Abie's Irish Rose,' 'Kosher Kitty Kelly,' in the two dramatic masterpieces Jews and Irish are sweethearts and in 'Abie,' they marry to the vast amusement of audiences who know nothing about Jewish life."[15]

But with *The Jazz Singer*, Broadway now had a show that offered a counternarrative to the rampant stage stereotypes. It also didn't hurt that Jessel was already a well-liked presence in the world of Yiddish entertainment. Jessel sat on the board of a number of Jewish theatrical organizations and performed for Jewish fundraising events. He was also an active supporter in the economic uplift of the Lower East Side (both he and Yossele Rosenblatt were investors in the doomed Libby's Hotel).

On September 14, 1925, just a few days before Rosh Hashona, *The Jazz Singer* opened. Among the mainstream critics, two words characterized the play: "hokum" and "racial." For example, *Variety* declared at the start of its review "on analysis it's all hokum" while damning the production with faint praise about the mechanics behind the show's runaway success: "The play is a shrewd and well-planned excursion into the theater . . . so assuredly written that even the slowest of wits can understand it."[16]

Other reviewers were also unamused. "Jessel has a great many friends and followers cultivated thru his undoubted talent in the popular song line," sniffed *Billboard* critic Don Carle Gillette, explaining the large and enthusiastic turnout. Gillette apparently understood little about Orthodox Jewish life; in his complaint of the staging, he noted that "very few of the visitors who call upon the cantor and his wife ever take off their hats." He boiled down *The Jazz Singer*'s greatest crime: "It is too essentially and too exclusively racial" (i.e., "Jewish")."[17] The "racial" aspect of the show annoyed another reviewer: "Many of the spoken lines which were spoken in dialect, while wholly unintelligible to us, were received with enthusiasm by an audience almost entirely composed of those of the Jewish race."[18]

The critics, who knew Jessel from vaudeville, were not prepared for his ability to command a dramatic stage thanks to his visceral, unwavering belief in the character he portrayed. Jessel's ability to drive a "seen-it-all" opening night Broadway audience to their feet with tears streaming down their cheeks (as a reviewer for *Brooklyn Times Union* noted) was attributed to his "ability so marked in actors of Jewish origin to be supremely pathetic, almost tragic while at the same time being able almost simultaneously to evoke laughter."[19]

Despite jabs at the production, even the *Variety* reviewer who noted it was all "hokum," ended the review: "A sure fire hit! . . . a full house enthusiastically applauded the play, Jew and Gentile uniting in their praise."[20]

The Yiddish language press was uniformly ecstatic.

It was none other than *Forverts* editor Abe Cahan who gave *The Jazz Singer* his *hekhsher*, his kosher endorsement: "The appearance of Raphaelson's 'The Jazz Singer' is a most noteworthy phenomenon. This is Yiddish theater in English, not just a Jewish drama in English. This is the Yiddish theater on Broadway." Cahan, a canny critic of American culture (he had had his own hit crossover English-language novel, *The Rise of David Levinsky*), also called out the play's low and pandering elements, and its cheap sentimentality. However, it was the far more important ever-present humanity of its stars that moved Cahan, particularly Jessel. Cahan noted, "His portrayal is lip smacking which he plays with great feeling." Cahan marveled at Jessel's powerful depiction of the passionate cantor given "he had no religious background, and all his Jewish friends in the theater were of an atheistic bent." Cahan also called out Sam Jaffe as Yudelson by saying "he IS an East Broadway *gabbai* (synagogue sexton) . . . from head to toe."[21]

Even Gentile actor Howard Lang (who played Cantor Rabinowitz)—Broadway's go-to "Jew" (this being his fourth stage portrayal as one)—was praised in the Yiddish press: "If Jews can successfully portray non-Jews on the stage, shouldn't it be possible for non-Jews to successfully portray us?"[22]

Advertisements in the Yiddish press emphasized Jessel's Jewish character in cantorial raiment accompanied by context or commentary: "Come see how American actors present realistic Jewish life," read one. Another asked, "Will Jacob Rabinowitz become Jack Robin and forsake his people or become cantor Jacob Rabinowitz and sing *Kol Nidre* on Yom Kippur?" This ad was accompanied by a picture of Jessel, synagogue garbed, hands clasped, and slightly pained looking, with the caption "George Jessel, as the Jazz Singer who took his father's place in the synagogue on Yom Kippur to sing *Kol Nidre*."

Jewish visibility was immeasurably helped when Edvin A. Relkin was hired by Lewis and Gordon. One of Relkin's PR ideas was a *Jazz Singer* Yiddish newspaper serial in the run up to the show's opening. To do this, he hired poet Yankev Glatshteyn of the *Morgn Zhurnal*, an unusual choice given Glatshteyn's being a leading avant-garde experimental poet.[23] Glatshteyn was faced with the inherent difficulty of creating weeks of storyline from a play where most of the action famously takes place within a single day. The poet—whose name did not appear in the serialization's byline—elegantly solved this problem by crafting elaborate backstories for all its main characters.[24]

The Jazz Singer would run for forty weeks and give over three hundred performances before closing on June 5, 1926. In its afterglow, Jessel's fortunes were seemingly made. He had already booked nearly a half year with a road company and a possible extended tour in England. There were also reports that financier Otto Kahn was underwriting a *Jazz Singer* opera for Jessel with music by George Gershwin.[25] But to top it all off, Jessel was on his way out to Hollywood to make a movie of it.

It is widely asserted that the idea for *The Jazz Singer* was born at a 1917 performance of Al Jolson's musical *Robinson Crusoe, Jr.* at Chicago's Garrick Theater, where university student Sampson Raphaelson saw it and was duly inspired.[26] By this time, it was commonly accepted that Jews were well represented in high-end/tail-end blackface performance as noted in *The American Jewish World* from March 26, 1926:

> The most successful blackface comedians are of the Jewish faith—notably Al Jolson and Eddie Cantor and a score of lesser prominence. No one has been able to figure this out. The truest delineators are also those who have not studied the darkey in his native habitat. Eddie Cantor, for instance is a product of the east side tenements and was essaying blackface roles before he ever talked to a colored person. Jolson, who made the "Mammy" song an institution had never been in Dixie until a few years ago, when he visited Georgia and Louisiana.[27]

Al Jolson

On the legitimate stage in the 1920s, no Jewish blackface performer was bigger than Al Jolson. Called "The World's Greatest Entertainer," Jolson (Asa Yoelson 1886–1950) was one of the only famous mainstream Jewish entertainers not born in America, arriving at the age of eight from Lithuania following his father, Rabbi Moishe Rubin Yoelson. Much was made of Jolson having learned and sung cantorial music with his father, and it becoming a conflict with him. (The front page of *The Jazz Singer* movie press kit ballyhooed: "Al Jolson Relives His Own Life.")

In 1898, Jolson appeared as a "Hester Street urchin" in a Washington, DC, production of Israel Zangwill's Jewish-themed play *Children of the Ghetto*. In a scene that would be echoed in the 1927 film, the bar mitzvah–aged Jolson had a stage career that lasted three performances, until he was discovered by his father and "an understudy finished his work."[28] Yet his father, who was the rabbi and cantor at Baltimore's Orthodox Talmud Torah, unlike his movie doppelganger put no pressure on his son to sustain the family cantorial tradition. Despite Asa subsequently running away from home only to return under duress, father and son had no rupture over Jolson's theater success: on the heels of signing with the Warner Brothers Jolson was widely reported to have bought a new home for his parents in their Washington, DC, Anacostia neighborhood.[29]

An impatient adolescent, Jolson escaped his Baltimore surroundings and ended up in New York. By 1906, he chanced into burnt cork when he joined Lew Dockstader, the last of the late nineteenth-century minstrel magnates, and in whose show Jolson made his blackface bones.[30] Jolson's ascent was so dramatic that by 1911 he crossed over to Broadway with a succession of hit shows followed by long national tours, one of which Raphaelson saw in Chicago.

Al Jolson and the Film

From its earliest iteration, it was widely repeated that *The Jazz Singer* had, as its inspiration, the life of Al Jolson. Raphaelson and Jolson are said to have spoken about the entertainer starring in the play, but Jolson's insistence on it being a musical featuring his songs caused Raphaelson to drop the idea because he envisioned it as a "comedy-drama."

The Warner Brothers did not immediately choose between Jolson and Jessel to play the lead. In retrospect, it's clear that Warners was hedging its bets, having both Jessel and Jolson making films around the same time as a kind of screen test. In late 1926, as part of the program of its latest silent comedy feature *The Better 'Ole* starring Charlie Chaplin's brother, Syd, Warners released two Vitaphone shorts to test audience reaction. One was *A Few Minutes with George Jessel* (a.k.a. "A Theatrical Booking Office") featuring his banter and singing Irving Berlin's "At Peace with the World." The other was *A Plantation Act*, featuring Jolson's blackface rendering of a trio of his current hits: "April Showers," "When the Red, Red Robin Comes Bob-Bob Bobbin' Along," and "Rock a Bye Your Baby with a Dixie Melody." Warner Brothers knew the value of these performers, as it paid Jolson $25,000 ($350,000 in today's dollars) for *A Plantation Act* as opposed to Jessel's $7,250. Yet Jessel's sound shorts were showcasing well. The monologue after his song "caused the audience to laugh more than they were expected to."[31] Warner Brothers continued to groom Jessel, with two 1926–1927 shorts (*Private Izzy Murphy*, *Sailor Izzy Murphy*), supposedly a running jump into production of *The Jazz Singer*.

Yet ultimately the studio gave the part to Jolson. Angered by this decision, Jessel signed with the upstart (and short-lived) Tiffany-Stahl studio, where he made several films including his own low-rent *Jazz Singer* remake *Lucky Boy*.

The reasons Jessel lost the part in the film all appear to be contradictory and all appear to be true. On the one hand, Jolson had long been associated with *The Jazz Singer* and was a far bigger draw than Jessel. After noting the play's huge success, Jolson was said to be actively lobbying for *The Jazz Singer* film. There were also claims made—even maintained today—that Jessel, seemingly unaware that *The Jazz Singer* was to be made using the Vitaphone system, demanded extra money for making a sound picture, an incongruous explanation given that he had already successfully filmed and released sound shorts.

Jessel insisted it was the altered ending of the play that caused him to bolt, as he did in his autobiography seventeen years later: "My first look at the motion picture scenario *The Jazz Singer* threw me into a fit. Instead of the boy's leaving the theater and following the traditions of his father by singing in the synagogue, as in the play, the picture scenario had him return to the Winter Garden as a blackface comedian, with his mother wildly applauding in the box. I raised hell. Money or no money I would not do this." Yet while Jessel could afford to turn his back on the film, another cast member could not: Cantor Yossele Rosenblatt.

Figure 23.1. "What the world renowned Cantor Rosenblatt says about *The Jazz Singer*" (1925). Yossele Rosenblatt (*left*) and George Jessel. *Source:* National Library of Israel, Historical Jewish Press website (www.jpress.org.il), founded by the National Library and Tel Aviv University. Used with permission.

Yossele Rosenblatt

Much of what we assume about Rosenblatt's involvement with *The Jazz Singer* comes from the 1954 biography *Yossele Rosenblatt: The Story of His Life as Told by His Son*, Samuel Rosenblatt. For example, he claimed his father's first contact with *The Jazz Singer* came when Warner Brothers' agents visited him in the spring of 1927 with an offer to appear in the film.[32] But Yossele Rosenblatt's connection goes back to even before it was a play or a film. If Al Jolson was the inspiration for Jakie Rabinowitz, then it was Yossele Rosenblatt (1882–1933) who was the model for Cantor Rabinowitz. As noted, in the original story, Raphaelson named Jakie/Jack's cantor father "Yossele," the by then internationally recognizable diminutive nickname for Joseph Rosenblatt. Raphaelson goes further and inserts Rosenblatt as a cultural touchstone in a scene when Jakie is leading services: "The rabbi, a rotund little man in the front pews, turned to his neighbor and remarked: 'Even Rosenblatt, when I heard him in Moscow, didn't give a *Yaaleh* like this. *Aza Singen nehmt by die Harz* (such singing grabs you by the heart).'"[33] In an era that lionized great voices and great voices ruled the great concert stages and record sales, Yossele Rosenblatt was one of the greatest.

Rosenblatt was already a world-famous cantor when he emigrated to the United States in 1912. While short of stature, Rosenblatt possessed a towering voice that leapt out of the horns of the early phonographs and made his record sales rival those of opera giants like Chaliapin, Galli Curci, and Caruso with whom he performed at war bond rallies, and is said to have thanked God that Rosenblatt had chosen a field other than opera in which to share his great gift.[34]

Yossele Rosenblatt, who would sing in the synagogue and in concert, famously refused to appear in the 1918 Chicago Civic Opera's production of *La Juive* for which he was offered $1,000 a night ($20,000 today) because it debased the sanctity role of the *sheliakh tzibur* (messenger of the people).[35]

With the success of *The Jazz Singer*, Jewish eyes turned to Yossele to see what the greatest cantor of the age thought of the new cantor-themed play. In a signed letter dated October 14, 1925, and reproduced in many Yiddish papers, Rosenblatt is shown shaking hands with Jessel, and exults about his performance ("a great gift to all Jews"). Rosenblatt most notably praised the actor's "Kol Nidre." In the show, "Kol Nidre" was accompanied by Rosenblatt's own twenty-voice men and boys choir led by Meyer Posner, a star in his own right in the Jewish music world and who probably coached Jessel's performance.[36]

When talk turned to a film and Rosenblatt's part in it, the *Forverts* commented:

> Whispers in *muvink piksher* circles assert that the famous Yossele Rosenblatt replete with his beard and yarmulke,—and especially with his Yossele Rosenblatt voice—will shortly become a *muvink piksher* actor.
>
> It is said that the Warner Brothers have completed a contract with the renowned cantor that he should appear in the *muvink piksher* "The Jazz Singer," in the drama George Jessel first made famous.
>
> Jessel will, in fact, play the same role in the movie that he is currently playing on the stage: he will be The Jazz Singer, who has inherited his father's voice but became a jazz singer and that Yossele Rosenblatt would play the role of the old cantor.
>
> So why do they need such a famous cantor for a *muvink piksher* role?
>
> Understand: the *muvink piksher* will be made with the Vitaphone, with talking *pikshers,* so the scenes with the old cantor and his son, The Jazz Singer, which require them to sing, you will hear them.
>
> They say that the Warners offered Yossele a tidy sum to appear and sing in the *piksher*. Yossele has already appeared and sung in vaudeville despite never having performed on the Sabbath. The *muvies* will be much easier for him to make. The *piksher* production can easily be accommodated to his schedule.
>
> The Warner Brothers plan to make this *piksher* so: with a strong, positive Jewish character. Their plan is making an authentic Jewish character, their plan is to place the religious scene in the synagogue including the chanting of "Kol Nidre." Yossele Rosenblatt would be a big *etrekshin* for such a *piksher*.[37]

The next month, on June 14, 1927, in a continued build toward the film, Warner Brothers on its station KFWB, featured George Jessel and Yossele Rosenblatt (who were appearing at a Los Angeles Jewish philanthropy event), in songs and stories associated with *The Jazz Singer*.[38]

But Jessel's sudden departure from *The Jazz Singer* put Rosenblatt in a bind. As Rosenblatt's personal connection to *The Jazz Singer* predated the Warners, it was to Jessel and to the original story he was loyal and not to the new denouement, which also went against Rosenblatt's beliefs. Yet the offer was decidedly a temptation for Rosenblatt, who was in desperate need of money: in 1924 he had been famously victimized in an elaborate scam around funding an Orthodox Yiddish newspaper the *Iddishe Likht* (*The Light of Israel*). Not only did Rosenblatt personally invest $100,000, but he also encouraged others, who also lost everything. Rosenblatt's loyalty was such that despite not being legally liable for anyone's investment losses, he solemnly pledged that he would pay back those who took his advice, even if it took the rest of life. Sadly, he died before he could.

So starting in January 1925, and despite a number of firm demands (no Sabbath performances; no synagogue prayers; only songs in Yiddish, Russian, and English; simple white lights; and no entrance or exit music), Rosenblatt now performed in vaudeville settings even more deeply antithetical to the music he was singing than would have been his appearance with the Chicago Lyric Opera. Among a bevy of jugglers, animal acts, and comedians, one 1925 performance had him splitting a bill with Daisy and Violet Hilton, Siamese Twins best known for their appearance in the 1932 Tod Browning horror film *Freaks*.

A brilliantly observed eyewitness account of Rosenblatt's descent into vaudeville and perhaps the best account in English of a period cantorial performance was in Gypsy Rose Lee's 1957 memoir:

> The garish white lights made him look even more shabby. His suit was wrinkled and one trouser leg was caught up in the top of his high-laced shoe. The silence in the audience and the stillness in the orchestra pit were strange and untheater-like. He blinked his eyes at the brightness, then suddenly, almost frighteningly, one note broke through the silence. It was a high, piercing sound, like a wail. There was a sadness in it that choked me. The note faded away and I could hear the audience catch its breath almost as though it was one person.
>
> The orchestra played softly as the Cantor began to sing. It wasn't a song I had ever heard before and I couldn't understand the Hebrew words but I knew he was singing about all the sadness in the world. He had the clearest, purest voice I had

ever heard. There was a gentleness and strength and warmth to it. I felt that if God were to sing to us, this is how His voice would sound.

Abruptly, and much too soon, it was over. The Cantor just stopped singing and without a nod or a bow he turned toward the wings and walked slowly off the stage. The cheap, coarse material of his coat brushed against my arm as he passed me. He walked straight toward the stage door and out onto the street. The stage door closed behind him.

The hushed silence in the audience broke as though someone had cracked a whip. Applause filled the theater. Then someone shouted "More! More!" and someone else began to stomp his feet. Soon, the theater rang with the noise of their shouting and stomping. The aisles began to fill with people rushing toward the stage. "Encore. Encore, more!" they yelled.

Backstage there was panic. The stage manager was shouting out orders. "I don't care where he went, find him! He's got to go out there and take a bow! Find him for God's sake before we have a riot on our hands!"

The applause and shouting from the audience were a deafening roar. The musicians crouched close to the wall in the pit away from the railing where the audience pushed and shoved as they shouted for the Cantor to come back. The moving-picture screen was quickly lowered behind the front curtain, the stage manager screaming into a phone to the front booth. "Get that newsreel on, hurry! We've got to quiet this mob!"

Then the orchestra leader tapped the stand with his baton and the musicians came to attention. "The Anthem," he said hoarsely and as they played "The Star-Spangled Banner" the audience quieted down, and in a little while they filed reluctantly out of the theater.

Before the show that night, the stage manager told the Cantor that singing in a theater was different from singing in a synagogue. "You have to take bows," he explained. "You have to sing an encore or two."

The Cantor listened patiently, nodding his head from time to time in agreement. But when he finished his act that night he walked straight across the stage and out the stage door. But this time the stage manager was prepared. The moving picture screen was in position and the newsreel flashed on the screen the moment the Cantor exited. Every show that week, it was the same way. The newsreel would go on and the audience would applaud all through it, shouting and screaming for an encore, but the Cantor had gone back to his Synagogue.

Mother said it was the greatest piece of showmanship she had ever seen. Later, she agreed with Gordon that the Cantor had more than just showmanship. "He could be the biggest thing in vaudeville," she said, "if he'd just dress up the act a little."[39]

While Rosenblatt could ill afford to turn down any payday, a sticking point remained the singing of "Kol Nidre" in the film, where Samuel Rosenblatt quotes his father: "Did you say *Kol Nidre*, the hallowed prayer that is chanted by the cantor at the inauguration of the holiest day of the year? Under no circumstances would I permit that to pass my mouth anywhere but in a house of God."[40] However, Rosenblatt already had sung it outside of a "house of God." Shortly after his arrival in America, it was Yossele Rosenblatt's inaugural 1913 commercial record for Victor followed in 1915 for Columbia. They each sold tens of thousands of copies. Samuel Rosenblatt later said that his father finally agreed "provided he was not photographed, to sing Rachem and several other such non-liturgical Jewish melodies for the Vitaphone project. But even that necessitated his presence in Hollywood to make certain that there would be no snag in the synchronization . . . and so for eight weeks in the summer and in return for $10,000 plus expenses my father came . . . to Los Angeles as the guest of the Warner Brothers."

Actually, the non-cantorial pieces, were not filmed in Hollywood but at the Vitaphone studios in Midwood, Brooklyn. In May 1927, Rosenblatt made two titles he had previously recorded for both Victor and Columbia, "Hallelujah" and "Eli, Eli." And while not "Kol Nidre," Rosenblatt did film an actual Sabbath prayer, the now-lost "Omar Rabbi Elosor" ("So Said Rabbi Elosor"). Set in the cantor's study (and not in a synagogue), the shorts were made for use in theaters in Jewish neighborhoods in advance of the forthcoming *Jazz Singer* release. However, problems with four of the songs made them unacceptable to Warners' front office for general release and had to be specifically requested and so languished in its vaults.[41] When Warners did finally release "Hallelujah" in 1929, it got outstanding reviews in *Variety* and other show trade magazines.

What Rosenblatt shot in Hollywood was his compromise feature film appearance: a three-minute shoehorned-in "concert" segment that allows Jolson an opportunity to flashback to his father, played by the Swedish actor Warner Oland (better known for his later Charlie Chan films). And despite the irresistible marquee ballyhoo "Sacred Songs/Popular Prices," the offering was hardly "sacred": despite the stage setting with a stained glass background and flanked by large candelabras and Rosenblatt (presumably) holding a prayer book, he sings "Yortsayt" ("In Memoriam"), a new Yiddish concert song he had only recently recorded for Columbia.[42]

Rosenblatt's refusal to sing "Kol Nidre" was actually no problem for Warner Brothers, whose tacked-on appearance in the film was a slight of hand meant to distract from the mangled ending. While pre-film press periodically dropped hints that Rosenblatt would sing the "Kol Nidre" sequence, what finally comes out of the mouth of Cantor Rabinowitz was the voice of uncredited Hungarian Jewish art singer Joseph Diskay. Diskay had appeared with Jessel and Rosenblatt in the June 14, 1927, KFWB *Jazz Singer* broadcast and for the film provided the Warners with a spot-on impersonation of Rosenblatt's "Kol Nidre."

Vitaphone and the Jews

Although it was not the first invention to allow films to "talk," it was the Vitaphone, the crude Rube Goldberg–like contraption whose extremely fragile sixteen-inch discs were synchronized to the corresponding film through a series of pulleys and turntables, that first popularly demonstrated the efficacy of talking pictures. Yet the cranky and finnicky Vitaphone system quickly outlived its usefulness, revealing the limits of a system with many moving—and easily disjoined—parts.

Despite switching over to feature length films in its Hollywood location in the early 1930s, Warner Brothers continued to use the Brooklyn Vitaphone studios into 1940 for its more than one thousand musical and comedy short films, a unique high-quality peek at the otherwise undocumented variety American theater tradition that sound films were, even at that moment, successfully killing off. Vitaphone shorts that featured Jewish dialect ("Hebe" characters) such as Willie and Eugene Howard, Nat Carr, Benny Rubin, and so on outnumbered the offerings that featured performers from the Yiddish world.

One was the March 1927 short *Isa Kremer: The Supreme Interpreter of Ballad and Folk Songs* for which she was paid $2,000 ($30,000 today). Kremer would return to make two more shorts in March 1929. Despite a diverse program of foreign songs, and her singular visibility in the Jewish world, none were Yiddish.

Other than Rosenblatt, the biggest Yiddish star to appear in Vitaphone shorts was Molly Picon, but again, not in Yiddish. In December 1929, Picon filmed *The Celebrated Character Comedienne*, her first English-language film, starring as an actress retelling her life in an East Side tenement. It included songs "Yiddishe Blues" (neither Yiddish nor a blues) and "Temperamental Tillie," both co-authored by Picon with Murray Ruminsky, son of Yiddish composer Joseph Rumshinsky. In September 1933, Picon returned in *A Little Girl with Big Ideas* a "30-minute featurette" fantasy about a waitress (Picon) who wins the Irish sweepstake and funds her sister's Broadway musical. The two-reeler, again in English with Jewish overtones, has songs by Picon's new collaborator, pianist Abe Ellstein. Their character piece "The Woiking Goil" (later reworked into the Yinglish dialect patter song "Busy Busy" for Banner records in the 1950s) is a highlight of the short. A kind of vest-pocket Busby Berkley choreography, set atop a giant cash register on which twenty dancers (some sporting "No Sale" costumes) hoof. Sadly, though she would appear in a number of major films and on TV, Molly Picon never got the nod from Hollywood for a starring role in her own English-language feature.

The Screenplay

How different film history might have been had *The Jazz Singer* been made by the director who first imagined it as a *muving piksher*: Ernst Lubitsch. The Jewish Lubitsch, whose singular German film training added the sophisticated "Lubitsch touch" to the Hollywood lexicon, had seen the play in New York. Thrilled with what he experienced, he crafted his own script and brought it to the Jewish Warner Brothers, who upon seeing the play remarked, it's "too Jewish."

However, taking no chances, Warners bought the property for $50,000 the day before the show closed.[43]

But instead of assigning it to Lubitsch, on April 3, 1927, Warners announced that Alfred A. Cohn was to adapt "The Jazz Singer" stage script, no doubt thanks to his successful string of recent screenplays depicting Jews: Eddie Sloman's drama *His People* (1925), an *Abie's Irish Rose*–inspired *Cohens and Kellys* feature (1926), and the lost 1927 MGM silent comedy *Frisco Sally Levy* (yet another Irish-Jewish mashup), starring former Yiddish stage actor Eli "Tenen Holtz" Tenenholtz.[44] Cohn's treatment buried what few Jewish cultural nuances remained in Raphaelson's play, most significantly giving it its new "Hollywood ending."

Cohn's script heats up the father-son conflict by breaking with the previous establishing scenes of introducing Jewish characters to make them sympathetic (e.g., while the story and play opened with a small and warm moment of Yossele teaching the young choristers the nuances of cantorial singing, Cohn revised a scene from the story where Jakie suffers at the hands of his Rebi by making his father the tormentor). By combining these scenes—and their implied meaning—the Cantor is robbed of his more humanized and nuanced character, so making it easier to sympathize with Jakie's his decision to leave. Even the Cantor's choir, who in the story and play show sincere deference to the old Cantor, in the film function more like "Dead End Kids" with circumcisions.

The stereotyping was furthered by quotidian director Alan Crosland, who had just come off directing the Warner Brothers/Vitaphone first synchronized sound feature, *Don Juan* with John Barrymore. *The Jazz Singer* was actually two interspersed films: the first, the stale, silent assimilationist melodrama, and the second, a series of audience-tested Jolson musical shorts, each one barely able to contain the ebullient Jolson.

But it was the ending that served two functions: it fulfilled the Warners' symbolic arrival of their own assimilation. It was also a way to replace Jessel with the far more marketable Jolson.[45]

The Critics

No question that enthusiasm in the Yiddish press for Jolson and the film was unwaveringly positive, but it was of a kind of level 2 enthusiasm: the general good feeling that "one of us" successfully crossed over to mainstream popularity. But the quantity and tone of the outpouring of Yiddish press toward Jessel and the play was level 1, nothing less than *kvelling*, the kind of beaming with delight that one only gets from the success of a child (*nakhes*).

Just as the narrative trajectory was changed for the film, so was its advertising. In the stage show ads, Jessel was not portrayed in blackface, only in cantorial robes, while for the film PR Jolson was mainly portrayed in blackface. But for the Jewish market, Warner's PR department made sure to always include an image of Yossele Rosenblatt in all the ads, even when it resulted in a bizarre visualization: a key scene where Jolson is being given an intimate pep talk by love interest Mary Dale Cantor for the Yiddish ads now had Yossele Rosenblatt bluntly inserted, creating a freakish menage a trois.

In the pages of the *Tog* on October 17, 1927, B. I. Goldstein wrote, "My readers may recall that previously in the pages of the *Tog* we wrote about *The Jazz Singer* when it played on Broadway with George Jessel in the starring role and we said how well he portrayed a cantor's son, as if it were his own life, well this time it's true as Al Jolson *is* a cantor's son. And Jolson portrayed the role correctly. But that's all." Goldstein was naturally wowed by Jolson's Vitaphone segments but saves the greatest praise in his

Figure 23.2. Ads in the Yiddish press for *The Jazz Singer* on Broadway did not show George Jessel in blackface. Ads for the Jolson film did. *Source:* National Library of Israel, Historical Jewish Press website (www.jpress.org.il), founded by the National Library and Tel Aviv University. Used with permission.

last paragraph for Yossele Rosenblatt ("a real cantor"), noting how his brief appearance was a highlight of the film. The Yiddish press was appreciative but also gimlet-eyed. The religious *Morgn Zhurnal* commented, "It now appears that what 'Abie's Irish Rose' was to theater, 'the Jazz Singer' is to film."[46]

The Aftermath

Faced with the imminent *Jazz Singer* film premier, Jessel returned for one last-hurrah East Coast tour opening in New York's City Theater on October 6, 1927, the night Yom Kippur ended. By then, Jessel had played the part one thousand times.[47] This last production was enhanced by hiring not only a professional cantor (Joseph Shengold) to play Cantor Rabinowitz but several veteran Yiddish theater actors. Taking a nod from Jolson, Jessel now stepped out to the stage apron to sing two songs with which he would forever be identified: "My Mother's Eyes" and "Home Pals," the second by Joe Young and Sam E. Lewis, who also wrote "Where Did Robinson Crusoe Go with Friday on Saturday Night" for Al Jolson. For several weeks in October, in perhaps the only place on earth, New York newspapers carried ads for both *Jazz Singers*: Jessel's final shows and Jolson's new movie.

Despite Jessel's subsequent popularity on radio, on the variety stage, and as a much sought after after-dinner speaker, his *Jazz Singer* debacle proved a curse in which he was never again offered a part in a major Hollywood feature film, though he would return as a producer, including the classic 1947 Tyrone Power film noir *Nightmare Alley*.

Jessel, now "America's Toastmaster General," delivered the main eulogy at Jolson's Hollywood funeral as much to bury Jolson as a part of American entertainment itself.

> In 1910 the Jewish people who emigrated here from Europe were a sorry lot, their humor came out of their own troubles . . . when they sang they sang with laments in their hearts . . . and then there came on the scene a young man, vibrantly throbbing with life and courage who marched on the stage, head high . . . and told the world that the Jew in America could shout happily about Dixie, about the night boat to Albany and about his mammy. . . . Jolson is the happiest portrait that can ever be painted about an American of the Jewish faith.

Raphaelson the playwright would pen another ten plays, with two challenging *The Jazz Singer*'s Broadway longevity, while Raphaelson the screenwriter racked up several dozen workman-like credits with two notable back-to-back triumphs: *The Shop Around the Corner* (1940), directed by his early champion Ernst Lubitsch, and a script that he considered his best, *Suspicion* (1941), directed by Alfred Hitchcock.

At the end of his life, both Raphaelson the playwright and Raphaelson the screenwriter ruefully and rightfully acknowledged his *Jazz Singer* legacy: "I'm not ashamed of the play, but the movie embarrasses me."[48]

The Remakes

There was talk of Jolson remaking *The Jazz Singer* on the film's tenth anniversary, but instead, on August 10, 1936, it appeared on CBS's *Lux Radio Theater*. While it ends the same as the film, the radio version more closely follows the structure of the stage play. In 1943, there were rumors of a remake starring Danny Kaye, but it was the fictionalized 1946 *The Jolson Story* and its *Jazz Singer* scene recreation that led to plans for a full-blown *Jazz Singer* remake. The lead, which came with Jolson on the soundtrack, was offered to a number of actors including Frank Sinatra, but eventually went to Larry Parks.

While Jolson's death in 1950 scuttled plans for a Larry Parks remake (that and Park's 1951 HUAC blacklist), on the heels of the seven-day *shiva* period to mourn Jolson, studio head Harry Warner tapped comedian/singer Danny Thomas for the role. Born Amos Alphonsus Muzyad Yakhoob, the Lebanese Christian from Deerfield, Michigan, came up through the nightclub circuit and scored a success as a screen cantor in the 1948 MGM musical-drama *Big City*. The Yiddish press, which touted "The Jazz Singer" as "a new film about Jewish life with Danny Thomas," already liked him. Like Jessel, Thomas was highly regarded for his philanthropy ranging from hospitals to support for the new state of Israel.

The 1952 *Jazz Singer* was also a breakout role for actual jazz singer Peggy Lee though not her first brush with Jewish music. Her 1942 OKeh record *My Little Cousin* with the Benny Goodman Orchestra was based on the hit 1922 Yiddish sweatshop pop song "Di grine kuzine" ("The Greenhorn Cousin") by fiddler Abe Schwartz. In an ironic break with the High Holiday release history of the play (opening before Rosh Hashona) and original film (the night Yom Kippur ended), *The Jazz Singer* remake was released during Christmas week 1952.

Its first small screen remake would be for *Broadway Television Theater*, a locally produced live show on New York's WOR, aired the episode on April 28, 1952, starring Yiddish theater royalty Celia Adler, daughter of actor Jacob P. Adler, as Sara Rabinowitz and Lionel Ames as Jack.

The second TV remake was on *Ford Startime*, an NBC anthology series on October 11, 1959, starring Jerry Lewis. In this, the first of his two tragically misbegotten Jewish-themed projects (the second being the famously unfinished 1972 Holocaust film *The Day the Clown Cried*), Lewis stars as Joey Robbins, transformed from a singer to a comedian, with Yiddish theater star Molly Picon as his mother and Eduard Franz (born Schmidt) reprising his cantor role from the Danny Thomas version. While Lewis earned some favorable press for his taken-from-life-performance as the tortured, egocentric comic, most critics used the word "shmaltz" when describing his scenes with Picon and Franz.

On the fiftieth anniversary of *The Jazz Singer*, plans were made for another updated big-screen remake. Like Jolson, they chose a popular Jewish singer making his first big-screen appearance: Neil Diamond, then a triple threat on record, in concert, and on TV. The Brooklyn-born Diamond was offered $1 million and a guarantee for even more for the soundtrack revenue. Once production began, chaos reigned when Diamond, who hated everything about the filmmaking process, regularly discarded scripts, leading ladies (he finally settled on number six, Lucie Arnaz), and directors (at one point, Barbra Streisand), but the helm eventually went to Richard Fleischer, son of Jewish animation pioneer Max Fleischer (Popeye, Betty Boop, and Superman).

Like the original film whose B-picture plot left critics yawning, here too the inept script featured some truly appalling touches: the "solution" for how to update Jolson's burnt-cork turn was to have Diamond's character Jess Robin, in an attempt to help a friend who needed a replacement for his Black vocal ensemble, fill in wearing blackface). Roger Ebert gave the film a one-star review, marveling at the star's persistent acting unavailability: "His fans apparently think Neil Diamond songs celebrate worthy human qualities," he quipped. "I think they describe conditions suitable for treatment." But like the original *Jazz Singer*, it was the star's singing power that powered the film, with Diamond racking up three top-ten hits ("America," "Hello Again," and "Love on the Rocks") and multiplatinum sales.

Lawrence Olivier, who portrayed the Cantor, hated the film ("This piss is shit," he is reputed to have said), and it showed. Olivier lazily recycled the pseudo middle-European accent used for his Academy Award–nominated performance as Nazi war criminal, Szell, in *Marathon Man*. One *Jazz Singer* review characterized Olivier's performance as "Mr. Kitzel [Jack Benny's Jewish accented radio foil] with an Oxford education."

But in what is a brilliant sideways reference to *The Jazz Singer*'s jagged production history, co-screenwriter Herbert Baker (son of Yiddish theater/Broadway star and Jessel confidante Belle Baker) includes a character who, when he refers to Diamond's "Jess" character, does so using the Yiddish diminutive *L* suffix, repeatedly calling him "Jess'l."

Notes

Chapter 1

1. *Jewish Messenger*, May 29, 1874, 3.
2. "In the Jewish World," *Hebrew Standard*, Oct. 1903, 7.
3. "A Well-Conducted Restaurant," *Hebrew Standard*, Sept. 4, 1903, 5.
4. *Arbeter Tsaytung*, Mar. 7, 1890, 4.
5. Advertisement, *Yiddishe Bine*, Nov. 26, 1909, 3.
6. Mrs. Esther Levy, "Jewish Cookery Book," *King and Baird* (Philadelphia), 1871.
7. W. M. Rosenblatt, "The Jewish Dietary System," *The Galaxy: A Magazine of Entertaining Reading*, Nov. 1874, 670–79.
8. *Jewish Voice*, May 17, 1895, 6.
9. "San Francisco, Cal.," *Jewish Voice*, June 7, 1895, 4.
10. "Meat Riots in New York Kosher Markets on East Side Raided by Hebrew Women," *Hartford Courant*, May 16, 1902, 9.
11. "Meat Riots in New York," 9.
12. "Women Open Butcher Shops," *Hebrew Standard*, June 13, 1902.
13. "Beef Poisoned by the Strikers," *Bisbee Daily Review*, Aug. 24, 1904, 4.
14. Upton Sinclair, "Zump" (trans. Mark Fogelman), *Farlag Sh. Goldfarb* (Warsaw), 1928.
15. Chaim Ehrenreich, "Vos yidn in Amerika hobn gegesn mit 50 yor tzurik, un vos zey esn haynt," *Forverts*, May 4, 1946, 2.

Chapter 2

1. Glendon Allvine, "'None Genuine Without This Signature' Trotzky," *New York Tribune*, May 25, 1919, G8.

2. Eichler, "Another Arts Center Built in Fun City," *Daily News*, Feb. 20, 1972, 21S.

3. Frederick C. Griffin, "Leon Trotsky in New York City," *New York History*, Oct. 1968, 393–95.

4. Advertisement, *Morgn Zhurnal*, Jan. 1, 1914, 8.

5. Eichler, "Another Arts Center Built in Fun City," 21S.

6. "Farewell Luncheon to Mr. Max Manischewitz," *Jewish Monitor*, July 23, 1920, 6.

7. "For Orthodox Jews," *Daily National Hotel Reporter*, Aug. 15, 1923, 7.

8. "Broadway Central," Talk of the Town, *New Yorker*, Oct. 6, 1934, 18.

9. Advertisement, *Forverts*, Apr. 13, 1925, 5.

10. Danton Walker, "Broadway," *Daily News*, Oct. 13, 1938, 63.

11. Eichler, "Another Arts Center Built in Fun City," 21S.

Chapter 3

1. "City Items," *American Israelite*, Dec. 10, 1875, 6.

2. "Miss Fream's Crusade," *New York Times*, Jan. 22, 1895, 16.

3. Trow's New York City Directory 1897–1898, 458.

4. "Throng at Hebrew Funeral 500 Policemen Out to Guard the Mourners for the Late Isaac Gellis," *New York Sun*, Mar. 22, 1906, 10.

5. Eddie Cantor and David Freedman, *My Life Is in Your Hands* (New York: Doubleday, 1957), 15.

6. *Variety Radio Directory*, New York, 1957, 902.

7. "An emese inshurens policy der Isaac Gellis sayn," *Forverts*, July 25, 1933, 7.

8. "For Those Who Want the Best," *New York Times*, Apr. 4, 1949, 16.

9. "Krainin-Rabenowitz," *Brooklyn Daily Eagle*, July 25, 1896, 7.

10. "Moyde Rabe!" *Morgn Zhurnal*, Feb. 26, 1909, 8.

11. *Jewish Daily Bulletin Index*, Jan.–Dec. 1925, 116.

12. "Tankhum krainin der eygntimer fun *hibru neshonel* kosher vurst fabrik," *Morgn Zhurnal*, Feb. 2, 1911, 2.

13. "Something New for the Jewish Housewife," *American Hebrew & Jewish Messenger*, Dec. 6, 1912, 174.

14. "Beblekh," *Morgn Zhurnal*, June 18, 1915, 3.

15. Sholem Aleichem, "In Amerike, motl peisie dem khazn's un andere mayses," Farlag Varhayt (New York), 1918, 142 (trans. Henry Sapoznik).

16. "Der velt berimte *hibru neshonel*," *Morgn Zhurnal*, July 15, 1919, 11.

17. Samuel Tenenbaum, "All About Coney Island: Thirty Years Ago You Took Your Life in Your Hands When You Came to Coney Island," *Forverts*, Aug. 8, 1926, E2–4.

18. Advertisement, "Yayin gefen kosher l'mehadrin min hamehadrin," *Morgn Zhurnal*, July 14, 1922, 10.

19. "Mercantile Appraisement," *Scranton Republican*, May 6, 1919, 15.

20. "Kosher Plant to Receiver," *New York Times*, July 6, 1928, 37.

21. "Mecktav golu lakol," *Tog*, Aug. 29, 1928, 2.

22. "Bakantmakhn fun der *hibru neshinel* kosher vurst fabrik," *Forverts*, May 30, 1934, 8.

23. Bernard Postal, "New York's Jewish Mayors," *American Jewish World*, Jan. 30, 1931, 2.

24. "I. Pinckowitz Dies; Charity Leader," *Brooklyn Times Union*, Nov. 9, 1936, 22.

25. "Di Yidishe Shtunde/The Jewish Hour," *Tog*, Oct. 11, 1931, 2.

26. "Hebrew National Puts 90% of Wine Budget on Radio," Broadcasting Telecasting, Mar. 22, 1954, 7.

27. William Freeman, "The Old Stand-By Becomes a Luxury," *New York Times*, May 14, 1961, F1.

28. *Sponsor Magazine*, Sept. 22, 1952, 76.

29. "Spot TV Brand Figures," Broadcasting Telecasting, April 6, 1957, 61.

30. "Island Business," *Newsday*, July 11, 1968, 95.

31. Star of David Memorial Gardens, North Lauderdale, FL, Garden of Gan Shalom, Plot 43, Grave 2.

32. "Losing Lines, Bought in the 70s, Were Sold Fast," *New York Times*, Apr. 12, 1980, 31.

33. Stewart Ain, Larry Sutton, "131 Fired Hebrew National Strikers Lose Jobs in Firm's Move," *Daily News*, Aug. 6, 1986.

34. "Conagra Acquires National Foods," *New York Times*, Feb. 2, 1993, D4.

35. *Official Gazette of the US Patent Office*, Washington, DC, Feb. 22, 1927, 684.

36. *Haggadah shel peysakh*, Hebrew Publishing Company, 1912. Maxwell House Coffee would later build on this idea when desperately lobbying rabbinic courts to have coffee (a.k.a. "beans," forbidden among Ashkenazim during the holiday) made kosher for Passover. It worked.

37. Advertisement, *Forverts*, May 4, 1936, 7.

38. Advertisement, *Forverts*, Jan. 24, 1938, 7.

39. "Hot Dogs for Moslems," *Buffalo Evening News*, May 8, 1940, 42.

40. George H. Roeder, *The Censored War: American Visual Experience During World War Two* (New Haven, CT: Yale University Press, 1993), 69.

41. Diane Kolyer, "Kosher Meat Sales Soar in Black Neighborhoods," *Daily News*, May 29, 1971, 9C.

42. "Conagra Buys Mogen David Trademarks," *New York Times*, Dec. 19, 1995, D4.

43. New York City Directory, 1915, 832. Until around 1955, Katz's was

listed at 183 Ludlow Street, but since then, 207 East Houston.

44. Federal census, 1920.

45. "Katz's delikatesn *stor, a yunion stor*," *Forverts*, July 1, 1918, 2.

46. Sanborn Fire Insurance Map, 1903.

47. New York City/WPA Tax Photo, 1940.

48. Craig Clairborne, "Meal Is Anytime at Delicatessen," *New York Times*, Apr. 25, 1961, 31.

49. The scene was recreated for a 2025 Super Bowl ad for, of all things, mayonnaise, something *never* found at a Jewish delicatessen.

50. Rona Kaysen, "Alongside the Pastrami, Luxury Condos a New York Institution Stays Put and Gets a New Neighbor in a $17 Million Deal," *New York Times*, Apr. 24, 2016, RE1.

51. Michele Clark, "Schmulka Bernstein and His Children," unpublished, n.d., 17.

52. Clark, 56.

53. Robert Sylvester, "Shanghai Knishes," *Daily News*, May 19, 1960, 70.

54. Clementine Paddleford, "Bernstein's Innovation: Chinese Kosher Cooking," *Herald Tribune*, Oct. 27, 1962, 9.

55. Heyman Zimel, "Chinese Food For Americans," *Forverts*, Dec. 2, 1928, 24.

56. Sylvester, "Shanghai Knishes," 70.

57. Paddleford, "Bernstein's Innovation," 9.

58. Sylvester, "Shanghai Knishes," 70. During World War Two, Shanghai was the home of more than 20,000 refugee European Jews.

59. Clark, "Schmulka Bernstein and His Children," 73.

60. In the 1970s, the author and Chinese American historian John Kuo Wei Tchen ate at Shang Chai, causing a sensation when the Chinese cook staff all came into the dining room to gawp at the first Asian to ever eat there.

61. Correspondence, Jeff Feinberg, Jan. 3, 2025.

62. Al Wendel Jameison Baker, "Gunned Down Making a Deposit," *Daily News*, Mar. 5, 1996, 2.

63. Bob Sylvester, "Dining By the Deli," *Daily News*, Feb. 11, 1973, 128.

64. "It's No Baloney," *Philadelphia Inquirer*, Oct. 30, 1975, 3.

65. Peter Coutrous, "Laughter, Dancing Spice Purim Feast For the Blind," *Daily News*, March 17, 1976, 4.

66. Israel Shenker, "Delicatessen Puts Clock Back 20 Years," *New York Times*, Mar. 12, 1974, 41.

67. Charlotte Astor, "Posters and Pasta for Picon," *Miami News*, July 11, 1980, 14.

68. "Yiddish Stardom," *New York Times*, July 10, 1985, B3.

69. Harry Berkowitz, "Deli Man in a Moscow Pickle," *Newsday*, Sept. 13, 1991, 15.

70. D. J. Saunders, "They Want to Live," *Daily News*, Mar. 18, 1988, M1.

71. Paul Richter, "Nothing Helps N.Y. Restaurants Like the Mob: Brush with Gangsters as Valuable as a Great Chef and Ambience," *Los Angeles Times*, May 30, 1989, C1.

72. Baker, Jamieson, "Gunned down making a deposit," *Journal News*, Jan. 6, 2006, 18.

73. "Famed 2nd Avenue Deli Shuts Down," *Journal News*, Jan. 6, 2006, 18.

74. Correspondence with Corey Brier, president of the Yiddish Theatrical Alliance, Oct. 17, 2023.

75. Rocco Parascandola, "New Push in Cold Case," *Daily News*, Mar. 4, 2019, 10.

Chapter 4

1. "Recipes," *Forverts*, Apr. 8, 1950, 10.
2. "Rivington Street Sees War," *New York Times*, Jan. 27, 1916, 7.
3. "The Advance on Knish," *The Literary Digest*, Mar. 4, 1916, 595.
4. "Rivington Street Sees War."
5. "The Advance On Knish."
6. "Hot Dogs Un Knishes" (words: Louis Gilrod, music: Peretz Sandler), Aaron Lebedeff Vocalion 13043, Nov. 3, 1926 (translation by Henry Sapoznik).
7. Lenny Bruce, "I Am Not a Nut, Elect Me!" Fantasy 7007, 1960.
8. "Yonah Schimmel's: An Unlikely Shrine," *Pensacola News*, July 10, 1981, 17.
9. "Der untersheyd tsvishn varshe un lemberg," *Forverts*, June 21, 1920, 6.
10. New York City Directory, 1916, 1412.
11. "Getzel tararam, yonah knish un motl bok loyfn nokh a dokter," *Forverts*, June 19, 1913, 7.
12. Federal Census, 1930.
13. Advertisement, *New York Times*, Dec. 27, 1950, 18.
14. Vic Ziegel, "Knishes Here, Gone Tomorrow," *Daily News*, Mar. 11, 1995, 15.
15. "Another Building Collapses," *Journal News*, July 14, 2000, 3A.
16. Advertisement, "Far ayer kinder's gezunt!" *Forverts*, July 19, 1925, 16.
17. Advertisement, *Tog*, June 28, 1925, 8.
18. "Dissolution Notice," *Standard Union*, Feb. 2, 1926, 15.
19. Israel Shenker, "Taste for Business, Builds Brooklyn Knish Empire," *New York Times*, May 9, 1971, BQ80.
20. *The Soda Fountain*, November 1922, 62.
21. Shenker, "Taste for Business."
22. "Serves Knishes at Inquiry," *New York Times*, Mar. 6, 1928, 19.

23. Shenker, "Taste for Business."
24. Shenker, "Taste for Business."
25. Tom Incantalupo, "LI Blaze at Knish Factory Touches Off National Shortage of Square Treat," *Newsday*, Nov. 12, 2013, A2.
26. Incantalupo, "LI Blaze at Knish Factory."
27. Neal Ashby, "The Old Neighborhood," *Daily News*, May 25, 1975, 11.
28. Mort Shatzkin, interview by Tricia Vita, Coney Island History Project, Feb. 25, 2023.
29. "Coney Island Fading? It Can't Be Noticed," *Akron Beacon Journal*, July 1, 1953, 46.
30. Shatzkin, interview by Tricia Vita.
31. "'Knish King' Royally Crowned," *Daily News*, Oct. 23, 1956, 1K.
32. Shatzkin, interview by Tricia Vita.
33. Arthur Schwartz, "A Guide to Seaside Noshing," *Newsday*, Aug. 21, 1970, 70.
34. Eric Newby, "Time Off," *London Observer*, May 28, 1972, 34.
35. Clint Marcia Kramer Roswell, "Knowing Noshers Nosh Knishes," *Daily News*, June 3, 1979, B1 (B1/B3).
36. Suzanne Hamlin, "Knowing the Knish New York's Favorite Nosh," *Daily News*, Jan. 19, 1983, GL 1/3.
37. Bea Lewis, "Knishes Are Hot Again," *Newsday*, Mar. 6, 1985, B7.
38. Julie Wheelock, "'Taste of New York' Store Flies In East Coast Knishes to Whet West Coast Appetites," *Los Angeles Times*, Oct. 3, 1991.
39. "*Hit him* in di kishkes," *Forverts*, July 11, 1921, 3.
40. "A lakh un a shmeykhl," *Forverts*, July 1, 1923, 13.
41. "Hail Papa Burger's Moveable Birthday," *New York Times*, Mar. 15, 1911, 15.
42. David Gordon, "Politics Among the Kishkes, Or How Sohn's Bubble Broke," *Daily News*, Aug. 31, 1949, KL9.
43. David Gordon, "Kishke King Puts Real Art Into Ancient Viand in Café," *Daily News*, May 29, 1949, B8.
44. Gordon, "Kishke King."
45. "Kishke King to Be Mayor," *Daily News*, Oct. 21, 1949, B1.
46. *Amsterdam News*, Sept. 17, 1949, 11.
47. Margaret Mara, "Living in Brooklyn Brownsville, East Side Counterpart," *Brooklyn Daily Eagle*, Mar. 30, 1949, 23.
48. Judith H. Bernstein, "Light & Shadows," *Newsday*, Aug. 29, 1999, D16.
49. Bret Senft, "After 50 Years, Looking for Fresh Images," *New York Times*, Dec. 22, 1996, LI10.

Chapter 5

1. Henry Sapoznik, "Klezmer: Jewish Music From Old World to Our World," *Schirmer* (New York) 1999, 41–3.
2. "Champion Cymbalist Is Playing Here Now," *New York Times*, Apr. 26, 1908, C4.
3. Richard Spottswood, *Ethnic Music on Records: A Discography of Ethnic Recordings Produced in the United States, 1893–1942*, vol. 3 (Urbana: University of Illinois Press, 1990).
4. O. O. McIntyre, "New York Day By Day," *Buffalo Inquirer*, Dec. 15, 1919, 6.
5. "Recorded Leases," *New York Tribune*, June 10, 1919, 21.
6. Michael Gold, *Jews Without Money* (New York: Horace Liveright, 1930).
7. *Forverts*, Sept. 10, 1926, 8.
8. *New Masses*, May 1, 1931, 21.
9. Advertisement, *Forverts*, Feb. 8, 1929, 8.
10. *Daily Worker*, Feb. 9, 1929, 2.
11. Lewis Sobol, *New York Evening Journal*, June 21, 1932.
12. *Yiddishes Togblatt*, Apr. 3, 1929, 7.
13. Lucy Jeanne Price, "New York Letter," *Muncie Evening Press*, Nov. 15, 1921, 7.
14. "Society Has Ghetto Fad," *Spokane Chronicle*, Apr. 7, 1903, 5.
15. Stephen Graham, "New York Nights," *George H. Doran* (New York) 1927, 150–51.
16. Graham, 150–51.
17. "The Gypsies Come to Town," *Kansas City Star*, Dec. 25, 1930, 14.
18. Graham, "New York Nights," 155.
19. Graham, 152–53.
20. Graham, 155.
21. "Joseph Moskowitz, 76, Dies; Noted Player of Gypsy Music," *Washington Post*, June 29, 1954, 16.
22. Dr. Isidor Lhevinne, "He Says Lower East Side Has Become Vulgarized," *Forverts*, June 2, 1929, 12.
23. Abel, *Variety*, Apr. 10, 1935, 48.
24. *Forverts*, July 4, 1929, 6.
25. "19 Places Here Padlocked for Dry Law Violations Twelve Alleged Speakeasies Padlock for a Year," *New York Herald Tribune*, June 4, 1929, 22.
26. "Jack Silverman, Operated Old Roumanian Restaurant," *New York Times*, June 16, 1974, 46.
27. Theodore Straus, "Late Events in the Nightclubs," *New York Times*, Oct. 15, 1939, 2X.

28. "Bolan to Copy Mulrooney in Handling Reds," *New York Herald Tribune*, Apr. 19, 1933, 3.

29. "2nd Ave. Fan Dancer," *Variety*, Feb. 27, 1935, 1.

30. "Dining and Dancing," *Women's Wear Daily*, Feb. 23, 1934, 23.

31. Don O'Malley, "New York Inside Out," *Stockton Independent*, Oct. 19, 1934, 12.

32. "Thomashefsky, Once Idol of the Stage, Sings in Cabaret," *Detroit Free Press*, Oct. 15, 1934, 3.

33. "The Night Club," *Women's Wear Daily*, Oct. 12, 1934, 14z.

34. "*Variety*'s Broadway Guide," *Variety*, Feb. 27, 1935, 67.

35. Joseph Rachlin, "Vu iz di heymishkayt fun dem amolikgn yiddishn restoranen?," *Forverts*, Jan. 15, 1957, 2.

36. "Everything's Silver," *Brooklyn Citizen*, Feb. 19, 1938, 9.

37. "Old Roumanian Is Rendezvous of Celebrities," *Farmingdale Post*, Oct. 29, 1936, 6.

38. "Old Roumanian of the East Side Offers 'Uptown Downtown Scandals,'" *Women's Wear Daily*, Jan. 25, 1935, 14.

39. "News of the Clubs," *New York Times*, Jan. 15, 1939, X2.

40. "Old Eatery Changes Over to Night Club," *Daily News*, June 30, 1957, M4.

41. Obituaries, *New York Times*, June 16, 1974, 47.

42. "Business Records," *New York Times*, Feb. 25, 1936, 27. Assertions that Anzelowitz worked his way up from kitchen help, butcher, chef, and finally owner of Moskowitz & Lupowitz are anecdotal and otherwise unprovable.

43. "Cuisine, Host Excel at 2nd Ave. Restaurant," *Women's Wear Daily*, Jan. 14, 1949, 51.

44. *Daily Worker*, Oct. 23, 1937, 5.

45. *Brooklyn Citizen*, Dec. 30, 1937, 3.

46. Martha Neumark, "Lights of New York: The Yiddish Cabaret," *American Israelite* Aug. 22, 1935, 2.

47. Regarding the Second Avenue Roumanian Kretchma, 285 AD 877 (1st Dept. 1955).

48. Sid Caesar and Bill Davidson, *Where Have I Been? An Autobiography* (New York: Crown Publishers, 1982), 52.

49. Robert Sylvester, "Dream, Street," *Daily News*, Dec. 12, 1961, 80.

50. "The Tragic Success of Alfred Tiloff," Naked City, WABC, Nov. 8, 1961.

51. Francis Sugrue, "30 Loyal Yiddish Sons of Erin Want to March With the Others," *Herald Tribune*, Nov. 21, 1962, 3.

52. "Chatter Broadway," *Variety*, Feb. 24, 1965, 76.

53. Vic Ziegel, "When Second Avenue Was King," *Daily News*, Mar. 10, 1996, 17N.

54. In the interest of full disclosure, around 1980, the author's klezmer band, "Kapelye," unsuccessfully auditioned to be the restaurant's house band.

55. Pete Wells, "Come. Eat. There's Plenty of Food," *New York Times*, Sept. 23, 2014, D8.
56. Mimi Sheraton, "Heart-and-Soul Jewish-Rumanian," *New York Times*, Sept. 17, 1976, 61.
57. Wells, "Come. Eat."
58. "Steakhouse Heifitz Dies at 81 from Heart Ailment," *Daily News*, Apr. 8, 1998, 57.
59. "Steakhouse Heifitz."
60. Corey Kilgannon, "Lower East Side Troubadour," *New York Times*, June 2, 2013, NJ4Side.
61. Lisa Keys, "Sammy's Roumanian, Famed Lower East Side Restaurant, Will Reopen with a Passover Seder," *Jewish Week*, Apr. 2, 2024.
62. Arthur Schwartz, "The Young & The Yiddish, a Truly Schmaltzy Tale at Triplet's," *Daily News*, Mar. 27, 1987, 19.

Chapter 6

1. "Form American Beverage," *Brooklyn Times Union*, Jan. 4, 1929, 12.
2. "Obituary," *Journal of the American Chemical Society* 19, part 2 (1897): 678–79.
3. "Obituary," 678–79.
4. Carl Schultz, "Mineral Spring Waters Their Chemical Composition, Physiological Action and Therapeutic Uses," *Baker and Godwin* (New York), 1865.
5. Daniel J. Watermeir, *Between Actor and Critic: Selected Letters of Edwin Booth and William Winter* (Princeton University Press, 2015), 26.
6. "Carl H. Shultz Dead," *New York Times*, May 30, 1897, 3.
7. "Local Intelligence: The Central Park," *New York Times*, May 29, 1866, 8.
8. "Central Park 'Spas' Is Now a Candy Shop," *New York Times*, Sept. 11, 1927, SM17.
9. Sol Etyinge Jr., "Sunday Morning in Central Park Jews Drinking Mineral Water," *Harper's Weekly*, Sept. 14, 1872, 720.
10. "Central Park 'Spas' Is Now a Candy Shop."
11. Correspondence with Dennis Smith, Oct. 24, 2021–Oct. 24, 2023.
12. Correspondence with Dennis Smith.
13. *American Carbonator and American Bottler*, June 15, 1905, 22.
14. "Death of Fred Schoneberger," *Brooklyn Daily Eagle*, April 26, 1890, 8.
15. *Trade-Mark Record*, May 20, 1907, 251.
16. "Seleri tonik helft fardayen dos essen," *Morgn Zhurnal*, Sept. 22, 1921, 10.
17. "Dr. Brown's Fame Travels," *Re-LY-On Bottler: A Monthly Magazine of Ideas and Ideals for the Bottling Trade*, Aug. 1922, 9.
18. *Official Gazette of the United States Patent Office: Trademarks*, Washington, DC, April 14, 1973, TM100.

19. "Di *union* hot nokh alts *trobl* mit Dr. Brown's seleri tonik," *Forverts*, May 15, 1924, 9.

20. It is commonly repeated that Dr. Brown's changed its name to Cel-Ray due to FDA disapproval of its use of the word "tonic," but there is no evidence to support that.

21. Advertisement, *Morgn Zhurnal*, Apr. 3, 1933, 2.

22. "*Onkle* abe's radio program iz di beste *skul* far kinder af *steyshn* WEVD," *Forverts*, June 14, 1936, 18.

23. "Juvenile Success, Over 10,000 Join Local Club in Short Period," *Broadcasting, Broadcast Advertising*, Aug. 1, 1936, 48.

24. P. A., "Robinson Crusoe, Jr.," *Billboard*, May 28, 1938, 9.

25. "Cel-Ray from Benay," *Motion Picture Daily*, June 17, 1939, 514.

26. "Warrants Issued for 3 in Musica Probe," *Hartford Courant*, Feb. 6, 1939, 1.

27. Thomas J. Maier, "A Federal Case Of Soda: Distributors Sue Bottler to Open Up Market," *Newsday*, Jan. 28, 1991, 29.

28. Charles Hillinger, "Drink of the Deli People," *Los Angeles Times*, July 4, 1986, 75.

Chapter 7

1. "The Food Shop," *Tampa Bay Times*, Dec. 26, 1917, 2.
2. "The Food Shop."
3. Michael Pollack, "Appetizing Indeed," *New York Times*, June 27, 2004, CY2.
4. Communication Aliza Gans, PR, Russ & Daughters, Mar. 14, 2023.
5. "Berger's Amphibious Steed When Swimming Days in Rockaway Were Over. He Swam Out to Sea," *New York Times*, Sept. 13, 1911, 7.
6. E. V. Durling, "On the Side," *San Francisco Examiner*, Oct. 9, 1943, 21.
7. Linda Abrams, "The Mom-and-Pop Store: Can It Outlast Its Founding Parents?," *Daily News*, July 7, 1974, 141.
8. Joan Wilen and Lydia Wilen, "An Appetizing Story," *Newsday*, Apr. 25, 1994, 4.
9. "Manhattan Transfers," *New York Times*, Aug. 2, 1949, 33.
10. Communication Aliza Gans, PR, Russ & Daughters, Mar. 2, 2023.
11. Communication Aliza Gans, PR, Russ & Daughters, Mar. 2, 2023.
12. Craig Clairborne, "Food News," *New York Times*, Mar. 10, 1964, 40.
13. Walter Winchell, "In New York," *Philadelphia Inquirer*, Nov. 7, 1945, 28.
14. Charles B. Driscoll, "New York Day By Day," *Alexandria Daily Town Talk* Jan. 10, 1939, 6.
15. Paul A. Peters, "And the Lamp Post," *Jewish Advocate*, July 22, 1938, 1.
16. Kay Gardella, "Burns' Humor Cuttingly Sharp," *Daily News*, Sept. 18, 1985, 51.

17. Burt Boyar, "Best of Broadway," *Philadelphia Inquirer*, Mar. 8, 1956, 11.

18. Leonard Lyons, "Business Dept.," *Washington Post*, Mar. 3, 1941, 14.

19. Douglas Martin, "Moe Greengrass, 84, King of a Sturgeon Shrine," *New York Times*, Jan. 5, 2002, B7.

20. Alex Witchel, "Counterintelligence: The Comfort of Sturgeon," *New York Times*, Sept. 23, 2001, ST2.

21. Merrill Shindler, "A Religious Experience New York Expats Find Heaven at Barney Greengrass," *Rave!*, Jan. 27, 1995, K39.

22. Jenn Harris, "A New Haute Lunch Spot," *Los Angeles Times*, Sept. 7, 2014, 62.

23. "Sam Bernstein, Founder of Murray's, the Store Specializing in Sturgeon," *New York Times*, May 18, 1977, 94.

24. Douglas Martin, "Murray Bernstein, West Side Sturgeon King, Dies at 87," *New York Times*, Feb. 3, 2000, C27.

25. Craig Claiborne, "Food News: Smoked Fish Delicacies," *New York Times*, Mar. 10, 1964, 40.

26. Martin, "Murray Bernstein."

Chapter 8

1. Josie Glausiusz, "Jewish Genetics: 75% of Jews Are Lactose Intolerant and 11 Other Facts," *Haaretz*, July 8, 2015.

2. "Jewish Coffee and Tea Houses," *Hebrew Standard*, Nov. 16, 1900, 1.

3. E. L., "The Melting Pot," *American Hebrew and Jewish Messenger*, June 23, 1916, 206.

4. *Forverts*, May 27, 1916, 6.

5. Ad, *American Hebrew and Jewish Messenger*, Nov. 18, 1921, 27.

6. "Mrs. Schildkraut, A Vegetarian Cook: Her Methods in Preparation of Meals Led to Opening of 15 Restaurants," *New York Times*, June 5, 1937, 17.

7. Despite being the entire reason there was a restaurant, Sadie Schildkraut's 1915 and 1920 census reports gave her profession merely as "housewife," unlike her husband Herman, who listed "restaurant" as his work.

8. Business card, n.d.

9. Business card, n.d.

10. Clement Wood, *The American Soul as Revealed by its Poetry* (New York: Frederick A. Stokes, 1929), 226.

11. Ad, *Brooklyn Daily Eagle*, Nov. 22, 1927, 32.

12. "Prof. J. C. Chatterji: The Greatest Hindu Scholar in America," *Brooklyn Daily Eagle*, Dec. 10, 1927, 10.

13. *Morgn Zhurnal*, June 23, 1922, 14.

14. "Mrs. Schildkraut, A Vegetarian Cook," June 5, 1937, 17.

15. "Fete in City Today to Be Third of War," *New York Times*, Nov. 23, 1944, 24.

16. Kenneth O. Smith, "The Vegetarian's Cue," *Philadelphia Inquirer*, Nov. 10, 1946, 10S.

17. Chaim Ehrenreich, "In a kleyninkn restoran oyf *pit strit*, hoybt zikh on di geshikhkte fun'm groysn *east sayder* restoran," *Forverts*, May 8, 1946, 2–3.

18. *Morgn Zhurnal*, May 22, 1927, 22.

19. *Forverts*, Oct. 22, 1928, 2.

20. Richard F. Shepard, "Abraham Harmatz of Ratner's Is Dead: Absorbed in East Village Reopening Hinted," *New York Times*, May 30, 1974, 40.

21. *New York Times*, June 19, 1977, W29.

22. Classified ad, *New York Times*, June 19, 1977.

23. Bob Foley, Fillmore stage crew, Sept. 6, 2022.

24. Corey Kilgannon, "Harold Harmatz, 91, Dies; Owned Ratner's Restaurant," *New York Times*, May 3, 2004, B8.

25. Lukas I. Alpert, "Famous N.Y. Kosher Eatery Fades with Time," *Ithaca Journal*, July 15, 2002, 11A.

26. "Picketing at Hammer's Enjoined," *New York Hotel Record*, Sept. 20, 1921, 3.

27. Florence Bergson Goldberg, "History of the B&H," *Jeremiah's Vanishing New York*, Dec. 5, 2011, https://vanishingnewyork.blogspot.com/search?q=B%26H.

28. Stanley Mieses, "Counterman," *New Yorker*, May 15, 1978, 28.

29. Mieses, 28.

30. Marcia Kramer, "An Eatery in the Soup, Inspectors Look Sharp," *Daily News*, Apr. 1, 1988, 7.

31. Arthur Schwartz, "Blintz Back Tears," *Daily News*, Jan. 1, 1991, 22.

32. Susan Heller Anderson and David W. Dunlap, "New York Day by Day," *New York Times*, Apr. 5, 1985, B3.

33. Jim Dwyer, "Unharmed by a Gas Explosion, but Choked by the Red Tape," *New York Times*, July 10, 2015, A21.

Chapter 9

1. Virginia Sheward, "Disappearing Cafeterias No One Wants to Carry His Own Load," *Newsday*, Dec. 14, 1972, 3A.

2. "Fire in a Broadway Cafeteria," *New York Times*, May 11, 1926, 16.

3. "Theft by the Women, Petty Pilferings By Those Who Should Know Better," *Chicago Daily Tribune*, Oct. 10, 1895, 12.

4. "In yam fun vitzn/in a kafeterye," *Forverts*, Nov. 3, 1946, 14.

5. "Speedy Bandits, Hold Up Cafes, Shoot Cashier," *New York Tribune*, Aug. 7, 1922, 5.

6. "1 Killed, 2 Wounded in Theater Holdup," *New York Times*, Feb. 24, 1931, 1.

7. "17 Communists Seized in Cafeteria Melee," *New York Times*, Oct. 28, 1930, 23.

8. Richard Massock, "About New York," *Herald Statesman*, July 8, 1929.

9. "Vus far a takhles di komunistn hobn gemakht fin tsvey arbayter kooperativn," *Forverts*, Dec. 24, 1929, 3.

10. Interview, Red Buttons *Yiddish Radio Project*, 2002.

11. Advertisement, *Tog*, Dec. 10, 1918, 7.

12. Advertisement, *Forverts*, Sept. 6, 1927, 6.

13. Radio ad, WEVD, ca. 1939.

14. Milton Danley, "Joseph Rumshinsky Defends Yiddish Musical Comedy," *Forverts*, Sept. 11, 1927, 14.

15. "Der yidl fun mizouri firt milkhome mit nu york," *Forverts*, Aug. 27, 1926, 5.

16. Joseph Opatoshu, "In a kafeterye," *Tog*, Feb. 25, 1933, 5.

17. Miriam Raskin, "In a kafeterye," *Forverts*, Feb. 1, 1938, 3.

18. I. B. Singer, "Di kafeterye," *Forverts*, Oct. 14–Nov. 3, 1977.

19. Murray Schumach, "Cafeterias Becoming Casualties of Age of Affluence," *New York Times*, Aug. 18, 1969, 37.

20. "Seek to Evict Café as Lair of Policy Mob," *Daily News*, December 7, 1942, B7.

21. "Armed Bandits Get $6,500."

22. "Bandits Seek Cash, Get a Bag Of Dough," *New York Tribune*, June 20, 1946, 10A.

23. "Babchik Clews Are Offered by His Chauffeur," *New York Tribune*, Sept. 27, 1941, 28.

24. "Amen Seeking Police Link to Slain Racketeer," *New York Tribune*, Sept. 26, 1941, 33.

25. "$15,000 Stolen as 400 Eat in Brooklyn Cafeteria," *New York Herald Tribune*, Jan. 8, 1952, 15.

26. Advertisement, *Women's Wear Daily*, Sept. 19, 1952, 7.

27. David Lawrence, "Curious Goings-On," *Times Recorder*, July 4, 1949, 4.

28. Robert Metz, "Loss Leaders Draw Cafeteria Customers," *New York Times*, Oct. 26, 1971, 59.

29. Jane Allison, "Dubrow's Cafeteria Is Sardi's of Seventh Avenue," *Indianapolis News*, May 17, 1972, 55.

30. Richard F. Shepard, "Singer Story Filmed Cafeteria-Style," *New York Times*, Aug. 20, 1983, 9.

31. Shawn Kennedy, "End of an Era, Dubrow's to Close," *New York Times*, July 14, 1985, R1.

32. "Beaten Up," *Daily News*, May 1, 1920, 10.

33. Advertisement, *Fraye Arbeter Shtimme*, July 29, 1932, 4.

34. Advertisement, *Forverts*, June 16, 1941.

35. Richard F. Shepard, "About New York: An Immigrant's Parish On the Lower East Side," *New York Times*, Dec. 30, 1978, 23.

36. "Where Socialists Kibitzed Yuppies May Follow," *New York Times*, Aug. 8, 2004, RE2.

37. "Two Food Landmarks of Very Different Ilk," *New York Times*, Mar. 10, 1972, 24.

38. "Cafeteria Holdup Nets $1,000," *New York Times*, March 30, 1965, 33.

39. Jack Roth, "C.P.A. Accused of $108,085 Swindle at Cafeteria," *New York Times*, April 3, 1963, 49.

40. Arthur Schwartz, "Restaurant Review," *Daily News*, Apr. 10, 1981, M3.

41. Irene Sax, "The Last Cafeteria," *Newsday*, June 12, 1985, part 2/15.

42. "Obituary, Charles Metzger," *New York Times*, Mar. 23, 1977, 51.

Chapter 10

1. "Silvershein Sells Jobbing Firm; Concentrates on Candy Making," *Confectionary Ice Cream World Weekly*, Aug. 1, 1947, 1/7.

2. "Silvershein Sells Jobbing Firm."

3. Correspondence with Shereen Silvershein-Willens, May 27, 2003.

4. Advertisement, *Tog*, Oct. 26, 1947, 17.

5. Broadcast, WEVD, June 28, 1947.

6. *Tog*, Oct. 26, 1947, 17.

7. Joselle Galis-Menendez, "Murray Silvershein Ran Own Ad Agency, Sold Real Estate," *Miami Herald*, Apr. 6, 2005.

8. "New Candytown Co. Expands," *Variety*, July 10, 1948, 98.

9. Correspondence with Lauren Rubbo, Nestlé PR, Nov. 21, 2023.

Chapter 11

1. "Veteran Banker of East Side Is Dead," *New York Sun*, June 3, 1912, 14.

2. New York City Directory 1875, 701.

3. "The State Bank Annoyed," *New York Times*, April 22, 1898, 12.

4. "A Pleasant Banking Operation," *Washington Post*, June 7, 1880, 4.

5. "A Pioneer East Side Banker," *Maccabean*, June 1912, 321.

6. "Real Estate Transfers," *New York Times*, Dec. 27, 1901, 12.

7. "Strike of Tailors May Be a Short One," *Brooklyn Daily Eagle*, July 23, 1901, 18.

8. "Appeal for Self-Defense," *American Hebrew & Jewish Messenger*, Dec. 8, 1905, 62.

9. *American Israelite*, Aug. 17, 1905, 6.

10. Advertisement, *Morgn Zhurnal*, Jan. 19, 1906, 4.

11. "Banking on the Densely Populated East Side Is a Serious Business, but Has Amusing Features," *New York Tribune Illustrated Supplement*, Mar. 15, 1903, 4.

12. "Of All Banks Most Gorgeous New Jarmulowsky Place One of the City's Sights," *New York Sun*, Mar. 4, 1903, 9.

13. "Banking on the Densely Populated."

14. "Banking on the Densely Populated."

15. "Shall Private Banking Houses Be Subject to Supervision?," *Wall Street Journal*, Jan. 17, 1914, 2.

16. "Unionizing Banks," *Montpelier Morning Journal*, Jan. 23, 1911, 7.

17. "'Be a Factor in the Business World," *New York Age*, Dec. 26, 1912.

18. Singer, Barry, *Black and Blue: The Life and Lyrics of Andy Razaf* (New York: Schirmer Books, 1992), 82.

19. "Banker Sues His Brother," *New York Times*, July 27, 1910, 16.

20. *Bridgemen's Magazine*, Feb. 1911, 112.

21. "More Lights on the East Side," *Edison Monthly*, Feb. 1913, 341–42.

22. "Notable Improvements on the East Side in Sanitary Loft Buildings," *New York Times*, Jan. 29, 1911, X10.

23. "Only $501,051 Left By Jarmulowsky," *New York Times* Aug. 14, 1913, 9.

24. "Half His Business to His Wife for Her Advice," *New York Sun*, Aug. 14, 1913, 1.

25. "Only $501,051 Left By Jarmulowsky."

26. "Banking News," *Wall Street Journal*, Jan. 17, 1914, 2.

27. "Private Banker in Bankruptcy," *Wall Street Journal*, Aug. 15, 1914, 8.

28. "5,000 Riot in Front of Closed Banks, Reserves Called to Disperse East Side Depositors Who Demand Their Money," *New York Times*, Aug. 30, 1914, 10.

29. "Jarmulowsky Besieged in Home by East Siders," *Evening World*, Sept. 22, 1914, 3.

30. "Tush, Says Sulzer Foiling Assassin," *New York Tribune*, Apr. 3, 1915, 6.

31. "Jarmulowsky's Bank Closed by State," *New York Tribune*, May 12, 1917, 16.

32. Advertisement, "The North American Bank," *Forverts*, Oct. 30, 1920, 2.

33. Marissa Meltzer, "Dimes Square Gets the Hotel it Deserves," *New York Times*, July 25, 2022.

34. "Not Edwin Jarmulowsky," *New York Times*, July 4, 1922, 24.

35. *Tulsa Daily Legal News*, Feb. 27, 1922, 4.

36. "Rites Today for Dr. Jarmulowsky," *The News*, Jan. 28, 1947, 51.

Chapter 12

1. Thomas Clapp Cornell, *Adam and Jane Mott: Their Ancestors and Descendants* (Poughkeepsie, NY: AV Haight, 1890), 377.
2. "Real Estate," *Evening Post*, Dec. 29, 1831, 4.
3. "In the Real Estate Field," *New York Times*, Dec. 31, 1903, 14.
4. "'The Forward' in Trouble," *New York Sun*, May 25, 1907, 11.
5. "Notice Bids Wanted for New 10-Story Building," *New York Times*, Jan. 25, 1911, 13.
6. Shirley Zavin, "Landmarks Preservation Report," New York Landmarks Preservation Commission, March 18, 1986, 11.
7. Zavin, 10.
8. "Workingmen and Employers," *New York Sun*, Dec. 28, 1885, 3.
9. "Tap East Side Spring, Water, Crystal Clear Now Free for the Thirsty Ones," *New York Tribune*, Aug. 12, 1911, 9.
10. "Spring of Ice Water in East Side Cellar," *New York Times*, Aug. 12, 1911, 3.
11. "Spring of Ice Water."
12. "Toyzinte menshn kumn trinken, kalte frishe vaser fun 'der forverts' fundament," *Forverts*, Aug. 13, 191, 1.
13. *Forverts*, Nov. 29, 1925, 17. At his death, playwright Herb Gardner (*A Thousand Clowns, I'm Not Rappaport*) was at work on a play part of which concerned an incident in the late 1930s when members the Communist *Freiheit*, following the Soviet Party Line of a nonaggression pact with Hitler, grew aggressive over the *Forverts* strident advocacy to aid the Allies, stole into their building and disabled the *Jewish Daily Forward* sign to read "Jewish Daily Forwar."
14. "Where Socialists Kibitzed Yuppies May Follow," *New York Times*, Aug. 8, 2004, RE2.
15. Christopher Gray, "A Capitalist Venture With a Socialist Base," *New York Times*, July 19, 1998, MB RE5.
16. Classified, *New York Times*, Aug. 6, 2006, RE18.

Chapter 13

1. *American Israelite*, Feb. 19, 1903, 5.
2. "Uncle Tom In Yiddish," *New York Sun*, May 26, 1901, 29.
3. "Floyd Johnson Now a Real Stage Performer," *Fresno Morning Republican*, Feb. 6, 1923, 13.
4. Exhibitor's Trade Review, Mar. 7, 1925, 55.
5. *Motion Picture News*, Apr. 19, 1926, 1068.
6. "Combine On," *Film Daily*, Aug. 13, 1926, 5.
7. "Loew's Commodore East Side," *Variety*, Aug. 10, 1927, 36.

8. "A Second Avenue Theater Project," *New York Times*, Apr. 16, 1925, 25.
9. *American Hebrew*, Dec. 3, 1926, 183.
10. "Yiddish Art Theater," *Brooklyn Times Union*, Nov. 14, 1926, 66.
11. "A Second Avenue Theater Project," *New York Times*, Apr. 16, 1925, 25.
12. Plans Yiddish Art Theater on Site of Peter Stuyvesant's Home," *Real Estate Record and Builder's Guide*, Sept. 26, 1925, 6.
13. "Sales on Second Avenue: Yiddish Art Theater Sold," *New York Times*, May 3, 1928, 54.
14. T. Edward Hambleton, Founder of Phoenix Theater, Is Dead at 94," *Playbill*, Dec. 19, 2005.
15. Barbaralee Diamondstein-Spielvogel, *The Landmarks of New York: An Illustrated Record of the City's Historic Buildings* (Albany: State University of New York Press, 2011), 571.
16. "$1,000,000 Yiddish Theater To Be Built Here By Pioneer," *Brooklyn Daily Eagle* May 10, 1928, 13.
17. *Billboard*, Aug. 16, 1924, 96.
18. "$1,000,000 Yiddish Theater."
19. "The Rolland Theater Presents 'Senorita,'" *Times Union*, Dec. 23, 1928, 28.
20. "Opening Soon," *Brooklyn Daily Eagle*, Sept. 10, 1933, 38.
21. *Times Union*, Sept. 24, 1926, 15.
22. "Discuss Youth Needs," *Brooklyn Daily*, Nov. 7, 1956, 2.
23. "People You Know," *Exhibitor*, Feb. 9, 1944, 4b.
24. "Thomashefsky to Loew's," *Variety*, Jan. 18, 1928, 24.
25. Bill Jaker, Frank Sulek, and Peter Kanze, *The Airwaves of New York: Illustrated Histories of 156 AM Stations in the Metropolitan Area 1921–1996*, 115.
26. Murry Frymer, "The Yiddish Theater Is . . . Don't Ask," *Newsday*, May 16, 1966, c3.
27. "A Berry Concert," *The Record*, Nov. 11, 1965, 27.
28. *Asbury Park Press*, Nov. 13, 1966, 24.
29. Dan DeLuca, "Tribute to Rock Impresario at Jewish Museum," *Philadelphia Daily News*, Sept. 16, 2016, 14.
30. Harvey Varga, Nov. 22, 2019.
31. John Chester, interview by Keith Mueller, Oct. 12, 2023.

Chapter 14

1. *Asmonean*, Oct. 26, 1849, 8.
2. *Hebrew Leader*, Feb. 18, 1881, 12.

3. "Der yiddisher *vekeyshan* vegvayzer," *Federeyshn* fin yiddishe *farmers* in amerike, New York, 1916.

4. "Oyf delensey *strit* veys men nit fun yikirus," *Yiddishes Togblatt*, Sept. 7, 1919, 9.

5. "Zol 'Libby's' veren a natzionaler yiddisher hotel iz di forderung fun amerikaner yudentum," *Forverts*, Mar. 11, 1922, 12.

6. "Tsulib dem vus a bridzhporter yid iz ayngeshlofn in a nu yorker resturan iz geboyrn gevoren der gedank fun libby's *hotel un bets*," *Forverts*, Aug. 7, 1925, 6.

7. Advertisement, *Forverts*, Mar. 29, 1925, 23.

8. "An erklerung tsu ale yidn vegn der groyser delensy *strit* unternemung," *Forverts*, Dec. 9, 1921, 2.

9. "Jessel Holds Share in East Side Hotel," *Jewish Theatrical News*, May 25, 1926, 6.

10. "Libby's Interests Buy East Side Corner for Baths," *New York Tribune*, July 18, 1921, 15.

11. "For Jews," *Time*, May 31, 1926, 26–27. The high quality of Bernstein's appointments is attested to by the exceedingly rare Libby's items that occasionally surface on eBay such as candy dishes and ash trays by the prestigious International Silver Company, and plates and cups by the high-end Chesterton China company, all emblazoned with a handsome Libby's coat of arms.

12. *Architecture and Building*, Aug. 1926, 154–59.

13. "Opening Week May 18 to 24," *New York Herald Tribune*, May 20, 1926, 21.

14. "Christians Greet Jews on New Year," *New York Times*, Sept. 14, 1928, 15.

15. Zeligson, M. "Fun der alter yidisher bod biz dem new york libby's *hotel un bets*," *Forverts*, Aug. 28, 1925, 6.

16. "$250,000' Swimmin' Hole' For Lower Second Avenue," *New York Tribune*, May 1,1921, A15.

17. *Architecture and Building*, Aug. 1926, 154–59. To appreciate the scale and sweep of Libby's baths is to compare it to the last of the once prolific R&T baths, the quirky (and quotidianly named) Russian and Turkish Baths at 268 East Tenth Street. This Yonah Schimmel's of bathhouses that is owned by two alternating and *very* different proprietors originally opened in 1892 on a lot with twenty-five-foot street frontage with two of its four 1,100 square feet floors (basement and first floor) dedicated to the bathhouse. Bernstein also dedicated two floors to his Russian and Turkish baths, but Libby's had 110-by-110 foot street frontage on Chrystie and Delancey totaling more than 12,000 square feet, so over ten times the size of the still active and much beloved East Tenth Street baths.

18. *Time*, May 31, 1926, 26.

19. "15,000 Visit Libby's New Hotel On East Side," *Jewish Exponent*, Apr. 30, 1926, 7.

20. Kelley Allen, "Amusements," *Women's Wear Daily*, May 21, 1926, 4.

21. "Libby's March," words and music by Solomon Smulewitz, A. Teres, New York, 1926, translation by Henry Sapoznik.

22. "Jessel Holds Share in East Side Hotel," *Jewish Theatrical News*, May 25, 1926, 6.

23. "For Jews," *Time*.

24. "Libby's March," words and music by Solomon Smulewitz, A. Teres, New York, 1926, translation by Henry Sapoznik.

25. *Forverts*, July 20, 1927, 2.

26. *Groyser Kundes*, 1922.

27. "City Brevities," *New York Times*, Apr. 28, 1926, 11.

28. *Fraye Arbeter Shtimme*, Oct. 31, 1908, 7.

29. *Forverts*, Oct. 25, 1925, 24.

30. *Forverts*, July 14, 1926, 6.

31. "Hold Radio Wedding," *Brooklyn Daily Eagle*, June 7, 1926, 30.

32. J. T. W. Martin, "Outside Listening In," *Brooklyn Daily Times*, July 22, 1926, 17.

33. WFBH, Bill Jaker, Frank Sulek, and Peter Kanze, *The Airwaves of New York: Illustrated Histories of 156 AM Stations in the Metropolitan Area 1921–1996* (Jefferson, NC: McFarland, 1998), 70.

34. "Show and Bathing," *Variety*, Nov. 16, 1927, 1.

35. "Music While You Bathe Is the Newest Thing," *Bristol Herald Courier*, Nov. 7, 1927, 12.

36. *Forverts*, Dec. 12, 1927, 6.

37. "Owner Ejected, Ousting Guests of Libby's Hotel," *New York Tribune/Herald Tribune*, Feb. 24, 1929, 11.

38. "New Hotel and Baths Increases Real Estate Values in Lower East Side," *Real Estate Record and Builder's Guide*, Aug. 1, 1925, 6.

39. *Architecture and Building*, Aug. 1926, 154–59.

40. "Ghetto's New Kosher Libby's Hotel and Baths," *Variety*, May 19, 1926, 55.

41. "Mrs Sarah Bernstein," *Jewish Exponent*, Oct. 29, 1926, 7.

42. "'Go in Debt,' Is Advice of Money Expert to Young," *Oklahoma City Times*, Feb. 1, 1921, 5.

43. "Mrs. Crater Denies Criticism of Crain," *New York Times*, Sept. 21, 1930, 2.

44. "Street Project in Housing Plan Now Criticized," *New York Herald Tribune*, May 11, 1928, 44.

45. Daniel Breck, *Puke Lawin': Law Makin' And Law Breakin' In Missouri Especially* (St. Louis, MO: Mound City Press, 1933), 22.

46. "Libby's Hotel Auctioned," *New York Times*, June 22, 1929, 34.

47. "Owner Ejected Ousting Guests of Libby's Hotel," *New York Herald Tribune*, Feb. 24, 1929, 11.

48. "Senior Leverich Apparent Suicide in Hotel Failure," *Brooklyn Daily Eagle*, Dec. 23, 1928, 1.

49. "Libby Hotel Award by City Fought," *New York Times*, Sept. 4, 1930, 28.

50. "La Guardia Declares He Foiled Libby's Deal," *New York Times*, Sept. 11, 1929, 10.

51. "Losers in Libby Hotel to Ask for Lease," *New York Times*, Sept. 15, 1929, 5.

52. "Libby's Hotel Auctioned," *New York Times*, June 22, 1929, 34.

53. "Sift 'Debt' to Crater in Libby Hotel Case," *New York Times*, Jan. 24, 1931, 16.

54. "Federal Men Study Mortgage Concern," *New York Times*, Apr. 18, 1931, 4.

55. Richard Lee, "Girls, Gay Revels, Aided $100,000,000 Racketeers," *Daily News*, Apr. 17, 1931, 3.

56. "Libby's Hotel Deal Called Scandalous," *New York Times*, Nov. 29, 1930, 3.

57. "The East Side Looks Into the Future," *New York Times*, Mar. 13, 1932, SM10.

58. "Sara D. Roosevelt Is the Park's Name," *Daily News*, Mar. 14, 1934, 8.

59. "Mrs. Crater's Report Ends Libby Hotel Receivership," *Daily News*, Mar. 29, 1933, 12.

60. Denny Lee, "Sky Isn't Falling, Earth Is Sinking and Residents Are Worried," *New York Times*, Sept. 2, 2001, 4CY.

Chapter 15

1. "New Corporations," *New York Times*, Mar. 21, 1900, 11.

2. Advertisement, *Forverts*, July 14, 1901, 5.

3. Advertisement, *Fraye Arbayter Shtimme*, Dec. 27, 1901, 11.

4. *Fraye Arbeter Shtimme*, Apr. 30, 1904, 6.

5. "Emma Goldman and Katz," *Fraye Arbeter Shtimme*, Apr. 9, 1904, 6.

6. Advertisement, *Teglikher Herald*, Oct. 24, 1901, 7.

7. "Discharges From Bankruptcy," *New York Times*, Oct. 10, 1904, 9.

8. "Corporations," *Brooklyn Citizen*, July 8, 1904, 7.

9. Federal census, 1900.

10. Advertisement, *Forverts*, Apr. 1, 1904, 6.

11. Advertisement, *Forverts*, Mar. 14, 1908, 7.

12. Richard Spottswood, *Ethnic Music on Records: A Discography of Ethnic Recordings Produced in the United States, 1893–1942* (Urbana: University of Illinois Press, 1990), 366–67. Despite it being in the name, to date no United Hebrew Disc and Cylinder Record Company cylinder has ever been found.

13. "Sheriff Takes Possession," *Music Trade Review*, Jan. 1905, 16.

14. US Extracted Death Index, 1931.

15. Advertisement, *Hebrew Standard*, Apr. 11, 1919, 2.

16. *Times Union*, May 15, 1933, 20.

17. Obituary, *New York Times*, Apr. 2, 1966, 23.

18. Advertisement, *Forverts*, Feb. 10, 1914, 2.
19. "Capitol Records Strides into 1st Foreign Distrib Deal Via Tele-Funken," *Variety*, Oct. 13, 1948, 39.
20. "Yiddish Waxery Formed," *Variety*, Dec. 28, 1946, 16.
21. "S. Selsman Announces New Record Firm in New York," *Billboard*, Jan. 11, 1947, 102.
22. "Michel Rosenberg, Actor, Dies at 71," *American Israelite*, Dec. 21, 1972, 15.
23. Henry Sapoznik, "Was Andy Griffith's First Big Hit Really an Old Yiddish Vaudeville Act?," *Forward*, Oct. 26, 2021.
24. "Gilbert & Sullivan Disked in Yiddish," *Variety*, Apr. 29, 1950, 15. An earlier 1940s Yiddish Mikado was staged at Camp Tamiment in the Poconos including Danny Kaye, Imogene Coca, and Jerome Robbins.
25. "Banner Readies Yiddish 'Pirates,'" *Variety*, May 10, 1952, 18.
26. Marsha Halper, "Love for Language Inspired Translator," *Miami Herald*, May 24, 1987, 20.
27. "Banner Goes LP, Quits 12-In Shellac," *Variety*, Jan. 28, 1950, 40.
28. "Banner Reactivates to Do Jewish Disks," *Variety*, Dec. 23, 1950, 43.
29. Joe Martin, "Fractured Yiddish: Peerless Parodist Puts Pops Into Folksy, Catchy Yiddish," *Variety*, Oct. 20, 1951, 1/14.
30. "Banner Records: Yiddish Disks Good Listening," *Variety*, Dec. 12, 1964, 8.
31. Advertisement, *Billboard*, July 26, 1947, 21.
32. "Gaieties Start at Orpheum Tomorrow," *Morning Call*, Oct. 20, 1934.
33. Billy Hodes, Essen Parts 1 & 2, Carnival Records C-5000A/B A-257.
34. Advertisement, "Essen, Jubilee Records," *Billboard*, Oct. 18, 1947, 22.
35. Advertisement, *Newsday*, Nov. 24, 1944, 29.
36. Advertisement, *Billboard*, Oct. 25, 1947, 33.
37. The Barton Brothers, "Joe and Paul Parts 1&2," Apollo Records 138 C-2087, 78 rpm.
38. "General Gershelman," WLTH, Oct. 21, 1939.
39. Red Buttons Interview, Los Angeles, CA, Nov. 22, 2000, Yair Reiner (DAT).
40. Interview, Eddie Barton, Miami Beach, FL, Apr. 23, 2000, David Isay, Yair Reiner, Henry Sapoznik (DAT).
41. Interview, Eddie Barton, Miami Beach, FL, Apr. 23, 2000, Henry Sapoznik, David Isay, Yair Reiner (DAT).
42. Interview, Eddie Barton.
43. Interview, Eddie Barton.
44. "225G Suit Over 'Joe and Paul,'" *Billboard*, Nov. 20, 1948, 19.
45. Interview, Eddie Barton, Miami Beach, FL, Apr. 23, 2000.
46. "Ich Bin a Boarder By Mein Weib" ("I Am My Wife's Boarder"), words and music by Rubin Doctor, Fyvush Finkel with Abe Schwartz's Orchestra, Apollo Records 143 C-2106, 1949, 78 rpm.
47. "In the Fiddler's House," PBS 1995.

48. Interview, Dave Tarras, May 25, 1975, Barbara Kirshenblatt-Gimblett, Janet Elias, tape.

49. "Herman Lubinsky Pioneer and Instructor Developed the Radio Shop of Newark," *Radio Dealer*, Jan. 1923, 37/56.

50. Commercial and Government Radio Stations of United States, Dept. of Commerce, 1923, 80.

51. *Forverts*, Sept. 17, 1929, 7.

52. Record Review, "Beacon Brass Band Featured," *Daily News*, Aug. 15, 1943, 64.

53. "Music Popularity Chart," *Billboard*, July 6, 1946, 35.

54. Henry Sapoznik, *Klezmer! Jewish Music from Old World to Our World* (New York: Schirmer Books, 1999).

Chapter 16

1. Although men were first, the earliest woman to record in Yiddish in America was Lizzie Goldfinger in 1904.

2. *New York Clipper*, Oct. 7, 1893, 507.

3. Display ad, *Boston Daily Globe*, April 13, 1890, 11.

4. "Austin and Stone's," *Boston Post*, Sept. 20, 1892, 3.

5. "The City Children Enjoying Themselves," *American Hebrew*, July 2, 1897, 27.

6. "A Child's Tragic Death," *Brooklyn Daily Eagle*, July 25, 1893, 1. Amazingly, another daughter, Mollie, escaped death by fire in 1904 when her mother refused to let her attend an outing held on the steamship General Slocum which caught fire and burned in the East River.

7. New York City directory, 1901, 989.

8. Richard Spottswood, *Ethnic Music on Records: A Discography of Ethnic Recordings Produced in the United States, 1893–1942*, vol. 3 (Urbana: University of Illinois Press, 1990), 1508–12.

9. "Organized Exhibitors Want to Eliminate Film Renters," *Variety*, Oct. 10, 1908, 13.

10. George Burns, *I Love Her, That's Why*, with Cynthia Hobart Lindsay (New York: Simon and Schuster, 1955), 42–43.

11. "Frank Seiden Buried," *Film Daily*, May 19, 1931, 2.

12. J. Hoberman, *Bridge of Light Yiddish Film Between Two Worlds* (New York: Museum of Modern Art, 1991), 225.

13. Peter Tonguette, "Lee Dichter: Meticulous Mixer, Maestro, Magician, Mensch," *CineMontage*, Dec. 19, 2018.

14. Zalmen Zilbercweig, ed., "Lexikon fun der yiddish teyater," *Yiddish Actor's Union* (Mexico), vol. 6, 1969, 5741.

15. Spottswood, *Ethnic Music on Records*, 1524–28.

16. Irene Heskes, "Yiddish American Popular Songs 1895–1950" (Washington, DC: Library Of Congress, 1992).

17. Zylbercewig, ed., "Lexikon fun der yiddish teyater," 5741.

18. Solomon Smulewitz, "Er Hot Gelakht," Meyer Levin's Music Store, New York, 1903.

19. Heskes, "Yiddish American Popular Songs 1895–1950," 494.

20. "Tsu Gefellen Mener," *Attractive Hebrews: The Lambert Cylinder Recordings*, Henry Sapoznik, co-producer/translations, Archeophone 8001, 2016, 52–53.

21. Solomon Smulewitz, *Der teyater zinger*, New York, 1905–9.

22. Solomon Smulewitz, *Khurbn titanik oder der naser keyver* (New York: Hebrew Publishing Company, 1912).

23. Smulewitz, "Lexikon fun der yiddish teyater," 5741.

24. Solomon Smulewitz, *Originale retinishn, in ritm un ryme* (Brooklyn, NY: Self-published), 1938.

25. While Joseph Green's film *was* named after Shmulewitz's song, and his music *was* used in the opening and throughout the film, the plot had nothing to do with his lyrics and the music credit went to Abe Ellstein (who arranged the score and wrote incidental music). Smulewitz received no screen credit and, no doubt, no royalties, which must have pained but not surprised him.

26. "A brivele der mamen," "Fun folk tsu folk," *Forverts*, Oct. 23, 1941, 6.

27. "Solomon Small, Jewish Actor, Poet, Composer Wrote for Muni Thomashefsky," *New York Times*, Jan. 3, 1943, 43.

28. Solomon Smulewitz, headstone, Beth David Cemetery, Elmont, NY, translation by Henry Sapoznik.

29. "New Acts Bands Reviews," *Billboard*, Nov. 14, 1936, 19.

30. *Hollywood*, Jan. 1942, 64.

31. "Amusement Machines," *Billboard*, Oct. 23, 1943, 67.

32. Advertisement, *Billboard*, Nov. 2, 1946, 31.

33. "Blessing the Bride," Bell Novelty Records 120-A, 1946.

34. "Ship Ahoy," (Bell) Rose Marie with Hal Hastings Orchestra, Mercury 4919/5811, 1952.

35. "Reviews of New Pop Records," *Billboard*, July 23, 1955, 78.

36. *Billboard*, Feb. 3, 1962, 45.

37. "Shaving Cream," Paul Wynn, *Cocktail Party Songs* (words and music: Benny Bell), 202-B, ca. 1946.

39. "Winston on 'Shaving Cream' Mystery Singer Out of Closet," *Billboard*, Apr. 19, 1975, 58.

39. *Billboard*, April 5, 1975, 18.

40. David Hinckley, "Mild If Unsubtle," *Daily News*, Nov. 2, 2005, 56.

Chapter 17

1. David Gilbert, "The Product of Our Souls: Ragtime, Race, and the Marketplace in James Reese Europe's New York" (PhD diss., University of Wisconsin, Madison, 2011).

2. Rudi Blesh and Harriet Janis, *They All Played Ragtime: The True Story of An American Music* (New York: Grove Press, 1950).

3. Vince Giordano, personal correspondence, Apr. 12, 2019.

4. "Song of Omar," words and music by Leo Edwards, OKeh 4092, Apr./May 1920.

5. This would not be the last time a redolent Yiddish solo was tucked away in the middle of a full-throated jazz side. On an unissued alternate take of Gene Krupa's 1941 "Jungle Madness," the drummer gives his first reed chair Sammy Musiker a full chorus doina improvisation set against the tune's relentless tom-tom-driven underbeat. The unissued side was released in 2002 as part of the anthology "From Avenue A to the Great White Way."

6. Zishe Vaynper, "Dzhez (Lid)," *Tzukunft* (New York), Mar. 1924, 163, trans. Henry H. Sapoznik

7. *Forverts*, Nov. 24, 1919, 4.

8. Regina Frishvasser, "Khasene mit yunge un alte mener," *Forverts*, June 13, 1920, 2.

9. *Forverts*, Feb. 1, 1922, 3. When the Jewish connection to jazz was represented to a non-Jewish audience, it took on a completely different cast, as on Hebe comic Julian Rose's 1923 record *That's Yiddisha Jazz*, where the "jazz" in question is the sound made by Jewish musicians as they eat.

10. *Morgn Freiheit*, Mar. 9, 1924, 2.

11. "To Propagate Jewish National Music," *Pittsburgh Post*, Oct. 5, 1919, 38.

12. Henry Sapoznik, Peter Sokolow, and Shulamis Dion, *The Klezmer Plus Folio* (Cedarhurst, NY: Tara Publications, 1997), 12.

13. Richard Spottswood, *Ethnic Music on Records: A Discography of Ethnic Recordings Produced in the United States, 1893–1942* (Urbana: University of Illinois Press, 1990), 1315.

14. Sapoznik, "Klezmer!" 112.

15. *Forverts*, Sept. 7, 1924, 10.

16. "Cherniavsky Arrives," *Motion Picture News*, Sept. 22, 1928, 936.

17. "U and 'Show Boat,'" *Variety*, Nov. 21, 1928, 15.

18. "Southern Voices Please in 'Talkies,'" *Universal Weekly*, April, 20, 1929, n620.

19. Ralph Wilk, "A Little From Lots," *Film Daily*, Sept. 22, 1929, 14. While Universal scored a successful "do over" when they remade *Show Boat* in 1936, the failure of the first version may have been partly responsible for diverting the studio away from musicals and into horror films for which they became rightly famous.

20. Saginaw, Michigan city directory, 1958.

21. Victoria Secunda, *Bei Mir Bist Du Schön: The Life of Sholom Secunda* (New York: Magic Circle Press, 1982), 132.

22. Michael Brooks and Henry Sapoznik, notes, "From Avenue A to the Great White Way," Sony Legacy, 2002.

23. "Bublitchki (Russian Traditional Air-Fox Trot)," Ziggy Elman, Bluebird B-10103, 78 rpm, Dec. 28, 1938. The song had already been covered (as "Who'll Buy My Bublitchki?") in May by Emery Deutsch and his Orchestra.

24. "And the Angels Sing (Fox Trot)," Benny Goodman, Victor 26170, 78 rpm, Feb. 1, 1939. Goodman's playing on the big band versions of these tunes are an inverse example of the early jazz records recorded by klezmorim: here it is Goodman, whose clarinet can't speak klezmer, who hands off the authentic Jewish showcase to Elman.

25. "Amusement Machine (Music Section)," *Variety*, June 17, 1939, 76.

26. "American-Jewish Swing," *Variety*, Oct. 15, 1941, 27.

27. "Album of the Week," *Santa Barbara News Press*, Mar. 9, 1963, 30.

28. "Modern Jazz," *Daily Herald*, July 4, 1963, 8.

29. Matt Darriau, personal correspondence, Sept. 28, 2023.

30. Terry Gibbs, *Good Vibes: A Life in Jazz*, with Cary Ginell, vol. 44 (Malden, MA: Scarecrow Press, 2003), 5.

31. Tom Surowicz, "At 77, Vibraphonist Terry Gibbs Is Still a Restless Dynamo," *Star Tribune*, Apr. 11, 2002, E6–8.

32. Terry Gibbs, phone conversation, Oct. 15, 2023.

33. "Leonard Feather," *California Eagle*, Nov. 5, 1964, 31.

34. Terry Gibbs, phone conversation, Oct. 8, 2023.

Chapter 18

1. Federal census, 1920.

2. Joel E. Rubin, *Klezmer in the Early Twentieth Century: The Music of Naftule Brandwein and Dave Tarras* (Rochester, NY: University of Rochester Press, 2020), 66. Nearby, Metro Music on Second Avenue, opposite the Loew's Commodore/Ratner's, sold records and sheet music to the nonprofessional trade.

3. Sammy Cahn, *I Should Care: The Sammy Cahn Story* (Westminster, MD: Arbor House, 1974), 52.

4. "Engineers to Stage Parade Saturday AM," *Plattsburgh Daily Press*, July 18, 1941, 3.

5. *Brooklyn Daily Eagle*, Feb. 8, 1946, 17.

6. Mark Cantor, *The Soundies: A History and Catalog of Jukebox Film Shorts of the 1940s* (Jefferson, NC: McFarland, 2023).

7. Henry Sapoznik, *Klezmer: Jewish Music from Old World to Our World* (New York: Schirmer, 1999), 165. Shimele Blank did not only hire family. Neigh-

borhood boy George Shore (father of future poet Jane Shore) who played reeds in the Clyde McCoy and Paul Whiteman orchestras worked at the store before and after returning home from World War Two.

8. Bill Buchen, *East Village Rundown, Global Village Lowdown* (Morrisville, NC, Lulu.com, 2023).

9. Jose, Night Club Reviews, *Variety*, Aug. 6, 1947, 40.

10. Buchen, "East Village Rundown."

11. "Klezmer . . ."

12. "Wedding Bands Lots of Fun, Says Violinist," *Daily News*, 1950, 5–14, 43.

13. Interview, Dave Tarras, Barbara Kirshenblatt-Gimblett, Janet Elias, tape, Sept. 11, 1975.

14. "Wedding Bands Lots of Fun," *Daily News*, May 14, 1950, 43.

15. Douglas Martin, "Paul Ash President of Music Store Chain Dies at 84," *New York Times*, Feb. 11, 2014, A20.

16. Michael Levenson, "Sam Ash Music Stores to Close After 100 Years in Business," *New York Times*, May 3, 2024.

Chapter 19

1. Judith S. Pinnolis, "'Cantor Soprano' Julie Rosewald: The Musical Career of a Jewish American 'New Woman,'" *American Jewish Archives Journal* 62, no. 2 (2010). Historian Pinnolis has observed women were already cantors in the American synagogue in the nineteenth century, such as in San Francisco's Reform Temple Emanuel, which featured opera singer Julia Eichberg Rosewald, and later, Josephine Jacoby at New York's Temple Emanuel. And while these women predate the so-called khazntes, the phenomenon was not related, as Rosewald's and Jacoby's roles were only possible within the more relaxed religious environment of the Reform movement. They also did not have the same social or religious intention, nor the same performance style, as the khazntes and so are outside of the khaznte narrative.

2. B. Gorin, *Morgn Zhurnal*, Jan. 27, 1918, 8. The khaznte was also present in other media. A popular serial in the *Lubliner Togblatt* newspaper on April 23, 1928, ran the startling header: "A Former *Khaznte* Converts and Sells Her Child to a Rich Turk."

3. Mark Slobin, *Chosen Voices: The Story of the American Cantorate* (Urbana: University of Illinois Press, 1989), 119.

4. "Special Holiday Show to Be Seen at Beth Am," *Wisconsin Jewish Chronicle*, Mar. 23, 1956, 5.

5. Charles W. Bell, "Seminary OKs Women Cantors," *Daily News*, Feb. 6, 1987, C8.

6. David Gahr and Robert Shelton, *The Face of Folk Music* (New York: Citadel Press, 1968), 364.

7. Jeremiah Lockwood, personal correspondence, Apr. 27, 2023.

8. "Bar mitsve yubeleyum fun der tsionistishn organizatsye hatechiye," *Yiddishes Togeblatt*, Feb. 20, 1916, 2.

9. "Mysteries of the Sabbath: Cantorial Recordings 1908–1947," produced by Henry Sapoznik, notes by Henry Sapoznik and Sam Weiss, Yazoo, 1994.

10. *Yiddishes Togeblatt*, Sept. 21, 1920, 8.

11. "Tsu di froyen in nu york un umgegend: Un tsu di mener," *Yiddishes Togeblatt*, Dec. 13, 1920, 6.

12. "Oyb ir hot nokh nit gehert . . . ," *Yiddishes Togeblatt*, Nov. 11, 1920, 20.

13. "Zeyer vikhtig far *relif sosayetis* khevres un faraynen," *Yiddishes Togeblatt*, Aug. 31, 1920, 7, 199.

14. "New Acts," *Variety*, Oct. 26, 1921, 9.

15. "Concert Fund, Manager Flit, Crowds Riot. Artists Unpaid, Refuse to Give Concert," *Chicago Tribune*, Apr. 25, 1921, 17.

16. Z. Rubinzohn, "Shayke fun brownsvil baym lyric teyater," *Yiddishes Togeblatt*, Feb. 3, 1922, 4.

17. Headstone inscription, Montefiore Cemetery, New York. Translation David Weider.

18. "Mysteries of the Sabbath: Cantorial Recordings 1908–1947," produced by Henry Sapoznik, notes by Henry Sapoznik and Sam Weiss, Yazoo, CD, 1994.

19. Kapelye, "On the Air," Shanachie Records, produced by Henry Sapoznik Yazoo 67005, CD, 1995.

20. "N. E. Debut of Woman Cantor in Dorchester," *Jewish Advocate*, May 14, 1943, 1.

21. "In the Revue-Theaters," *Forverts*, Sept. 26, 1947, 8.

22. "At the Ambassador," *New York Times*, Jan. 28, 1950, 10.

23. "Revue Will Open Locally Tomorrow," *Los Angeles Times*, June 13, 1950, A7.

24. Walter Winchell, "Gossip of the Nation," *Philadelphia Inquirer*, Mar. 22, 1951, 17.

25. "Television Chatter," *Variety*, Apr. 4, 1956, 34.

26. Slobin, *Chosen Voices*, 120.

27. *Tog*, Feb. 15, 1960, 6.

28. Andy Lanset and Henry Sapoznik, interview, Nov. 5, 1991.

29. Freidele Oysher, "I Watched Little Plants That Were Growing," in *Wind Blowing Across a Field Wisdom and Tales From 25 Musicians*, eds. Evo Bluestein and Juliana Harris (Private publication, 2022), 44.

30. Andy Lanset and Henry Sapoznik, interview, Nov. 5, 1991.

31. Lipa Feingold, *Der Neier Yid* (New York: Self-published, 1934).

32. Oysher, "I Watched Little Plants That Were Growing," 45.

33. "A speshiyele forshtelung in Hopkinson teyater." *Tog*, May 14, 1935, 9.

34. A. M. W., "Wedding Comedy Delights Audience at Bushnell Hall," *Hartford Courant*, Mar. 8, 1949, 19.

35. Andy Lanset and Henry Sapoznik, interview, Nov. 5, 1991.

36. Advertisement, *Forverts*, Apr. 4, 1948, 12.

37. Joseph Levine, "Yossele's Protégé: Samuel Malavsky (1894–1985)," *Journal of Synagogue Music (Cantor's Assembly of America)*, Fall 2011, 91–93.

38. David Prager, Correspondence, June 17, 2023.

39. Levine, "Yossele's Protégé."

40. Spottswood, *Ethnic Music on Records*.

41. US Census, 1940.

42. "New York Cantor in Sacred Concerts," *Minneapolis Journal*, May 24, 1935, 17.

43. Advertisement, *Morgn Zhurnal*, Mar. 10, 1944, 6.

44. Advertisement, *Morgn Zhurnal*, Oct. 2, 1946, 7.

45. "In Yiddish Theater," *Morgn Zhurnal*, Jan. 10, 1947, 13.

46. "Nitery Reviews," *Variety*, Feb. 4, 1948, 54.

47. "Recording Blues," *Variety*, Apr. 14, 1948, 53.

48. *Ross Report*, Mar. 22, 1953, 10.

49. *Asbury Park Press*, Apr. 3, 1995, 5.

50. Ron Keller, "Jean Gornish, Female Cantor," *Record*, May 1, 1981, C-16.

51. "Downtown Orphan Home's Concert," *Jewish Exponent*, Dec. 22, 1932, 12.

52. "Free Loan Group to Hear Cantor," *Atlanta Constitution*, Feb. 10, 1939, 7.

53. *Forverts*, Jan. 13, 1941, 2.

54. Advertisement, *Forverts*, Oct. 5, 1943, 7.

55. Keller, "Jean Gornish, Female Cantor."

56. "Personal and Social Notes," *Jewish Exponent*, Feb. 6, 1953, 23.

57. *Jewish Exponent*, Mar. 22, 1963, 84.

58. Advertisement flyer, Manhattan Beach Jewish Center, Jan. 7, 1942.

59. Bernice Zuckerberg Gordon, "The Chazzen's Daughter," Medium, 2022, https://bernicezuckerberggordon.medium.com/the-chazzens-daughter-f39d80683ae5?-source=friends_link&sk=1550aa225c07f5f7f5fc1b8b744c25d4.

60. Correspondence, Bernice Zuckerberg Gordon, December 12, 2024.

61. "Vikhtig far hotel *kippers* in di *montens*," *Forverts*, May 15, 1949, 7.

62. Correspondence, Bernice Zuckerberg Gordon Aug. 30, 2023.

Chapter 20

1. Jacob S. Dorman, *Chosen People: The Rise of American Black Israelite Religions* (New York: Oxford University Press, 2016), 26.

2. Zev Chafetz, "Obama's Rabbi," *New York Times*, Apr. 5, 2009, SM34.

3. "4,000 Black Jews Hail Advent of Year 5698," *Baltimore Afro-American*, Sept. 11, 1937, 8.

4. Howard Waitzkin, "Black Judaism in New York," *Harvard Journal of Negro Affairs* 1, no. 3 (1986).

5. Dorman, *Chosen People*, 26.

6. Arnold J. Ford, *The Universal Ethiopian Hymnal* (New York: Privately printed, 1921), 3.

7. Z. Rubinzohn, "Mendel, der shvartzer khazn," *Yiddishes Togeblatt*, June 28, 1922, 4.

8. Z. Rubinzohn, "Dovid, di kollscritta, ha'koen der falash," *Yiddishes Togeblatt*, Sept. 20, 1920, 4.

9. Rubinzohn, 4.

10. "Colored Cantor," *Variety*, Dec. 9, 1921, 3.

11. Alice Cogan, "5 Minutes a Case Speeds Court as Divorce Mill," *Brooklyn Times Union*, Nov. 13, 1934, 2.

12. "Fairley to Speak at School Opening," *Pittsburgh Press*, Sept. 9, 1944.

13. "Colored Cantor Lectures at Ohava Zedeck," *Burlington Daily News*, Dec. 5, 1930, 3.

14. "Noted Cantor," *Vancouver Sun*, June 2, 1932, 13.

15. "Sam Wilson, Colored Comedian," *Variety*, Feb. 13, 1920, 16.

16. Advertisement, *Amerikaner familyen magazin un gazetn*, Nov. 1, 1929, 2.

17. Lucien White, "In the Realm of Music," *New York Age*, Apr. 8, 1922.

18. Commonwealth of Virginia Delayed Certificate of Birth, Mar. 18, 1942.

19. Federal census, 1910.

20. *Forverts*, Mar. 23, 1918, 17.

21. "From Across the Sea," *Harrisburg Telegraph*, Sept. 15, 1921, 14.

22. *Boston Globe*, Jan. 30, 1921.

23. Poster, *Dos khupe kleyd*, 1921.

24. Z. Karnblit, "Hot ir gehert fun dem barimten khazn r'toyvele," *Forverts*, Nov. 4, 1921, 3.

25. "The Impromptu Minstrel," *Jewish Chronicle*, June 6, 1923.

26. Sholom Secunda (music) and Isidore Lash (lyrics), *Farlir nor nit dein hofenung, reb yid*, trans. Henry H. Sapoznik.

27. "A khazn a neger," *Grodno Moment* (Grodno), Sept. 19, 1930, 3.

28. *Ilustrowana Republika* (Lodz), Nov. 26, 1930, 3; "Toy'velle, der shvartzer khazn un unzer redaktsye," *Naye Leben* (Bialystok), Oct. 24, 1930, 2.

29. *Unzer Grodner Moment* (Grodno), Nov. 21, 1930, 16.

30. "Der 'shvartzer khazn' hot nekhtn gehat in varshe a shvartzer sof," *Unzer Express* (Warsaw), Oct. 10, 1930, 13.

31. "Der 'shvartzer khazn,'" 13.

32. "Der 'shvartzer khazn,'" 12.

33. "Der shvartzer khazn baym 'palatz,'" *Naye Lebn* (Bialystok), Oct. 29, 1930, 4.

34. *Unzer Express* (Grodno), Nov. 20, 1930.

35. *Jewish Advocate*, Jan. 13, 1931, 1.

36. Shimen Harendorf, "Teyater karavanen mayselakh un epizodn fun mayne vanderungen in yiddish teyater," *Fraynt Fun Yidishn Loshn* (London), 1955, 188–91.

37. Harendorf, "Teyater karavanen mayselakh," 189.

38. "Bar-Mitzvah Fete Of Orphans Set One Week Hence," *Jewish Chronicle*, Jan. 22, 1937.

39. Gerald Deltz, "Black Yiddish," *Jewish News*, Feb. 11, 1988, B24.

40. "East Orange Temple to Hold New Year's Eve Party; Dinner Dance Planned By Ladies," *Jewish Chronicle*, Dec. 22, 1933, 5.

41. Draft registration, 1942.

42. *Patent Gazette* (Washington, DC), Jan. 18, 1927.

43. Advertisement, *Newark Jewish News*, Nov. 27, 1953, 17e.

44. Renee Ghert-Zand, "Headstone for long-forgotten Black cantor unveiled in NJ cemetery," *The Times of Israel*, September 1, 2021.

45. "Goldye, the Colored Cantor," *Jewish Criterion*, Mar. 9, 1925, 12.

46. *Wisconsin Weekly Advocate*, May 10, 1906, 1.

47. *Chicago Defender*, Oct. 2, 1915, 12.

48. "Professionals: Gladys Sellers to Teach," *Wisconsin Weekly Blade*, Jan. 4, 1917, 14.

49. "Negro Orchestra Rarest of Treats," *Milwaukee Sentinel*, Apr. 28, 1919, 5.

50. "Ginger Band," *Chicago Defender*, Aug. 19, 1922, 7.

51. *Chicago Defender*, May 31, 1913, 4.

52. "Goldye, the Colored Cantor," *Jewish Criterion*, Mar. 9, 1925, 12.

53. "Woman Cantor Will Sing Her Own Compositions," *Daily News* June 21, 1924.

54. Andrew Esensten and Shoshana McKinney Kirya-Ziraba, in *The Jerusalem Post* (Feb. 28, 2024) article reports on Black violinist and singer Jenni Asher, who is studying for cantorial ordination though the nondenominational Academy of Jewish Religion, California, for the spring of 2025.

55. L. Krishtall, "*Vodvil*, russishe, amerikanish un yiddish," *Fraye Arbeter Shtimme*, Jan. 23, 1925, 3.

56. "Di shvartzer khaznte in mont morris teater," *Forverts*, Jan. 14, 1925, 7.

57. "Baltimore ervart mit umgedult dem 17 dzhune," *Forverts*, June 11, 1925, 2.

58. "Happenings in Local Theaters," *Pittsburgh Courier*, Mar. 7, 1925, A2.

59. "*Him* Is Tried and Found Guilty," *Daily News*, Apr. 19, 1928, 37.

60. "The Serious Drama," *Honolulu Star Bulletin*, Jan. 23, 1928, 40.

61. *The Daily Worker*, Jan. 5, 1929, 13.

62. "Family Theater Will Have African Singer," *Democrat and Chronicle*, Oct. 27, 1928, 23.

63. Paul Harrison, "The Day in New York," *Muncie Evening Press*, Apr. 20, 1933, 3. The article appeared in hundreds of newspapers around the country.

64. "Dial Settings," *Brooklyn Jewish Examiner*, June 12, 1935, 2.

65. "From Swing to Opera On Urban League Bill," *New York Amsterdam News*, Apr. 23, 1938, 6.

66. "Feld Stars in Routine Show," *Daily News*, Mar. 21, 1939, 37.

67. Advertisement, *Forverts*, Mar. 6, 1939, 12.

68. "In Yiddish Play in Bushnell Hall Monday," *Hartford Courant*, Apr. 20, 1939, 9.

Chapter 21

1. Alexander Harkavy, *Yiddish-English-Hebreyish Verterbukh* (New York: Hebrew Publishing Company, 1928), 255.

2. Nahum Stutchkoff, "Oytser fun der yiddisher sprakh," YIVO (New York), 1950, 183.

3. Shmuel Niger and Yakov Shatzky, eds., "Lexikon fun der nayer yiddisher literature un presse," *Alveltlekhn yiddishn kultur-kongres* 1, New York, 1956, 24.

4. "Yente, kovner, a valgerholtz un a maskn-ball," *Forverts*, Feb. 7, 1916, 3.

5. "Yente bay der arbet," *Forverts*, Nov. 23, 1917, 3.

6. Hillel Rogoff, "Kovner's 'Yente Telebende' in Thomashefsky's Natsional Teyater," *Forverts*, Nov. 21, 1917, 4.

7. Telebende vert a soldat (I. Lillian), Telebende Quartet, Victor 69479, New York, May 22, 1917.

8. Yente Telebende (J. Jacobs-L. Cohen) Anna Hoffman Victor 73341, New York, March 21, 1922. Despite Hoffman having recorded over 25 Yente Telebende records, she apparently never portrayed her onstage.

9. "Tsum akhtn yor gang 'tog,'" *Tog*, Nov. 6, 1921, 4.

10. Reuven Brinan, "Di yiddishe froy fardint nit ernidrigt un oysgelakht veren fun di yiddishe humoristn als a 'yente,'" *Tog*, May 5, 1924, 5.

11. A. Drashner, "teyater feuillitondlakh," *Tog*, May 2, 1924, 3.

12. "Shpatziren iber dem yidishn teyater," *Tog*, Apr. 21, 1922, 3.

13. William Gropper, "Di goldene medine," *Freiheit Farlag*, 1927.

14. "Farvus kumen menshen zeyn eynige mol 'yente telebende?,'" *Morgn Zhurnal*, Feb. 17, 1922, 16.

15. B. Kovner, "Pinye's khaver, dos niger'l," *Forverts*, Jan. 17, 1920, 10.

16. *Forverts*, Mar. 23, 1918, 17.

17. B. I. Goldshteyn, "An andersh-geshlayete 'Yente,'" *Tog*, Jan. 13, 1922, 3.

18. Ab Cahan, "Yente un Yente's tokhter in Lenox Teyater," *Forverts*, Jan. 20, 1922, 3.

19. "Washington, Lincoln un Moishe Rabeynu," words by Isidore Lillian, music by Joseph Rumshisky (New York: Hebrew Publishing, 1917).

20. Young Blacks engaged with Jewish culture is underscored in a January 25, 1928, *Forverts* article that tells of an Orthodox Newark synagogue helping young Black Jewish boys prepare for their bar mitzvahs and to become cantors.

21. "Yente af yener velt," *Forverts*, Dec. 28, 1922, 9.

22. B. Kovner, "Yente Telebende iz toyt," *Forverts*, Mar. 31, 1931, 4.

23. "Gin Rummy with Yenta Telebende" (Jacob Jacobs-Abe Ellstein), Jacob and Betty Jacobs, Banner A-270/B-2063A, New York, ca. 1953.

24. "Vet 'Yente Telebende' geshpilt vern af brodvey?," *Forverts*, Feb. 17, 1922, 2.

25. Advertisement, *Forverts*, 3, 1922, 7.

26. Leo Rosten, *The Joys of Yiddish* (New York: Simon and Shuster, 1968), 421.

27. *Webster's New Collegiate Dictionary*, 8th ed (Springfield, MA: G&C Merriam, 1973), 1372.

28. Sholom Beinfeld and Harry Bochner, *Comprehensive Yiddish-English Dictionary* (Paris: Bibliothéque Medem, 2013), 343.

29. Gitl Schaechter Viswanath and Paul Glasser, *Comprehensive English-Yiddish Dictionary* (Bloomington, IN: Indiana University Press), 2016.

Chapter 22

1. Advertisement, *New York Daily Herald*, Apr. 4, 1859, 7.
2. Correspondence, Eli Rosenblatt, Sept. 2, 2023.
3. B. Goren, "Di shvartze shklafn," *Arbayter Tsaytung*, Dec. 23, 1900, 6.
4. "Some New Plays," *Buffalo Sunday Morning News*, June 2, 1901, 13.
5. Advertisements, *Forverts*, Apr. 30, 1901, 3.
6. "Uncle Tom in Yiddish," *New York Sun*, May 26, 1901, 29.
7. Ann Charters, *Nobody: The Story Of Bert Williams* (New York: MacMillan, 1970), 35.
8. "Uncle Tom Played in German-Yiddish," *Indianapolis Star*, Mar. 25, 1906, 25.
9. L. L. "Uncle Tom's Cabin," *American Hebrew & Jewish Messenger*, May 24, 1901, 14.
10. *American Israelite*, June 6, 1901.
11. "Simon Le Greesky Arrested for Failing to Support His Wife," *Democrat and Chronicle*, May 9, 1901, 1.
12. *Topeka State Journal*, May 18, 1901, 11.
13. "Uncle Tom's Cabin in Yiddish," *Chicago Tribune*, June 21, 1901, 4.
14. "Some New Plays," *Buffalo Sunday Morning News*, June 2, 1901, 13.

15. Edvin A. Relkin, "Lexikon of Yiddish Theater (Yiddish Actor's Union in America)," New York, 1963, vol. 4/3192.

16. Ashton Stevens, "Glickman On the Yiddish Stage," *San Francisco Examiner*, July 16, 1905, 41.

17. "Jewish Actors Present 'Uncle Tom's Cabin' in Yiddish to a Ghetto Audience at Glickman's Theater," *Chicago Daily Tribune*, Feb. 28, 1903, 3.

18. "Uncle Tom Played in German-Yiddish," *Indianapolis Star*, Mar. 25, 1906, 25.

19. "Mr. Thomashefsky As Uncle Tom," *Jewish Exponent*, Mar. 31, 1911, 13.

Chapter 23

1. *Arbeter Tsaytung*, Mar. 20, 1898, 3.

2. *Arbeter Tsaytung*, Mar. 27, 1898, 4.

3. J. Hoberman, "Bridge of Light," *Museum Of Modern Art*, 1991, 258.

4. Samson Raphaelson, Federal Census, 1930.

5. "Boy Who Tended Furnaces Now Successful Writer," *Boston Daily Globe*, Sept. 5, 1926, C10.

6. "Raphaelson Writes for the Chicago Herald Magazine," *Daily Illini*, Feb. 7, 1917, 4.

7. S. M. Raphaelson, "Co-Authors," *Oregon Daily Journal*, Feb. 4, 1917, 50.

8. Samson Raphaelson, "The Day of Atonement," *Everybody's*, Jan. 1922, 44–55. Subsequent quotes are from this source.

9. Raphaelson, 44.

10. Samson Raphaelson, "The Jazz Singer," *Brentano's*, 1925, 7. All subsequent quotes from the play come from this edition.

11. George Jessel, *So Help Me: The Autobiography of George Jessel* (Cleveland: World Publishing, 1944).

12. "Crowd of Kids at Orpheum," *Los Angeles Times*, Aug. 26, 1913, II7.

13. Brett Page, "Passing Show of 1923: Hits Speedy Stride on Broadway," *Great Falls Tribune*, July 1, 1923, 33.

14. Wood Soanes, "Curtain Calls," *Oakland Tribune*, June 26, 1925, 30.

15. Nathaniel Zalowitz, "Is Intermarriage a Growing Menace Among Jews?," *Forverts*, Nov. 15, 1925, 3.

16. "The Jazz Singer Has Heart Interest," *New York Times*, Sept. 15, 1925, 29.

17. Don Carle Gillette, *Billboard*, Sept. 26, 1925, 41/59.

18. "George Jessel Feature in 'The Jazz Singer,'" *New York Herald Tribune*, Sept. 15, 1925, 18.

19. "Religion vs. Theater," *Brooklyn Times Union*, Sept. 13, 1925, 18.

20. "A Sure-Fire Hit," *Variety*, July 22, 1925, 21.
21. Ab Cahan, "Tsvey forshtelungen oyf brodvey," *Forverts*, Jan. 29, 1926, 3.
22. *Forverts*, Oct. 9, 1925, 5.
23. Z. Zylbercweig, ed., Lexikon fun yiddishn teyater, *Yiddisher aktyorn yunyon in amerike* 4, 1963, 3192–3198.
24. Y. Glatshteyn, "Der dzhez zinger," *Morgn Zhurnal*, Mar. 2, 1926, 3.
25. "Kahn's Idea," *Daily News*, Jan. 1, 1926, 26.
26. "'Jazz Singer' Work of Youth Carried Away by Personality of Jolson," *San Francisco Examiner*, Mar. 4, 1928, 53.
27. *American Jewish World*, Mar. 26, 1926, 24.
28. "The Story of Al Jolson," *New York Times*, Feb. 24, 1918, 54.
29. "Jolson Buys Home for Old Parents," *New York Times*, Dec. 19, 1926, 26.
30. "The Story of Al Jolson."
31. Mordaunt Hall, "The Screen," *New York Times*, Oct. 8, 1926, 23.
32. Samuel Rosenblatt, *Yossele Rosenblatt: The Story of His Life as Told by His Son* (New York: Farrar, Straus and Young, 1954), 287–293.
33. Samson Raphaelson, "The Day of Atonement," *Everybody's*, Jan. 1922, 55.
34. Rosenblatt, *Yossele Rosenblatt*, 63.
35. "Shikago opera co. vil r' yossele rosenblatt," *Morgn Zhurnal*, Mar. 22, 1918, 9.
36. *Forverts*, Oct. 28, 1927, 7.
37. "Yossele rosenblatt vert a *muving piksher ektor*?," *Forverts*, May 11, 1927, 3.
38. "Dinner Opens Appeal Drive," *Los Angeles Times*, June 14, 1927, 22.
39. *Gypsy: A Memoir, Gypsy Rose Lee* (New York: Harper, 1957), 80–86.
40. Rosenblatt, *Yossele Rosenblatt*, 290.
41. Roy Liebman, *Vitaphone Films: A Catalog of the Features and Shorts* (Jefferson, NC: McFarland, 2003), 177.
42. Rosenblatt would have several appearances in feature length films: *The Voice of Israel* (1931) directed by Joseph Seiden and the travelogue *Khulem fun mayn folk* (*Dream of My People*) filmed in Palestine and released the year after his death in 1933.
43. Warner Brothers Buy 'Jazz Singer,' *Daily News*, June 3, 1926, 27.
44. *Pittsburgh Press*, Apr. 3, 1927, 105.
45. Part of the received narrative about the film is its ending. Is it literal that Jack Robin sang both Kol Nidre and the Broadway opening? (As noted, he could have.) Or is it ambiguous and there are two endings/two fantasies: the mother's, seeing him sing in the synagogue, and his, singing on Broadway with his enthusiastic *kvelling* mother in the front row? Jewish law, however, would have compelled his mother to have begun the seven day shiva [mourning] period, which, for the following year, precludes the listening of music for pleasure.

46. "Der dzhez zinger," *Morgn Zhurnal*, Nov. 13, 1927, 9.
47. "Lady Luck Played Big Part Here," *Washington Post*, Oct. 16, 1927, F3.
48. "I'm Not Ashamed," Creativity with Bill Moyers, PBS, Jan. 2, 1982.

Bibliography

Berger, Shulamith, and Jai Zion. *A Ritz with a Shvitz*. Albany: State University of New York Press, 2025.

Bluestein, Evo Juliana Harris. "I Watched Little Plants That Were Growing." In *Wind Blowing Across a Field Wisdom and Tales From 25 Musicians*, edited by Freidele Oysher. Private publication, 2022.

Breck, Daniel. *Puke Lawin': Law Makin' And Law Breakin' In Missouri Especially*. St. Louis, MO: Mound City Press, 1933.

Buchen, Bill. "East Village Rundown, Global Village Lowdown." Lulu.com, 2023.

Burns, George, with Cynthia Hobart Lindsay. *I Love Her, That's Why*. New York: Simon and Shuster, 1955.

Cahn, Sammy. *I Should Care: The Sammy Cahn Story*. Westminster, MD: Arbor House, 1974.

Caesar, Sid, and Bill Davidson. *Where Have I Been? An Autobiography*. New York: Crown Publishers, 1982.

Cantor, Mark. *The Soundies: A History and Catalog of Jukebox Film Shorts of the 1940s*. Jefferson, NC: McFarland, 2023.

Charters, Ann. *Nobody: The Story Of Bert Williams*. New York: MacMillan, 1970.

Cornell, Thomas Clapp. *Adam and Jane Mott: Their Ancestors and Descendants*. Poughkeepsie, NY: AV Haight, 1890.

Diamondstein-Spielvogel, Barbaralee. *The Landmarks of New York, An Illustrated Record Of the City's Historic Buildings*. Albany: State University of New York Press, 2011.

Eyman, Scott. *Ernst Lubitsch: Laughter in Paradise*. Baltimore: Johns Hopkins University Press, 2000.

Federman, Mark Russ. *Russ & Daughters Reflections and Recipes from the House That Herring Built*. New York: Schocken Books, 2013.

Ford, Arnold J. *The Universal Ethiopian Hymnal*. New York: Privately printed, 1922.

Gahr, David, and Robert Shelton. *The Face of Folk Music*. New York: Citadel Press, 1968.

Gibbs, Terry. *Good Vibes: A Life in Jazz*, with Cary Ginell. Malden, MA: Scarecrow Press, 2003.

Gold, Michael. *Jews Without Money.* New York: Horace Liveright, 1930.
Graham, Stephen. *New York Nights.* New York: George H. Doran, 1927.
Hapsgood, Hutchins. *Spirit of the Ghetto.* New York: Funk and Wagnalls, 1902.
Harendorf, S. J. *Teyater karavanen mayselakh un epizodn fun mayne vanderungen in yiddish teyater.* London: Fraynt Fun Yidishn Loshn, 1955.
Harkavy, Alexander. *Yiddish-English Dictionary.* New York: Hebrew Publishing Company, 1898.
Heskes, Irene. *Yiddish American Popular Songs 1895–1950.* Washington DC, Library of Congress, 1992.
Hoberman, J. *Bridge of Light Yiddish Film Between Two Worlds.* New York: Museum of Modern Art, 1991.
Jaker, Bill Frank Sulek, and Peter Kanze. *The Airwaves of New York: Illustrated Histories of 156 AM Stations in the Metropolitan Area 1921–1996.* Jefferson, NC: McFarland, 1998.
Jessel, George. *So Help Me: The Autobiography of George Jessel.* Cleveland: World Publishing Company, 1944.
Katz, Mickey. *Papa Play for Me.* With Hannibal Coons. New York: Simon and Shuster, 1977.
Levy, Mrs. Esther. *Jewish Cookery Book.* Philadelphia: King and Baird, 1871.
Liebman, Roy. *Vitaphone Films: A Catalog of the Features and Shorts.* Jefferson, NC: McFarland, 2003.
Roeder, George H. *The Censored War: American Visual Experience During World War Two.* New Haven, CT: Yale University Press, 1993.
Rosenblatt, Samuel. *Yossele Rosenblatt: The Story of His Life as Told by His Son.* New York: Farrar, Straus and Young, 1954.
Rubin, Joel E. *Klezmer in the Early Twentieth Century: The Music of Naftule Brandwein and Dave Tarras.* Rochester, NY: University of Rochester Press, 2020.
Rubenstein, Joshua. *Leon Trotsky: A Revolutionary's Life.* New Haven, CT: Yale University Press, 2012.
Sapoznik, Henry. *Klezmer! Jewish Music from Old World to Our World.* New York: Schirmer, 1999.
Sapoznik, Henry, Peter Sokolow, and Shulamis Dion. *The Klezmer Plus Folio.* Cedarhurst, NY: Tara Publications, 1997.
Schaechter-Viswanath, Gitl, and Paul Glasser. *Comprehensive English-Yiddish Dictionary.* Bloomington: Indiana University Press, 2016.
Schultz, Carl Mineral Spring Waters Their Chemical Composition, Physiological Action and Therapeutic Uses. New York: Baker and Godwin, 1865.
Secunda, Victoria. *Bei Mir Bist Du Schön The Life Of Sholom Secunda.* New York: Magic Circle Press, 1982.
Slobin, Mark. *Chosen Voices: The Story of the American Cantorate.* Urbana: University of Illinois Press, 1989.
Smulewitz, Solomon. *Originale retinishn in ritm un raym.* Brooklyn, NY: Self-published, 1938.

Spottswood, Richard. *Ethnic Music on Records: A Discography of Ethnic Recordings Produced in the United States, 1893–1942*. Vol. 3. Urbana: University of Illinois Press, 1990.

Watermeir, Daniel J. *Between Actor and Critic: Selected Letters of Edwin Booth and William Winter*. Princeton, NJ: Princeton University Press, 2015.

Zylbercweig, Zalmen, ed. *The Lexikon of the Yiddish Theater*. Vol. 1, *Hebrew Actor's Union* (New York) 1931; Vol. 2, *Hebrew Actor's Union* (Warsaw) 1934; Vol. 3, *Hebrew Actor's Union* (New York) 1959; Vol. 4, *Hebrew Actor's Union* (New York) 1963; Vol. 5, *Elisheva Press* (Mexico City) 1967; Vol. 6, Elisheva Press (Mexico City) 1969.

Index

Illustrations are indicated by page numbers in italics.

Abdelwahad, Fawzy, 96
Abramson, Herb, 171
Abyssinian descent of Black Jews, 232, 236, 243–44, 246, 249, 251
Adler, Celia, 307
Adler, Jacob P., 129, 260, 277, 281, 307
Adler, Jacob "Yankev." *See* Kovner, B.
Ahavath Zion (Newark Orthodox congregation), 237, 247
Aleichem, Sholem, 21, 131, 271
Allen, Woody, 94
American Beverage Corporation (ABC), 69–70, 73–74
American Bond and Mortgage (AB&M), 141, 152, 153–54
American Federation of Musicians (AFM), 164, 177, 211
American Folklife Center of the Library of Congress, 80, 111
The American Hebrew and Jewish Messenger, 85, 180, 276, 278
The American Israelite, 18, 240, 276
The American Jewish World, 292
Amsterdam, Morey, 209–10
Anderson, Max W., 25
Andrews Sisters, 201–2

Anistratov, Ellen, 37
Anzelowitz, Hyman and Max, 64
Anzelowitz, Louis ("Yehuda Leyb"), 58–64, 89, 316n42
Apollo Records, 171–73, 175–76. *See also* records; records and record companies/labels
appetizing stores, 77–84
Arbeter Ring (Workman's Circle), 128
Arbeter Tsaytung (*The Worker's Newspaper*), 274, 280
architecture, 8, 113–55; *Forverts* Building, 125–28, *127*; House of Jarmulowsky, 2, 115–23, *118*, *120*; Libby's Hotel and Baths, 139–56, *142*, *147*; New York Yiddish theaters, 129–38, *131–32*, *134*
Armstead, Richard, 255
Arnaz, Lucie, 307
Arnshteyn, Mark, 280
Arsenal building, 15
Arthur, Bea, 271
Art Shryer's Modern Jewish Orchestra, 198
Asch, Moe, 226
Asch, Sholem, 136, 289

349

Asch label, 226
Ash, Jerry and Paul, 213
Ash, Rose, 211
Ash, Sam (Shmuel Ashkynasye), viii, 207, 211–13, *212*
Ashkenazi Jews, 31, 40, 85, 179, 216, 232, 280, 311n36
Ashokan reservoir, 70
The Asmonean (Jewish newspaper), 139
Astor (kosher hotel), 227
Atlas, Charles, 144

B. Manischewitz Company, 177
Babchik, Abe ("Jew Murphy"), 104
bacon, kosher, 19, 30–31, 87
Bagelman, Claire and Merna (aka "Pert" and "Gaye"), 203
B&H Dairy (kosher restaurant), 1, 94–97
banjo, 160, 173, 195–96, 199, 273–74, 288
Bank of M&L Jarmulowsky, 117, 119, 121–22
Banks, Sadie, 60, 66
Banner Records, 166–70, 224, 269, 302
Barney Greengrass, 81–83
Barondess, Joseph, 117
Barry Sisters (aka Bagelman) Claire and Myrna/Pert and Gaye, 177, 203, 226
Bart, Jan, 177, 203, 220
Barton Brothers, 175, 222
Barugel, Marla Rosenfeld, 216
Bas Sheva (aka Bernice Kanefsky), 166, 217, 220–22, 226; Mickey Katz and, 220, 222; as lounge singer Beth Hunter, 220
baths and health spas: Max "Mac" Levy and physical culture movement, 144–46; Libby's, 139, 148; spa cures, 69–70, 87

Baxter, Les, 221
Beck, Vincent, 166
Beckerman, Shloimke ("Sam"), 195, 198
beef fry, 19. *See also* fry beef
Beinfeld-Bochner: *The Comprehensive Yiddish-English Dictionary*, 272
Belasco, David, 141, 252
Bellison, Simeon, 198
Belmore cafeteria, 101
Benny, Jack, 308
Benny Goodman Orchestra, 178, 193, 202, 254, 306
Bercovici, Konrad, 54
Berekson, Benem, 94
Berger, Isaac, 78
Berger, Joseph, and son Arthur Morris, 37
Berger, Lillian, 37
Bergson, Abraham, 94–95
Berlin, Irving, 287, 294
Berman, Bess, 173
Bern, Mina, 137
Bernstein, Bernard and Leonard, 155
Bernstein, Leah (aka Libby), 140, 148
Bernstein, Max, viii, 2, 101, 139–41, 146, 148–49, 187
Bernstein, Murray and Sam, 83–84
Bernstein, Schmulka (aka Dmocher), ix, 30–32
Bernstein-On-Essex Street, 30–32
Bertholoff, William Henry Joseph Bonaparte (Willie "The Lion" Smith), 234–35, *234*
Beth Shalom B'nai Zaken Ethiopian Hebrew Congregation (Chicago), 232
Beys Hamedresh Ha'Godol (Lower East Side Orthodox synagogue), 9, 281
Black cantors (*shvartze khazonim*), 2, 231–55, 340n20; African American synagogues, 231–35,

350 | Index

234; Franklin as, 236; Goldye, Di Shvartze Khaznte (aka Gladys Mae Sellers, Steiner), 2, 248–55, *248*, *253*; Milton Grossman as, 236; Dovid Kollscritta as (aka "Dovid, di Kollscritta Ha'Cohen der Falash"), 235–36, 250; LaRue Jones as, viii, 2, 150, 177, 231, 237–47, *238*, *243*, *263*, 265, 267–68; *Lulu Belle* on Broadway (play), 252; "Mendel, der shvartzer khazn" as 232, *233*; R'Toyvele Ha'Cohen as, 237, 239, 243–45; Willie "The Lion" Smith as, 233–34, *233*
blackface performances, 252, 255, 268, 273–75, 294, 304, *304*, 307
Blanc, Manny Menashe, 204, 206, 209
Blank, Morris ("Murray," "Blimpy"), 209–11, 213
Blank, Shimele (aka Yankl, Shimen "Shimele" Blankleder), viii, 204, 207–11, *208*, 213
Blank's Bargain Music Store, 209–10
blintzes, 85–86, 96, 105
Bloom, Rube (ragtime pianist), 194
blue laws (Sunday laws), 18, 27, 182–83
B'nai B'rith, 8, 117
Bock, Jerry, 271
Boehm, George (*Forverts* building architect), 126
Bonus, Ben (actor), 136–37
Boop, Betty, 307
Boris Thomashefsky's Roumanian Village, 60
Borscht Belt, 32, 44, 66, 88, 170–71, 223
Brady, William A., 274–75, 277
Brandwein, Naftule, 198
Branin, Joseph (*Forverts* cartoonist), 261

Breakers (Atlantic City kosher hotel), 227
Breindele (Bernice Zuckerberg Gordon), 215, 228–30, *229*
Brice, Fanny, 147
Bringing Up Father (comic strip), 260
Broadway Central Hotel. *See* hotels
Broadway shows. *See* plays and shows
Broder Zinger, 181, 240
Brody, Joseph, 274
the Bronx, 14–15, 25, 73, 116, 137, 149, 174, 177, 195, 247, 253, 255, 288
Brooklyn, iv, ix, 10, 23, 26, 32, 38, 40–48, 72–74, 78, 94, 100, 102, 104–5, 128, 133, 135–36, 144–46, 153–55, 167, 169, 174–75, 188–91, 204–5, 209, 211–13, 217, 220, 222, 224, 228, 230, 236, 254, 291, 300, 307
Brooklyn Daily Eagle, 46, 88
Brooklyn Jewish Center, 230
The Brooklyn Jewish Examiner, 254
Browning, John Moses, 163
Bruce, Lenny, 36
Burger, "Papa" Joseph, 45
Burns, George, 81, 182, 288
Buttons, Red (aka Aaron Chwat), 101, 174

Cafeteria Employees Union of AFL, 100
cafeterias, 90, 99–108; as motif in Yiddish arts, 102–3. *See also specific names of cafeterias*
Cahan, Abe: *Forverts* editor, 125–27, 260–61, 264–67, 291; on Thomas LaRue Jones, 267–68; *The Rise of David Levinsky* (novel) by, 291; Yente Telebende and, 260–61, 264–66, *266*. See also *Forverts*
Cahn, Sammy, 84, 201, 207–8

Canada Dry Bottling Company, 74
Cantor, Eddie, 19, 81, 147, 292
cantors. *See* Black cantors; women cantors of the stage
Cantor's Assembly, 222
Capitol Records, 165–66, 173, 220–21, 226
Carney, Art, 210
Carter Family, 224
Casman, Nellie, 133, 201, 224; "Yosl, Yosl" (with Steinberg), 201
Catskills, 44, 103; hotels, 44, 139, 170–71, 175, 220, 230
celery tonic, vii, 69–76, *71*
Chaplin, Charlie, 199
Chaplin, Saul, 201
"The Chazzen's Daughter" (Gordon), 228
Cherniavsky, Joseph, 148, 150, 198–201, *199*; Hasidic American Jazz Band, 148, 198, *199*, 200–1
Cherniavsky, Lara, 198
Chichinsky, Esther (sister of Bill Graham), 137
Chinese kosher cuisine, 31–32
Chunky Milk Chocolate, vii, x, 109–11, *109*
Claiborne, Craig, 29, 84
Clef Club (Harlem), 193, 232, 234
Club Society Orchestra (Sam Ash), 212–13
Cohen, Jacob (Harlem hotelier), 139
Cohen, Julie (filmmaker), 80
Cohn, Alfred A., 302–3
Collector's Guild label, 169–70
Columbia Records, 160, 163, 165–66, 226, 240, 242, 262–63, 300
Commandment Keepers Ethiopian Hebrew Congregation, 232
Commodore: Loew's, 63, 90, 131, *131*, 136–37, 333n2; M&S, 130–31

Communist Cooperative Movement, 101
Communist Food Workers Industrial Union, 100
Como, Perry, 286
ConAgra, 24
Concord Hotel (Catskills), 230
Coney Island, 22, 38, 46, 75; knish, 38–39, *39*, 40–44; kosher food, 22; Steeplechase Park, 46
Congregation Ahavat Shalom (Lakewood, NJ), 227
Congregation Beth B'nai Abraham, 232
Congregation Beth Shalom B'nai Zaken Ethiopian Hebrew Congregation, 232
Cook, Will Marion, (composer) 193, 249
Co-Operative Sausage Co., 20
Costello, Lou, 171
Crater, Joseph Force, (shyster) 153–55
Cronyn, Hume, 133
Crosland, Alan: *Don Juan* (film director), 303; *The Jazz Singer* (film director), 303
Cugat, Xavier, 202
cummings, e.e., 252–53
Curtis, Tony, 36
cymbalom (Joseph Moskowitz's instrument), 50–53, 55–56, 62, 251

dairy and vegetarian restaurants, vii, 1, 7, 31, 49, 65, 79, 85–97; B&H Dairy, 1, 94–97; Famous, 107; Garfein's, 31; Hammer's Dairy Restaurant, 93–94, *93*; Lansky's Lounge, 92; Ratners, 79, 89–92, *91*, 106; Schildkraut's Vegetarian Restaurants, 86–89, *86*; Triangle (the Bronx), 14

352 | Index

"The Day of Atonement" (story), 280–84
Decca Records, 201
Delancey Rendez-Vous (Romanian restaurant), 57
Delicatessen Counterman Union Local 302 of the American Federation of Labor, 27, 29
delicatessens, viii, ix, 1, 17–34, *17*, 38, 44, 46, 72, 77–78, 82, 93, 103; Hebrew National, 19–24, *21*; Katz's delicatessen, 1, 27–30, *27*, 93; ix, Schmulka Bernstein/ Bernstein-On-Essex Street, 30–32; Second Avenue Delicatessen, 32–34; unions in kosher food industry and, 26–27; Zion National, 25
Diamond, Neil, 279, 307–8
Dichter, Murray and son Lee, 184
Dickstein, Sol, 137
dictionaries: Beinfeld-Bochner, 272; Harkavy, 259, 272; Merriam Webster, 272; Modern Yiddish-English, 1, 272
Die Freie Gesellschaft (The Free Society, magazine), 117
Dik, Isaac Myer, 274
Di kafeterye (Isaac Bashevis Singer), 103, 105
Di Shvartze Khaznte. *See* Sellers, Gladys Mae
Di shvartze shklafn (*The Black Slaves*, serial translated into Yiddish), 274
Diskay, Joseph, 301
Di Yiddishe Fon (The Jewish Flag, newspaper), 117
Doraine, Pete, 166
Dorsey, Tommy, 194, 206–9
Dr. Brown's Celery Tonic, vii, ix, 69–74, *71*
Dr. Brown's Cel-Ray, ix, *71*, 73–74

Dress and Cloak Maker's Union, 117
Dubrow, George F., 103
Dubrow, Irwin, 105
Dubrow's Cafeteria, 100, 103–5, 107
Dubson restaurant, 105
Dymow, Ossip, 102

Earl Fuller's Jazz Band, 194
Edison, Thomas, 161, 163; *Edison Monthly* (magazine), 120; records, 160, 163, 184
Edwards, Gus, 288–89
egg creams, 65
Ehrenreich, Chaim, 89
Eisland, Hyman and Morris, 28–29
Eldridge Street Synagogue, 18, 20, 108, 116
Ellington, Duke, 220, 240, 254
Ellstein, Abe, 25, 90, 167–68, 202, 224, 228, 302, 331n26
Elman, Mischa, 82, 211
Elman, Ziggy (aka Harry Finkelman), 202–3, 333n24
Epstein, Max (klezmer clarinet), 190, 205
Epstein Brothers, 175, 190
Ethiopian lineage of Black Jews. *See* Abyssinian descent of Black Jews
Ethiopian Spiritual Church of Christ (Pittsburgh), 236
Europe, James Reese, 193, 232
"Eyn Keloheynu" ("There Is None Like Our God," prayer), 286

Falk, Louis (Apollo Records), 172
Famous (dairy restaurant), 99, 107
Faye, Joey, 94
Federman, Anne Russ, 79
Feig, Perele (khaznte), 216
Feinberg, Irving, 73–74
Feingold, Lipa, 222–23
Ferber, Edna, 200

A Few Minutes with George Jessel (aka *"A Theatrical Booking Office,"* film), 294
fiddlers: viii, Sam Ash, 207, 211–13; Hirsh Gross, 23, 253; Abe Gubenko, 204–5, *205*; Abe Schwartz, 56, 166, 202; Solomon Smulewitz (Small), 184
Fillmore East, ix, 90, 131, 137–38
Finkel, Fyvush, 176
Finkelman, Harry (aka Ziggy Elman), 202–3
Finkle, Ruchele, 216
Fisher, Eddie, 226
Flagler Hotel, 171
Fleischer, Dave, 147
Fleischer, Max, 147, 307
Fleischer, Richard, 307
Ford, Rabbi Arnold Josiah, 232
Ford Startime (1959 TV remake of *The Jazz Singer*), 307
Forverts, 12, 20, 29, 31, 35–37, 60, 86–87, 89, 100, 103, 105, 107, 143, 149, 151, 160, 166, 180, 187, 195–96, 200, 237, 251, 260–61, 265–68, 291, 297. *See also* Cahan, Abe
Forverts Building, viii, ix, 117, 122, 125–28, *128*, 143
Forward Hour, 110, 150
Franklin, Abraham Ben Benjamin, 236
Fraye Arbeter Shtimme (Yiddish anarchist newspaper), 106, 160, 251
Freedman, Theodore Leopold (aka Ted Lewis), 194, 208
Freiheit, Morgn Freiheit (*The Morning Freedom*), 54, 88, 100–1, 196, 265, 324n13
Freiman, Louis, 134, 224
fry beef, 30; *see* beef fry
Friedman, Debbie, 216
Friedman, Mirele and Malkeleh, 216
Frishvasser, Regina (*Forverts* columnist), 196
Fuchs, Leo, 254
Fuchs, Sammy (Sammy's Bowery Follies), 67
Fun groys New York (From Big New York, newspaper column), 232
Funnye, Rabbi Capers, ix, 232

Gabay, Elia and Bella, 40–41
Gabila, 40–42, 44
The Garden Cafeteria, 105–8, *106*, 117
Garden Restaurant and Broilings, 57
Gardner, Herb, 324n13
Garfein, Oscar and son David, 31–32
Garfein's Dairy Restaurant, 31
Garfein's Jewish Family Restaurant, 31
Gelbart, Michl, 222
Gellis, Isaac, 17, *17*, 18–20, 22, 24–25, 27, 38
Gene Krupa Orchestra, 178, 332n5
Germansky, Joseph (choir director), 239
Gershwin, George, 147, 287, 292
Gershwin, Ira, 147
Getz, Stan, 193
Gibbs, Terry (aka Julius Gubenko), 204–6
Gillette, Don Carle, 290
Gilrod and Sandler (songwriters), 36
Gin Rummy (Yente record), 269–71
Giovanonni, David, 161
Glatshteyn, Yankev, 292
Glickman, Ellis S., 161, 277–78
God of Vengeance (Asch), 289
Gold, Michael, 51
Goldberg, Rube, 147
Goldfaden, Abraham, 110, 129, 131, 136, 181, 188
Goldman, Emma, 160

Goldstein, B. I. (*Tog* journalist), 304
Goldstein, Gus, 262
Goldstein, Jennie, 284
Goldye, Di Shvartze Khaznte (aka Gladys Mae Sellers), viii, ix, 2, 231, 248–55, 231, *248*, *253*
Goodman, Benny, 178, 193, 202–3, 254, 306, 333n24
Gordon, Bernice Zuckerberg. *See* Breindele
Gordon, Max (Broadway producer), 283, 292
Gordon, Sheldon ("Shelley"), 230
Goren, B. (aka Yitzhkok Goida-Hoida), 274, 280
Gornish, Jean (Sheindele di Khaznte), 227–28, 230
Gotti, Harry (aka Hershel Gottleib), 149–50
Gotti, John, 34
Graham, Bill (aka Wulf Grajonca), 90, 137–38
Graham, Stephen, 54–56, 65
Green, Victor H.: *Green Book* (for Black travelers' accommodations), 140
Greenblatt and Meyers Roumanian Gardens, 57
Greengrass, Barney (aka Berl Gringrass), 81–83
Greengrass, Gary, 83
Greengrass, Marvin (Moe), 82–83
gribenes (crispy minced chicken skins), 35
Gronenberg and Leuchtag (architects), 143
Gropper, William (cartoonist), 265, *266*
Gross, Hirsh (fiddler), 23, 253
Gross, Milt (cartoonist), 147
Gross and Lindenboim (Traffic cafeteria), 101

Grossman, Milton (Black child cantor), 236
Groyser Kundes (The Big Stick Yiddish magazine), 149
Gubenko, Abe (fiddler), 204–5
Guinan, Texas, 60

H. W. Perlman Pianos, ix, 122, 162–64, *164*
Hackley, Mme. E. Azalia, 249
Hadassah, Kadima chapter of, 167
Hammer, Max ("Mekhl"), 93
Hammer's Dairy Restaurant, 93–94, *93*
Hancock, David (*Collector's Guild* recording engineer), 169
Harendorf, Sh.: *Theatrical Caravans* (memoir), 246
Harkavy, Alexander, 259, 272
Harlem, Jewish community in, 27, 77, 81, 101, 117, 133, 139–40, 152, 193, 231, 234, 239, 246, 251, 264
Harlem Renaissance, 232, 252
Harmatz, Abe, 90
Harmatz, Fred and Robert, 92
Harmatz, Harold, 79, 91–92, 108
Harmatz, Harry, 89–90
Harmatz, Jacob, 89–90
Harmatz Brothers Restaurant, 89
Harnick, Sheldon, 271
Harry's Chop House and Roumanian Paradise, 61
Hart, Madame Bertha, 284
Hebrew Actor's Union, 136
The Hebrew Leader (newspaper), 139
Hebrew National, 19–24, *21*
The Hebrew Standard (newspaper), 11, 85
Hegamin, Lucille (blues singer), 252
Heimowitz's Oriental Roumanian, 57
Helfenbein, Joe, (Cherniavsky drummer), 200

Heller, Joseph, 41
Henry's delicatessen, 29
Herman, Rabbi Mordechai (Moorish Zionist Temple), 232
Herman, Woody, 205–6
Herzl, Theodore, 51, 141
Hilton, Daisy and Violet (Siamese twins), 298
Hirshfield, Harry, 147
Hochman, Israel J. (klezmer bandleader), 219
Hochman's Roumanian Restaurant and Broilings, 57
Hodes, Billy ("Essen"), 170–71
Hoffman, Anna, 263–64, 339n8
Holiday, Billie (singer), 241
Holocaust and Holocaust survivors, 1, 3, 90, 103, 137, 307
Home of the Sages of Israel, 128
Honickman, Harold, 74
hotels, 2; Borscht Belt, 32, 171, 223; Broadway Central, 14–16; early Jewish hotels, 139–56; Flagler, 171; Leverich Towers Hotel, 153–54; Manischewitz-owned Broadway Central, 15, 149; Normandie, 223; St. George, 144. *See also* Libby's Hotel and Baths
Houseman, Al, 221
Howard, Willie and Eugene, 301

Iceland, Hyman and Morris, 28
Iddishe Likht (*The Light of Israel*, Orthodox Yiddish newspaper), 298
Impossible Burgers, 87
independent record labels, 176–78
International (night club), 61, 64
International Union of United Brewery and Soft Drink Workers of America, 72

In the Fiddler's House (TV program), 176
Irving Place Theater, 129
Isa Kremer: The Supreme Interpreter of Ballad and Folk Songs (film), 301
Island, Hyman and Morris, 28
Itzkowitz's Original Roumanian Inn, 57

Jackson, Mahalia, 173
Jacobs, Betty, 269
Jacobs, Jacob, 133–35, 201, *238*, 239, 247, 264, 269
Jaffe, Ida, 289
Jaffe, Louis N., 131–33. *See also* Louis N. Jaffe Theater
Jaffe, Sam, 289, 291
Jaffee, N. Jay, iv, 46–48
Jarmulowsky, Alexander ("Sender"), 2, 18, 115–21, *120*, 125. *See also* S. Jarmulowsky
Jarmulowsky, Harry, 115, 122–23
Jarmulowsky, Rebecca, 115, 117, 121
Jarmulowsky (aka Jarmel), Albert, 115, 122
Jarmulowsky (aka Jarmel), Louis, 105, 115, 117–19, 122, 125. *See also* M&L Jarmulowsky bank
Jarmulowsky (aka Jarmuth), Edwin, 123
Jarmulowsky (aka Jarmuth), Fanny, 122
Jarmulowsky (aka Jarmuth), Meyer, 105, 115, 117–19, *118*, 121–23, 125. *See also* M&L Jarmulowsky bank
jazz, 31, 35, 59, 169, 173, 176–78, 187, 191, 193–206, *197*, 231, 234, 238, 245, 254; *brodvey dzhez bend*, Cathedral of the Underworld, 254; Cherniavsky's

Hasidic Jazz Band, 148, 150, 198–201, *199*; Earl Fuller's Jazz Band, 194; Hirsh Gross and his Famous Yiddish-English Jazz Band, 253; later Jewish hybrids, 203–6, *205*; Prof. Nodelman's Union Double Jazz Band, 198; Prof. Schiller's Jazz Band, 198; Prof. Schulman's Jazz Band, 198; rag-a-jazz, 194, 250; Raphaelson and, 286–88; "Tekiah gedoylah," 194

The Jazz Singer, 147, 200, 279–308; critical reception of, 291–93, 303–4; "The Day of Atonement," 280, 282–85, 290; film version, 200, 293–94; Jessel and, 147, 288–94, *295*, 296–98, 303–5, *304*; Jolson and, 292–96, *295*, 300, 303–7, *304*; philosophy behind, 286–88; play version, 147, 279, 283–92, 302; remakes of, 306–8; Rosenblatt and, 294–301, *295*; Vitaphone, 293–94, 297, 300–2

Jessel, Charlotte, 288
Jessel, George, 141, 288–92; *The Jazz Singer and*, 147, 289–91, *295*, 296–98, 303–5, *304*; "My Mother's Eyes" and "Home Pals," songs identified with, 305; *Nightmare Alley* (film), 305
Jewish Anarchists, 106, 117, 160, 251
Jewish Cookery Book (Levy), 8
Jewish Daily Forward, 128, 324n13. See also *Forverts*
Jewish Defense Fund, 117
The Jewish Exponent (newspaper), 278
Jewish Mobile Theater, 136
The Jewish Press Bureau, 117
Jewish Socialist Farband, 128

Jewish Theological Seminary, 116, 216
Jews Without Money (Michael Gold), 51
Jim Crow, 231, 273
Joe and Paul, 171–76, *172*, 222
Joe's Roumanian, 57
Jolson, Al (aka Asa Yoelson), 73, 81–82, 202, 221, 233, 244, 289, 292–93; *The Jazz Singer* and, 287, *294*, 300, 303–6, *304*; *The Jolson Story* (film), 306
Jones, Quincy, 205
Joplin, Janis, 137
Joplin, Scott, 288
Joseph, Rabbi Jacob, 9–10, 26, 116
Joys of Yiddish (Rosten), 271–72
Jubilee records, 171. See also records
Juvelier, Kalmen, 162, 277

Kandel, Harry, 198, 202; Kandel's Jazz Orchestra, 198
Kanefsky, Bernice. See Bas Sheva
Kanefsky, Yossele, 217–18, 220
Kantrowitz and Katzenelenbogen (publishers), 274
Kapelye (klezmer group), 176
Karnblit, Z., 239–40
kashrus practices. See kosher
The Kate Smith Hour (TV show), 227
Katz, Mickey, ix, 36, 166, 203, 220, 222; *Papa, Play for Me* (memoir), 151
Katz, William (Katz's Delicatessen), 28
Katz's delicatessen, 1, 27–30, *27*, 93
Kaufman, George S., 289
Kaye, Danny, 306, 329n24
Kellogg, Dr. J. H., 87
Kellogg's cafeteria, 101, 174
Kessler, David, 129, 131, 274, 280
Kessler's Thalia Theater, 129, 233, 274–75, 280

Index | 357

khazntes. *See* women cantors of the stage
"Kid Twist" (Abe Reles), 74
"Kid Twist" (Max Zweifach), 74–75
Kishiniev pogroms, 119, 181
kishkes. *See* knishes and kishkes
The Kishke King, 44–48, *47*
klezmer music, 2, 23, 44, 50, 165–66, 175–78, 190–91, 195–96, 198–99, 202–5, 219, 230
klezmorim, 193, 195, 333n24
Klugman, Jack, 95
knishes and kishkes, 21, 35–48; Gabila, 40–42, 44; history of knish, 35–36; "Papa" Joseph Burger, 45; The Kishke King, 44–48, *47*; Mrs. Stahl's, 42–44; Potatola, 38, *39*; Schwartz's Famous Potatopie, 38–39, *39*; Shatzkin's Famous, 41–42; Yonah Schimmel, 1, 36–38, 42, 67, 211
Kofsky, Paul Emanuel, 174–75. See also *Joe and Paul*
Kollscritta, Dovid (aka "Dovid, di Kollscritta Ha'Cohen der Falash"), 235–36, 250; aka David Kohl, 150, 236
Kol Nidre: film, 184; *The Jazz Singer*, 283, 285–86, 288, 292, 296, 300–1, 342n45; prayer/service, 280, 286, 288, 342n45; recording, 201, 241; in *Der vilner balabesl*, 280
Koninsky, Sadie (ragtime composer), 193–94
kosher (*kashrus*), 7–12, 20, 77, 232; bacon, 19, 30–31, 87; meat riot, 10–12, *11*; unions and crime in kosher food industry, 26–27. See also kosher restaurants
kosher butchers, 10–11, 23, 30, 45, 128, 225; Chinese kosher cuisine, 31–32; Hebrew National Restaurant and Lunch Rooms, 22–23; restaurants, 7–10; Second Avenue Delicatessen, 32–34; Shang Chai (Brooklyn), 32; Trotzky's Kosher Restaurant, 13–15, *13*
Kovner, B. (Jacob "Yankev" Adler), 218–19, 260–61, 264, 266–69, 271–72
Kovner, Samuel ("Little Kishke"), 104
Krainin, Theodore (Tanchum), 20–23, 25
Krishtal, L., 251
Kroll, Max, 171
Kurtzer, Aaron ("Arnold"), 217
Kurtzer, Sophie (aka Khaye Sore Kanefsky), 217–20, *217*, 224, 251
Kwartin, Cantor Zevulun ("Zavel"), 170, 239

Ladies Bikkur Cholim Society Hebrew Industrial School, 117
Laemmle, Carl, 200
LaGuardia, Fiorello, 154–55
Lambert cylinders, 160–62
Lando, Dr. George, 159–62, *159*
Lansky, Meyer, 92
Lansky's Lounge, 92, 105
LaRue Jones, Demosthanes (Demos), 237
LaRue Jones, Herbert Socrates (HS), 237
LaRue Jones, Thomas, 2, 150, 177, 237–47, *238*, *243*, 249–51, 255; burial site and headstone for, 247; in *Forverts* salons, 267–68; Jewish circuit, 237, 247, 250; records of, 240–42, *243*, 247; R'Toyvele Ha'Cohen (European tour), 243–46; war work and patent of, 247; *Yente Telebende* production with, *263*, 265, 267–68

Latner, Helen Stambler, 169–70
Lebanon Hospital (now Bronx Lebanon Hospital), 18, 116
Lebedeff, Aaron, 36, 50, 90, 226
Lebewohl, Abe, 32–34
Lee, Gypsy Rose, 298–300
Lee, Peggy, 306
Leibowitz and Tuckeroff Roumanian Village, 57
Lenox Theater (Harlem), 133, 239, 264
Leonard, Benny ("The Ghetto Wizard"), 146
Levensohn, Joel David, 280
Levenson, Sam, 33, 176
Levitsky, Mitchell, 110
Levy, Esther, 8
Levy, Max ("Mac"), 144–46
Lewis, Albert, 283–85, 288–89, 292
Lewis, Jerry, 173, 307
Lewis, Ted (aka Theodore Leopold Freedman), 194, 208
Libby's Hotel and Baths, viii, 26, 139–55, *142, 147*; Max Bernstein and, 2, 101, 139–41, 143–44, 146–49; birth of, 140–46, *142*; destruction of, 152–55; Max "Mac" Levy and physical culture movement, 144–46; Lower East Side improvement and, 152; Mickey Katz, 151; musical director, 200; Music Hall, 150–51; opening night, 146–49, *147*; theater and radio of deluxe accommodations, 149–51
Libby's Lunch, 101, 140, 152
Lippitz, Erica, 216
Lippman, Martin (Judge Crater lawyer), 154
Liptzin, Keni, 277; Irving Place Theater and, 129
Little Club Orchestra, 195
Little Romania (Michl Rosenberg's Miami Beach club), 226

Lockett, Lou, 178
Loew, Marcus, 136, 181
Loew's Commodore, 63, 90, *131*, 136–37, 333n2
Loew's Delancey, 90, 136
Loew's Kameo, 135
Loew's Oriental, 135
Lomax, Alan, 173
Louis N. Jaffe Theater, 131–33, *132*, 135, 138
Lowenwirth, Sam, 150
Lower East Side, 9–10, 18, 23, 27, 33, 35–37, 53–54, 59–61, 64, 67, 74, 78, 80–81, 85–86, 89–91, 115–18, 122, 128, 130, 139, 141, 143, 151–55, 164, 175, 180, 193, 210, 251, 274, 280–81, 286, 288, 290
Loyal League of Yiddish Sons of Erin, 64
Lubinsky, Herman, 176–78
Lubitsch, Ernst, 302, 306
Lupowitz, Samuel, 50, 61, 63
lynchings of African Americans, 241
Lyric Theater, 133

M1 Garand rifle, 163
Mac Levy. *See* Levy, Max ("Mac")
MacLevy, Montague ("Monty") (son of Max "Mac" Levy), 146
Magnes, Judah, 117
Malamut, Max, 227
Malavsky, Abraham (Albert), 224
Malavsky, Goldele and Gittele, 224–27
Malavsky, Minnie and Ruth, 226
Malavsky, Morton, 224
Malavsky, Shmuel ("Samuel"), 224–27
Malavsky family, 224–27
Malini, Max (aka Max Katz), 180
M&L Jarmulowsky bank, 105, 117, 119, 121–22
M&S Circuit, 130, 136

Manhattan, 22, 29, 32, 38, 43, 57, 103, 105, 128, 130, 141, 146, 149, 174, 200, 203
Manhattan Special soda, 75
Manischewitz, Rabbi Meyer ("Max"), 15
Manischewitz Matzos, 40, 203
Manne, Shelly, 203–4, 206
Manny Blanc Plays Jewish Jazz, 204, 206
Mansky, M. (Newark music store), 240
Markowitz, Louis, 168
Marlin Sisters, 226–27
Martin, Dean, 173
Martin, Leo (last Dubrow's owner), 105
Marx, Felix, (pioneering kosher restaurateur), 7
Mathis, Johnny, 286
Matthew, Rabbi Wentworth Arthur (Commandment Keepers), 232
Maud, Zuni (artist), 261
Max Gabel's Bowery Theater, 54, 133
Mayer, Elias, 130, 136–37
Mayfield's Celery Cola, 71
McKinley Square Theater (the Bronx), 247, 253
McLeod, Alice (Coltrane), 206
McManus, George, 260
Meara, Anne, 74
meat riots, 10–12, *11*
Medoff, David, 177
Medoff, Raisa, 177
Medoff, Sam, 177, 203, 206
Meeropol, Abel, 241
"Mendel, der shvartzer khazn," 232–33, *233*
Mendelsohn, Fred, 176–78
Mercer, Johnny, 203
Metzger, Beatrice, 106
Metzger, Charles (Garden Cafeteria), 106–8

Mezzrow, Mezz, 193
Michaels, Marilyn ("Toni Michel"), *223*, 224
Michalesco, Michal, 134
Midnight Rose Candy Store (Murder, Inc.), 104
"The Million Dollar Yiddish Theater" (Rolland Theater), 133–35, *134*
minstrel shows, 245, 247, 273–74, 287–89. *See also* blackface performances; vaudeville
Misses Palache's Boarding and Day School for Young Ladies of the Jewish Persuasion, 139
Miss Gefilte Fish Queen New York, 64
Mme. Levy's Mosaic Accommodations and Boardinghouse, 139
The Modern Yiddish-English Dictionary (Weinreich), 1, 272
Mogelewsky, S. P., 222
Mogen David Kosher products, 25–26
Mogen Dovid Delicatessen Corporation, 26
Mogulesco, Sigmund, 131, 274
Moishe Peking (kosher Chinese), 32
Moishe's (kosher baker), 91
Molly Picon Dining Room, 33
Moorish Revival theme, 70, 118, 132
Moorish Zionist Temple, 232
Morgenstern, Dan (jazz historian), ix, 234–35
Morgn Freiheit. See *Freiheit*
Morgn Zhurnal (The Morning Journal), 20, 26, 36, 107, 225, 239, 265, 292, 305
Morse, Gerald J. (Banner records), 167–68
Moses, Robert, 92, 154–55
Moskowitz, Abe, 55–56
Moskowitz, Joseph ("Yossele"), vii, 49–58, *53*, 61–62, 65

Moskowitz, Rebecca, 51
Moskowitz & Lupowitz, 50–52, 58, 61–64, *62*
Moskowitz's Little Roumanian Rendezvous, 52, *53*, 54
Mount Morris vaudeville theater (Harlem), 251
Mrs. J. Kampus' Restaurant, 86
Mrs. Stahl's knishes, 42–44
Muni, Paul (aka Muni Weisenfreund), 147
Murder Inc., 104
Murray's Sturgeon Shop, 83–84
music: Black cantors, 2, 219, 231–55, *233–34*, 235, *238*, *243*, *248*, *253*; first Yiddish recording artists, 179–81, *189*; first Yiddish records, 159–78, *159*, *164*; Lambert cylinders, 160–62; music stores, 204, 207–13, *208*, *212*; novelty music, 36, 168, 190–92, 194, 206, 209–10; women cantors of the stage, 215–30, *217*, *223*, *229*. *See also* banjo; fiddlers; jazz; klezmer music; songs; *specific singers and composers*
music stores, viii, 207–13, *208*, *212*
Musiker, Ray, 206
Musiker, Sammy, 177–78, 204, 206, 332n5

Nathan's, 42
Nathanson, Julius, 135, 261
National League, 15
National Library of Israel, ix, 2
Naye Leben (*The New Life*, Bialystok newspaper), 244–45
The Negro Motorist Green Book (Green), 140
New Masses (magazine), 54
New York Board of Education, 212
New York Bottling Company, 71

New York Yiddish theaters, 129–38, *131*; Clinton theater, 255; The Commodore, 90, 130–31, *131*, 136–37; Folksbeine, 128, 149; Hopkinson theater, 224, 271; Irving Place, 129; Kessler's Thalia, 129, 233, 274–75, 280; Lenox, 133, 239, 264; Louis N. Jaffe Theater, 131–33, *132*; McKinley Square theater, 247, 253; National theater, 220, 224, 255; Parkway theater, 135, 220; Public theater, 95, 135; Rolland theater, 133–35, *134*; Satz's Folks Theater, 227; Seiden's Columbia Street theater, 182; Seiden's Willett Street theater, 183, *183;* Thomashefsky's National theater, 261; Village theater, 90, 136
Nodiff, David, 165–66
Noonan, Tom (Bishop of Chinatown), 254
Normandie Hotel (Borscht Belt), 223, *223*
Nowak, Amram (*The Cafeteria*), 105

OKeh record label, 194, 240, *243*, 261, 306
Old Roumanian Restaurant, 58–61, *58*, 63, 65
Olivier, Lawrence, 308
Olshanetsky, Alexander, 187, 202, 254
Opatoshu, Joseph, 102–3
Original Dixie Jazz Band (ODJB), 194
Original Moskowitz restaurant, 52–53
Orpheum Theater (NJ), 171
Osterman, Edward ("Monk Eastman"), 75
Ostfeld, Barbara Jean, 216
Oysher, Freidele, 222–24, *223*
Oysher, Moishe, 167, 222, 224, 280

Pabst, H. W., 71
Packer, Victor, 136
Painters, Decorators, and Paperhangers Union, 160
Parks, Larry, 306
The Parkview, 135
Parkway Cafeteria, 102
Parkway Theater, 135, 220
  party records, 170–71, 173, 176
Pemberton, John (Coca Cola inventor), 71
Perlman, Harry Wolf (HW), ix, 122, 162–64, *164*
Perlman, Itzhak, 176
Petrillo, James C., 164, 168, 177
Picon, Molly, 33, 95, 102, 133, 147, 167, 223, 271, 278, 302, 307
Pinckowitz, Isidore, 23
Pines, Isidore ("Skip"), 24
Pines, Leonard, 23–24
plays and shows
  Abie's Irish Rose, 290, 303, 305
  Bagels and Yox, 222
  Borscht Capades, 220, 222
  The Daughter of a Lost Tribe, 248, 254
  Der poylisher rebbe (*The Polish Rabbi*, musical comedy), 254–55
  Der rebetzin's dzhigalo (*The Rabbi's Wife's Lover*, musical comedy), 255
  Der shirtz (Yiddish *HMS Pinafore*), 167–68
  Der vilner balabesl (The Little Vilna Boss), 280–81, 286
  Die yom banditten (The Pirates of Penzance), 167
  Di khaznte (musical drama), 215
  Dos khupe kleyd (*The Wedding Dress*, musical), *238*, 239
  The Dybbuk: Schwartz production, 198; Vilna Troupe, 133
  Falshe tokhter (False Daughter), 247
  Freidele's khasene (*Freidele's Wedding*, musical), 224
  Goldene kale (musical), 110
  Helen of Troy, New York (musical comedy), 289
  Him, 252–53
  Ir ershte libe, 220
  Katinka (musical), 110
  A khazndl af shabbos, 224
  Der khazn's tokhter, 224
  "Kiddie Kabaret," 288
  Kosher Kitty Kelly, 290
  Let's Sing Yiddish, 137
  Lomir beyde zingn (*Let's Both Sing*, musical), 224
  Lulu Belle (Broadway play), 252
  A malke af peysakh, 224
  Mentshn shtoyb (*Human Dust*), 102
  Molly dolly (musical), 102, 110
  A nakht in gan eyden revue (A Night in the Garden of Eden), 150
  Passing Show of 1923, 289
  Reizele, 102
  Robinson Crusoe, Jr.: musical, 292; radio show, 73
  Shayke fin bronzvil (Shayke from Brownsville), 219
  Showboat (musical), 285
  Uncle Tom's Cabin, 129, 268, 273–78, *276*
  Vik-end (Bas Sheva), 220
  The War Song (Broadway show), 289
  Yente af brodvey, 253, 271
  Yente af yener velt (*Yente from Beyond*), 268–69
  Yente Telebende, 219, 253, 259–65, *263*
  Ziegfeld Follies, 275, 289
  Zing, freidele, zing, 224
  See also specific actors/actresses, playwrights, and producers
Poggi, Louis ("Kid"), 75
pogroms, 3, 117, 119, 241

Poland, 14, 19, 37, 43, 61, 78, 81, 83, 93–94, 115, 168, 207, 241, 243
Port Arthur Chinese restaurant, 31
Powell, Walter ("Mousy"), 209
Prager, Regina, 162, 215
Pressman, Barney, 83
Printer's Ink (magazine), 145
Prof. Nodelman's Union Double Jazz Band, 198
Prof. Schiller's Jazz Band, 198
Prof. Schulman's Jazz Band, 198
Progressive Dramatic League, 160
Prolectos Cooperative Cafeteria, 100–1
Property Owner's Improvement Corporation, 119

Qualitessen, 26, 40
Queens, 38

Rabinowitz family as characters in Raphaelson's work, 281, 291–92, 296, 301, 305–6
Raderman, Elias and Max, 194
Raderman, Harry, 194–95
Radical Reading Room, 160
radio shows
  American Jewish Caravan of Stars, 23
  Amerikaner familyen magazin un gazetn (The American Family Magazine and Gazette), 236
  Buccaneers, 73
  The Chunky Theater of the Air, 110–11
  Forverts Hour, 110, 150
  Libby Hotel's radio show, 149–50
  Lux Radio Theater, 306
  Major Bowes Amateur Hour, 205
  Name It and Take It, 73
  Ratner's Dairy Restaurant, 89–90
  Robinson Crusoe, Jr., 73
  Uncle Abe's Mogen Dovid Club, 73
  Uptown, Downtown, 25
  Yiddish Melodies in Swing, 177, 203, 206, 226
  The Yiddish Radio Project (NPR series), 111
  Zion Variety Hour, 25
  See also radio stations
radio stations
  KFWB, 297, 301
  WABC, 89–90, 150
  WBBC, 174
  WBNX, 73, 174, 177
  WBNY, 89
  WBVD, 171, 174
  WEVD, 33, 73, 110, 150, 174, 228, 230, 254
  WFBH, 149–50
  WHN, 73, 150, 177, 203, 226
  WJZ, 73
  WLTH, 136, 150, 163, 174
  WMCA, 25, 175, 254
  WMGM, 23
  WNYC, 254
  WOR, 73
  WRAZ, 176
ragtime, 160, 193–94, 231, 283, 287–88
Rainbow Music and Gift Shop, 172
Raphaelson, Samson, 280–93, 296, 303, 305–6
Rappoport's restaurant, 95
Raskin, Miriam (writer), 103
Ratner's Restaurant, 79, 89–92, *91*, 96, 108, *131*, 137
Ratnofsky, Leo (B&H counterman), 95
Ray cafeteria, 106, *106*
Ray Carter's Catskill Cowboys, 170
Rechtzeit, Seymour, 150, 168, 253
recording artists, 179–92, *183*, *189*
records and record companies/labels, 159–78, *159*, *164*, *172*
  Apollo, 171–73, 175–76
  Banner, 166–70, 224, 269, 302

records and record companies/labels (*continued*)
   Capitol, 165–66, 173, 220–21, 226
   Collector's Guild, 169–70
   Columbia, 56, 160, 163, 165–66, 181, 184, 225–26, 240, 242, 261–63, 300–1
   Decca, 201
   Edison, 160–61, 163, 184
   Lambert, 160–62
   RCA/RCA Victor, 168–70, 202–3, 220, 235
   Standard, 159–62, *159*
   United Hebrew Disc and Cylinder Record Company (UHD&C), 162–63
   Victor, 50, 160, 162–63, 181, 184, 225, 240, 261, 263, 300
   Zion Records, 226
Reed, Napoleon (Black Yiddish singer), 222
Reform Hebrew Union College, 9, 216
Regensberg, Rabbi (celery tonic swindler), 76
Reiner, Rob, 30, 93
Relkin, Edvin A. (Yiddish theater impresario), 134, 136, 237, 239, 243, 251, 255, 277–78, 292
Rich, Buddy, 205
Rippel, Mendel (Yiddish translator of "Uncle Tom's Cabin"), 274
Ritt, Martin, 93–94
Robboy, Ron, ix, 279
Robinson, Bill ("Bojangles"), 60
Rogoff, Hillel (*Forverts* columnist), 261
Rolland, William (Theater owner), 133–34
Rolland Theater (Brooklyn), 133–35, *134*
Romanian restaurants, 49–67. *See also* specific names of restaurants
Rosansky, Louis (UHD&C), 162–63
Rosenberg, Israel (Yiddish playwright), 255
Rosenberg, Michel (Yiddish actor), 167, 226; Romanian restaurant (Miami Beach) and, 167
Rosenblatt, Henry, 150
Rosenblatt, Samuel, 296, 300
Rosenblatt, W. M., 8
Rosenblatt, Yossele, 15, 141, 215, 225, 239, 250, 267, 294–301, *295*, 304, 342n42; aka Joseph, 150
Rosten, Leo, 271–72
Rothstein, Shloimele (cantor), 242
Rouse and Goldstone (S. Jarmulowsky architects), 120
Roxy Theater, 130
"Rozhinkes mit Mandlen," 110–11, 181
Rubinzohn, Z., 219, 232–33, 235
Ruminsky, Murray, (aka Rumshinsky), 302
Rumshinsky, Joseph, 102, 110, 187, 215, 227, 261, 302
Russ & Daughters, 1, 78–80, 83

S. Jarmulowsky, 2, 18, 115–22
Sam Ash (music store), 211–13, *212*
Sammy's Bowery Follies, 67
Sammy's Roumanian Steakhouse, 64–67
Sandler, Peretz (composer), 36, 280, 286
Sapoznik, Cantor Zindel, *223*
Sapoznik, Henry H.: *Attractive Hebrews*, 160–62; *Klezmer! Jewish Music from Old World to Our World*, 2; *Mysteries of the Sabbath* (anthology), 219; *The Yiddish Radio Project* (NPR series), 111
Satz, Ludwig, 133, 227
Savoy Records, 176–78
Say It in Yiddish (Weinreich), 1, 3

Schildkraut, Herman and Sadie, 2, 86–88, *86*
Schildkraut's Vegetarian Restaurants, 86–89, *86*
Schimmel, Yonah. *See* Yonah Schimmel
Schimmel (daughters): Bessie, 67; Rose, 37
Schneider, Louis (M&S theater), 130, 136–37
Schoneberger, Frederick, and son Adolph, 72–73
Schultz, Carl H. (seltzer), 69–70
Schwartz, Abe (fiddler/composer), 56, 166, 176, 202, 306
Schwartz, Arthur (food writer), 42, 96
Schwartz, Maurice, 95, 102, 131–35, 147, 160, 167, 198, 271
Schwartz, Morris, 38–40, 42
Schwartz's Famous Potatopie, 38–39, *39*
Scooler, Zvee, 228
Second Avenue Delicatessen, 32–34
Secunda, Sholom, 61, 134, 174, 201, 222, 224, 230, 240
Seiden, Frank, 130, 137, 179–84, *183*, 188, 288
Seiden, Joseph, 184, 227
Sellers, Gladys Mae (aka Goldye, Di Shvartze Khaznte), 2, 231, 248–55, *248*, *253*, 255
Selniker, Evelyn, 216
Selsman, Sam (Banner founder), 166
seltzer, 60, 65, 69–70
Sforim, Mendele Moykher, 136
Shang Chai (Brooklyn kosher Chinese restaurant), 32, 312n60
Shanghai Orthodox Jews, 32, 312n58
Shapiro's Little Roumanian Casino, 57
Shatzkin, Sam, 41–42
Shatzkin, Yosl ("Alex"), 41–42
Shatzkin's Famous, 41–42
Shavous (holiday), 85
Shaw, Artie, 193
"Sheba of Gza," 249
Sheikowitz, Jacob and Nina, 149, 253
Sheindele di Khaznte (aka Jean Gornish), 215, 227–28
Shengold, Joseph (cantor), 305
Sheraton, Mimi, 65
Sherman, Allan, 203
Shimele Blank, 204, 207–11; Bargain Music Store, 207–11, *208*
Shore, George, 334n7
shows. *See* plays and shows
Shryer, Art, 198
Shvartze mame [Black Mother], (drama), 255
Silverman, Jack ("Rowdydow"), 58–61, 63–65, 89, *58*
Silvershein, Phil, 109–10, *109*, 111
Silvershein, Roberta, 111
Silvershein, William, 109
Silvershein-Willens, Shereen, 111
Simonoff, Betty, 90
Sinai Kosher Wurst Company, 23
Sinclair, Upton, 12
Singer, I. J., 135
Singer, Isaac Bashevis, 103, 105, 107
Sirota, Gershon, 162, 215, 239, 244
Skulnik, Menashe, 28, 133, 167
Sloman, Eddie, 303
Smack, Albert, 249
Smith, Alfred E., 153–54
Smith, Kate, 227
Smith, Willie ("The Lion"), 234–35, *234*
Smulewitz, Solomon (aka Small), 2, *147*, 148, 162, 184–89, *189*, 331n25
Sohn, Eleazar ("Louis"), 45
Sohn, Jacob ("Kishke King"), 45–48
Sokolow, Pete, v, 210

songs
- "And the Angels Sing" ("Der shtiller bulgar"), 202–3, 333n24
- "Baym rebin's tish" ("At the Rabbi's Table"), 166
- "Bei mir bistu sheyn," 134, 177, 201, 207–8, 240
- "A brivele der mamen," 148, 185, 187, 267
- "Bublitchiki," "Beigelakh" ("Little Bagels"), 202–3
- "Busy Busy," 302
- "Der nayer yid" ("The New Jew"), 223–24
- "Di babe ligt in kimpet" ("Grandma's Pregnant"), 166
- "Di grine kuzine" ("The Green Cousin"), 56, 202, 306
- "Dixie Mammy," 285–86
- "Doina," 50, 194, 202, *208*, 332n5
- "Eli, Eli," 201, 239, 241, 254, 267, 280, 286, 300
- "Eli Green's Cakewalk," 194
- "Farlir nor nit dein hofenung reb yid" (Don't give up hope, Mr. Jew), 240
- "Fight Illian," 280
- "Freilach in Swing: And the Angels Sing," 202–3
- "Grine kuzine," 56, 202, 306; "My Little Cousin," 306
- "Hallelujah": Kurtzer, 219; Rosenblatt, 300
- "Home Pals," 305
- "Hot dogs un knishes," 36
- "Huliet, huliet kinderlakh" ("Dance, Dance Children"), 56
- "Ich bin a boarder by mein weib" ("I Am My Wife's Boarder"), 176
- "Ikh hob dikh tsufil lib," 168
- "Joseph, Joseph"/"Yosl, Yosl," 202
- *Kol Nidre*, 184, 201, 241, 280, 283, 285–86, 288, 292, 296–97, 300–1, 342n45
- "Libby's March," 148, 187
- "Love Sings a Song in My Heart," 200
- "Make That Trombone Laugh," 194, 208
- "Mayn shtetele belz" ("That Wonderful Girl of Mine"), 63, 168, 202
- "Mayn yiddishe mame," 204
- "Misratzeh berach'mim" ("Become favorable through compassion"), 241–42
- "My Mother's Eyes," 305
- "Oi Vey, Titina," 198–99
- "Omar Rabbi Elosor" ("So Said Rabbi Elosor"), 300
- "Red Hot Mama," 285
- "Roumania, Roumania," 50
- "Song of Omar," 194–95
- "Strange Fruit," 241
- "Swim-Music-Swim," 150
- "Temperamental Tillie," 302
- "The Thing," 168
- "V'chol Ma'aminim," 230
- "Victory Tantz" (wartime song), 226
- "Vi iz dus gesele" ("Where Is the Street"), 56
- "Wedding Samba," 202
- "Where Did Robinson Crusoe Go with Friday on Saturday Night," 305
- "Yiddishe Blues," 302
- "Yortsayt" ("In Memoriam"), 301

spa cures, 69–70, 87. *See also* baths and health spas
Spottswood, Dick, x, 165, 242
St. George Hotel (Brooklyn), 144

Stahl, Fannie, and Mrs. Stahl's knishes, 42–44
Stambler, Benedict and Helen, 169–70
Standard Records, 159–62, *159*, 184
Stang, Arnold, 111
Stars on Parade (Black movie), 184
Steinberg, Joseph (composer), 201
Steinberg's Restaurant, 95
Stiller, Jerry, 74
Stiner, Goldye Mae. *See* Goldye, Di Shvartze Khaznte
Stowe, Harriet Beecher, 273, 276–77
Sturtz, Phil (Apollo co-founder), 172
Stutchkoff, Nahum, 259
Sumac, Yma, 221
Sunday laws. *See* blue laws

T. L Neff and Sons Celery Tonic, 71, 73
tallis, 215, 279, 284
Tammany Hall, 23, 74–75, 153–54
Tandy, Jessica, 133
Tarlow, Leopold, and sons (Zion National), 25
Tarras, Dave, 166–67, 176–78, 198–99, 203, 211
"Tekiah gedoylah," 194
Telebende Quartet, 262–63
Teller, Maurice (last Dubrow's owner), 88–89
Temkin, Louis ("the cloak maker with the golden voice"), 90
Temple Sharey Tefillo (NJ), 247
Tenenbaum, Samuel (*Forverts* food writer), 22
Tenenholtz, Eli ("Tenen Holtz"), 303
Tepel, Rudy, 170, 190–91
"Tevye" stories (Sholem Aleichem), 79, 89, 271
Thalia. *See* Kessler's Thalia Theater
Theological Seminary of the Conservative Synagogue, 116, 216

Thomas, Danny, 306–7
Thomashefsky, Bessie, 275
Thomashefsky, Boris, 59–60, 95, 129, 136, 198, 261, 265, 268, 274–75, 278
Thomashefsky, Max ("Mike"), 278
Thomashefsky's Roumanian Village, 60
Thompson submachine gun, 163
Tin Pan Alley, 194, 250
Tlomackie synagogue (Warsaw), 244
Tobin, Max (Dubrow's ill-fated manager), 104–5
Tog (newspaper), 20, 36, 107, 111, 196, 265, 267, 304; *Tog-Morgn Zhurnal*, 107
Top Notch Candy Inc., 109–11
Torrio, Johnny ("Terror"), 73
"Toyve Ha'Cohen." *See* LaRue Jones, Thomas
Traffic (cafeteria), 101
Trillin, Calvin, 80
Trotsky, Leon (aka Bronstein), 13–16
Trotzky, Hyman, 13–16
Trotzky's Kosher Restaurant, 13–16, *13*
Tucker, Sophie, 60, 287
Tully, Lee ("Essen"), 171

Uncle Tom's Cabin: revivals, 274–75, 278; Stowe's book, 273–74
Uncle Tom's Cabin shows, 129, 268, 273–78, *276*; Black performers in, 275–77; Jewish interest in, 274–78, 278; press on, 275–78, *276*; productions of, 268, 274–78
unions: kosher food industry, 26–27. *See also specific unions*
United Hebrew Disc and Cylinder Record Company (United Hebrew Record/UHD&C), 162–63, *164*
United Hebrew Trades, 128
United Knish Factory, 35

United Orthodox Congregation, 116
Unzer Express (newspaper), 244
Unzer Grodner Moment (newspaper), 244

Van Camp's pork and beans, 21
Vargas, Herman (Russ & Daughters), 80
vaudeville, 94, 99, 130, 136–37, 149–50, 182–84, 198–99, *199*, 216, 218, 222, 226, 236–37, 249, 251, 253, 262, 269, 278, 282, 289, 291, 297–98, 300
Vaynper, Zishe, 195, 199
Victor Records. *See* records
Vilna (city), 9, 184, 274, 280–81
Vilna Troupe, 133
Vitaphone, 130, 294, 297, 300–4
Vizhnitsky's New Roumanian Paradise, 58
Vodery, Will ("Showboat"), 201
Volfman, Alex (Yonah Schimmel's), 37
Volstead Act (1919), 52

Waiter's Union Local Number One, 94
Waldman, Leibele, 167
Walker, Jimmy ("Gentleman Jimmy"), 147, 153–54
Waller, Fats, 254
Walowit, Miriam (Yiddish Gilbert and Sullivan), 167–68
W&A Roumanian Oriental Restaurant, 61
Warner Brothers, 293–94, 296–98, 300–4, 306
Waverly (theater), 136
Weingast, Morris and Sam (Mrs. Stahl's), 44
Weinreich, Uriel, 1, 3, 272
Weinreich, Beatrice, 1
Wells, Pete (*New York Times* food writer), 65

White, Lucien H. (*New York Age* columnist), 237
Whiteman, Paul, 195, 334n7
Willett Street Theater, 183, *183*
Williams, Bert, (Black stage comedian)275, 289
Wilson, Sam (Black Yiddish singer), 236
Winchell, Walter, 81, 288
Wiseman, Harrison G., 2, 129–35, 138
"The Woiking Goil" (character piece), 302
women cantors of the stage (*khazntes*), 215–30, *217*, *223*, *229*, 248, 250–52, 285, 334nn1–2
World War I, 22, 77, 121–22, 165, 176, 187, 196, 235
World War II, 28–29, 46, 61, 88, 163–65, 171

Yankovic, Frankie, 226
yenta (yenta, definition of term and English use of), 80, 259, 271–72
Yente (name), 259
Yente Telebende: criticism of, 265, *266*; newspaper series, 219, 260–61, 265–69; plays, 253, 261, *263*, 264–65, 268, 271–72; records of, 261–64, 269–71
Yiddish Art Theater, 95, 102, 131, 135, 160, 166–67
Yiddish dictionaries, 1, 259, 272
Yiddishe Mame, 204, 220, 284, 286
Yiddisher Dilettante (Hebrew Amateur, magazine), 149
Yiddisher Farmer's guide (*The Jewish Vacation Guide Hotels, Boarding Houses and Rooming Houses Where Jews Are Welcome*), 140
Yiddishes Togblatt (*Jewish Daily News*), 219; Fun groys New York, 232, 235

Yiddish Gilbert and Sullivan Light Opera Company, 168
Yiddish recording artists, 179–92. *See also* recording artists
Yiddish regional theater circuit, 44, 136, 226, 230, 247, 251–53, 255, 268, 278
Yiddish theater, 129–38. *See also* New York Yiddish theaters; plays and shows; *specific actors/actresses, playwrights, and producers*
Yiddish Times Square (Lower East Side), 141
Yoelson, Rabbi Moishe Rubin (Al Jolson's father), 293
Yom Kippur, 280, 288, 292, 305–7
Yonah Schimmel, 1, 21, 36–38, 42, 67, 211
Yoshe Kalb (I. J. Singer), 135
Youngman, Henny, 175
Yudelson, Moisha (character in "The Jazz Singer"), 282, 284, 289, 291

Zankel brothers (sausages), 89
Zavin, Shirley (architecture historian), 126
Zimbalist, Efrem (actor), 286
Zimbalist, Samuel (cymbalist), 251
Zionism, 14, 117, 132, 232, 240, 242
Zion National, 24–25
Zion Records, 226
Zuckerberg, Regina, 59–60
Zuckerberg Gordon, Bernice, 228–30, *229*; daughter of Israel Zuckerberg, 228–30

About the Author

Henry H. Sapoznik is an award-winning author, radio and record producer, and performer of Yiddish and American traditional and popular music. A child of Holocaust survivors and native Yiddish speaker, Sapoznik was one of the architects of the 1970s klezmer revival and in 1985 founded and directed the internationally renowned KlezKamp for thirty years. Sapoznik was nominated for five Grammy awards as a performer and producer. He co-produced the Peabody-award-winning NPR series *The Yiddish Radio Project* in 2002.

In addition to his work as a writer, Sapoznik is a banjoist, lap steel guitarist, and a nationally ranked bullseye pistol competitor. He is currently working on a book on the history of Yiddish radio.

To hear the recordings mentioned in the book, for additional information and primary research materials, and to subscribe to my blog, go to: henrysapoznik.com.

www.ingramcontent.com/pod-product-compliance
Lightning Source LLC
Chambersburg PA
CBHW070335240426
43665CB00045B/1994